JUST MARRIED

JUST MARRIED

Same-Sex Couples, Monogamy
& the Future of Marriage

Stephen Macedo

PRINCETON UNIVERSITY PRESS
PRINCETON AND OXFORD

Requests for permission to reproduce material from this work
should be sent to Permissions, Princeton University Press
Published by Princeton University Press,
41 William Street, Princeton, New Jersey 08540
In the United Kingdom: Princeton University Press,
6 Oxford Street, Woodstock, Oxfordshire OX20 1TW
press.princeton.edu
ISBN 978-0-691-16648-3
Library of Congress Control Number 2015937044
British Library Cataloging-in-Publication Data is available
This book has been composed in Adobe Caslon Pro
Printed on acid-free paper. ∞
Printed in the United States of America
1 3 5 7 9 10 8 6 4 2

For
David

CONTENTS

PREFACE AND ACKNOWLEDGMENTS

My direct engagement with some of the issues discussed below, especially in part 1, began in September 1986. Robert P. George, newly appointed assistant professor at Princeton University, was an examiner for my doctoral thesis in Princeton's Department of Politics. Noting that I defended a constitutional right to privacy for gay and lesbian Americans, he recommended that I address the arguments in an article on sexual morality by John Finnis, which I did. That led to a series of exchanges over a decade or so, from which I benefited greatly.

When I came back to these questions more recently, it was clear that a wider debate had emerged not only on same-sex marriage but on the public status and justifiability of civil marriage itself and also monogamy. I was lucky enough to be able to discuss these issues in several classes at Princeton University: in my lecture course, Ethics and Public Policy, sponsored by the Woodrow Wilson School, the Politics Department, and the University Center for Human Values; in several versions of an upper-level undergraduate seminar on Moral Conflicts in Public and Private Life; and in a first-year seminar on Religion and Politics in the fall of 2013.

I want to offer my hearty thanks to the terrific students in these classes, whose thoughtful engagement with the issues contributed greatly to whatever progress I have been able to make. I have often felt that I should be paying the university for the privilege and pleasure of teaching such great students. This book is indebted to Princeton University in many other ways as well.

Various undergraduate and graduate students at Princeton have served as research assistants on this book: Haidar Abbas, Paul Baumgartner, Emily de La Bruyere, Kathy Chow, Sarah Cotterill, Manuel Marichal,

Madhu Ramankutty, Miranda Rehaut, and Han Tran all provided extensive assistance. Karen Ku and Thompson Zhuang spent time during the spring of 2013 and then returned to Princeton during part of the summer and helped me work through a number of issues. I am grateful to them and to all the students with whom I have discussed these issues in classes and at various forums on campus.

I first sketched the argument below in the annual Walter F. Murphy Lecture on Constitutionalism sponsored by Princeton's James Madison Program on American Ideals and Institutions, and more recently in a debate on gay marriage with Sherif Girgis cosponsored by the Princeton Anscombe Society, the Program on Gender and Sexuality Studies, and several other groups. I have benefited from several discussions sponsored by the Program on Law and Public Affairs (LAPA), directed by Professor Kim Scheppele. Robby George served as commentator at one of those events, and I am grateful for his generous and helpful comments on that early draft paper. A roundtable seminar discussion of an early draft, cosponsored by the Madison Program and LAPA, included helpful comments by Linda McClain, Elizabeth Brake, Laurie Schrage, and Matthew Franke.

I presented an early version at the Center for Advanced Study in the Behavioral Sciences at Stanford University, where I was a visiting fellow in 2009–10. I am grateful to the center and to the other fellows in residence that year. It was and is, as many others have said, the perfect place to work. I especially benefited from a discussion group with Gillian Hadfield, Victoria McGeer, Philip Pettit, Dan Posner, and Dan Ryan.

Later versions were presented at the Department of Law at Pompeu Fabra University in Barcelona; the Political Science Department at the University of Chicago; the Faculty of Philosophy at the Autonomous National University of Mexico; the University of Birmingham; Shandong University; the University of Palermo in Buenos Aires; and the University of Miami School of Law. My sincere thanks to the audiences, commentators, and my hosts at these various places: Jose Luis Marti, John McCormick, Itzel Mayans, Jeremy Williams, Julio Montero, and Fred Frohock.

I was able to present versions of chapters at professional meetings, including the Western Political Science Association and two annual meetings of the American Political Science Association. My thanks to fellow panelists and commentators, including Sonu Bedi, Elizabeth Brake, Wendy Brown, Andrew March, Tamara Metz, Nancy Rosenblum, Dennis Thompson, and Ralph Wedgwood.

Several friends and colleagues provided often extensive written comments on late drafts, and I am extremely grateful to them: Sotirios Barber, Sonu Bedi, Jameson Doig, George Kateb, Michael Lamb, Jeffrey Tulis, and Alex Zakaras. Professor Robert Katz of the University of Indiana's Robert H. McKinney School of Law provided extensive and helpful written comments on several drafts in the summer of 2014, above and beyond any call of duty, for which my heartfelt thanks.

Conversations at various points with colleagues at Princeton and elsewhere were very helpful, including with Charles Beitz, Christopher L. Eisgruber, James Fleming, Elizabeth Harman, Will Harris, Nan Keohane, Andy Koppelman, Alan Patten, Gideon Rosen, Alan Ryan, Annie Stilz, Caleb Yong, and Everett Zhang. I want to add, finally, that there are terrific books and articles that helped shape my thinking early on, including (but not only) ones by John Corvino, Mary Lyndon Shanley, and E. J. Graff, which deserve greater acknowledgment than I have given them in the text and notes.

William A. Galston and Linda McClain were the two perfect reviewers of the draft manuscript for Princeton University Press. Both offered extremely helpful and constructive suggestions; I am deeply grateful to them. McClain, in particular, has provided me with innumerable suggestions and resources.

Anita O'Brien has been a terrific copyeditor. Ali Parrington has ably managed the book's production. Scott Wayland has also provided additional assistance on the manuscript, serving as a very helpful and generous sounding board for many ideas presented below.

Rob Tempio has been the perfect editor: encouraging, helpful, and knowing when to put his foot down. He deserves credit for the final title, along with several other good titles we did not use.

Needless to say, the mistakes that remain are entirely my own.

My thanks finally to my partner of many years, David Bernhardt, for giving me the time, space, and support I have needed, and for also knowing when to put his foot down.

JUST MARRIED

WHY MARRIAGE MATTERS

This book defends same-sex marriage, marriage (as a distinctive relationship defined by law), and monogamy. It upholds and extends the emerging common sense of the American public and American law against those who would arrest and reverse the historic movement toward a more inclusive institution. It also argues for the justness and goodness of preserving marriage against those who demand something radically new in our law.

But why do we need such an argument now?

INTRODUCTION

Marriage, the family, and gender relations have changed remarkably over the past sixty years. The changes include greater gender equality, with women working in far greater numbers, better access to contraception, and greater reproductive freedom; higher rates of divorce; more permissive attitudes toward premarital sex; delayed marriage; and many more children being raised by single parents. Marriage was once a precondition for having licit sexual relations and for having children. But sexual activity, procreation, and childrearing increasingly take place outside marriage, and far fewer Americans are currently married than in the past. Nevertheless, while Americans now marry later in life and half of these marriages end in divorce, they still marry in impressive numbers. The vast majority of Americans marry at some point in their lives, and 95 percent of American adults are either married or would like to be. So, in spite of all the changes, Americans still aspire to marriage, and marriage still matters.[1]

The intensity of the debate over same-sex marriage in the United States reflects the importance that Americans ascribe to this institution. And while young people have recently expressed somewhat less inclination to marry than other age-groups, the keen interest of many same-sex couples has given the institution a boost.[2]

Consider Jacques Beaumont and Richard Townsend, 86 and 77 years old, respectively, who were featured in the Weddings/Celebrations section of the *New York Times* in August 2011.[3] Beaumont worked for decades with a refugee organization, and Townsend was a playwright who also taught playwriting at the YMCA. They had met thirty-nine years ago and lived together for many years. Townsend had developed Parkinson's disease some time ago, and they spent much of their time caring for each other. At the time the story ran, Beaumont had recently been diagnosed with leukemia, and the prognosis was not good. A few days after celebrating the signing of New York State's same-sex marriage legislation, they were forced to call an ambulance and together check in to the Beth Israel Medical Center, where they insisted on sharing a room. There, in a patient lounge on August 2, they were wed. "When he got sick," said Mr. Townsend, "it changed everything. We said we must get married. It's vitally important."

It is left to our imaginations to fill in the details. Townsend's sense of marriage's vital importance may have referred only to particular legal rights. As we will see, marriage brings with it a wide range of rights and obligations under law that reflect and support couples' shared lives together. Very likely he also referred, in part at least, to the significance of the status of marriage as a way of publicly declaring and solemnizing their mutual commitment. The symbolic and expressive dimension has, indeed, been at the center of what some call our "culture war" over marriage.

In the litigation in California over Proposition 8 (which overturned a California Supreme Court decision extending marriage rights to same-sex couples[4]), a conservative justice observed that, as a matter of state law, same-sex couples in California already had domestic partnerships with nearly all the same legal entitlements of marriage, so the protracted litigation there was over the word "marriage." Charles Cooper, a lawyer defending Proposition 8, responded that the word "is essentially the institution."[5] That may be an overstatement, but it captures an important truth: the institution of marriage in the United States is freighted with social meaning and moral, cultural, and religious significance; these words and their public meanings, and the recognition that "marriage" entails, are a crucial part of what is at stake.

To Kristin Perry, the lead plaintiff in the constitutional challenge to Proposition 8, marriage provides access to the language to describe her relationship with her partner: "I'm a 45-year-old woman. I have been in love with a woman for 10 years and I don't have a word to tell anybody about that. . . . Marriage would be a way to tell our friends, our family, our society, our community, our parents . . . and each other that this is a lifetime commitment . . . we are not girlfriends. We are not partners. We are married."[6]

Marriage is a singular institution. The law of marriage sets out a host of legal rights and obligations that bind and enable those who enter into it. As we will see in chapter 4, over a thousand federal laws touch on these legal aspects, though marriage is defined mostly by state law. The profound meaning of marriage in people's lives and its resonance in our culture are also shaped deeply by religious traditions that variously define the terms on which they will recognize marriages and their dissolution. While state laws allow members of the clergy, along with judges, court clerks, and others, to officiate at marriage ceremonies, the rules governing civil and religious marriages are independent of each other: to be married in the eyes of the state is not necessarily to be married in the eyes of any particular church, and vice versa. The deep resonance of "marriage" in law, religion, and culture intensifies the conflicts around it while also enhancing its capacity to solemnize and stabilize the commitments that underlie the most important relationship in the lives of most people.

The conflicts inherent in our long-running debate are intensified by two sets of issues that are closely bound up with marriage: sexual ethics and children's well-being. Many opponents of same-sex marriage regard same-sex sexual relations as inherently immoral; exactly why is a question we will need to investigate in part 1. In addition, most Americans are troubled, and for good reason, about the impact of changes in family structure on children's well-being. It is frequently charged that same-sex marriage is a threat to children. This too is a matter we consider below.

In late June 2013, a slim majority of the U.S. Supreme Court insisted that the lawful marriages of same-sex couples are equal in "dignity and status" to traditional marriages under the U.S. Constitution and must be treated that way in federal law. In *United States v. Windsor*, the provision of the Defense of Marriage Act (DOMA) defining marriage as a relationship between one man and one woman—a law passed overwhelmingly by Congress and signed by President Bill Clinton in 1996—was held to rest on "a bare congressional desire to harm a politically unpopular group."[7] The "avowed purpose and practical effect of the law here in question are to impose a disadvantage, a separate status, and so a stigma upon all who enter into same-sex marriages made lawfully by the unquestioned authority of the States."[8] The Constitution, wrote Justice Kennedy for the Court, does not permit the federal government to tell same-sex couples, "and all the world, that their otherwise valid marriages are unworthy of federal recognition. This places same-sex couples in an unstable position of being in a second-tier marriage. The differentiation demeans the couple, whose moral and sexual choices the Constitution protects."[9] On the same day that it struck down the federal Defense of Marriage Act, the Supreme Court let stand lower federal and state court rulings that made same-sex marriage legal in California by invalidating Proposition 8.[10]

In the months and years after *United States v. Windsor* was decided, a steady cascade of state and federal courts and electorates extended *Windsor's* rationale and reach by finding DOMA-like requirements in state law unconstitutional. These courts found, as the Supreme Court had in *Windsor*, that state officials failed to offer good reasons and evidence to justify denying same-sex couples access to a public institution as important as civil marriage. Several other courts disagreed, however, and held that the reasons advanced were sufficient to warrant continued deference to state legislatures. Writing for the Sixth Circuit Court of Appeals, whose decision finally prompted the U.S. Supreme Court to take up the same-sex marriage question, Judge Jeffrey Sutton upheld the constitutionality of same-sex marriage bans while observing that marriage equality appears inevitable.[11]

FOR BETTER OR WORSE?

The rapid ascent of same-sex marriage makes further questions inescapable: What next? What does same-sex marriage portend for the meaning and future of marriage? Many on the political right and left who disagree vehemently on most issues agree on one thing: *same-sex marriage is an unstable way station on the road to more radical change*. So this book asks: Does victory for same-sex marriage sound a death knell for marriage as we have known it? Do the moral and practical arguments for same-sex marriage also compel us to enact other, more radical reforms? Are civil marriage and monogamy still justifiable and viable?

Conservatives have long warned that recognition of same-sex marriage rights puts us on a slippery slope to unions both abhorrent and outlandish. Professor Hadley Arkes, a scholar and advocate of natural law, put it this way in his 1996 testimony in favor of DOMA:

If we detach marriage from that natural teleology of the body, on what ground of principle could the law confine marriage to couples? On what ground would the law say no to people who profess that their love is not confined to a coupling, but woven together in a larger ensemble of three or four? . . . If that arrangement were made available to ensembles of the same sex, it would have to be made available to ensembles of mixed sexes, which is to say we'd be back in principle to the acceptance of polygamy.[12]

"Legal recognition and social acceptance" of people who are gay would leave us with no grounds for excluding from marriage "a father and daughter who want to marry. Or two sisters. Or men who want (consensual) polygamous arrangements," said William Bennett. "We'll become more accommodating to man-boy associations, polygamists and so forth," added Robert H. Bork. Gary Bauer, president of the Family Research Council, similarly claimed that if same-sex marriage were permitted, it would be logically indefensible to prohibit polygamy and logically inappropriate to continue "the limitation of the [marital] relationship to human beings."[13] The slippery slope to polygamy, incest, and even bestiality has been deployed against even the basic right of gay and lesbian adults to be free of criminal prosecution for engaging in sexual acts in the privacy of their own homes: "If the Supreme Court says that you have a right to consensual (gay) sex within your home," warned former U.S. senator Rick Santorum in 2003, "then you have the right to bigamy, you have the right to polygamy, you have the right to incest, you have the right to adultery. You have the right to anything."[14] Weeks later, in *Lawrence v. Texas*, a majority of the Supreme Court extended the Constitution's privacy right to gays, prompting Justice Antonin Scalia to declare: "called into question by today's decision" are "state laws against bigamy, same-sex marriage, adult incest, prostitution, masturbation, adultery, fornication, bestiality, and obscenity."[15]

The specter of polygamy was raised frequently by defenders of California's Proposition 8, which sought to reverse marriage equality for same-sex couples by defining marriage as the relationship of one man and one woman.[16] That was not the end of it. Writing in *National Review* in August 2014, Ryan T. Anderson warned that "redefining" marriage to include same-sex couples "leads to the dissolution of marriage, to a social mess of adult love of manifold sizes and shapes. Defenders of the truth about marriage should redouble our efforts while there is still time to steer clear of that chaos."[17] In upholding Puerto Rico's same-sex marriage ban in October 2014, U.S. District Judge Juan Pérez-Giménez conjured up the specters of polygamy and "the marriage of fathers and daughters."[18] In upholding Louisiana's same-sex marriage ban, Judge Martin C. Feldman asserted that

inconvenient questions persist. For example, must the states permit or recognize a marriage between an aunt and niece? Aunt and nephew? Brother/brother? Father and child? May minors marry? Must marriage be limited to only two people? . . . All such unions would undeniably be equally committed to love and caring for one another, just like the plaintiffs. Perhaps in a new established point of view, marriage will be reduced to contract law, and, by contract, anyone will be able to claim marriage.[19]

In late 2014, in the wake of dozens of court decisions and decades of debate, Professor John Finnis argued that "concerns about polygamy go unreported and unanswered" in even the most celebrated of decisions in favor of same-sex marriage. And Judge Sutton, penning the opinion that led the Supreme Court to take on same-sex marriage, affirmed that, "If it is constitutionally irrational to stand by the man-woman definition of marriage, it must be constitutionally irrational to stand by the monogamous definition of marriage. Plaintiffs have no answer to this point."[20]

Sometimes, or perhaps often, such arguments amount to right-wing "fear mongering," but not always. The shift in public opinion on gay marriage has been swift but far from unanimous. Many continue to regard same-sex marriage as "preposterous ... something barely imaginable." For them, as David L. Chambers argues, these various unions are "moral equivalents, each repellant," and it is "the appropriate province of the law to discourage or prohibit" them.[21]

After all, *if marriage is not necessarily about procreation but is centrally about adult happiness, which individuals define for themselves, then why not grant people the freedom to choose not only the sex but the number of their marital partners?* Why not indeed, say many on the left, in order to entertain rather than restrain the manifold forms of "self-definition" and "moral and sexual choice" that conservatives warn against.

"At the heart of liberty is the right to define one's own concept of existence, of meaning, of the universe, and of the mystery of human life," wrote Justice Anthony Kennedy in *Planned Parenthood v. Casey* (1992), the case that dramatically "reaffirmed the essential holding" of *Roe v. Wade*, upholding a woman's right to choose to have an abortion.[22] Many progressive academics argue that marriage ought to be "disestablished" or privatized because the state has no good basis for setting the terms of our most intimate and important relationships and the number of participants. These ought to be left up to the free choice of the parties, as in other contracts.

Indeed, feminists have long argued that the magnetic power of marriage in our culture and the bundling of so many benefits into marriage lead people to overinvest in this one form of caring and caregiving relationship. It ill serves most people's interests to put all their eggs in the basket of marriage, an institution whose fragility in the real world mocks fantasies of lifelong permanence.[23] Feminists and queer theorists brand traditional marriage as "heteronormative," charging that it unfairly enshrines in law "heterosexist" values such as monogamy. From this point of view, same-sex marriage is "an alarming movement toward assimilationist erasure of Gay identity" that undermines the liberationist potential of gay relationships. Gay marriage, like marriage generally, "privatizes energies into the family unit" and "results in the dismantling of support systems found in the community." Gays were once ready to recognize all other gays as "family"; now they are abandoning this "communitarian conception of family in favor of the heterosexualized, privatized, monogamous family model found in marriage."[24]

Yet others assert that monogamous marriage's preferred status unjustly privileges Western and Christian models of family life. Prejudice against polygamy is held to reflect racism as well as religious and civilizational chauvinism. The state has no business encouraging its citizens "to couple, but only to couple," argues one Canadian scholar.[25] Many now embrace the idea that principled consistency requires legal recognition and protection for polygamous or "polyamorous" unions of three or more.

But is the embrace of "poly" marital unions sufficiently inclusive? Many theorists say no. One set of progressive proposals would replace marriage with a new, more inclusive, and more ethically neutral model of relationships. This could be done by extending support to caring and caregiving relations, whether monogamous or amorous or not.[26] Philosopher Elizabeth Brake, in a widely cited argument, brands marriage as "amatonormative," meaning that it unfairly privileges amorous or romantic relationships.[27] Rather than extend such relationships to groups larger than two, she would radically broaden the character of marriage and refound it on a more ethically neutral and inclusive basis. "Minimal marriage," as she calls her proposal, should recognize and support "adult care networks" or "caring relationships" of any number and combination of persons, with or without a romantic component.[28]

Some philosophers go so far as to invoke principles of liberty, fairness, and state ethical neutrality to argue for the legal recognition of adult incestuous relations. Professor Sonu Bedi of Dartmouth College provocatively asks what is wrong with an adult incestuous relationship in which procreation is not intended, or indeed where it is impossible—in, for example, an adult gay or lesbian incestuous relationship.[29] Bedi is not alone.

Participants in these debates are often strangely inarticulate. In the past, conservatives frequently fell back on the moralistic assertion that homosexuality is "unnatural," and in many parts of the world such sentiments are expressed even now with great vehemence. In the West, we more commonly hear that polygamy is simply "abhorrent" and inconsistent with American, Canadian, and European traditions.[30] Yet feelings of that sort are frequently unreliable and do not in themselves provide a good reason: Why is it abhorrent? What is the harm? And traditions are frequently revised, so why not the one pertaining to monogamy? On the left, academics and intellectuals are typically alert to the importance of choice, diversity, and free self-definition but less willing to acknowledge that some choices and ways of defining oneself are less conducive than others to one's own well-being and that of others.

Whereas conservatives see gay marriage as the infiltration of destructive radicals, radicals see it as a surrender to conservatives. The marriage issue is very personal, and the most important human interests are at stake. That makes the questions urgent and fascinating, but it can also derail clear thinking.

As I explain at the beginning of chapter 1, there is also a deep global divide on the various issues discussed here, and in many places the arguments for and against equal rights for gay people have yet to be aired. That is yet another reason for considering the arguments advanced by opponents of same-sex marriage.

"I tell my students that it is difficult to think about sex," a wise Jesuit has observed. "People can fairly easily pant, picture or pontificate about sex. But it is hard to think deeply, clearly and cogently about it." He adds that with respect to sexual ethics, and, I would add, the marriage question, "most of us begin with our conclusions" and then, "if ever, we seek reasons to justify our conclusions."[31] Father Edward Vacek seems to me on the mark. We need to do better.

*****

Many conservatives and progressives agree that same-sex marriage is an unprincipled and unstable stopping point on the path to marriage abolition or radical reform. Their disagreement is about whether to condemn or welcome this prospect.

The debate over marriage and its future will not be ended by the inclusion of gay and lesbian Americans. I argue in what follows that both sides fail to appreciate the good reasons and considerable evidence in support of marriage reform and preservation, not abolition. Justice requires the extension of marriage to same-sex couples. It does not require adopting a privatized "contractual" model, the extension of marriage to groups of three or more, or other radical reforms. There is a sensible, liberal, and democratic case for monogamy and against legal recognition of polygamy, which I elaborate below. Monogamy helps advance core values of liberal democracy. At the same time, I agree with those progressives who argue that the law should do more to recognize and support a variety of forms of nonmarital caring and caregiving relationships; not as substitutes for monogamous marriage but as supplements.

Indeed, the argument goes an important step further: the core liberal democratic values of equal liberty and opportunity for all argue for monogamy as the preferred social form. Monogamous marriage helps to secure everyone's fair access to the great good of family life and is conducive to social well-being in a wide variety of ways. The case for marriage, as we will see, remains intact and even strengthened after same-sex marriage: it rests on liberal democratic justice as well as the good of individuals and society.

There are other steps that ought to be taken by those concerned about marriage and the wider forms of caring and caregiving on which all of us depend. Large numbers of disproportionately poor children and adults are no longer living within intact marriages, and there is no serious prospect of this changing soon. The value of marriage and the legitimacy of public recognition and support for it are called into question by the increasingly dire plight of those whom our society is leaving behind. Stable marriage is increasingly associated with socioeconomic privilege: along with the declining economic fortunes of the less educated has come declining marital prospects.[32] Feminist and other progressive critics of marriage have been right to insist that marriage must not be made an excuse for failing to attend to the needs of those outside of marriage.

If the assertions just advanced sound overly confident, let me assure the reader that I am aware that there are many difficult questions to be addressed here about which reasonable people of good will disagree.

LIBERALISM AS PUBLIC PHILOSOPHY

The debate over marriage raises wider and deeper questions concerning our governing political philosophy. Virtually all Americans are "liberals" in the broadest sense: committed to the values of individual freedom and equality that are enshrined in the Declaration of Independence, the Constitution, and many later sources. We interpret our founding values differently, however, and those differences animate our politics. The "conservatives" among us place greater emphasis on private property, personal responsibility, and sexual restraint. Progressives, whom we tend to call "liberals," emphasize the need for an active government to secure fair opportunity in the face of inherited inequalities. Those on the free-market right are often radicals nowadays, but true conservatives are cautious in the face of proposed reforms to complex institutions. Liberals are insistent on the need to extend equality and freedom to those who have been marginalized, including women and sexual minorities. Our public debates tend to be dominated by those who argue stridently for one side or the other, but most Americans care about values on both sides of these divides, and I think they are right to do so.

The polarization that plagues our politics is too often reflected in academic debates. Conservatives tend to caricature "liberalism," and many on the left seem all too ready to embrace the caricature. The caricatures may be based on the ideas of "neutrality" or "political liberalism" and associated with particular writings of John Rawls and Ronald Dworkin, the two greatest defenders of progressive liberalism over the past half century. Among many on the left, radical marriage reform is thought to be required by the vast religious and ethical diversity of America today and our government's obligation to be fair or "neutral," as some would say, among citizens with different beliefs about what makes for a good life. We cannot publicly justify, they say, a law of civil marriage that bestows a "special" status and benefits on monogamous pairings because not everyone values such pairings. Indeed, Professor Bedi, whom I have already quoted, lampoons the position I defend as "natural law but with a gay spin."[33]

So along the way, and especially in the conclusion, I make the case for a moderate and flexible approach to liberalism (by which I shall henceforth mean progressive liberalism): one that allows the state to promote such widely if not unanimously valued goods and activities as health, happiness, knowledge, prosperity, the preservation of areas of great natural beauty, progress in science, humanistic understanding, and excellence in the arts and athletics. The liberal democratic state should, in short, favor all genuine human goods but do so within a constitutional framework that gives priority to the defense of equal basic liberties and the fair distribution of resources and opportunities. Fairness among citizens and their worthwhile conceptions of the good life is a moral imperative but not one that requires the elimination of civil marriage.

I argue against those who believe that liberal principles impose narrow limits on the state's authority. Core liberal values of equal liberty and fairness among citizens allow support for widely, if not unanimously, valued institutions such as marriage, along with many other broadly public goods. Justice and equal liberty are at the core of our public morality, but they are not the whole of it: they leave space for public institutions to promote a wide array of broad-based human goods. We can honor fairness by recognizing the value of marriage along with other nonmarital caring relations that people also wish to enter and that also advance their good and the good of society. The idea of an ethically neutral state has been misconceived: democratic institutions have a wider scope for discretion than marriage's critics have allowed.

Admittedly, and as we shall see, marriage is unlike other institutions that liberal states routinely support in order to make a wide and inclusive array of human goods available to citizens. Unlike museums, parks, and concert halls, monogamous marriage imposes a certain ordering on the most intimate aspects of almost everyone's personal life. It shapes and constitutes the most important and most personal relationships in the lives of individuals. It creates certain kinds of families and rules out other forms of family life that have prevailed across most human societies in the past and much of the world today. Monogamous marriage imparts a common shape to most people's deepest aspirations for their lives as a whole. And all this in spite of the great diversity that is supposed to characterize modern societies.

The moderate reformism defended here holds that justice and respect for equal basic rights leave *significant scope* for democratically accountable legislatures to facilitate widely valued and generally beneficial institutions such as marriage. This approach respects the values of democratic deliberation, social learning, and incrementalism in the face of complex social changes. Those values are especially important when contemplating reform of an institution as complex and central to so many people's lives—and the life of our society—as marriage. I defend an understanding of justice, rights, and the public good that is sensitive to empirical evidence and our evolving public understandings of human sexuality and family life.

We should embrace a moderate and flexible liberalism that is closer to the common sense of ordinary citizens and takes seriously the "formative project" of liberal constitutionalism: the need to fashion institutions that cultivate the virtues on which a liberal society depends.[34] The case for marriage advanced here incorporates sensible conservative concerns, including incrementalism in the reform of complex institutions. I urge, further, that we proceed on the basis of widely available reasons and evidence and acknowledge the importance of democratic deliberation and social learning. We can be fair to the diversity of reasonable conceptions of the good life and extend new forms of recognition and support to caring and caregiving relationships while continuing to recognize the special role of monogamous marriage in a liberal democracy.

The focus of the book is most directly on marriage in the United States and, with respect to polygamy at least, Canada. Marriage cultures vary, and marriage has a distinctive resonance in the United States. Part of my argument is that we ought to respect the particularity of democratic law and culture, at least to a point, and within the limits of basic rights and distributive fairness.[35] Nevertheless, while my particular focus is marriage here and now in America, the discussion can illuminate inquiry elsewhere. Indeed, much of the evidence and argument concerning polygamy is drawn from a wider historical and anthropological record.

THE PLAN OF THE BOOK

This book asks: what does the recognition of same-sex marriage portend for the future of marriage as an institution? I ask, in effect: *what's next for marriage?*

The debate over same-sex marriage has been at the center of our public life for over two decades. Those who defend what they call the "traditional" conception of marriage as necessarily and inherently heterosexual portray same-sex marriage as a deeply destructive development that subverts an institution on which the good of children, spouses, and society as a whole depends. As marriage equality spreads rapidly and the arguments against it are rejected, the question becomes: where does that leave us with marriage?[36]

Specifically:

- Why has the conservative case against same-sex marriage collapsed so quickly, and where does this leave the defense of monogamous marriage?

- How can we, after same-sex marriage, justify preserving marriage as a *status* institution in law, that is, as a relationship whose terms are defined in advance by law rather than negotiated by the parties to the arrangement? Can we justify a "one-size-fits-all" institution of marriage given the great diversity of American society?

- What, if any, is the principled argument for monogamy, or limiting marriage to two people only? What sorts of relationships should count as marriage, and why?

- Which of the traditional legal privileges and obligations of marriage should be kept, which should be eliminated, and which should be made available on another basis, say, to unmarried couples or groups in various caregiving relationships?

These are complicated questions, and any attempt to pursue them comprehensively could fill many volumes. I examine the main issues only. One also needs to decide where to begin, and how to organize the journey. I proceed by asking three interrelated questions in each of the successive parts of this book: *Why same-sex marriage? Why marriage? Why monogamy?*

My contention is that the case for marriage and monogamy remains intact and in many ways strengthened after same-sex marriage. I examine these matters from the standpoint of ethics and political theory, or what some would call public philosophy, considering the merits of the debates in light of ordinary standards of soundness and rigor, as well as the available evidence.

*****

Part 1 traces the trajectory of conservative moral arguments against same-sex marriage over the past three decades, including the arguments featured in prominent court decisions and state and federal legislative battles. It is important to reexamine these arguments because, irrespective of what courts decide, many harbor objections to same-sex marriage, and their concerns will shape other debates going forward.

In chapter 1 I trace the arc of three decades of conservative arguments against same-sex marriage and gay rights more broadly, distinguishing several different strands. The debate over gay rights has been shaped by the repeated articulation of a demand for public reasons and evidence to justify the shape of the law touching on gay rights and marriage. The demand for reasons was laid down by the dissenters in *Bowers v. Hardwick* (1987), and it has shaped and elevated the subsequent debate.

In chapter 2 I give more extended treatment to the most philosophically sophisticated opponents of same-sex marriage. The New Natural Law defense of marriage as necessarily the relation of one man and one woman is linked to an account of sexual morality that few Americans entertain. These arguments will seem somewhat academic, but their influence extends to the center of American politics. In his dissenting opinion in *United States v. Windsor* (2013), Justice Samuel Alito referred to these arguments to buttress his assertion that the merits of same-sex marriage remain unsettled, and others have also done so.[37] I show that natural law arguments fail to provide a reasoned basis for excluding same-sex couples from the civil institution of marriage.

Other conservatives oppose gay wedlock because they say it will weaken marital commitments and fidelity and degrade parenting, to the detriment of spouses, children, and society as a whole. We take up a variety of such charges in chapter 3. Concerns about children and families can be addressed far more effectively once they are disentangled from the injustice of discrimination on the basis of sexual orientation. Extending marriage to same-sex couples will allow them to make the sorts of stabilizing commitments that marriage stands for, which is exactly what conservatives should want.

*****

Having made the case for same-sex marriage in part 1, I turn in part 2 to the even broader complaints of a variety of critics who regard civil marriage in its current form as unjust. Invoking libertarian, feminist, and liberal political principles, critics charge that the "special status" of marriage in our law unfairly favors some people's conceptions of the good life over others. It fails the principle of state ethical neutrality. Instead of a one-size-fits-all marital arrangement whose specific terms are defined in advance by law, we would be much better off with a contractual arrangement whose terms are set out by the parties, or a much more flexible and open institution.

There are two broad aspects of the civil institution of marriage: the symbolic dimension, which has in many ways been at the center of the controversy surrounding same-sex marriage, and the specific legal "incidents": the obligations, benefits, and entitlements that spouses acquire in marriage.

After laying out the complaints of marriage critics, chapter 4 focuses on the symbolic dimension of marriage, which is one source of the complaint that marriage's special status is problematic. I explain and defend the practical work done by this symbolism: it allows people to publicly declare their commitment to each other in a way that will be well understood in society as a whole, and not only in their church or local community. Marriage as a status relation whose terms are set out in law facilitates people's reasonable desire to enter a socially legible committed relationship surrounded by expectations and norms that can help stabilize and support their commitment.

Chapter 5 sets out, in broad terms, the many "legal incidents" of marriage: the specific rights and responsibilities created by the law of marriage. My brief overview makes the case that these usefully recognize and support the spouses' mutual commitments and lives together. While critics focus on the special privileges or benefits that spouses acquire in marriage, those are balanced by special obligations. I suggest that the whole package seems reasonably appropriate for both opposite-sex and same-sex couples. This chapter also describes the ways in which marriage seems to promote the good of spouses, children, and society, and it describes the astonishing class divide that now characterizes marriage and parenting. This class divide, not same-sex marriage, is the great challenge for the future.

Chapter 6 considers a variety of reform proposals that have been advanced as alternatives to the current law of marriage. These include marriage "privatization" and a much greater emphasis on contractual choice and personalization. Relatedly, some recommend enhancing the use of "prenuptial" agreements. While allowing that such suggestions are worth taking seriously, I also explain and defend the comparative advantages of an open-ended marital commitment. I cast doubt on the proposal to leave the term "marriage" to churches and other nonpublic associations as a way of avoiding both confusions and conflicts between "church and state." I also consider the conditions of just marriage, which include extending greater support to those in nonmarital relationships of care, and to singles.

*****

Parts 1 and 2 make the cases for same-sex wedlock and marriage as a special status in civil law. If marriage continues to make sense in the wake of same-sex marriage, what about monogamy? This is one of the most interesting and least examined questions, which we take up in part 3. Critics on the political right have repeatedly warned that if equal rights are extended to same-sex couples, there will be no principled basis for denying equal rights to polygamists. Polygamy has received increased attention in the popular media, thanks in part to television shows such as *Big Love* and *Sister Wives*. It has figured in debates concerning the rights of Muslim minorities in Western countries, and it has been the subject of notable court cases in Canada and the United States. We consider polygamy, both its traditional form—of one husband with multiple wives—and the new, supposedly "postmodern" form of egalitarian "polyamory."

Why monogamy? Is it simply a matter of unthinking traditions rooted in Christianity, and racial and civilizational prejudices directed at practices associated with non-Western family forms? Part 3 explores these questions in part by using two important legal cases on the rights of polygamists, in British Columbia and Utah, and their surprising results, to make the case that polygamy is an unwelcome social practice.

Chapter 7 lays out the variety of forms of plural marriage and provides some historical background and context, focusing on the long-running conflict around polygamy in the Mormon Church in North America. As we will see, the large majority of human societies in history have practiced plural marriage in one form or another, and opposition to the practice over the past two centuries has often been rooted in religious, civilizational, and racial chauvinism. Is there a good public case against polygamy?

Chapter 8 lays out a variety of principled factors that help to distinguish plural marriage from same-sex marriage as a matter of both justice and constitutional principle. I also explore the impressive array of evidence that led the Supreme Court of British Columbia, in a landmark case decided in December 2012, to uphold Canada's criminal prohibition on polygamy. I argue that this evidentiary record, while certainly not beyond challenge, stands in contrast to the abstract and moralistic arguments advanced against the rights of gay and lesbian citizens. There is a good case for not extending equal rights to plural marriages, and for in some manner discouraging polygamy.

One year after the Canadian decision, a federal court in Utah came to the opposite result and struck down that state's criminal prohibition based on considerations altogether different from those relied on in British Columbia. This surprising case, introducing a number of complications, involved none other than the polygamous family that stars in *Sister Wives*. Kody Brown and his four wives present polygamy in a far more favorable light than do the other polygamists who have been the subjects of other legal actions since the 1950s. Their case also raises the difficult question of whether law enforcement officials can be trusted with the discretion supplied by general criminal prohibitions on polygamy. The chapter explores the issues raised by polygamy today. It also considers whether legal prohibitions against adult incest can be justified when partners avoid having children, and it closes by considering the new, "postmodern" form of plural relationship known as polyamory.

*****

Conservatives have long warned that gay marriage would change marriage for all, ultimately spelling the death of marriage and monogamy. It is undeniable that marriage and monogamy face new and ongoing challenges. While same-sex marriage is likely to affect the wider marriage culture, the clearest changes seem likely to be for the good. In the concluding chapter, I argue that monogamous marriage is made stronger as a liberal and democratic social institution by same-sex marriage. With respect to other complex aspects of law pertaining to marriage and family relations, when issues of basic justice and the public good are unclear, consequences are uncertain, and many people have come to rely on and build their lives around existing institutions and rules, the law should change incrementally.

PART I

WHY SAME-SEX MARRIAGE?

CHAPTER 1

GAY RIGHTS AND THE
CONSTITUTION OF REASONS

The public debate over gay rights generally and marriage rights specifically has ranged far and wide for over two decades: across courtrooms, legislatures, and political campaigns; in churches, schools, universities, the military, homes, workplaces, and clubs and associations such as the Boy Scouts of America; in the news media and on the Internet. Scholars have revisited and revised older debates and generated new arguments and evidence, with the humanities and sciences playing important roles. Movies, literature, music, photography, the theater, popular television, and other art forms have all played important roles in the ongoing debate, as have professional sports, beginning with women's tennis and finally reaching to men's professional football. It is no exaggeration to say that every department of American life has joined our national conversation on gay rights. The upshot? The national tide has clearly shifted, and the victories for same-sex marriage in the nation's courts and legislatures have turned from a trickle to a broad tide reaching much of the country.

Just as astonishing as changes in the law are those in the public mind. In 1988, when first asked about this in a national poll, only 12 percent of Americans agreed that "homosexual couples should have the right to marry one another."[1] Same-sex marriage was opposed in 1996 by a margin of 68 percent to 27 percent, according to Gallup polls. In 2004 the margin had closed to 55 percent against, 42 percent in favor. By 2011, 53 percent *favored* recognition of same-sex marriages, and in 2014, 55 percent favored and only 42 percent were against. Americans over 50 years of age still opposed same-sex marriages, but younger respondents—those 18–29 years of age—were in favor by 78 percent to 22 percent. Public opinion is currently shifting at the rate of approximately 1.5 percent per year.[2] I am aware of no similarly fraught public moral question that has ever witnessed so sudden and dramatic a shift.

This chapter and the next two present the main arguments that have been advanced by conservatives in opposition to gay rights and same-sex marriage. Given the profound changes in law and public opinion, why reconsider the arguments against and for same-sex marriage now? One reason is that our political community is and will remain deeply divided. Large majorities of "conservative" Americans, older Americans, those who attend church very regularly, and those who live in rural areas are opposed to same-sex marriage.[3] In addition, Americans often seem divided within themselves, and many who favor same-sex marriage seem to have serious reservations. When a poll in May 2012 offered Americans the option of allowing gays and lesbians to get "a legal partnership similar to but not called marriage," *only 37 percent of those polled favored legal marriage for same-sex couples*: fully 33 percent of those polled selected "legal partnership ... not called marriage," while 25 percent favored "no legal recognition."[4] As recently as 2012, roughly the same number of Americans polled described sexual relations between two adults of the same sex as "always wrong" as said it is "not wrong at all."[5] Genuine enthusiasm for marriage equality likely remains a minority position. Whatever particular courts and legislatures decide, Americans will likely remain deeply divided for many years to come. It still matters not simply *that* our politics is shifting but *why*.

The global divide is even more profound. While large majorities of citizens across western Europe and Canada affirm that homosexuals should be "accepted by society," according to recent Pew Research polls, only a small minority of Russians do so. Lack of acceptance generally prevails across Africa, with the partial exception of South Africa. In the Middle East, only Israel exhibits a fairly high level of acceptance, and in many Middle Eastern and African nations, gay and lesbian people are subject to horrible forms of prejudice, discrimination, and violence. In Asia and around the Pacific, there are vast differences between very accepting countries, such as Australia and the Philippines, and large countries like Pakistan and Indonesia where only 2 or 3 percent of people say homosexuality should be accepted. In Latin America, Argentina and Chile are very accepting; El Salvador and some other countries, less so.[6] The world is deeply divided on gay rights, with poorer and more religious countries tending, though not always, to be less accepting. Same-sex couples aside, the status of monogamous marriage is under pressure in China and up for grabs in some other Asian societies. I hope this book may contribute to the wider debate. Indeed, the "natural law" argument that I focus on exerts global influence via the teachings of the Roman Catholic Church.

I take up the conservative side of the argument, finally, because I share many of their concerns. I hope that some thoughtful dissenters from gay marriage will be provoked into fresh thinking by what follows: this book is addressed to them. Conservatives are right that not all effects of the sexual revolution that culminated in the late 1960s and 1970s have been good. Greater equality for women and greater acceptance and freedom for sexual minorities are among that era's most positive legacies. But there have also been negative consequences for many children of a weaker family structure, lower levels of marital stability and commitment, and a highly sexualized public environment. Rates of suicide among young people appear to be three times what they were in the 1950, and there are two hundred to four hundred attempts for every successful suicide.[7] Rates of emotional distress and mental illness appear, by some measures at least, to have increased for many children, and these appear correlated with higher rates of divorce and single parenting.[8]

Conservatives are rightly concerned about the difficulties that many of us face in integrating our sexual lives with deeper and long-lasting friendships, meaningful relationships, and family life. Marriage is a strategy for managing that integrative project as part of a profoundly important and life-shaping commitment. It conduces to greater health and happiness, especially for men. Defenders of same-sex marriage have long noted that marriage is in many ways a conservative institution. Libertarians, liberationists, and some liberals, as we shall see, doubt that marriage is fair given the diversity of people's conceptions of meaning and value in life. Many adopt an unnecessarily critical posture toward civil marriage. I seek to offer a sympathetic account of marriage that recognizes the importance for many people of marital commitment while also honoring, and indeed helping to secure, the equal liberty and fairness prized by liberals.

We begin by tracing the arc of conservative arguments against gay rights and same sex marriage since the 1980s. We will see the emergence of a demand for better reasons and evidence to justify settling the bounds of constitutional rights, and the emergence of the stated worry that affirming rights for gays and lesbians opens the door to other claims that cannot then be resisted. Such assertions were never well grounded.

CONSERVATIVES IN SEARCH OF AN ARGUMENT

For most Americans in the 1970s and 1980s, the subject of gay rights was both novel and generally regarded as distasteful.[9] Many would have allowed that gay men and lesbians should be left alone, but few endorsed equal rights or moral approval. The subject was not much discussed, and when it was, there was often a level of hostility and incomprehension that now seems astonishing.

Consider a symposium in 1984 on "Sex and God in American Politics," published in *Policy Review*, the journal of Stanford University's Hoover Institution. The participants were heads or founders of flagship institutions of the political right, including the Heritage Foundation, *National Review*, *Wall Street Journal*, *Public Interest*, American Conservative Union, Committee for the Survival of a Free Congress, Conservative Caucus, Eagle Forum, and Hoover Institution. Consider a sampling of the published comments of these conservative movement leaders:

> Homosexuality . . . is a form of life-denying death ethic in our society. If the homosexual ethic prevailed, that would be the end of the human race.—M. Stanton Evans[10]

> Homosexuality is one of the ultimate acts of rebellion against God and godly law. It is an act of rejection of traditional authority, an act of self-centeredness and selfishness. It is part of a humanistic world-view . . . which encourages people to . . . act in non-productive, existential, self-destructive, and sinful ways. Government should stop . . . trying to treat homosexuality as something other than wrong.—Howard Phillips[11]

> "It is an abomination unto the Lord." It is not normal, it is against nature, it produces a social evil. [Gays' sexual practices are] absolutely sickening. . . . The people who engage in it need to be pitied, counseled, reached out to in a way that will bring them back, because there is no question that homosexuality is a choice.—Paul M. Weyrich

> [T]he homosexuals are trying . . . to force the rest of us to respect their lifestyle. . . . We can't acquiesce in that. It's like prostitution. . . . [Y]ou are not going to force us to say that it is morally acceptable.—Phyllis Schlafly[12]

> I do not like homosexuality. I think it is a misfortune for a person to be a homosexual. . . . I don't want to see homosexuals persecuted by the law or by society. But I believe it is the responsibility of homosexuals . . . to keep their sexual life as private as possible. No society, certainly not our society, is going to accept homosexuality as being as morally and socially acceptable as heterosexuality. This is something homosexuals must come to realize.—Irving Kristol[13]

Other participants affirmed that homosexuality "is a learned lifestyle, and can be unlearned";[14] that it "goes against the obvious purpose of creation" and "is contrary to Biblical values and guidelines, and contrary to human nature"; and that measures must be taken to "establish a social environment in which homosexuality becomes less alluring."[15] And then there was Milton Friedman, God bless him: "I don't think it is any business of the government, so long as it's purely voluntary."[16]

Midge Decter, executive director of the important-sounding Committee for the Free World, concluded thus:

> One reason for so much homosexuality is the terror that angry, truculent girls and women have introduced into the relations between the sexes. I see young boys absolutely terrified of girls. . . . So, in my view, homosexuality is a means of escaping from girls, from women. [A]nother factor—and no doubt I could get slaughtered for saying this—is that homosexuality provides a handy escape from manhood, which is to say, fatherhood. It is inevitable, when you have women attempting to escape from womanhood, that you will have men attempting to escape from manhood. I couldn't say with any assurance that I know which came first. . . . But they are certainly interconnected.

She ended with an apparent attempt to reassure: "I don't have any special passion about homosexuals, I live in peace and amity with all sorts of homosexuals. But homosexual activism must be resisted."[17]

*****

Academics who addressed the issue often did no better. Consider Harry V. Jaffa, late professor emeritus at Claremont McKenna College and Claremont Graduate University, and distinguished fellow of the Claremont Institute. An arch moralist, Jaffa developed the "unnaturalness" theme in the 1980s and 1990s with particular vehemence. Gay and lesbian sexual love is "the very negation of anything that could be called a right according to nature," he wrote, because "the very root of the meaning of nature is generation." It "violates the order of nature" to use "men as if they were women, or women as if they were men." Marriage cannot be conceived "apart from the possibility of generation," and neither should legitimate sexual activity.[18] Jaffa warned that by rejecting the basic guideposts that "nature" offers to human conduct, homosexuals strike at the root of *all morality*. Indeed, there is no more reason to doubt that sodomy should be a criminal offense than that rape should be. I quote at length because this now seems so hard to fathom: "To release sodomy from such social restraints as still surround it . . . would be to adopt a neutral attitude toward the family and ultimately toward all morality,"[19] opening the door to incest and to those who "have uncontrollable cravings that can be gratified only by rapes and murders of their victims." "Homosexuals even more than Communists are enemies of every good thing we associate with the Declaration of Independence," which Jaffa reads as embodying natural law. "If sodomy is not unnatural, nothing is unnatural. And if nothing is unnatural, then nothing—including slavery and genocide—is unjust."[20]

Other conservatives were more elliptical. In 1993 Harvey C. Mansfield of Harvard, one of the most influential and important conservative political philosophers in America, testified in Colorado in favor of Amendment 2, which invalidated government policies designed to protect gay and lesbian citizens from discrimination. Shortly after his expert testimony, he wrote that homosexuality is an "open challenge to society's sense of shame, as the gays recognize quite well. For if the practices of homosexuals are not shameful, what is?"[21]

Well, lots of things actually, but no matter. A question that comes naturally to mind is: of what *should* people be ashamed? "Shame is variable and seems arbitrary," allowed Mansfield, and it should be guided by reason. Good, but how can we distinguish what is genuinely shameful from what prejudiced, misguided, or unreasonable people merely think is shameful? The best guide, said Mansfield, is traditional natural law, "Protestant as well as Catholic," and "the Christian, Jewish, and Muslim religions," which approve of sex for procreation.[22]

The problem is that Catholics and Protestants do not agree on contraception, abortion, or any number of other aspects of sexual morality. Some Orthodox Jews, Muslim fundamentalists, and others regard the pleasures of sex as deeply problematic even in marriage, a position that most everyone else (including the Catholic hierarchy) rejects. There are many versions of natural law; one of them needs to be specified and defended, a task that Mansfield has never undertaken. However, he did opine that

> this does not mean necessarily that all sex not for procreation is wrong; contraception might be justified as a way of intending procreation rather than letting it happen. In either case procreation is considered to be part of a perfect or complete human life. Sex without procreation is imperfect, even though it's fun and permissible (it's never safe). But sex in which procreation is inconceivable is not permissible and is shameful.[23]

Let's get this right: procreation must be possible for sex to be permissible. Therefore, homosexual conduct is not permissible. Contracepted heterosexual sex is permissible because procreation is then at least possible.

Why exactly? Because the contraceptives might fail? Because contracepted intercourse can be a way of "warming up" for actual procreation? (Incidentally, Catholic natural law rejects all use of contraception as immoral, for reasons we will see.) And what about postmenopausal women and their partners?

One key claim in Mansfield's version of natural law seemed to be that "procreation is considered to be part of a perfect or complete human life." Let us grant the great goods of procreation and child rearing. On that basis, one could argue that homosexuality is a misfortune since with gay and lesbian couples, and also sterile heterosexual couples (though in somewhat different ways), "natural" childbirth in which each parent contributes equally to the child's genetic makeup is unavailable. But that is no reason to regard sexually active gays and lesbians as *immoral*, or their practices as "shameful," any more than sexually active sterile men and postmenopausal women, nor does it furnish a respectable ground for discrimination.[24]

GAY RIGHTS AND MARRIAGE RIGHTS IN THE COURTS AND CONGRESS?

The U.S. Supreme Court spoke first in a dramatic way on gay rights in 1986, when, in *Bowers v. Hardwick*, a five-to-four majority of the justices upheld Georgia's criminal prohibitions on same-sex sodomy in the privacy of the home.[25] The background was that the Court had, more than twenty years earlier in *Griswold v. Connecticut*, announced constitutional protections for married couples' decision to use contraceptives.[26] The Court extended those privacy rights to the decision of unmarried heterosexual couples to use contraceptives, and later to the reading of pornography at home.[27] The most controversial extension of the privacy right was *Roe v. Wade*'s recognition of a woman's right to have an abortion under a doctor's supervision in the early stages of a pregnancy.[28]

The tone and substance of the majority opinions in *Bowers* now seem astonishing. Justice Byron White, writing for the majority, simply declared that the freedom to engage in "homosexual sodomy" bore no resemblance to the Court's previous privacy cases. Gay sex had "no connection" with "family, marriage and procreation." "Proscriptions against that conduct have ancient roots." To claim otherwise was "at best facetious." Never mind that those earlier privacy rights cases included the right to have an abortion, the right of married and unmarried couples to use contraceptives, and the right to read pornography at home. White insisted that the law "is constantly based on notions of morality," and "majority sentiments about the morality of homosexuality" are a fully adequate basis for law.[29] Chief Justice Warren Burger wrote separately to underscore that state criminalization of gay sex was "firmly rooted in Judeo-Christian moral and ethical standards." "Homosexual sodomy was a capital crime in Roman law." Blackstone described it as an "'infamous crime against nature' as an offense of 'deeper malignity' than rape, a heinous act 'the very mention of which is a disgrace to human nature,' and 'a crime not fit to be named.'"

White's opinion echoed the views set out by the eminent British jurist Lord Patrick Devlin in his famous defense of the *Enforcement of Morals* in 1965. Devlin wrote in opposition to the recommendations of the Committee on Homosexual Offenses and Prostitution, also known as the Wolfenden Report, which recommended in 1957 that "homosexual behaviour between consenting adults in private" and prostitution should no longer be criminal offenses.[30] Against the report's liberal conclusions, Devlin argued that societies are held together by moral codes based on the sentiments of the great mass of people. Legal prohibitions may simply reflect and give voice to social consensus. We need not determine that the underlying judgments are rationally defensible or backed by reasons and evidence. Reasoning, insisted Devlin, allows us to rule out only patently irrational assertions, such as that homosexuality is "the cause of earthquakes." Among "a number of rational conclusions," the "ordinary man has to rely upon a 'feeling' for the right answer. Reasoning will get him nowhere." It is sufficient, argued Devlin, to know that the laws are backed by an "intensity of feeling" and the moral judgments of the "reasonable man," or, as he put it, "the man in the Clapham omnibus."[31]

One of the most crucial questions animating the debate over gay rights since Devlin's time is whether good reasons and evidence need to be offered in support of the majority's moral sentiments. Devlin himself drew on a U.S. Supreme Court decision for support, albeit one that had already been discredited: "The ultimate foundation of a free society is the binding tie of cohesive sentiment."[32] The question is whether it is sufficient for a political majority to believe and hold that particular practices are morally abhorrent or offensive, perhaps because they are rooted in religious prohibitions, without any particular good explanation as to why or what harm they do.

Justice John Paul Stevens, dissenting in *Bowers*, took the liberal line, which I also defend, that "the fact that the governing majority in a State has traditionally viewed a particular practice as immoral is not a sufficient reason for upholding a law prohibiting the practice." This is especially the case, he insisted, when the laws in question were written, as in Georgia and elsewhere, to prohibit heterosexual as well as homosexual sodomy, and those laws would be unconstitutional if enforced against the heterosexual as well as gay citizens.[33] Justice Harry Blackmun agreed, remarking: "It is revolting to have no better reason for a rule of law than so it was laid down in the time of Henry the IV."[34] If the constitutional right to privacy "means anything," Blackmun continued, "it means that, before Georgia can prosecute its citizens for making choices about the most intimate aspects of their lives, it must do more than assert that the choice they have made is an 'abominable crime not fit to be named among Christians.'"[35]

Blackmun laid down a principle that became a challenge: "The legitimacy of secular legislation depends instead on whether the State can advance *some justification for its laws beyond its conformity to religious doctrine.*"[36]

The conservatives won in *Bowers*, but the majority opinions were derided by some as unreasoned and mean spirited.[37] Since *Bowers* the question has been: what good reasons and evidence can be offered to justify denying equal basic rights to gay and lesbian Americans?[38]

*****

If the justification for laws denying privacy rights to gays was murky, the political advantages of the gay rights issue was very clear. In the early 1990s, opinion polls showed support for gay marriage at only between 11 and 23 percent, but a State Supreme Court decision in Hawaii in 1993, and the conservative reaction against it, thrust the issue to the fore.[39] By overwhelming majorities, the U.S. House of Representatives and Senate passed the federal Defense of Marriage Act, which President Clinton signed in 1996, defining marriage in federal law as the relation of one man and one woman. Thirty-four state legislatures followed suit and passed "mini-DOMAs" inserting similar definitions into state law.[40]

During debate on the proposed federal legislation, Congressman Henry Hyde exploded with indignation when Congressman Barney Frank suggested that the Right was using same-sex marriage to score political points:

> Political! I wish I had never heard of this issue. This is a miserable, uncomfortable, queasy issue. . . . Nobody wants to talk about it. We are forced to by the courts. . . . If two men want to love each other, go right ahead. If you want to solemnize your love affair by some ceremony, create one. But don't take marriage, which has been a union between man and woman, and certainly is in this country, and try to say what you're doing is American.[41]

The fact is that in 1996 and for a long while thereafter, the gay marriage issue played very well for Republicans in electoral politics. The decision of the Supreme Judicial Court in Massachusetts upholding the right to same-sex marriage was initially extremely unpopular in most of the rest of the country. In the 2004 presidential election, George W. Bush and other Republican candidates emphasized their support for traditional marriage in campaign ads and speeches, while Democrats from John Kerry on down typically sought to avoid the issue. The presidential contest, and several Senate races, wound up being extremely close—a swing of sixty thousand votes would have given Ohio and the presidency to Kerry. Evidence suggests that the same-sex marriage issue may have proved a decisive mobilizer for the political Right, giving George W. Bush a second term as president.[42]

LIFESTYLE TO IMMUTABILITY

Why the change in public sentiment on gay rights? Why was homosexuality so long regarded as an immoral perversion? Why did public sentiment shift, dramatically and speedily, after centuries of disapproval, including several decades (after World War II) during which that disapproval was quite intense?[43]

To the extent that people gave it any thought at all, most once regarded homosexuality, explicitly or implicitly, as a *lifestyle choice*: a choice to give in to sexual perversity or "insatiable desire," or to escape from the responsibilities of adulthood, as illustrated in many of the remarks quoted above. The sexual radicalism among some—straight and gay—during the 1960s and 1970s, and the AIDS epidemic of the 1980s and 1990s, no doubt unnerved many, especially older, Americans.

The "older" view of homosexuality, says Judge Posner, was that it is a "selfish" choice "because male homosexuals have on average more sex partners (because men on average are more promiscuous than women) and didn't have to worry about pregnancy."[44] Only lately have most people confronted the fact that gays and lesbians typically experience their sexuality as *given* rather than *chosen*: as an orientation rather than a preference. The vast majority of gay men and lesbians report having "little or no choice" about their sexual orientation—95 percent for men and 84 percent for women.[45] And yet the older, discredited "lifestyle choice" view has persisted: it reappeared in the "ballot argument" submitted in 2008 to California voters summarizing the argument in favor of Proposition 8.[46] Judge Martin C. Feldman's opinion upholding Louisiana's ban on same-sex marriage also uses the language of "lifestyle."[47]

Writer and culture critic Edmund White observes that "most out gays in the 1970's would have resented" the argument that sexual orientation was genetic, or otherwise given by nature. That might suggest that one is making an excuse for something regrettable rather than affirming the equal goodness of same-sex love. "Defensible as that position seemed to us then," says White, "the genetic argument has in fact persuaded mainstream America to accept us. If the poor buggers can't help being pansies, then why persecute them? You might as well persecute someone for the color of his skin."[48] Radicals also often want to play down the role of human nature in shaping our dispositions and behavior. But the consensus of experts now confirms the experience of gay and lesbian people: that same-sex attraction is something one discovers as an adolescent, often, thanks to social prejudice and discrimination, with horror.

Indeed, the Google Books Ngram Viewer shows that the phrases "sexual preference" and "sexual orientation" were used with roughly comparable frequency in published books through the early to mid-1980s, but in the late 1980s and 1990s, "sexual orientation" skyrocketed, leaving "sexual preference" far behind.[49] Yet, more impressive, when the question was first asked in a Gallup Poll in 1977, only 13 percent of Americans described homosexuality as something "a person is born with," while 52 percent attributed it to "other factors such as upbringing and environment," and 14 percent to "both." Those figures began to shift in the 1980s and 1990s, until, by 2001, roughly equal numbers of Americans attributed homosexuality to nature and nurture/environment. Somewhat larger percentages of Americans say that one's sexual orientation "can't be changed," or that it's "just the way they are." In any event, the shift in view appears enormous.[50]

The shift in attitudes concerning same-sex desire came in parallel with the emergence of millions of Americans from the closet. Whereas 25 percent of Americans knew someone who was openly gay in 1985, by 2000 that figure was 75 percent. As Judge Jeffrey Sutton has observed, a large majority of Americans have now been "forced to think about the matter through the lens of a gay friend or family member."[51]

The spread of the idea of sexual orientation as an "immutable characteristic" rather than a lifestyle choice likely had several consequences.[52] It helped many to begin to accept that "that's just how some people are." If it is not a choice and there is nothing people can do about it, then not accepting gay people as such seems mean and cruel. It also made it far easier for gay and lesbian citizens and their advocates to assert that they were being denied the equal protection of the law. The Supreme Court has never added sexual orientation to its list of "suspect classifications," meriting "heightened scrutiny." Nevertheless, discrimination on the basis of sexual orientation has increasingly been treated as similar to discrimination on the basis of other "immutable characteristics," such as race, national origin, and gender, at least in requiring genuine scrutiny of whether laws discriminating against homosexuals can be supported by good reasons and real evidence.[53] The idea of inborn sexual orientation has undoubtedly lent support to the conviction that discrimination against gay men, lesbians, and, increasingly, transgender people ought not to be allowed unless there is some overriding reason requiring it.

THE *ROMER* REVOLUTION

In 1996 the Supreme Court decided its second major gay rights case. The background was this: In the 1970s, a few liberal cities, towns, and counties enacted ordinances banning discrimination against gays in housing, employment, public accommodations, and other matters. Conservatives often labeled these "special rights" for gays and lesbians and mobilized to reverse the ordinances. Nevertheless, antidiscrimination laws were enacted in greater numbers in the 1980s and 1990s, including in the Colorado cities of Aspen, Boulder, and Denver.

Conservatives responded by getting a popular initiative—Amendment 2—on the Colorado ballot in 1992. It held that no subdivision, agency, or municipality within Colorado could enact or enforce any law or policy "whereby homosexual, lesbian or bisexual orientation, conduct, practices or relationships" shall entitle any person or group to "claim any minority status, quota preferences, protected status or claim of discrimination."[54] A trial ensued in the Colorado Supreme Court that featured testimony from leading political philosophers, including Harvey C. Mansfield, Robert P. George, and John Finnis (and the present author, who was paired against Finnis).

The U.S. Supreme Court struck down Colorado's Amendment 2 by a six-to-three vote in *Romer v. Evans* (1996). The language of Justice Anthony M. Kennedy's majority opinion was a world away from *Bowers*, only nine years earlier. This Reagan-appointed justice invoked iconic language from the landmark civil rights case of 1896, *Plessy v. Ferguson*: "One century ago, the first Justice Harlan admonished this Court that the Constitution 'neither knows nor tolerates classes among citizens.'"[55] Kennedy pointed out that Amendment 2 did not simply rescind the ordinances but prohibited "all legislative, executive or judicial action at any level of state or local government designed to protect the named class."[56] He noted that protections from discrimination had become common and were extended to people on the basis of "age, military status, marital status, pregnancy, parenthood, custody of a minor child, political affiliation, physical or mental disability," among other characteristics. Amendment 2 "withdraws from homosexuals, but no others, specific legal protection from the injuries caused by discrimination." It enacted a "disqualification of a class of persons from the right to seek specific protection from the law," which "is unprecedented in our jurisprudence." "Its sheer breadth is so discontinuous with the reasons offered for it that the amendment seems inexplicable by anything but animus toward the class that it affects; it lacks a rational relationship to legitimate state interests." Kennedy concluded that Amendment 2 violated the Constitution's guarantee that no person should be denied the "equal protection" of law: "the government and each of its parts" must "remain open on impartial terms to all."[57]

This was the first Supreme Court judgment protecting gay and lesbian Americans from discrimination. It precipitated, perhaps surprisingly, no great public outcry; by 1996 most Americans agreed that gays should be protected from discrimination in housing, employment, and some other matters.[58]

The response from conservative intellectuals and academics was intense, and they were led by Justice Antonin Scalia's vehement dissent. Amendment 2 did not deny gays general legal protections, he argued, and, moreover, "moral disapproval of homosexual conduct" is a perfectly legitimate basis for law. Otherwise, he warned, there is no basis for disfavoring polygamy, "unless, of course, polygamists for some reason have fewer constitutional rights than homosexuals."[59]

Strikingly, Scalia never considers whether there are commonsense reasons and evidence that justify moral concerns about polygamy or homosexuality. No reasons or evidence are needed to support or justify these moral judgments: they are long-standing and deeply felt, and that is sufficient. He simply asks, rhetorically, "Has the Court concluded that the perceived social harm of polygamy is a 'legitimate concern of government,' and the perceived social harm of homosexuality is not?"

Leading conservative intellectuals, including Hadley Arkes, Robert George, and Charles Colson, writing in the conservative journal *First Things*, joined Scalia's excoriation of Kennedy and *Romer*. "Law, as it is presently made by the judiciary, has declared its independence from morality," wrote the editors, "especially traditional morality, and most especially morality associated with religion." Robert H. Bork referred to the *Romer* majority as a "band of outlaws." Russell Hittinger advised that if the courts prevent "the elected representatives of the people" from enacting "traditional morals legislation," on the basis of "the citizens' moral or religious motivation"—he did not distinguish—the righteous should engage in "civil disobedience."[60]

*****

Seven years later, the other shoe dropped, as Justice Scalia predicted it would. In *Lawrence v. Texas* (2003), the Supreme Court overruled *Bowers* and struck down a state criminal statute targeted at what Texas law called "deviate sexual intercourse with another individual of the same sex." Writing again for the Court's majority, Justice Kennedy insisted that constitutional "liberty gives substantial protection to adult persons in deciding how to conduct their private lives in matters pertaining to sex," at least "absent injury to a person or abuse of an institution the law protects."[61] Along with fundamental liberty, Kennedy emphasized that criminal laws targeting gays "demean" and "control" them "by making their private sexual conduct a crime."[62] "When homosexual conduct is made criminal by the law of the state, that declaration in and of itself is an invitation to subject homosexual persons to discrimination both in the public and in the private spheres."[63]

Older criminal statutes prohibited sodomy without regard to the sexual orientation of the parties, as we observed above, but any such prohibition applied to heterosexuals nowadays would violate the constitutional right to privacy and cause considerable outrage. Statutes targeting gays specifically date only to the 1970s. Kennedy emphasized that singling out gays in this way has no good public justification: it suggests an "animus" or animosity directed against gays that advances no legitimate public interest and therefore violates the Constitution's guarantee of "equal protection" of the law.[64]

This last point is extremely important. Hadley Arkes insisted in 1996 that "there persists in the public a residual moral sense that there is something about homosexuality that is not quite right."[65] That was certainly true for many Americans in 1996, and for a smaller but still significant number now. The crucial question is whether such judgments have a publicly reasoned basis and the support of evidence, accessible to the common sense of the political community. Or do these sentiments rest on the religious convictions of some in the community, and also lingering prejudice?

Justice Scalia dissented once again in *Lawrence*, asserting, as had the Court in *Bowers*, that popularly elected legislatures should be able to make "essentially moral choices" about what should and should not be criminalized without providing substantial reasons and evidence. He insists repeatedly that "moral disapproval of homosexual conduct" is in itself a "legitimate state interest."[66] Indeed, he goes out of his way to (apparently) torpedo the only serious philosophical defense of those moral judgments (in natural law).[67] Unless a majority of Texans has the right to pass laws based simply on their "belief . . . that certain forms of sexual behavior are immoral and unacceptable," and Coloradans have the right to express sheer "moral disapproval of homosexual conduct" without supplying any further justification,[68] then there will be no way to sustain laws against "fornication, bigamy, adultery, adult incest, bestiality, and obscenity." If majority convictions concerning sexual morality are not, standing alone, a "*legitimate* state interest, none of the above mentioned laws can survive rational basis review." To require substantial reasons, asserts Scalia, "effectively decrees the end of all morals legislation."[69]

Justice Scalia here echoes Lord Devlin, who also insisted that the criminal law may prohibit certain moral offenses widely held to be essential to society's existence, or at least, "necessary to preserve its integrity." To discern these standards, argued Devlin, we can look to "the generally accepted morality." If a principle of individual liberty is favored with respect to homosexuality and prostitution, then what, Devlin asked, of polygamy, incest, and bestiality?[70] The question posed half a century ago still reverberates in our time.

The skeptical insistence that reasons and evidence cannot be asked for in support of *any* such laws lest *all* such laws be swept aside is itself unsupported by reasons. Why should we believe that all moral restraints will fall away unless the state has the right to enact into law the sheer moral disapproval of the majority, without offering substantial reasons and evidence to justify those judgments? It is as if our only choices are unthinking traditionalism or sexual chaos. Reasons and evidence on these matters are not so opaque or fugitive, as I show below.

And there is another problem: one of most honored and valuable constitutional traditions is the insistence that reasons should be offered to publicly justify important political decisions touching on people's vital interests. The Declaration of Independence sets out an argument to justify America's separation from Britain. In the first number of the *Federalist Papers*, Publius addresses his fellow citizens, promising to "frankly acknowledge to you my convictions" and "freely lay before you the reasons on which they are founded."[71] The judiciary plays an important role in helping to identify and overturn laws grounded in no more than long-standing prejudice.[72] This is especially important when those distinctions "proceed along suspect lines": "suspect" because the group discriminated against is a minority defined by an immutable characteristic and a history of discrimination.[73]

GOD AND GAY MARRIAGE

The *First Things* Symposium from 1996, in which conservative academics and intellectuals railed against the Court's decisions in *Bowers* and *Romer*, is replete with appeals to religious beliefs and biblical morality. Charles Colson there predicted that the Supreme Court "may likely require states to recognize homosexual marriage. Christians therefore would be forced to live under a government whose actions violate the biblical ordering of social life and threaten the first institution ordained by God." Hadley Arkes refers repeatedly to the sexual ethic "imprinted on our natures" when humans were created male and female, and he worries that the Supreme Court has disenfranchised "people who bear these religious and moral sentiments."

Indeed, as this book goes to press, the Chief Justice of the Alabama Supreme Court, Roy S. Moore, has written a very public letter to the governor of Alabama, urging him to remember that the state constitution recognizes marriage as a "sacred covenant, solemnized between a man and a woman." Chief Justice Moore has further opined that, "The laws of this state have always recognized the Biblical admonition stated by our Lord," namely that, "'God made them male and female. For this cause shall a man leave father and mother, and cleave to his wife; And they twain shall be one flesh. . . .' (Mark 10:6–9)."[74]

Attempts to justify civil laws by invoking particular religious convictions, or particular interpretations of scriptural passages, cannot succeed. The reason is not that we disrespect religion but because Americans disagree so profoundly about their religious beliefs. And yet the law that binds all should be justified to all: that requires that we seek out reasons and evidence that we can examine in common, subject to widely accepted methods of inquiry. The Supreme Court has repeatedly recognized that laws are illegitimate if they are based only on the majority's favored religious convictions. In the debate over same-sex marriage, public officials have frequently expressed support for this principle of public reasoning. Judges, legislators, and citizens have repeatedly asked, "What is society's interest in marriage?"[75]

There was ample evidence of religiously based claims on behalf of Proposition 8 in California: promotional and advocacy materials contained many references to "God's plan for marriage" and the authority of the Bible. One of the lead defendant interveners, Hak-Shing William Tam, wrote to supporters of Proposition 8 warning that if it were not approved, other states would also "fall into Satan's hand."[76] When the proposition was challenged in federal court, Tam denied playing a leadership role on the measure's behalf.[77] A study of public opinion from the Pew Forum on Religion and Public Life in 2003 found that "religious beliefs underpin opposition to homosexuality."[78]

Obviously, many people's ethical and political views concerning marriage, family, and sex are shaped by their religious convictions and upbringing. There is nothing wrong with that. Religious communities and leaders played an important part in the struggle for civil rights, and they now participate in the debates over gay marriage, immigration reform, and other matters. Political analysts in New York attributed the success of Marriage Equality legislation in 2011 partly to the "concerted, sustained efforts by liberal Christian and Jewish clergy," who countered "the language of morality voiced by foes."[79] The moral energies generated by faith-based communities are to be welcomed in our politics, especially when religious citizens recognize their obligation to go beyond the teachings specific to their faith tradition and consider whether civil laws can be justified to citizens of other faiths.

When confronted with the question of same-sex marriage in the summer of 2011, state legislators in New York, as elsewhere, grappled directly with how their religious convictions about marriage should "bear on their obligations as lawmakers" deliberating and voting on a civil marriage bill.[80] In a closely divided New York State Senate, several Republicans provided the crucial votes in favor of same-sex marriage, while one Democrat voted with the Republicans in opposition. The Democrat, Senator Ruben Diaz, who is also a Pentecostal minister, proclaimed that "God, not Albany, has settled the definition of marriage a long time ago," as the union of husband and wife. "Same-sex marriage," he insisted, "is a government takeover of an institution that government did not create and should not define."[81] Senator Diaz was opposed very publicly by his granddaughter: "I am not asking to be married in church, I am simply asking to reinforce my right to marry in a consensual manner with the woman who I love and who I want to spend the rest of my life with."[82]

On the other side, Senator Mark Grisanti, a Republican from Buffalo, explained that "As a Catholic I was raised to believe that marriage is between a man and a woman. I'm not here, however, as a Senator who is just a Catholic." He said that his "background as an attorney" also shapes how "I look at things and I apply reason." When running for election, Grisanti had previously pledged his opposition to same-sex marriage. His change of mind was, he said, based on "conscience," "fairness," "research," and the conviction "that same-sex couples should have the same right that I enjoy with my wife that I love."[83]

Assembly Member Deborah Glick emphasized that "everybody is entitled to their religious belief. But they are not, according to our Constitution, entitled to impose those religious beliefs on others." Civil marriage, said Glick, "is the recognized and consistent shorthand that we all use to recognize and acknowledge committed, loving relationships and the families that exist within them."[84] The recognition that is being sought is civic rather than religious. As Assembly Member Daniel O'Donnell said, referring to his own long-term relationship, "What I'm seeking is nothing from a church, or from a synagogue, or from a mosque; what I'm seeking is a piece of paper from my government . . . that conveys responsibilities and rights, which I am currently deprived from getting."[85]

The religiously orthodox have every right to decide who is validly married within their particular communities of faith. The civil law of marriage, however, belongs to all of us as citizens of the political community: it is instituted by us and answerable to us as political equals. At our best we answer to one another by seeking and providing reasons and evidence that can be shared and assessed in public. It is not enough to point to the mere fact of the majority's moral sentiments or feelings, or the religious convictions that define our particular communities of faith. The proper question is: what are our reasonable public grounds as citizens?

CONCLUSION

One of the most salutary features of the argument over gay rights generally and same-sex marriage in particular has been the constant tug of the demand for reasons. What reasons are there for discriminating against gay and lesbian couples seeking the same kinds of rights enjoyed by heterosexuals? What public purposes are served by excluding gay and lesbian couples from the civil institution of marriage? Those questions reflect the demand that our law represent more than the private preferences and convictions of the powerful. The rule of law insists that "like cases should be treated alike," or distinguished by principles, reasons, and evidence that hold up to critical public scrutiny. Collective decisions governing access to important civil institutions such as marriage should be accompanied by public reasons and evidence sufficient to justify the way that power is being used to all the members of the political community.

Our subject is the law of marriage for a large and diverse political community in which citizens pursue a variety of reasonable conceptions of the good life, often under the influence of their deepest religious beliefs. Enshrining a sectarian ideal of marriage in law would fail to respect the range of reasonable opinions in our society. As Justice Kennedy observed in *Lawrence v. Texas*, many people condemn same-sex relations based on religious and ethical ideals "to which they aspire and which thus determine the course of their lives.... The issue is whether the majority may use the power of the state to enforce these views on the whole society."[86]

David Moats, editorial page writer and editor at the *Rutland Herald*, observed the conflict over same-sex unions in Vermont, earning a Pulitzer Prize. Looking back, he reports that "I had not read John Rawls at the time, but the editorials I wrote on the question of private morality and public justice reflected a Rawlsian concept of secular democracy." He offers a homespun analogy that seems altogether apt:

> The village green of a typical Vermont town was emblematic of my view. The green might be surrounded by a Congregational church, an Episcopal church, a Unitarian church, a Catholic church, a public library, and a tavern. Citizens would enter each place for their own personal reasons, and they would be free to fashion their own moral codes from what they learned inside. But when it came time to develop public policy, the citizens would have to emerge onto the village green and meet together to pass laws that a majority could support. No individual sect would have the authority to force its moral view on the others. Somehow, the separate groups would have to find common ground on which to act. What Rawls called a "comprehensive" view of morality—as embodied in religion, philosophy, or other moral teachings—is not the business of government.[87]

We next turn to the philosophical argument, grounded in natural law, for regarding marriage as necessarily the union of one man and one woman. Later, in chapter 3, we will consider arguments from the gendered nature of marriage as a relation of husband and wife, and others based on children's interests.

CHAPTER 2

TRADITIONAL MARRIAGE
AND PUBLIC LAW

"Marriage is the union of one man and one woman."[1] So say the federal Defense of Marriage Act and California's Proposition 8. And that is the crux of the matter for conservatives opposed to marriage rights for gay and lesbian couples. But why? And what is the harm of same-sex marriage to heterosexual marriages? Why do many conservatives continue to think that same-sex couples must be barred, by definition or moral necessity, from being married in the eyes of the law?

The conservative arguments presented in the previous chapter were notable for their lack of subtlety and persuasiveness. This may be one reason why Justice Scalia insists that the majority's bare "moral choices" and long-held disapproval of homosexuality are enough to make discriminatory laws legitimate in a democracy.

Other conservatives insist that to justify excluding gays from marriage and other rights, reasoned accounts must be offered that appeal to our common human sense, not to religious convictions. John Finnis observes that "embarrassment" makes "most people more than usually inarticulate" with respect to homosexuality. Nevertheless, he insists, "public policies should indeed be based on reasons, not merely emotions, prejudices, and biases."[2] Robert P. George joins Finnis in denying the legitimacy of laws prohibiting equal rights for gays and lesbians if they are based only on long-held convictions that lack the support of reasoned argument. Taking direct aim at Lord Patrick Devlin, who defended "traditional" morals legislation based only on widely held moral sentiments, George argues that "morals laws are morally justified only when the morality they enforce is true."[3]

Ryan T. Anderson, one of the younger advocates of natural law, insisted in 2014 that most Americans had "never heard a rational case for" traditional marriage as necessarily the union of one man and one woman.[4] He and his coauthors argue that when the New Natural Law case is explained correctly, its truth becomes "luminous."[5] The reader can judge.

WHAT IS MARRIAGE?

The group of philosophers, ethicists, and legal scholars whose views we now consider have worked tirelessly for decades to refine and disseminate the argument that marriage is necessarily heterosexual because it is inherently and by nature ordered to procreation. These scholars are associated with the tradition of natural law central to Catholic teachings on sex, marriage, and family life, but their argument appeals to our common human reason rather than specific religious claims. The scholars on whom I focus call their approach the "New Natural Law" (NNL, or "natural law" for short in what follows), and they are widely regarded as the most philosophically sophisticated contemporary representatives of this tradition. They include Finnis, George, Germain Grisez, Patrick Lee, and others.

The most recent restatement of this position is a short but tightly argued book that Justice Samuel Alito cited in his *Windsor* dissent: *What Is Marriage? Man and Woman—A Defense*, by Sherif Girgis, Ryan T. Anderson, and Robert P. George.[6] Girgis, Anderson, and George play down their larger debt to New Natural Law, saying little about sexual ethics more broadly, but, as we will see, their view of marriage is embedded in a wider account of sexual ethics.[7]

Those who subscribe to natural law generally link ethical judgments to our common human nature and argue that it is by virtue of that nature that we know what is good for human beings.[8] Hence, Hadley Arkes refers to the "natural teleology of the body." They argue further that the law ought to be based on these ethical truths, especially when touching on morally significant matters of personal ethics such as sex and marriage.

Girgis, Anderson, and George argue that marriage has a specific and *inherent nature* that is prior to and independent of law and culture:

> Marriage is, of its essence, a comprehensive union: a union of will (by consent) and body (by sexual union); inherently ordered to procreation and thus the broad sharing of family life; and calling for permanent and exclusive commitment, whatever the spouses preferences. . . . [I]t is also a moral reality: a human good with an objective structure, which is inherently good for us to live out.

Marriage is comprehensive, because, "unlike ordinary friendships, marriage unites people in all their basic dimensions. It involves a union of minds and wills that unfolds in a sharing of lives and resources." It unites two people "in their minds *and* bodies . . . it unites them with respect to procreation, family life, and its broad domestic sharing . . . permanently and exclusively." We are, after all, embodied creatures. If marriage didn't include bodily union, "it would leave out—it would fail to be extended along—a basic part of each person's being."[9]

Girgis, Anderson, and George go on to describe various familiar and widely valued benefits associated with marriage. Marriage is *good for children*: it helps provide a stable and healthy environment in which to have and to raise them. Second, marriage is *good for spouses* "financially, emotionally, physically, and socially." Husbands and wives "gain emotional insurance against life's temporary setbacks." With their exclusive commitment, spouses withdraw from the "sexual marketplace" and settle down; men spend less time in bars, and they enjoy the benefits of a "sharpened sense of purpose at home and work." Marriage signals and promotes maturity, and the benefits seem to be especially pronounced for men. And marriage is, finally, *good for society*: it promotes economic growth and "limited government," they say, by settling spouses in their relationship and facilitating their focus on economically productive and responsible endeavors. In addition, the "decline of marriage," they say, most hurts the least well off.[10]

These commonsense claims about marriage are all on the right track, and only some qualifications are needed with respect to several. While Girgis, Anderson, and George speak repeatedly of "permanence" as a norm, stability in marriage is not an unconditional good: separation and divorce can serve everyone's interests in high-conflict marriages. Children and spouses benefit from stable, *healthy* marriages, in which open conflict is reasonably low and the long-term happiness of the spouses is advanced.[11]

If we leave such qualifications aside for the moment, along with the references to "essences" and "nature," then we can endorse as plausible and familiar these observations concerning marriage and its benefits to children, spouses, and society. These are the terms on which gay and lesbian Americans are making the case for inclusion in the institution of marriage. People aspire to marriages understood as comprehensive, permanent, and unconditional mutual commitments that unite two people—bodily and spiritually—in building a common life together. This is notwithstanding the fact that approximately half of marriages end in divorce. That common life involves coordination across all aspects of their lives: a shared household, coordinated work lives, mutual friendships and extended family lives, shared sexual intimacy, caring for one another and being there in time of need. And of central importance for many or most, but by no means all, married couples is the common project of having and raising children together.[12] Those who espouse natural law are right that it is marriage so understood to which people aspire, and they are also right that the good of children, spouses, and the wider society is advanced by marriage so understood. All this seems right, and none of it (again aside from the language of "essences" and "nature," yet to be unpacked) is distinctive to New Natural Law.[13]

Obviously, there are important and legitimate variations in people's marriages: some marriages are cut short by death or some other tragedy, or by choice and mutual agreement. Some couples could, but choose not to, have children. And there are married couples in "blended families" raising children from previous marriages.

The obvious question arising from all this is: *Why not extend marriage so understood to same-sex couples?* Why do Girgis, Anderson, and George insist that same-sex marriage is not simply wrong but impossible?

IS MARRIAGE BY NATURE HETEROSEXUAL?

The authors of *What Is Marriage?* argue that marriage can be understood as a comprehensive, permanent, and exclusive union of two persons only if it consists of a man and a woman. Why? Because, they say, only a man and a woman can *consummate* their marriage via a sexual act that is ordered to procreation: "spouses unite only by coitus [or sexual intercourse], which is ordered toward the good of bringing new human life into the world."[14]

> [M]arriage is ordered to family life because the act by which spouses make love also makes new life; one and the same act both seals a marriage and brings forth children. That is why marriage alone is the loving union of mind and body fulfilled by the procreation— and rearing—of whole new human beings.[15]

And later,

> Having consented to sharing in the generative acts that unite them organically (as "one flesh"), spouses cooperate in other areas of life (intellectual, recreational, etc.) in the broad domestic sharing uniquely apt for fostering the all-around development of new human beings.[16]

Or, as George has put it elsewhere (writing with Patrick Lee), in coitus, male and female "become literally one organism" for the purpose of generating new life, and so, marital union is "the kind of community distinguished by its openness and orientation to procreation."[17]

On this view, it is the *twoness of coitus* (or intercourse) and its aptness for (or "orientation to") procreation that uniquely make sense of monogamy and other central features of marriage. Coitus holds all the elements of marriage together as a comprehensive (bodily and intellectual) relation of two people who commit to share one another's lives on the basis of *permanence* and *exclusivity*.[18] The norms that define marriage—"twoness," permanence, and exclusivity—depend on coitus and its natural orientation to procreation and new life. In the absence of coitus, say Girgis, Anderson, and George, *none of the distinctive elements of marriage makes sense*: not the bodily dimension (why should sex be so central to marriage?), nor the twoness and exclusivity (why not married groupings of three or more?), nor the permanence, for merely emotional bonds are transient, but coitus is by its nature oriented to the good of children and family, which call for permanence.

The focus on sexual intercourse or coitus is striking. Common sense affirms that *children* benefit from a stable home life and the emotional security, time, and resources that two devoted parents can most easily provide. So procreation provides one very good reason for public concern about marital stability: bringing a child into this world provides a profound rationale for a couple to make a serious long-term commitment to each other. Of course, marriage is not only about children, and marriage without children still serves the good of the spouses and society, as proponents of natural law affirm.

These commonsense claims are not what advocates of natural law have in mind, however, for they assert that coitus or intercourse is the sine qua non of marriage even if, owing to the sterility of one or both partners, actual procreation is impossible.[19] They say that marriage is necessarily formed by "only a man and a woman," because marriage is "a union whose norms and obligations are decisively shaped by its *essential dynamism* toward children," and crucially, "*that dynamism* comes not from the actual or expected presence of children, which some same-sex partners and even cohabiting brothers could have, and some opposite-sex couples lack, but from the way that marriage is sealed or consummated: in coitus, which is organic bodily union."[20]

In other words, according to these philosophers, it is the baby-making sex and *not the babies* that makes sense of marital norms of twoness (monogamy), permanence, and exclusivity.

It is on this basis that Girgis, Anderson, and George insist that same-sex couples are not "denied a right to marriage." They are, rather, *ineligible* for marriage by nature. Same-sex marriage is a moral impossibility because same-sex couples cannot mate.[21] *No coitus, no marriage.* This is (presumably) why Maggie Gallagher calls same-sex marriage "a lie": it obscures what Girgis, Anderson, and George call the "luminous" truth, and universal "moral reality," that marriage is a "two-in-one-flesh communion."[22]

The argument fails to capture the meaning and value that civil marriage has for Americans today, and it provides no comprehensible public argument for excluding same-sex couples from marriage. Let us consider some of these problems in turn.

Children, spouses, and society benefit, as we have already observed, from stable, healthy marriages (we explore these benefits at greater length below). But it seems bizarre to say that coitus, with no babies or possibility of babies, "require[s] permanent and exclusive commitment." The tendency of baby-making sex to actually make babies could furnish a reason for thinking that sex and marriage should go together; this is the "channeling argument," which we will consider below. But New Natural Law insists that marital norms come "not from the actual or expected presence of children."

Similarly, it seems very strange to suppose that it is the nature of coitus or intercourse that explains marital norms such as "twoness" or monogamy. Girgis, Anderson, and George advance the startling claim that "marriage is possible between only two because *no act can organically unite three or more*, or thus seal a comprehensive union of three or more lives" (emphasis added).[23] In other words, marriage is possible only between two because only two people can have intercourse at the same time? No defender of polygamy would be moved by that observation, which seems irrelevant. The reasons for favoring monogamy over polygamy are otherwise: there is substantial evidence, set out below, that polygamy as a social form tends, as compared with monogamy, to give rise to greater inequality and conflict within families and in society. The admitted fact that only two people can have intercourse at the same time is tangential.

*****

Many have now remarked on the oddness of New Natural Law's focus on the *nature of the consummating act* (coitus or intercourse) as the sine qua non of marriage and the thing that calls for twoness, permanence, and exclusivity in marriage. It seems much more sensible to locate the essence of marriage in the nature of the marital commitment, aptly expressed in familiar marriage vows: "to have and to hold, for better for worse, for richer for poorer, in sickness and health, til death do us part."

Loving commitment allows two people to build a life together in ways that tend to enhance their health and well-being, and the good of society. For most people, though not for everyone, sharing one's life with another provides an anchor of stability and support that is comforting in times of trouble and enhances happiness and success. The common good of the spouses, and the well-being of actual children for whom parents are profoundly responsible, furnish good grounds for working at sustaining the commitment. We explore at greater length below, in part 2, the nature of marriage and marital commitment and, in part 3, the reasons for favoring monogamy, reasons that are altogether consistent with marriage equality.

With respect to the natural law argument, however, puzzlement has now been registered not only in academic journals but in popular online publications, courtrooms, and legislatures.

Jason Lee Steorts, writing in the conservative *National Review*, observes of Girgis, Anderson, and George's view of marriage that it seems strange that "the value of a relationship between two persons in love [would depend] on the structure of their genitals."[24] Marc Joseph Stern, writing in *Slate Magazine*, has remarked on the oddness of the view that "only sex acts with a 'dynamism toward reproduction'—that is, penile to vaginal intercourse—create true marriages." He correctly observes that "the broad sharing uniquely fit for family life—is embraced by both sides of the marriage debate": those arguing "in favor of same-sex marriage speak of 'commitment' and the 'stability' of a 'multifaceted intimate relationship.' What's in dispute is how you get there. According to [same-sex marriage] opponents, to achieve this sharing, commitment, and stability, a penis must ejaculate in a vagina."[25]

In response to Steorts, Girgis, Anderson, and George complain that, "with the right (unfair) description, any view can be ridiculed." It is unclear, however, what the right (fair) description is of "organic bodily union" that renders the argument persuasive.

DOUBLE STANDARD FOR INFERTILE HETEROSEXUALS?

Critics have long flagged an apparent inconsistency in the natural law position. New Natural Law endorses sex within the marriages of sterile heterosexuals as not only permissible but good: "marital union itself fulfills the spouses." Natural law proponents consistently hold that even when it is impossible for spouses to conceive a child, marital union itself is a great good "joining mothers to fathers in friendship."[26] But if there is no possibility of procreation, then what makes the sex acts of sterile heterosexual couples part of their marital good? Why do sterile heterosexual sex acts, unlike homosexuals, have "procreative significance"?

Of course, sterility is an unchosen condition beyond the control of sterile heterosexual couples. But New Natural Law allows that the same is typically true of homosexuals. Gays and lesbians do not have the physical equipment (the "biological complementarity") such that anyone could have children by doing what they can do in bed. Yet the same thing true of sterile couples. The crucial difference, assert these scholars, is that infertile heterosexual couples can still have intercourse—behavior "suitable for procreation"—and thereby experience "organic bodily union." Because of that, their relationship is inherently "oriented toward begetting, nurturing, and education of children together" (even when there are no children). On the other hand, because same-sex couples lack the physical complementarity needed to engage in behavior suitable for procreation, they simply cannot share in a marital kind of community, and their sex cannot be anything but immoral.[27]

What is the point of sex in an infertile marriage? If the partners have sex, knowing they are infertile, it is for pleasure and to express their love, or friendship, or some other shared goods that are available to them. It will be for precisely the same reasons that committed, loving same-sex couples have sex. Why are these good reasons for sterile or older married couples but not for gay and lesbian couples? If, on the other hand, sex detracts from the real goods of intimacy, love and friendship that can be shared by two men or two women, as advocates of natural law say, why isn't the same true for sterile heterosexual couples?

Strangely enough, and precisely because "the sterile and the elderly are allowed to marry," Justice Scalia has asserted that "the encouragement of procreation" cannot be the reason for excluding gays from marriage. The reason for excluding gays, he says, has to involve moral disapproval of "homosexual conduct."[28] Justice Scalia is right. And yet, if we inquire into the sexual ethics of the New Natural Law, the only sophisticated conservative moral theory on offer, we will see that it provides no justification for singling out gays for moral disapproval.

WHEN IS SEX GOOD?

In *What Is Marriage?* Girgis, Anderson, and George keep the discussion firmly fixed on marriage. They do not articulate the larger natural law sexual ethic. Given the immediate aim of defeating same-sex marriage, it makes sense to avoid taking stands that would give many political allies pause. But *What Is Marriage?* relies on and refers to central aspects of the wider New Natural Law sexual ethic, which Robert George has ably defended for decades.[29] "Organic bodily union" and "two-in-one-flesh communion" seem puzzling taken on their own, but these formulas are central to the distinctly Catholic ethics of sex: "Conjugal love," as Grisez puts it, is "the central principle of sexual morality."[30] Or, as Stephen J. Pope, professor of theology at Boston College, puts it in describing the Catholic Church's authoritative teaching, "same-sex marriage is impermissible because 'homosexual activity' is always wrong," this principle "is the center of its general argument against same-sex marriage."[31]

Let me cut to the chase. In the New Natural Law view, whenever persons, *married or unmarried and of whatever sexual orientation*, seek sexual pleasure in a way that is intentionally severed from *openness to new life (babies) in marriage*, those sexual acts are valueless and immoral. Sexual acts must be open to new life, as Pope Francis has recently reiterated.[32] Therefore, the use of contraceptives is always immoral in the same way that homosexual sexual relations are. Germain Grisez, whose important multivolume work *The Way of the Lord Jesus* provides the most detailed account of New Natural Law's sexual ethics, is quite clear: "*such heterosexual activities—including contracepted intercourse, within or outside marriage—are morally similar to sodomy*" (emphasis added).[33] Similarly, George and his sometime coauthor Gerard Bradley argue for the moral wrongness of all "nonmarital orgasmic acts . . . irrespective of whether the persons performing such acts are same or opposite sexes (and even if those persons are validly married to each other)." In all such acts the persons involved "cannot form one complete organism,"[34] as do husband and wife in coitus: their acts are not only, then, not marital but (these scholars assert) antimarital and immoral.

The implication of New Natural Law sexual ethics is that all use, including by married couples, of condoms or intrauterine devices or morning-after pills, or intentional withdrawal and ejaculation outside the vagina, masturbation, mutual masturbation, and so forth, *artificially* blocks the natural dynamism of intercourse toward procreation and is, once again, immoral. Immoral *in the same way as gay sex* because all these acts "violate the good of marriage itself,"[35] by damaging our capacity to appreciate and understand marriage properly: as ordered by intercourse to procreation.

Only "natural family planning" (as the Roman Catholic Church calls it) in the form of the "rhythm method"—avoiding sexual activity on those days when the woman is fertile (and taking account that sperm may last three or four days in the genital tract)—is permitted. Contracepted sex is "contralife" and "contrary to marital love," whereas the "choice of the natural rhythms involves accepting the cycle of the person, that is the woman, and thereby accepting dialogue, reciprocal respect, shared responsibility and self-control," according to Grisez, quoting another authority on natural law, John Paul II.[36]

New Natural Law proponents often support restrictions on the marketing and sale of contraceptives, the revival of laws against extramarital and premarital sex, or fornication, and much tighter legal restrictions on divorce and remarriage, as well as the overturning of whatever judicial rulings stand in the way.[37] This is not a "conservative" agenda: it would require the reversal of many decades of legal reforms that are largely very widely accepted.

Just why all the various sexual acts described above are inherently always immoral is obscure. The reason given is that heterosexual married couples engaged in uncontracepted intercourse (or in acts leading up to it) experience a "real good in common," while all of the other sexual acts (all contracepted and all nonmarital sexual acts) instead involve "the partners in treating their bodies as instruments to be used in the service of their consciously experiencing selves," with no real common good.[38] Their experiences of pleasure are private and incommunicable. These impermissible sex acts involve a self-destructive "mind-body dualism" because they treat "one's sexuality and another's as a mere extrinsic instrument" of the conscious self.[39]

These are extremely abstract and broad generalizations about classes of sexual acts that would seem, in lived reality, to be very diverse. While one might agree with natural law advocates that, for example, promiscuous anonymous sex seems likely to involve treating one's own and others' bodies as mere instruments of pleasure in a way that is self-destructive, it seems implausible to characterize all nonprocreative and contracepted sex, including between married and otherwise loving couples, as necessarily immoral and self-destructive in these ways. At the very least such claims are speculative, counterintuituve, and unproven.

Paul J. Weithman, a professor of philosophy at Notre Dame, expresses sympathy with parts of the natural law view, taken in the abstract: "I am inclined to agree that there is something both alienating and morally bad about treating one's body as nothing more than an instrument for producing one's own or another's pleasure." But he also asks why we should suppose that two people can share real goods in common *only* if they "complement or complete one another with respect to the function of procreation." Same-sex couples, he observes, may share other forms of complementarity.[40] Professor Pope of Boston College agrees: New Natural Law "fails to build a logical case for the claim that" all homosexual acts are reducible to "the pursuit of individual self-gratification." He charges New Natural Law proponents with "gross overgeneralization," insisting that "Gay people are more diverse, and in morally relevant ways, than is recognized by the 'new natural law.'"[41]

The sexual ethics of the New Natural Law is implausible on its own terms, and deeply at odds with the beliefs and practices of the vast majority of Americans, Democrat or Republican. The unpopularity of these wider views certainly furnishes a tactical reason for keeping mum about them when trying to stop same-sex marriage. But the sexual ethics is at the core of the natural law account of marriage.

The Guttmacher Institute reports that "virtually all American women aged 15–44 who are sexually experienced have at some point used a contraceptive method other than natural family planning." By "virtually all" they mean 99 percent. The same study suggests that this is true of 98 percent of Catholic women.[42] Other polls suggest that 93 percent of Americans, and 90 percent of Catholics, accept contraceptive use.[43] Furthermore, almost all Americans have sex before marriage: "almost all" here means 97 percent.[44] Reasonable people can disagree about many aspects of sexual morality, but virtually all unite in rejecting New Natural Law sexual ethics.

New Natural Law condemns all these behaviors common among heterosexual Americans on the same grounds as it condemns gay and lesbian sexual relations. And if one dismisses natural law's broad sexual ethic, then its account of marriage loses its crucial prop. Americans overwhelmingly reject, as concerns themselves, the primary ground offered by natural law for morally condemning gay and lesbian sex and for rejecting same-sex marriage.

MARRIAGE AND THE ORIENTATION TO CHILDREN

New Natural Law proponents claim that only heterosexual couples can be married because only their unions can be oriented toward having and raising children, and toward the permanence, monogamy, and fidelity that are best for children. But when we shift our attention from natural law's strange focus on coitus to the lives and marriages of actual people, the claim seems obviously wrong.

Consider a marriage in which the heterosexual spouses could have children but decide they do not want to. They commit to "have and to hold [or, to love and cherish], from this day forward, for better for worse, in sickness and in health, til death." They have sexual relations, but they use contraceptives assiduously because they value their careers and travel, say, or they seek to devote their lives to some larger cause such as treating infectious diseases in Africa. For them, these other projects are not compatible with raising children. In the natural law view, as we already saw, when spouses interpose artificial means to prevent conception, their sexual relations are no longer marital but rather are morally similar to sodomy and not "shaped by" any "essential dynamism toward children." Their sexual acts are immoral: valueless and damaging to themselves and society. This strikes me as absurd: it seems obviously wrong to regard as necessarily and categorically immoral those heterosexual marriages in which contraceptives are used to avoid conceiving children.

On the other hand, many same-sex couples—including those who have adopted or conceived children somehow—view their partnership as centrally about raising children together in a loving home environment. If we want to think of marriage as involving an "essential dynamism toward children," it seems strange to exclude all married gay parents, but to include those heterosexual couples who *could* have children but *do not*. If we shift our attention away from the sexual act to the nature of people's marriages, then it seems clear that many heterosexual marriages are much less oriented toward the good of raising and nurturing children than are those homosexual couples raising children together.[45] It seems obvious to me that neither same-sex couples nor the childless by choice should be excluded from marriage.

I see no problem with allowing that sexual relations in marriage have a *special sort of significance* as a consequence of the connection with the act of procreation; a special meaning.[46] This is how new human life begins. That's wonderful. Precious. But why is everything else valueless and immoral? Why is such singular significance attributed to sexual acts that are procreative in type (even if not procreative in effect) while everything else (unless a prelude to coitus) is condemned as immoral? If ever there were a case of *the best* being the enemy of *the good*, this would be it.

PLAIN FAIRNESS

If the procreative—or coital—argument for excluding gays from marriage is obscure, the fairness argument for including gays has been stated clearly by no less a philosopher than Alec Baldwin: "Beyond any issues of infertility or illness, there are men and women who are married in the eyes of the state, enjoying all of the legal benefits, who have no intention of having children. They seek only companionship and all of the entitlements that come with marriage. Sex, joy, partnership, caring. All of that is theirs, even though they will never bear children and willfully so. If the state says they are free to do that, why aren't gay couples, as well?"[47]

Evidence and common sense suggest that Baldwin is right: the same benefits of marriage to heterosexual couples are also available to homosexual couples. Numerous studies show that people in reasonably happy marriages have better physical and psychological health, lower mortality rates, and increased longevity compared to single people. The benefits of marriage seem to be especially great for men, and these benefits flow not only to them (in the form of greater longevity and better health) but to society in the form of lower rates of violence, drug and alcohol abuse, and crime. Many of the same benefits seem to flow to same-sex couples from the legal recognition of their marriages, including reduced social stigma and psychological stress.[48] Natural law advocates remain unmoved and respond by repeating the formula that heterosexual intercourse is behavior *oriented toward procreation*.

As Chief Justice Margaret Marshall of the Supreme Judicial Court of Massachusetts observed: "Fertility is not a condition of marriage, nor is it grounds for divorce. People who have never consummated their marriage, and never plan to, may be and stay married. . . . [I]t is the exclusive and permanent commitment of the marriage partners to one another . . . that is the sine qua non of civil marriage." Moreover,

> The "marriage is procreation" argument singles out the one unbridgeable difference between same-sex and opposite-sex couples, and transforms that difference into the essence of legal marriage. . . . [T]he marriage restriction impermissibly "identifies persons by a single trait and then denies them protection across the board." *Romer v. Evans* (1996). In so doing the State's action confers an official stamp of disapproval on the destructive stereotype that same-sex relationships are inherently unstable and inferior to opposite-sex relationships and not worthy of respect.[49]

ABSTRACTIONS AND EXPERIENCE

Natural law proponents like Lynn D. Wardle claim that their philosophy reveals the "true, real, actual nature of homosexual relationships in general."[50] Such advocates impose a set of descriptions on sexual acts and relationships of different types, and these are asserted to represent their *essential nature*. The burden of the argument is then carried by selective descriptions of the favored and disfavored forms of marriage and sex.

One thing that is striking about this teaching, as should now be evident, is how distant it is from anything resembling sympathetic engagement with the lives of actual people. For example, even if a gay couple loves and commits to care for and support each other, and also to raise a child together, Girgis, Anderson, and George insist that there is no resemblance between them and a married couple. They dismissively remark, "Just deciding to rear children together is not enough to make you married: three monks who commit to caring for an orphan do not thereby marry."[51] Why say such a thing? Because "marriage is a special kind of friendship uniquely embodied in coitus."[52] Without coitus, "shared domestic life would be at best an optional bonus, and at worst a suffocating hindrance, to non-familial bonds, just as surely as raising a child with your college roommate would be."[53]

Maggie Gallagher, who is an ally rather than a proponent of natural law, also describes gay men (lesbians are left out) so as to defy their inclusion in marriage:

> The gay marriage idea is based on a lie.... A gay man does not wish to be a husband in the sense of taking responsibility for a woman and any children their unions create together, a responsibility that necessarily includes eschewing all others sexually. I do not criticize him for this. This is probably a very reasonable decision on a gay man's part.... But people who choose not to marry do not therefore have a right to redefine marriage.[54]

Gallagher here turns "the gay man" into a stereotypical object, presumably, the irresponsible narcissist.

Most conservatives do not proceed in this manner, which is one reason that conservatives so infrequently articulate or defend New Natural Law. When bioethicist Leon R. Kass argues that "marriage, procreation, and especially child-rearing are at the heart of a serious and flourishing human life," he is sensible enough to add, "if not for everyone then at least for the great majority." He also observes that many people are denied these blessings, while others choose childlessness without regret, and he urges conservatives to "acknowledge that there will be no going back to the more traditional views and practices regarding sex and marriage."[55]

Talking about child-rearing monks and college roommates allows some opponents of same-sex marriage to avoid addressing themselves to actual litigants. Holly Puterbaugh and Lois Farham were among the plaintiffs in the Vermont civil unions case in 1999. At the time, Puterbaugh and Farham had been living together for nearly thirty years, leaders in their church, active in community groups, and caretakers over the years of fifteen foster children and one adopted child.[56] What about them and their children?

Making moral judgments about the questions that lie before us requires a modicum of openness to the quality of the lives that actual people live. More and more Americans have friends and family members who are gay. Plaintiffs seeking marriage equality could be, and increasingly stand in for, one's own child, friend, cousin, or coworker. When asked to describe his partner, whom California's Proposition 8 barred him from marrying, Jeff Zerillo, a plaintiff in the case, said: "He's the love of my life. I love him probably more than I love myself. I would do anything for him. I would put his needs ahead of my own. I would be with him in sickness and health, for richer, for poorer, till death do us part, just like the vows. I would do anything for him. And I want nothing more than to marry him."[57]

Sandy Stier, who was married to Kris Perry during a brief window of opportunity, only to see their marriage invalidated by California's Proposition 8, leaving them with a domestic partnership, remarked, "There is certainly nothing about domestic partnership . . . that indicates love and commitment that are inherent in marriage. . . . It's just a legal document. . . . It has nothing to do with marriage. Nothing." Marriage, she insisted, means something different in our society: "We have a loving, committed relationship. We are not business partners. We are not glorified roommates. . . . We want to be married. It's a different relationship." In addition, Sandy continued, and of course this is important for gays as well as straights, being married "would provide me with a sense of inclusion in the social fabric. . . . I would feel more respected by other people and I feel like our relationship is more respected and that I could hold my head up high . . . our family could feel proud." And then she reflected on the two sons she is raising with Kris: "I want our kids to have a better life than we have right now. When they grow up. . . . [I] think about that generation and the possibility of having grandchildren someday and having them live in a world where, when they grow up and whoever they fall in love with, it's okay, because they can be honored and they can be true to themselves and they can be accepted by society and protected by their government."[58]

The devotees of New Natural Law assert that its formulas are obviously true. But in my experience, most people find their assertions to be ethereal, opaque, and oblivious to the "so what?" question. Detached from ordinary experience, these seem like exactly the sorts of arguments that would be generated in the academy and stay there.[59]

New Natural Law advocates sometimes say that theirs is "the *only principled*" argument for monogamous marriage and its norms of twoness, permanence, and exclusivity. That is clearly wrong: the view I defend below is a *principled argument* because it is consistent with all sound moral principles. But I do not try to derive an account of civil marriage from claims as abstract as those relied on by natural law; I offer a commonsense defense of the legal institution as it exists in America today. Similarly, I do not argue that plural marriage is inherently immoral in principle; I draw conclusions from evidence and historical experience concerning plural marriage as a social form.[60]

Natural law's reliance on *in principle* arguments is not an advantage. Part of the weight of the natural law argument is carried by unfair descriptions of the lives of those who reject its sexual ethic, *as if a complex reality is being forced to conform to preordained patterns.*

Precisely this point is developed in a self-colloquy penned in 2003 by Catholic professor of moral theology Edward Vacek, S.J., "The Meaning of Marriage: Of Two Minds." Vacek directly engages with the Congregation for the Doctrine of the Faith (CDF), headed by Cardinal Joseph Ratzinger, later Pope Benedict XVI, and its recently issued "Considerations Regarding Proposals to Give Legal Recognition to Unions between Homosexual Persons."[61] The document's teachings are similar to those of New Natural Law.

On the one hand, says Vacek, "my early life in the pre–Vatican II church, my Jesuit training, and my study of Thomistic philosophy strongly bias me toward" what he calls the "essentialist mindset" of official church teachings such as those contained in New Natural Law. And so, "I lean toward the view that anything less than the best is not good enough." On the other hand, he says, "as a priest, I have learned that human life is messy and that the best is often the enemy of the good." He contrasts the "unambiguous conclusions about what marriage is and which sexual acts are right or wrong," which can be found in the "realm of the textbook," with the "fallible human wisdom" that tries to cope with the "ever changing mix of reality" in "the morning newspaper." For the essentialist, "God created the institution of marriage, and so its terms are not open to human modification. Sexual activity is either natural and good or unnatural and evil." But back in the realm of the everyday, "our categories are more or less adequate, they are mental groupings for pragmatic purposes." There, one "sees similarities between homosexual and heterosexual unions," whereas essentialists who formulate official doctrine see "no similarity whatsoever."

And so, continues Vacek, then Cardinal Joseph Ratzinger "knows with 'certainty that marriage exists solely between a man and a woman.'... Yet most people have found it difficult to say what, apart from reproductive capacity, is essentially different in women and men." Nowadays, "tough-minded wives go to the law office, and gentle husbands stay home to nurture their children." Psychological and spiritual differences between men and women exist sometimes but not always. So "we find it hard to say why, on the all-important interpersonal level, the marriage covenant of a man and a woman is significantly different from a covenant between, say, two women." This is especially the case, he observes, because "most American marriages are primarily whole-life unions of persons and only secondarily genital unions." Vacek also observes, as my students have, that these matters become even more difficult when we acknowledge that "some people feel they are men trapped in female bodies, and vice versa."

And so he goes on, offering questions from the perspective of common sense that challenge the certainties of official church teachings. Whereas the "official Church position says children should be conceived through sexual intercourse by married couples," common sense asks, "why is this the only moral way to have children?" Whereas for "the essentialist mind, sex by its very nature requires that the right male organ engage the right female organ in the right manner under the right circumstances and for the right reasons." Anything else "is unnatural and therefore immoral." But many heterosexual married couples consider a variety of "'unnatural' acts to be within the broad pale of what is acceptable, so they are hard pressed to insist that such acts are wrong for homosexual partners." Since the 1960s, "Catholics began to connect sexual activity more strongly with expressing love than with making babies," and so it "became harder to see how homosexual acts are completely different from heterosexual acts."

The questions and observations that Father Vacek advances are apt, and might usefully be addressed to those who espouse the "essentialist mindset" in the academy as well as in the Catholic hierarchy. Attempts to justify the law of civil marriage must be addressed to ordinary citizens, and should be attentive to the lives they live, and the range of choices they reasonably make.

PHILOSOPHY, NATURE, AND PUBLIC REASON

The absence of commonsense arguments and evidence has been the main shortcoming of those opposed to same-sex marriage. David Boies and Theodore B. Olson, the attorneys who challenged Proposition 8 in order to preserve marriage equality in California, report that their aim was to "establish a public record," a "definitive record," via a public trial, in order to both preserve same-sex marriage rights and influence public opinion.[62] In contrast, "Our opponents plainly and viscerally did not want a trial in the *Perry* case. They did not want the pro–Proposition 8 (defining marriage as necessarily one man and one woman) campaign planning and rhetoric exposed, and they did not want to respond with actual evidence to" the "questions that Judge Walker had raised."[63]

Girgis, Anderson, and George nevertheless insist that "there is a true description" of their position "that highlights" the "special value of conjugal acts": "*Organic bodily union* and *life-giving act*, both related to the concept of *comprehensive union*, make the special value of marriage luminous, but apply only to husband and wife."[64] If the truth of these arguments is "luminous," why are intelligent conservative lawyers and judges so reluctant to endorse them? The natural law argument is not very complicated, and yet Justice Alito referred to it, in his *Windsor* dissent, without articulating it, which he presumably could easily have done. Why? Is it because it is not very persuasive? Conservative political philosopher Harvey C. Mansfield is much closer to the mark when he observes that "our nature in the sense of our human good is not easy to discern or to convey in a manner that closes off arguments."[65]

Paul J. Griffiths, a Catholic theologian at Duke University, observes of the New Natural Law arguments considered as public arguments addressed to a diverse citizenry: "I think the orthodox view is true," the arguments are valid, and

> it would be better if everyone thought so. . . . [But] there are not, as a matter of fact, arguments available that do or should convince those who do not hold that orthodox view (whether Catholics or non-Catholics) that they should. The lack of such arguments— I'll call them public arguments—is empirically obvious. . . . [T]he premises are rationally disputable. . . . The truth about none of these things is obvious or self-evident, which is among the reasons that thoughtful, well-meaning people differ so profoundly about them.[66]

Griffiths goes on to ask, as a Catholic addressing the church hierarchy: "Is it part of Catholic orthodoxy to have a particular view about the nature and efficacy of public argument?" He says no. So Catholics as citizens should be free to support same-sex marriage as a matter of civil law. This displays not only political but moral sense.

It is now common to read younger conservatives saying what Jonah Goldberg recently wrote in *National Review*: "Opponents of same-sex marriage insist gays have the same right to marry a person of the opposite sex as anyone else. It's a clever line, but it overlooks the fact that romantic love has been the paramount reason for marriage for quite some time. Telling people they're free to be unhappy isn't all that persuasive."[67]

Natural law proponents have generated little sympathy in the wider political community for their views on sexual morality generally and marriage specifically. Americans would regard it as outrageous if our government set out to establish by legislation that contraception is generally immoral, inside and outside marriage. It would make the law an object of contempt and ridicule. It is in truth more outrageous to suggest that the law should seek to enforce the sectarian ethic of New Natural Law with respect to gay and lesbian Americans only.

All this is a shame because some ethical judgments associated with the natural law tradition are valuable and relevant to today's problems. Ethicists associated with natural law and the more "conservative" side of the political spectrum are correct to emphasize the moral dimensions of our sexual lives and the importance of the institution of marriage and the social norms that surround it. Grisez rightly observes that "sexual appetite is a powerful, continuing motivator, not easily restrained."[68] Many people face difficulty in integrating their sexual urges into loving spousal and family commitments, and this is especially true in the hypersexualized environment in which we live. The purpose of civil marriage is to allow people to enter into "a solemn, publicly given and legally supported mutual commitment," which is, as John Finnis emphasizes, often a "much-needed framework for sustaining" spouses' mutual commitment "through years of changing, perhaps very unfavorable circumstances."[69] Valuable observations such as these will be ignored when embedded in accounts that condemn millions to immorality without attending sympathetically to their actual lives and experiences.

FROM OBSCURITY TO FARCE

In the early stages of the litigation in federal court over California's Proposition 8, Attorney Charles Cooper sought a summary judgment in favor of the constitutionality of Proposition 8, that is, without a full-scale trial. He insisted that limiting marriage to a man and a woman "furthered the state's interest in procreation." Judge Vaughn Walker observed, "Well, the last marriage that I performed, Mr. Cooper, involved a groom who was ninety-five and the bride was eighty-three. I did not demand that they intended to engage in a procreative activity. Now, was I missing something?" Amid the ensuing laughter, Cooper offered that the "central purpose" of regarding marriage as necessarily heterosexual is the "simple biological reality that same-sex couples do not naturally procreate."

But Judge Walker persisted and went to the core of the matter: if "the state's interest in marriage is procreative," how does "permitting same-sex marriage impair or adversely affect that interest"? Cooper's eventual response, after being pressed, was: "Your honor, my answer is: I don't know. I don't know."[70]

Cooper was the lawyer for those seeking to exclude gays from marriage, and he could not or would not articulate the reasons. Why? Perhaps because the reasons are obscure, even to a smart and experienced lawyer like Charles Cooper.

Cooper defended the constitutionality of Proposition 8 once again in oral arguments before the U.S. Supreme Court in spring 2013. He advanced, once again, the argument that marriage is essentially between a man and a woman because at its core it is oriented to procreation.[71] And once again the going was rough.

Justice Elena Kagan asked: if the state's interest is in keeping marriage focused on procreation, would it be constitutionally permissible if a state decided that couples in which both people are over the age of 55 may not marry?

Well no, Cooper replied, "with respect to couples over the age of 55, it is very rare that" both "are infertile." The transcript records laughter in the courtroom.

Justice Kagan: "I can assure you, if both the woman and the man are over the age of 55, there are not a lot of children coming out of that marriage."

More laughter.

At which point, Justice Antonin Scalia joins in: "I suppose we could have a questionnaire at the marriage desk when people come in to get the marriage—you know, are you fertile or are you not fertile?"

Laughter again. But Cooper comes back: one spouse may be fertile.

At which point, Justice Scalia can't resist himself: "Strom Thurmond was."

Interesting choice of examples.[72]

CONCLUSION

At every step of the debate over gay marriage, and gay rights more broadly, over the past thirty years, in court rooms, legislatures, and elsewhere, the arguments on both sides have been aired, probed, challenged, and revised. A great many ethicists and political theorists, social scientists, political and religious leaders, and ordinary Americans have been involved. The arguments have been ably summarized in magazines and journals fully accessible to literate Americans, such as *National Review*, *New Republic*, and *Slate*.

Have the astonishing shifts in public opinion occurred because of the merits of the arguments we have examined? I am in no position to parse for causality. The intellectual debate has certainly helped shape a segment of elite opinion. The most important spur to the changing opinions of ordinary Americans has likely been the widening cascade of people "coming out" and putting a face on gay people and their rights, which makes it harder to think of them as a "disgrace to human nature." Some came out as a result of the political activism after Stonewall; others were forced out by the AIDS crisis, which helped humanize gays by making vivid their suffering and the profound commitment that many brought to their relationships. Some emerged from the closet out of a sense of duty or hope, and with widening prospects for acceptance and even affirmation. In 1985 only 25 percent of Americans said they knew someone who was openly gay; by 2000 the figure was 75 percent. For all the public controversies, there have been many more private dramas of disclosure and acceptance or rejection.[73]

It is now common to read about ministers in conservative Protestant denominations, like the Southern Baptists or United Methodists, who struggle with the question of whether to officiate at a son or daughter's same-sex wedding. Many are choosing love over age-old convictions and amending old doctrines in light of what they are learning.[74] This is the reasonableness of everyday life.

Positive portrayals in the media must also have helped. When public television broadcast the British dramatization of Evelyn Waugh's *Brideshead Revisited* in 1981, its sympathetic portrayal of two young men's romantic and sexual relationship was a jolting novelty. *Will & Grace* debuted seventeen years later, and in explaining his support for same-sex marriage on *Meet the Press* in 2012, Vice President Joe Biden said the show "did more to educate the American public than almost anything anybody has ever done."[75] In the 2000s gay, lesbian, and transgendered characters proliferated and became more diverse.

Public support has clearly shifted away from conservative marriage opponents, and it is striking how few conservatives in politics have rallied to the arguments just discussed, the only philosophically sophisticated arguments for "traditional marriage" on the right. Justice Alito referred to the New Natural Law argument of Girgis, Anderson, and George without explaining or defending them.

The law of a diverse political community ought not to be based—indeed, it *may not legitimately be based*—on philosophically or religiously sectarian systems of thought such as that supplied by New Natural Law. New Natural Law's conception of marriage and sex is perfectly respectable if conceived as the perfectionist ethic of those who embrace its system of ideas and commitments. If asserted as a guide to the law that will be imposed on all, then it fails to respect the range of reasonable views concerning marriage and sexuality in our society.

The arguments against same-sex marriage advanced by natural law proponents is, as we have seen, notable for its focus on sexual acts. Other conservatives oppose same-sex marriage based on assertions concerning broad social consequences including the well-being of children. We take these up in the next chapter.

CHAPTER 3

MARRIAGE, GENDER JUSTICE, AND CHILDREN'S WELL-BEING

The natural law argument discussed in chapter 2 situates the case for marriage within a broader sexual ethic that is both inherently implausible and widely unpopular. Attorneys defending state marriage bans in federal courts in recent years have generally not relied on natural law or claims about the inherent immorality of gay sex. Instead, partly driven by norms of public reason and the insistent question, "what is the harm of gay marriage?," opponents have focused on the supposed impact of same-sex marriage on the health of marriage and, especially, children's well-being.

How will gay marriage affect marriage as an institution? Is it plausible to think that same-sex marriage will undermine marriage as an institution, promote more out-of-wedlock births, and harm children and society? This chapter concludes our survey of conservative opposition to same-sex marriage by considering several versions of these claims.

MARRIAGE AS A GENDERED RELATIONSHIP

When political activists carry signs reading "marriage = 1 man + 1 woman," it is unlikely that they seek to represent the New Natural Law conception of marriage as essentially conjugal and consummated by coitus or intercourse. More likely, they seek to express the idea of marriage as an *essentially gendered* relationship of husband and wife. Those signs seem to convey the thought that marriage is founded on, and its success depends on, the distinct and complementary contributions of husband and wife.[1]

In contrast with the New Natural Law argument, whose appeal seems to be limited mainly to scholars and activists associated with traditionalist

Catholicism, the idea of marriage as an essentially gendered relation of husband and wife has found wider expression in the popular culture and in conservative policy writings, though this argument too is waning. It gains support from sociobiological theories of evolved differences in the innate dispositions and mating strategies of males and females. Men can sow their seeds widely (and thereby maximize the chances of having genetic offspring), whereas women's optimal "mating strategy" is to invest intensively in their young. Evolved differences are also said to contribute to higher levels of sexual aggression in men, and their greater taste (as compared with women) for multiple and younger sexual partners.[2]

According to this view, taming and channeling the male sexual impulse is a primary task of civilized social institutions. Part of the success of marriage as an institution is in the way it responds to and shapes sex-based differences by constructing different and complementary gender roles.[3] The "male problematic" can be addressed by fostering responsible fatherhood, and that requires a complementary (and differentiated) idea of motherhood.[4] In this view, it is not marriage alone (or even principally) that civilizes men, it is women.

Since same-sex relationships and partnerships cannot partake of the gendered complementarity of husband and wife, they cannot succeed as marriage. Many conservatives view same-sex marriage as the last nail in the coffin of gendered marriage because it dramatically dispenses with sex-based gender complementarity.

Claims about psychological differences between men and women and the good of differentiated roles for husbands and wives often overlap with natural law claims about biological complementarity in relation to procreation. The normally sober John Finnis charges that equality-based demands for same-sex marriage also require, "just as imperiously," that "all social recognition of the distinction between mothers and fathers— of the paternal and the maternal, the masculine and the feminine . . . must be systematically expunged from our schools and social life, to be replaced by the lies and seductions of 'gender identities' on the ever more blurry rainbow spectrum. The resultant miseries and losses will reach into every family."[5]

Let us get a grip. The breakdown of sharply differentiated roles for husbands and wives is due to the women's movement and feminism: since the 1970s, men and women are formally equal in marriage. Older traditions sharply distinguishing the feminine and masculine were called into question by women, not gays. Women work in much greater numbers, and more men participate in housework and childcare. Gender equality in marriage predates and prepares the way for same-sex marriage, as we will see in chapter 5. Conservatives should beware of unloading all of their anxieties concerning family and gender relations onto same-sex marriage. It is common to observe differences in the relationships and marriages of gay men and lesbian women. Same-sex marriage does not require and is very unlikely to lead to the erasure of gender identities. Liberal justice does require real equality of opportunity for men and women, and the erasure of artificial boundaries excluding women from certain fields.

There is considerable evidence that evolved biological and psychological differences between men and women shape some differences in observed behavior; higher levels of testosterone in young men are linked to greater aggression and more risk taking.[6] All observed differences are also shaped deeply by cultural norms, values, and upbringing, including the different signals and opportunities that boys and girls, men and women, encounter from a very early age. Underlying differences rooted in our evolved natures give rise only to tendencies that are neither inevitable nor immutable.

The pertinent practical issue is, *what difference does this make with respect to marriage law and policy?* For some conservatives, men's and women's distinctive natures provide a cornucopia of implications: they define a central task of marriage, namely, to control unruly male impulses, and provide a rationale for differentiating the roles of husband and wife, and also a ground for excluding gay and lesbian Americans from marriage. There are obvious problems with this strategy, as thoughtful conservatives increasingly acknowledge.

Scholars such as Steven Rhoads and Harvey C. Mansfield, for example, point to research suggesting that men tend to be more reluctant than women to participate in domestic tasks like doing the dishes and changing their children's diapers.[7] It is conceivable that something about being a male contributes to the reluctance to do housework, but it seems very unlikely that this is impervious to conscientious effort and encouragement.

For some, a key to successfully addressing the male problematic is not mere gender role differentiation but gender *hierarchy* in marriage. George Gilder nicely illustrates the stronger claim when he asserts that "the provider role accords with the deepest instincts of men," but "it is hard for men to meet the claims of familial and sexual love 'without a sense of masculine dominance.'"[8] Most others writing in this vein call for gender role differentiation but not male dominance.

David Blankenhorn, in his 1995 book *Fatherless in America*, bemoaned the decline of responsible fatherhood and called for its renewal. He was (and is) right that children benefit from having committed and nurturing fathers as well as mothers. Unfortunately, he also disparaged as "androgyny" the idea of equal sharing of husbands and wives in housework and paid work outside the home. Blankenhorn characterized this as a "puerile desire for human omnipotentiality in the form of genderless parenthood."[9] "I dispute the New Father's imperative of gender role convergence," says Blankenhorn, "because I do not credit its promise of greater human happiness." He insisted, instead, that the "division of parental labor is the consequence of our biological embodiment as sexual beings." He identified fatherhood and masculinity with being the "breadwinner," and with "toughness, competition, instrumentalism, and aggression."[10]

James Q. Wilson called the model of equal responsibilities at home and work "nonsense," and Wade Horn, who was assistant secretary of health and human services for youth and family services under President George W. Bush, derided as "androgyny" the idea that "mothers and fathers should share equally in all childrearing activities."[11]

Why should we suppose responsible fatherhood is incompatible with equality in marriage? Why should the one go with the other? Gender equality is, in the first instance, a claim of justice. Recognition of women's equality has led to an insistence on equal rights in public as well as private life. The fragility of modern marriages, and women's fully understandable desire to enjoy the benefits of careers as well as home life, have also contributed to the insistence on more egalitarian marital arrangements. If Blankenhorn wants to call this "gender role convergence," so be it. But convergence need not be sameness. Nor is it necessarily a "desire for omnipotentiality," "narcissism," as he also calls it, or the "ultimate triumph of radical individualism as a philosophy of life."[12]

Ironically, the more traditional gender role expectations that Blankenhorn defended seem now to be contributing to a greater reluctance to marry among the less well educated. The reason is, as we will see in chapter 5, that changes in the economy, including the decline of well-paying and stable manufacturing jobs, has undermined working men's capacity to act as the family breadwinner, and this has undermined their willingness to marry and also their attractiveness as marriage partners. Meanwhile, among the college educated, marriage is shaped by the "androgynous" tendencies Blankenhorn bemoaned, and it also flourishes! Among the college educated, two-career marriages have become the norm along with impressive levels of marital stability.

Linda McClain convincingly shows that the preference of some policy makers for gender-differentiated roles in marriage and their opposition to "androgyny" play a prominent role in many of the arguments advanced by supporters of the self-styled "marriage movement," which aims to promote marital "stability" by affirming and reinforcing traditional gender roles. McClain rightly argues that "governmentally sponsored" programs aimed at educating people about, or promoting, healthy relationships (including marriages) should "not embrace models of marriage premised on gender hierarchy."[13]

The aim of public policy should not be to promote stable marriages, irrespective of their quality; it should rather be to promote marriages that are just and healthy: low-conflict, equal partnerships that provide respect, status, and opportunity for men and women. Insofar as there is evidence for a special "male problematic"—a problem of responsible fatherhood—governments "should address the problem in a way that respects women's equal citizenship," as McClain argues, and does not make women responsible for "taming men."[14]

Public policy must reflect basic principles of liberal democratic justice, which require that we give priority to each citizen's status as free and equal. It is of fundamental importance that we arrange our institutions and policies to guarantee everyone—women as much as men—the fair opportunity to pursue the great goods of family life and public life. The latter include the opportunity to pursue a meaningful career and positions of leadership and service in civil society and public affairs. With respect to marriage, what we owe to men and women, whether heterosexual, gay, or lesbian, is an equal opportunity to marry the one you love. None of this, however, spells the end of gender differentiation, masculinity and femininity, though the meaning of the masculine and the feminine will no doubt continue to change.

In her widely discussed *Atlantic Monthly* article, "Why Women Still Can't Have It All," Anne-Marie Slaughter describes her decision to leave her high-level State Department position, "because of my desire to be with my family and my conclusion that juggling high-level government work with the needs of two teenage boys was not possible." Interestingly, she then goes on to question "the proposition that women can have high-powered careers as long as their husbands or partners are willing to share the parenting load equally (or disproportionately) [which] assumes that most women will feel as comfortable as men do about being away from their children, as long as their partner is home with them. In my experience, that is simply not the case." She adds that "I've come to believe that men and women respond quite differently when problems at home force them to recognize that their absence is hurting a child, or at least that their presence would likely help." Men and women seem to frame their choices differently, says Slaughter, partly owing to "a maternal imperative felt so deeply that the 'choice' is reflexive."[15]

Justice for women requires real equality of opportunity, and that in turn demands affirmative efforts on the part of government and other institutions to overcome and counteract the stereotypes and differential encouragement and support confronting boys and girls, men and women. Justice does not require that men and women make exactly the same choices.

THE FEDERAL MARRIAGE AMENDMENT AND CHILDREN'S WELL-BEING

Alarmed by both the *Lawrence* decision and the decision of the Supreme Judicial Court of Massachusetts in *Goodridge v. Department of Public Health* (2004), which ordered state officials to issue marriage licenses to same-sex couples, the U.S. Senate in 2004 debated a Federal Marriage Amendment (FMA) to the U.S. Constitution. That amendment declared, in now-familiar terms, that "Marriage in the United States shall consist only of the union of a man and a woman. Neither this Constitution, nor the constitution of any State, shall be construed to require that marriage or the legal incidents thereof be conferred upon any union other than the union of a man and a woman."

Republican supporters of the FMA advanced two main claims on the Senate floor: first, that traditional heterosexual marriage tends to promote the well-being of children, which is true, and, second, that same-sex matrimony would damage or destroy heterosexual marriage. Senator Orrin Hatch assured his colleagues that "this amendment is not about discrimination. It is not about prejudice. It is about safeguarding the best environment for our children." Empirical evidence, argued Senator John Cornyn, shows that children who grow up outside the structure of traditional heterosexual marriage are "at higher risk of a host of social ills": they are more likely to drop out of school, abuse drugs or alcohol, and commit crimes.[16]

But how would same-sex marriage contribute to weakening of heterosexual marriage? Senators insisted that same-sex marriage would contribute to the "redefinition" of marriage and would disassociate marriage from parenthood in the public mind.

What is the evidence for these claims about the effects of recognizing gay marriage? Senators cited the work of Stanley Kurtz, who had published a series of articles in conservative intellectual journals arguing that the legal recognition of gay registered partnerships in Denmark (1989), Norway (1993), and Sweden (1994), and the eventual recognition of gay marriage in the Netherlands (2000), had led to higher rates of heterosexual cohabitation, out-of-wedlock births, and family disso-lution.[17] On this basis, Senator Cornyn claimed that same-sex marriage threatened to place "more and more children at risk through a radical social experiment."[18] Senator Santorum explicitly attributed the problem of out-of-wedlock births in Scandinavia to same-sex partnerships.[19]

Did the legal recognition of same-sex partnerships in Scandinavia help cause the rise in single parenting? William Eskridge and Darren Spaedele have offered a thorough refutation of Kurtz's argument. The rise in single parenting in Scandinavia *long preceded* the legal recogni-tion of same-sex partnerships. Rates of divorce and single parenthood rose sharply in those countries in the early 1970s—just as they did in the United States and Britain—as a consequence of several factors that included the passage of no-fault divorce laws and the availability of gen-erous welfare benefits for single mothers. In northern Europe generally, same-sex partnerships came much later, after single parenting increased. Moreover, same-sex "legal partnerships" are not marriages, and they also typically did not allow for adoption rights. Same-sex adoption rights and marriage came later—often ten years or more after partnership rights—and long after the rise in single parenting.[20] Kurtz's argument was never particularly plausible, and conservatives now rarely refer to it.

SAME-SEX MARRIAGE AND CHILDREN'S WELFARE: THE EVIDENCE

Children's welfare is a moral high ground in this debate, and properly so. The principal focus of Judge Walker's opinion in the Proposition 8 case in California was the question of whether evidence exists to support the contention that same-sex marriage would impair the state's interest in "encouraging parents to raise children in stable households."[21] Studies purporting to show that children on average do better when raised by opposite-sex couples instead of same-sex couples actually do not com-pare these couples. Instead, those studies compare married opposite-sex biological parents with families headed by single parents, unmarried mothers, step-families, and cohabiting families. The expert witness who testified for the proponents of Proposition 8 was David Blankenhorn. Judge Walker observed, "None of the studies Blankenhorn relied on iso-lates the genetic relationship between a parent and child as a variable to be tested." These studies have "no bearing on families headed by same-sex couples." Indeed, when questioned, Blankenhorn agreed that "adopted children or children conceived using sperm and egg donors are just as likely to be well-adjusted as children raised by their biological parents";

he even allowed that on some outcomes they do better.[22] Blankenhorn has subsequently abandoned his opposition to same-sex marriage.

Judge Walker acknowledged that "an initiative measure adopted by the voters deserves great respect" but insisted that "when challenged . . . the voters' determinations must find at least some support in evidence."[23] And this was found to be lacking.

Some conservatives on marriage argue that Walker was too hasty and challenge the thesis that same-sex parenting makes no difference to children's overall well-being and future prospects. The brief submitted by an arm of the House leadership, the Bipartisan Legal Advisory Group (BLAG), argued that "virtually no society anywhere has had even a single generation's worth of experience with treating same-sex relationships as marriages. There thus is ample room for a wide range of rational predictions about the likely effects of such recognition—on the institution of marriage, on society as a whole."[24]

A much-discussed study by Mark Regnerus of the University of Texas, Austin, Sociology Department concerns a random national sample of adults who turned 18 between 1990 and 2011 (18–39-year-olds at the time of the study), who report that their mother or father (or both) had had same-sex relationships. These now-adult children experienced when growing up a higher level of family instability: time spent in foster care, or living with grandparents, or living on their own. They now experience higher levels of unemployment and psychological problems, including depression and greater instability in their own relationships. Regnerus acknowledges that the adults in his study are overwhelmingly from failed heterosexual relationships, not from "planned" same-sex families. Indeed, these former children of lesbian and gay parents come disproportionately from socially conservative parts of the country with low concentrations of gay and lesbian people and also disproportionately from racial minorities, all of which suggest that the families in question confronted an abundance of challenges and low levels of social support.[25]

So what does the Regnerus study tell us about the prospects of children raised in the same-sex families of the future? The nature of his sample suggests that the families in question faced the same challenges associated with divorce and single parenting, plus additional ones owing to considerable discrimination and prejudice against gays, likely in many instances from family members and not only much of the rest of society. The study does show, as William Saletan points out, that "kids from broken homes headed by gay people develop the same problems as kids from broken homes headed by straight people." We need, no doubt, "fewer broken homes among gays, just as we do among straights."[26] Children need committed parents in a stable, low-conflict relationship and a stable home.

Regnerus's main point seems to be that we should not exaggerate the amount of positive evidence we have about the experiences of same-sex parenting. That may be true, but a wide variety of other studies paint more positive pictures. Denying rights to same-sex persons will not stop them from having children but will likely degrade their children's life prospects. Moving speedily toward greater acceptance of same-sex persons and their relationships seems likely to decrease the number of people encouraged by circumstances to enter unhappy heterosexual marriages and relationships, in which unplanned for children are one possible consequence. Based on its extensive survey of relevant data, the American Academy of Pediatrics has just concluded that "lack of opportunity for same-gender couples to marry adds to families' stress, which affects the health and welfare of all household members. Because marriage strengthens families and, in so doing, benefits children's development, children should not be deprived of the opportunity for their parents to be married."[27]

Regnerus suggests one inherent disadvantage of gay parenting: because the combined gametes of same-sex couples cannot produce an offspring, children born to such unions are bound to confront "a diminished context of kin altruism." Studies of adoption, stepfamilies, and cohabitation suggest that this kinship deficit has "typically proven to be a risk setting, on average, for raising children when compared with married, biological parenting." As Saletan points out in response, "homosexuals who want to have kids could emulate the biological model by using eggs or sperm from a sibling of the non-biological parent, though the effects of this practice on family dynamics are unknown." He also points out that same-sex couples have an inherent advantage over straight couples: their sexual acts cannot lead to unplanned pregnancies, so their families must be planned, and planned families are more successful.[28]

MARRIAGE AS CHANNEL FOR HETEROSEXUAL SEX?

Scholars have, following Carl M. Schneider, described one basic function of marriage as channeling heterosexual sex into a committed partnership that provides what is, other thing being equal, the most advantageous environment for the rearing of children.[29] Within marriage, the husband is presumed to be the father of any children that are born to his wife. This has been an important rationale for marriage, and it is certainly one that has connected marriage and procreation. The "channeling function" has been used as an argument against same-sex marriage rights by BLAG, a standing body of the House of Representatives that can intervene on legal and constitutional questions. In its *Windsor* brief to the Supreme Court, BLAG argued that "the link between procreation and marriage itself reflects a unique social difficulty with opposite-sex couples that is not present with same-sex couples—namely, the undeniable and distinct tendency of opposite-sex relationships to produce unplanned and unintended pregnancies." It further insisted that

> the core purpose and defining characteristic of the institution of marriage always has been the creation of a social structure to deal with the inherently procreative nature of the male-female relationship. Specifically, the institution of marriage represents society's and government's attempt to encourage current and potential mothers and fathers to establish and maintain close, interdependent, and permanent relationships, for the sake of their children, as well as society at large. It is no exaggeration to say that the institution of marriage was a direct response to the unique tendency of opposite-sex relationships to produce unplanned and unintended offspring.[30]

On the basis of these observations, the BLAG brief argued that "there is nothing irrational about declining to extend marriage to same-sex relationships that, whatever their other similarities to opposite-sex relationships, simply do not share" the "tendency of opposite-sex relationships to produce unintended and unplanned offspring."[31] The state has a special interest in "channeling" heterosexual couples into marriage because they might "produce unplanned and unintended offspring."

As other arguments have fallen away, the "channeling" argument in favor of keeping marriage heterosexual has come to the fore. It allows same-sex marriage opponents to avoid relying on moral disapproval of gay and lesbian couples.[32] "Because same-sex relationships do not naturally produce children," argues Texas attorney general Gregg Abbott, "recognizing same-sex marriage does not further these goals to the same extent that recognizing opposite-sex marriage does. . . . That is enough to supply a rational basis for Texas's marriage laws."[33] Judge Martin C. Feldman, for a time the lone federal judge to uphold same-sex marriage bans in the many months after *Windsor*, similarly agreed that states' "central" and "legitimate" interest is "linking children to an intact family formed by their biological parents."[34]

Interestingly, few claim that the channeling argument provides an especially good reason for excluding gays from marriage. The claim is only that it might be good enough if one assumes that legislatures deserve a great deal of deference on this issue.[35]

The channeling argument at least proceeds from a substantial national concern. As Judge Richard Posner bluntly explains, when pregnancies are "unintended," often "the mother is stuck with the baby—the father, not having wanted to become a father, refuses to take any responsibility for the child's welfare."[36]

What is difficult to see is how same-sex marriage hinders efforts to promote responsible procreation and parenthood. Forty percent of children are now born outside of wedlock. Why would letting same-sex couples marry encourage heterosexuals to behave less responsibly? The only rigorous statistical study finds that permitting same-sex marriage has no effect on the rate of heterosexual marriage, and it increases the overall marriage rate.[37]

Judge Posner lampooned the "channeling" argument in the course of striking down same-sex marriage bans in Indiana and Wisconsin. Indiana's lawyer, under questioning, said that "the assumption is that with opposite-sex couples there is very little thought given during the sexual act, sometimes, to whether babies may be a consequence." In other words, writes Judge Posner, "Heterosexuals get drunk and pregnant, producing unwanted children; their reward is to be allowed to marry. Homosexual couples do not produce unwanted children; their reward is to be denied the right to marry. Go figure."[38]

Even Justice Scalia, you will recall, dismissed the argument that marriage is about promoting procreation based on his observation that the sterile and the elderly are allowed to marry.[39] To defend "channeling" in those cases, the state answers that infertile heterosexual couples "model" the "optimal" relationship for other opposite-sex couples. But why, asks Posner, "wouldn't same-sex marriage send the same message?"[40]

Posner allows that the state might be concerned that it would be an "invasion of privacy" to make heterosexual marriage conditional on proof of fertility. Fair enough. But there is a further odd feature of state law in Indiana and Wisconsin (and other states) that suggests the state is prepared to extend marriage rights to some heterosexuals while explicitly *requiring that procreation is impossible*. The state generally prohibits marriage among close relatives, including first cousins, but it makes an exception for heterosexual cousins who are 65 or older *because they cannot procreate*. So the state has carved out a special permission for some heterosexual couples to marry because they cannot procreate, while excluding same-sex couples in general from marriage because they cannot procreate. The inconsistency is glaring. As Posner puts it: "Elderly first cousins are permitted to marry because they can't produce children; homosexuals are forbidden to marry because they can't produce children."[41] This defies the claim that the state law is animated by a general concern with channeling procreative sex for the sake of children. What makes it even worse, of course, is that many of those same-sex couples are actually raising children.

That the state is unwilling to apply to heterosexuals the reasons it invokes for excluding gays from marriage suggests clearly that something else is going on, and that the law is being shaped by reasons and motives that *the state is unwilling to own up to and defend.* The courts call this evidence of *animus*, or animosity, or some other illicit hidden motive.[42] It is in precisely such cases that the courts are supposed to cast a critical eye on the law in question and demand substantial reasons and evidence. As Judge Posner rightly observes, "homosexuality is not a voluntary condition and homosexuals are among the most stigmatized, misunderstood, and discriminated-against minorities in the history of the world, the disparagement of their sexual orientation, implicit in the denial of marriage rights to same-sex couples" is gratuitously injurious and unjust.[43]

The states claim to be concerned about children's well-being, Posner observes, but they appear to pay little heed to the well-being of the 200,000 children being raised by same-sex couples nationally, and the 400,000 children in foster care, many of whom might be adopted by same-sex couples if the law provided recognition and support for their families.[44] Indiana and Wisconsin, like most other states, allow same-sex couples to adopt but not to marry, denying these children the "emotional comfort" and security of knowing their parents are married, and exposing them to the taunts and ridicule that may well follow from other children's awareness of their family's second-class status in law.[45]

DO GAYS BEHAVING BADLY
DAMAGE MARRIAGE?

I am going to consider one final argument that is occasionally raised, and it relates to some of the sex-based differences we began with. Conservatives worry that greater acceptance of the marriages of gay males, in particular, could contribute to more permissive attitudes toward premarital and extramarital sex, and the weakening of marriage. Men generally and gay males in particular appear more prone to promiscuity. Some evidence suggests that gay males seem to have more frequent sexual partners,[46] and that even those living in committed relationships may be less sexually exclusive than is the case with heterosexuals.[47] Of course, samples based on "out" gay males in the 1980s and 1990s, especially, would certainly have contained a selective sample of the gay male population, given the reluctance of most homosexuals to be "out" until fairly recently; the more radical among gay and lesbian people were often the first to come out. So, the argument seems to run, gay marriage could, via a kind of "demonstration effect" (gay married men setting a bad example) contribute to the further loosening of heterosexual marital fidelity. These sorts of effects are highly speculative and seem quite doubtful. Nevertheless, let us consider the possibilities.

Conservatives sometimes point to specific cases. For example, sex advice columnist Dan Savage writes about the very qualified "open" relationship he had with his partner, which he describes as "conservative" nonmonogamy. According to his book, *The Commitment: Love, Sex, Marriage, and My Family*, he and his partner have had two "three ways" in ten years, based on mutual agreement.[48] This is an honest and fairly conservative version of "open marriage." Savage asserts that he and his partner were reluctant to discuss their arrangement but were pressed by others to do so.

Some studies report that gay males who are married or in committed relationships tend, more frequently than heterosexuals, to agree to more sexually open relationships.[49] So gay male relationships may be less sexually exclusive but more honest, and the same studies suggest that these consensual arrangements are less productive of conflict than is the heterosexual pattern, in which sex outside the relationship more often involves deception and betrayal. Where a couple agrees that one or both may have an outside sexual liaison, there is no betrayal. If it is truly consensual (and not a matter of duress or manipulation), then I doubt it should be classified as "infidelity." It may be bad for the relationship, or a sign that something is wrong, but neither spouse is failing to be true to the other if both agree to a "threesome." Admittedly, most spouses would probably find the proposal itself outrageous, but that depends, obviously, on the explicit and implicit mutual understandings of the parties.

I suspect that many who agree to have "open relationships" are playing with fire—underestimating the danger of jealousies and misunderstandings, and the possibility that one party will later regret the arrangement and feel betrayed.

Savage has been criticized by other gays, including one young man who had just come out to his family and who wrote:

> When I watched that one YouTube, it seemed like you were making monogamy out to be joke. . . . Frankly, Dan, it's the acceptance of open relationships in the gay community that makes me not

want to connect with the gay community AT ALL. Because now I have to wonder if my future partner is going to leave me because I don't want to "swing," or if I will never find a partner because I want a closed relationship.

Savage's reasonable response was, in part:

> An open relationship, like a closed one, can be good or bad, healthy or unhealthy, successful or not. (Laci Peterson was in a closed relationship.) . . . I'm interested in people being honest with themselves and their partners about what they want, what works for them, what makes them happy, and then finding someone who wants the same things. And finally . . . Straight people don't have to be monogamous to be married or married to be monogamous. Our fight is for equal rights . . . not double standards.[50]

Insofar as we are concerned with the stability of people's committed intimate relationships, excluding gay men from marriage will not help and almost certainly worsens the situation. As Jonathan Rauch and others have pointed out, extending same-sex marriage to gays seems likely to also extend marital norms to gays.[51] Of course, some on the left express the hope that gay marriage will undermine the expectation of monogamy in heterosexual marriage, but those voices were stronger in the 1970s and 1980s and seem to have been marginalized as the gay rights movement has matured and more gay Americans have come out.[52]

In addition, if you want to observe gay men having, or hoping to have, promiscuous sex, you need to go out and look for it. Gays in the popular media tend to be portrayed as upstanding citizens and decent people. Meanwhile, heterosexual extramarital sexual activity of all sorts fills popular music, movies, the tabloid media, television soap operas going back to *General Hospital*, and newer shows like *Desperate Housewives* and *Jersey Shore*.

The idea of open marriages is decades old and was spoofed in the popular American film *Bob and Carol and Ted and Alice* in 1969.[53] *Open Marriage: A New Life Style for Couples*, by Nena and George O'Neill, was published in 1972. Utopian communities and theorists, going back to Plato, have imagined overcoming the constraints of the marital relation.[54] And while we may disapprove and doubt their wisdom and stability, an "open marriage" is not a contradiction in terms. Newt Gingrich's second wife, Marianne, claimed that he asked for an "open marriage" prior to their breakup.[55]

The people who participated in the sexual revolution of the 1960s are now grandparents. *Playboy* magazine debuted in 1953. For four decades, the divorce rate has hovered around 50 percent, though it has declined in recent years. What exactly do heterosexuals have left to learn from gays? After Catherine the Great, Liz Taylor's eight marriages to seven different men, Wilt Chamberlain's boast of having sex with twenty thousand women, Silvio Berlusconi, Dominque Strauss-Kahn, Anthony Weiner, and Snooki? If we want to do more to shield children from exposure to explicit sexual content—which strikes me as a good idea—the main obstacles are the popular media and corporate America, not gays.

We observe a range of behaviors among both gay and heterosexual men and women. Relationship patterns and marital stability vary along various demographic lines, and increasingly by class. Young gay males and African American males both have more frequent sexual relationships and higher HIV rates than others. It was likely predicted that interracial marriages would be unstable, and some of them are. Fully 15 percent of new marriages are interracial. One study finds that marriages between a black husband and a white wife are twice as likely to experience divorce after ten years. Non-Hispanic Asian husbands and white wives are 59 percent more likely to experience divorce, but a white husband and a black wife are 41 percent less likely.[56]

A proper response to these findings, if they hold water, is not to ban types of marriages by category but to try to understand the special vulnerabilities of some couples and help them manage. There is no behavioral test for straight men and women who wish to marry, divorce, and remarry, as many times as they wish, often leaving disadvantaged children in their wake.

Civil marriage as organized by our law for heterosexual couples is a forgiving and inclusive institution. Heterosexual marriage is not reserved to the especially virtuous or those whose marriages measure up to the standards of ethical perfection advanced by natural law or other philosophies.

It is worth remembering that the right to marry is a fundamental one in the United States: this has been held repeatedly, including fourteen times by the U.S. Supreme Court. In *Loving v. Virginia* (1967), the Court held that "the freedom to marry has long been recognized as one of the vital personal rights essential to the orderly pursuit of happiness by free men."[57] The Supreme Court has also extended the fundamental right to marry to prison inmates, and to men who have fathered children and failed to pay child support, who have a constitutional right to marry. Public authorities may not require them to show that they can support additional children.[58] In *Lawrence v. Texas* (2003), the Court held that "our laws and tradition afford constitutional protection to personal decisions relating to marriage, procreation, contraception, family relationships, and education. . . . Persons in a homosexual relationship may seek autonomy for these purposes, just as heterosexual persons do."[59]

CONCLUSION

There simply are no good reasons and evidence to support the view that same-sex marriage will harm heterosexual marriage or children. Opposition to same-sex marriage does nothing to strengthen families or help children; to the contrary, it gives marriage a bad name, weakening it further. It is a distraction from important public conversations concerning the problems of single parenting and the need to strengthen families for the sake of children. It is precisely this worry that led David Blankenhorn to withdraw from the ranks of those opposing same-sex marriage.[60]

Accepting same-sex marriage in no way signals unconcern with the plight of disadvantaged children, nor with the behavior that brings them into existence. Marriage, as I explore in part 2, is about the public affirmation of commitment.[61] The desire of same-sex couples to marry is, in every obvious respect, a conservative impulse and a reaffirmation of tradition.

The only children directly affected by bans on same-sex marriage are the children of lesbian and gay couples, whose interests are seriously harmed by the failure to give equal recognition to their parents, and the consequent stigma they suffer. Same-sex marriage will improve the prospects of those hundreds of thousands of children being raised by gay and lesbian parents, and also those millions of children and young adults who are gay, or who will soon discover themselves to be.

Conservatives are right to be concerned about the decline of marital commitment and its negative impact on the well-being of many children. I agree with the BLAG brief that it is legitimate for the government to encourage, in reasonable ways, procreation and child rearing in marriage: stable, healthy marriages appear to be the optimal environment for children. There are many things we can and should do, consistent with respect for the equal rights of all, to promote a decent family life, and a good start in life for all children. Children being raised in single-parent homes and homes that have experienced marital disruption do face special challenges. As we will see later, a substantial class divide has opened with respect to marriage and family stability. More and more conservatives seem to be recognizing that opposition to same-sex marriage distracts us from a long overdue focus on support for responsible parenting and children's well-being.

PART II
WHY MARRIAGE?

CHAPTER 4

THE SPECIAL STATUS
OF MARRIAGE

Civil marriage is one of the cornerstones of our way of life. It
allows individuals to celebrate and publicly declare their intentions to form lifelong partnerships, which provide unparalleled
intimacy, companionship, emotional support, and security.
—*Bostic v. Schaefer* (2014)

Part 1 addressed our first question: why same-sex marriage? Answering
that question has become increasingly easy in recent years. We explored a
veritable panorama of implausible arguments against same-sex marriage.
Same-sex couples and their children benefit from marriage in all the
same ways as opposite-sex couples. The exclusion of gay and lesbian couples from marriage has become widely recognized as an invidious form
of discrimination, a badge of second-class status, an injury to same-sex
couples and their children, and a serious injustice. Justice requires their
inclusion, and, happily, constitutional law in America has moved toward
this recognition with remarkable speed.

So we move on to the next question: why marriage? Liberals and
others on the political left are increasingly divided on marriage. They
agree that if marriage is to be preserved, justice requires that it be extended to include same-sex couples on equal terms. But many now say
that same-sex marriage should be a mere halfway house to more radical reform. The marriage question splits the coalition behind same-sex
marriage, with many liberals, feminists, and advocates of greater respect
for diversity calling for the elimination of "marriage" in law, or for some
form of radical reform. Libertarians—on both sides of the political
spectrum—have long argued that government has no business defining

marriage for all: individuals should be free to voluntarily contract into domestic partnerships of their own defining. Advocates of minimally regulated religious liberty might also prefer to leave the term "marriage" to religious and private associations, while coining a new term for the legally recognized relationship.

Does fairness permit the retention of marriage as a status relationship in law, or does the special status that marriage has in American law unfairly favor some conceptions of the good life over others? Why, and under what conditions, is civil marriage permissible? In an era of increasing diversity and greater respect for diversity, does it even make sense for there to be one canonically defined template for the marital relation?

These are among the central questions I take up in the next three chapters. I begin by focusing on the symbolic meaning of marriage, in chapter 4, and then move on to consider the various legal aspects or "incidents" of marriage in chapter 5. There I also provide a brief account of the various ways in which marriage, in today's America, contributes to the well-being of spouses and children, and I explore briefly the astonishing class divide that has grown around marriage. In chapter 6 I consider a variety of reform proposals that seek to make marriage more ethically neutral by enhancing the contractual elements of marriage, introducing greater choice about the terms of marriage.

My aim in this part is to explain and clarify the public meaning of marriage today, both in its symbolic dimension and with regard to the specific rights and responsibilities that marriage law assigns. I make the case for a one-size-fits-all arrangement while also allowing that personalization of marital commitments can sometimes be useful. Without attempting anything like comprehensiveness, which would require many volumes, I make the case for this singular institution, constantly being revised to suit Americans' changing lives and values, from the standpoint of our deepest commitments to equality and freedom. Retaining "marriage" as a distinctive status in law serves both justice and the public good.

The liberal democratic political community has a serious interest in the shape of people's most intimate choices. In part 3 I will examine one of the most important and least examined dimensions of marriage: monogamy, or, why two?

AGAINST MARRIAGE

A growing chorus of scholars and activists argue that preserving marriage as a status relation in law unfairly favors some conceptions of the good life over others and so fails to be fair among citizens with different visions of how to live.[1] An ethically spare version of liberalism has persuaded many that the role of the state is to protect citizens' equal rights to freedom, especially religious freedom and freedom to craft and pursue their own conception of a good life. According to the more progressive strain of this view, the state should also ensure a fair sharing of income, wealth, and opportunity. But the state must strictly avoid enacting policies that seem to take sides on contested ethical questions about the best way to live. Fairness, the argument goes, requires that the state remain ethically "neutral."

So, as Sonu Bedi puts it, "liberal neutrality invalidates both prohibitions on same-sex marriage and marriage itself."[2] Preserving marriage and extending it to gays, says Bedi, takes sides "in a very personal decision about what constitutes the good life."[3] Lawrence G. Torcello agrees that this is both "unstable and unjust."[4] Our state lacks the "ethical authority" to define marriage as a "special status" for all, says Tamara Metz.[5] And so, argues Andrew March, the "liberal state should get out of the 'marriage business' by leveling down to a universal status of 'civil union' neutral as to the gender and affective purpose of domestic partnerships."[6]

In some ways these criticisms of civil marriage echo older critiques by feminists and queer theorists who branded traditional marriage as "heteronormative," meaning that it made the values and norms associated with heterosexual marriage authoritative for all, including those who reject the values. Elizabeth Brake, in an influential book, goes further, calling marriage "amatonormative," meaning that marriage unfairly elevates and celebrates romantic love or "amorous dyads."[7] Marriage contributes to the general expectation that a happy life involves settling down with a loving partner, and for many, suggests Brake, that expectation can be oppressive. By conceiving of marriage as "a cohabiting, financially entangled, sexually monogamous, exclusive, romantic, central relationship," we unfairly exclude many "relationship types," including various kinds of nonsexual friendship networks.

The key claim here is that the law of monogamous marriage is unfairly biased in favor of some conceptions of the good life and against others, and so that it fails to treat citizens with equal concern and respect.[8] For decades, progressives have been troubled by the fact that the law of marriage in effect institutionalizes a particular form of intimate relationship and family life. Here, more than anywhere, we might expect diversity rather than uniformity to be the rule. "Marriage is a great institution," Paula Ettelbrick once quipped, "if you like living in institutions."[9] According to Bedi, prohibitions on polygamy and adult incest rest "on the intrinsic moral superiority" of certain relationships, and that, he says, is no more than "natural law but with a gay spin."[10]

*****

These critics of marriage advance several different claims, which need to be unpacked so we can address them in the rest of part 2. One central concern of some critics is that the word "marriage" is too ethically freighted. It is an honorific that some perceive as demeaning for cohabiting couples and singles.[11] The law should abandon "marriage" as a legal status in favor of a less ethically charged category such as "civil union" or "domestic partnership." Unlike the older policy of reserving the word "marriage" for heterosexuals, it would be perfectly fair to get rid of the legal category of marriage for everybody—same-sex and opposite-sex couples—and to provide one broader and more inclusive legal status, such as domestic partnership or civil union, available on equal terms to gays and straights. Let churches and private associations confer the honorific "marriage" on whomever they wish.

Leaving the term "marriage" to churches and other private associations would have additional advantages. It would help to eliminate the (possible) confusion caused by using the same word for both the religious and the civil or legal relationships,[12] and it could help defuse some of the political conflict over marriage that our society has endured for two decades. It would better comply with the familiar idea of separation of church and state if we "disestablished marriage"—as we have disestablished religion—and created a distinct legal relationship with its own name.

A second concern of many critics is that, whatever label is retained in law—marriage, civil union, domestic partnership, or what have you—it should be made not only more inclusive but more *flexible*: the parties should be able to define the terms of their marriage to suit their own preferences. In place of marriage as a status relationship whose central terms are fixed by law, it would be better to move to a much more flexible contractual model in which the parties define the terms to suit their particular preferences. Individuals should be free to break up various parts of the bundle of relations we associate with marriage and parcel them out or share them with a variety of people.

The third broad concern is that marriage as traditionally understood misidentifies the public interest in people's intimate partnerships. The public's interest is in recognizing and helping to ensure that everyone has access to the *caring and caregiving* relationships that we all need and depend on.[13] For some, this will be traditional marriage; for others, it will be a network of friendships that substitute for marriage. Retaining marriage conceived as a comprehensive bond of two people privileges conjugal and other sexual relations over other, nonromantic forms of caring and caregiving. Law and public policy should recognize and support a much wider range of caring and caregiving relationships.

This is, obviously, quite a raft of challenges to marriage. Some are taken up in this part and some in part 3, which makes the case for monogamy. As we will see, critics of marriage are also often critics of monogamy. Both marriage and monogamy are now frequently challenged as inconsistent with liberal principles of fairness, and the obligation of the state to remain neutral on disputed ethical questions.

Can a liberal defense of marriage as a legal relationship of two adults be sustained in the face of these charges? Or does the law of civil marriage violate a weighty principle of equal respect for citizens with a wide plurality of religious and ethical ideals?

*****

Those who insist that state ethical neutrality and public reason require marriage disestablishment make several mistakes. First, they rest their case on *needlessly controversial* conceptions of "marriage as special."[14] No doubt, civil marriage is a distinctive and profound form of mutual commitment, but it need not be regarded as problematically "special" so far as the law is concerned.

Second, and relatedly, these critics fail to appreciate that there are *broadly public reasons* to recognize and support civil marriage.[15] Many people want to make a public commitment to each other, and the law of marriage enables them to do that. In addition, wanting to marry is very reasonable: ample evidence suggests that doing so promotes health and well-being in a variety of ways. The values of fairness and equality that underlie demands for neutrality can be satisfied by extending appropriate forms of public recognition and support to marriage along with other kinds of nonmarital but valuable caring and caregiving relationships that also serve the good of individuals, families, and society. If we attend in appropriate ways to the interests of those in valuable nonmarital caring relationships and those who are single, charges of nonneutrality can be addressed without disestablishing marriage as some prefer. Fairness to those who live outside of marriage argues for making some of the privileges and rights traditionally associated with marriage also available to people in nonmarital relationships. We can and should do this while preserving monogamous marriage as a distinct status relationship in law.

I defend a moderate policy of liberal marriage preservation. Justice, in this view, *requires* equal treatment of opposite-sex and same-sex couples, and it permits the retention of a reformed institution of marriage. Marriage is distinctive, and it promotes a wide variety of personal and public goods as well. Marriage preservation need not run afoul of any weighty requirements of state ethical neutrality. Going further, I argue in part 3 that monogamy helps secure basic interests associated with liberal democratic citizenship, including gender equality and the fair opportunity for all citizens to pursue the great goods of marriage and family life.

Defenders of neutrality are typically very concerned that when the state favors controversial institutions such as marriage, it is not being sufficiently fair to those who dissent from the majority's ethical ideals. The concern is admirable, but we must weigh the seriousness of the alleged unfairness and consider the various possible ways it can be addressed. It is true that the state ought not to *practice favoritism* among citizens' worthwhile conceptions of the good life, any more than it may among their differing religious beliefs. But the fact that not everyone can or does take advantage of particular publicly supported institutions—whether art museums, universities, or marriage—is not a sufficient reason to regard them as deeply unfair. The issues here go to the heart of debates in recent decades concerning liberalism as a public philosophy, and in the conclusion I argue that fairness does not preclude the liberal democratic state from promoting, through recognition and modest financial support, *widely appreciated and broadly based aspects of the human good.* The principle of state ethical neutrality (and the related idea of political liberalism) need not have radical implications. As James E. Fleming and Linda McClain argue, while political liberalism precludes public institutions from imposing a marital regime reflecting a "particular comprehensive conception of the good," such as that of New Natural Law, "it does not preclude government from pursuing moral goods or public values that are common to a number of competing comprehensive conceptions."[16]

Those who defend traditional marriage based on what they claim is a timeless natural law place too much confidence in abstractions and display too little sympathetic understanding of the lives of actual people or human experience. Progressive critics of marriage also make too much of a quite different abstract principle, namely, state ethical neutrality. They may be reacting against the excesses of some proponents of natural law or simply operating with a very finely honed commitment to fairness. In either event, I urge the importance of attending to actual political debates and also the institutional underpinnings of the lives that most actual people lead. It is not invidious, at least after the inclusion of same-sex couples, for our law to support a form of commitment as widely sought and esteemed, as useful, and as flexible as marriage, even if a considerable number of our citizens are not able to take advantage of it, and a smaller number do not wish to have anything to do with it. Fairness to those outside of marriage requires creative public policy responses. But it does not require the abolition of marriage, or so I will argue.

For now, let us proceed to the main issue: the public justification of marriage as a two-person status in law.

IS MARRIAGE SPECIAL?

As we have seen, many people think that marriage as a civil institution is tainted with illegitimacy on account of its special status in law. Marriage, say the critics, violates important principles of state neutrality because it is a "morally special status" that has "special value."[17] Tamara Metz refers to "the mysterious and troublesome special value of marriage."[18] Critics seem to mean that the law regards married life as especially honored, or distinctly excellent and choice-worthy, in a way that is unfair or invidious to the unmarried.

The "specialness" charge can apply to two different aspects of marriage. First is the public symbolic meaning of marriage in our law and culture, and second is the large and important array of benefits, rights, and obligations awarded by the state and by third parties specifically to married couples. Along both dimensions, I argue, the "specialness" charge can be disarmed.

For the benefits, we should address charges of unfairness or non-neutrality: which particular benefits really can be justifiably confined to married couples and which, in contrast, should be extended to people in nonmarital forms of caring and caregiving relationships? While some benefits may be specifically suited to marriage as compensatory or otherwise appropriate, given the kind of commitment married couples make to each other, we must also consider what forms of appropriate recognition and support we owe, in fairness, to people involved in caring and caregiving relationships that are not marital. I will return to this below.

I begin with the symbolic dimension, which has tended to be the focus of most of the controversy. One reason for this is that an important question has been whether governments satisfy constitutional and moral requirements of equal treatment by giving same-sex couples many or all of the tangible benefits of marriage under an alternative rubric, such as civil union or domestic partnership. At least some conservatives who object vehemently to calling gay unions "marriages" might be willing to consider extending some benefits and an alternative form of recognition. This became, indeed, the central point of controversy in Massachusetts and California.

One preliminary observation is that law and state policy are not fully (perhaps not even mainly) responsible for the meaning and resonance of marriage in our culture. The law may in some ways reflect, express, and reinforce the public meaning, but marriage is also a fabled part of culture and history, a long-standing social practice, and a religious rite that has enormous significance for people independent of the civil law of marriage. One student of public opinion has said that Americans put marriage "on a pedestal."[19] It is far from obvious that that would change (at least immediately) if marriage were wiped off the law books.

Nevertheless, the law of marriage also matters deeply to Americans, for political as well as personal reasons. As we saw above, while there were deep conflicts in Vermont (and other states) over its "civil unions" law, the national response was relatively muted. But a tremendous backlash was unleashed when Hawaii seemed on the verge of recognizing same-sex marriage in law, and then later when Massachusetts actually did so.[20] Charles Cooper, litigating same-sex marriage in California, observed that "the word is the institution." The Supreme Court of New Jersey observed that it was "mindful that in the culture clash over same-sex marriage, the word marriage itself—independent of the rights and benefits of marriage—has an evocative and important meaning to both parties."[21] To many ordinary Americans, the legal authorization to describe their relationship as a marriage is hugely significant.

Marriage retains its significance for Americans even though the stability of marriages has eroded. Indeed, Andrew J. Cherlin argues that the symbolic meaning of marriage may be greater than it was fifty years ago when nearly everyone married and it was "a mark of conformity" and "the only acceptable way to lead an adult life." Nowadays there are a variety of other acceptable alternative lifestyles, but marriage remains the "preferred way to have an intimate partnership," "a notable achievement," the "capstone" of a relationship, and "a mark of status."[22] And so, across "income and ethnic groups, the vast majority of young people report very positive attitudes about and aspirations for marriage."[23]

If marriage is widely regarded as significant, is it also, as critics charge, too ethically controversial for the law to be involved with?

MARRIAGE AS STATUS RELATION

Part of the "specialness" charge is associated with the idea of marriage as a status relation defined by law. Sir Henry Maine famously described the emergence of modernity as a movement from "status to contract." In premodern feudal societies, people were born into roles defined by their place in the social hierarchy, and these "fixed a man's social position irreversibly at his birth."[24] In the modern world, increasingly, individuals are born "free and equal," and choice and consent progressively supplant predetermined roles.

To many, marriage seems an anachronism: its terms are defined in important part by the law and also by inherited social meanings. Couples can shape many aspects of their relationship and establish their own particular ways of doing things. But marriage is also a singular social institution that shapes and limits people's deepest aspirations and the most intimate aspects of their lives.

"Marriage is entered by means of a contract, but turns into a status."[25] The parties enter into marriage by voluntary and publicly declared agreement, but the general terms of marriage—the spouses rights and obligations—are defined by state and federal law and may be altered by law if doing so would serve the public good. As the Supreme Court colorfully put it in 1888, "Other contracts may be modified, restricted, or enlarged, or entirely released upon consent of the parties. Not so with marriage. The relation once formed, the law steps in and holds the parties to various obligations and liabilities. It is an institution, in the maintenance of which in its purity the public is deeply interested."[26] Chief Justice Margaret Marshall of the Supreme Judicial Court of Massachusetts made a similar point when she observed, "In a real sense, there are three partners to every civil marriage: two willing spouses and an approving State."[27]

The marriage vows that are pronounced in public, and the documents that must be signed, are astonishingly brief when compared with the contracts that seal far less consequential commercial transactions, such as buying a home or a car, or the dozens of online service contracts we routinely enter into every year. The institutions of marriage and parenting are shaped largely by state laws, which vary. First-cousin marriage is allowed in some states but not in others. The age of consent for marriage is generally 18, but in Mississippi it is 17 for men and 15 for women. The legally permissible age generally drops to 16 with parental consent, but in Massachusetts the law says, rather astonishingly, that a 14-year-old boy could marry a 12-year-old girl![28] The most elaborate marital rules concern what happens to the couple's shared assets in the event of divorce.

Marriage contains important elements typical of contractual relations, and these have grown in recent decades as couples gain greater freedom to craft the terms of their marital relationship. Until the 1970s, courts refused to enforce prenuptial agreements, but courts are now far more apt to honor premarital (and postmarital, or simply marital) agreements, and even in some states to see them as superseding state law, so long as the court is assured that the agreement was truly voluntary, informed, and reasonably fair.[29] So the status dimensions of marriage are on the wane in some respects. But that is only part of the story. While there is a shortage of reliable data, it appears that prenuptial agreements remain rare in first marriages and have become more common in second marriages, especially when there are children from a first marriage, and for very wealthy people. A Harris survey in 2010 suggested that only 3 percent of people who have a spouse or are engaged have a prenuptial agreement. The figure was only 1 percent in a similar study in April 2002, so the frequency may be increasing but appears to remain low.[30] While many marriage reformers laud the growth of prenups, they can have important downsides, and fairness remains a touchstone for courts deciding whether to give effect to such agreements, as we will see later on. My point here is only that marriage retains important elements of a public status relationship defined in advance by law and social understandings.

PUBLIC USES OF MARRIAGE AS STATUS

Let us back up a step and consider the uses of marriage as a status relationship defined by law. "Marriage" is importantly a form of public declaration and social recognition entailing certain general expectations and entitlements on the part of the spouses, and of society. The traditional wedding vows, pronounced before a representative of the state and witnesses that typically include one's family and friends, express joint commitments that are familiar to us all:

> I, (name), take you (name), to be my lawful (wife/husband), to have and to hold from this day forward, for better or for worse, for richer, for poorer, in sickness and in health, to love and to cherish; til death do us part.

Even whimsical variations on the vows (such as ones inspired by Dr. Seuss) contain the same basic aspiration to lifelong and unconditioned commitment.

> Pastor: Will you take her as your wife?
>   Will you love her all your life?
> Groom: Yes, I take her as my wife,
>   Yes, I'll love her all my life.
> Pastor: Will you have, and also hold
>   Just as you have at this time told?

Groom: Yes, I will have, and I will hold,
   Just as I have at this time told. . . .
Pastor: Will you love through good and bad?
   Whether you're happy or sad?
Groom: Yes, I'll love through good and bad,
   Whether we're happy or sad. . . .
Pastor: Will you love her if you're rich?
   Or if you're poor, and in a ditch?[31]

You get the idea.

But does it really make sense, given the great diversity of the United States and other modern states, and the fluidity that seems to characterize people's marriages, to speak of a "public meaning" of marriage? No doubt, if there is a public meaning—a set of commonly recurring themes or "family resemblances"—it coexists with innumerable variations. This is entirely consistent with the idea of marriage as a hybrid of status and contract. There are, after all, variations in the ways that individuals inhabit all their roles, and that does not stop the role—whether police officer, judge, senator, mother, or father—from being publicly understood.

Accounts of modern marriage often describe it as "companionate."[32] Vice President Joseph Biden seemed to capture the core idea when discussing same-sex marriage: "This is all about is a simple proposition. Who do you love? Who do you love and will you be loyal to the person you love? And that's what people are finding out what all marriages at their root are about."[33] Companionate marriage is about the mutual love, loyalty, and commitment of two people.

So let us say this: *marriage in America is generally understood as an exclusive and long-term commitment, aspiring to permanence, between two people who love each other, share a household and sexual intimacy, and promise to love and care for each other through life's trials.* Spouses are expected to care for each other and be there in time of need, and to work at sustaining the relationship and the joint commitment.[34] For most younger couples, children are expected to be central: the having and raising of children together is profoundly meaningful, and children provide an extremely important reason to work at keeping a marriage healthy and stable. The well-being of children is one very good reason for the state to take an interest in marriage. But for some younger and many older couples, raising children together is not what their marriage is centrally about. As the Massachusetts Supreme Court put it, in extending marriage rights to same-sex couples, "While it is certainly true that many, perhaps most, married couples have children together . . . , it is the exclusive and permanent commitment of the marriage partners to one another, not the begetting of children, that is the *sine qua non* of civil marriage."[35]

One striking aspect of contemporary marriage is formal gender equality. This is, as I made clear in the last chapter, a huge change from the past when, for centuries, marriage was the relationship of husband and wife understood in terms of distinct rights and obligations. The husband was head of household and had a duty to provide a home and support for his wife, who in turn maintained the home, received his sexual advances, and raised the couple's children. Legally defined sex-based role differences are now a thing of the past, though gendered expectations still shape many marriages. Suzanne B. Goldberg exaggerates only somewhat when she says, "From a gender perspective . . . marriage today looks like a completely different institution than it did even a few decades ago."[36]

It does not seem wrong to speak of a common conception of marriage, so long as it is understood to coexist with variation and ongoing change. If we take as the baseline what marriage has become in America—this companionate conception—then same-sex marriage is not a fundamental revision to the institution.[37] It moves marriage further away from gender-differentiated roles and toward more equal spousal relations; how far remains to be seen. And it makes the institution more inclusive and fairer. Many same-sex couples share with heterosexual couples the wish to be married in the eyes of society: they want access to the public status of being married and want to signal and help secure their mutual commitment, to take on marital responsibilities, and to enjoy marital benefits. They can benefit from marriage in the same ways as straights. Justice Marshall explained in her opinion in *Goodridge*:

> Without question, civil marriage enhances the "welfare of the community." It is a "social institution of the highest importance." Civil marriage anchors an ordered society by encouraging stable relationships over transient ones. It is central to the way the Commonwealth identifies individuals, provides for the orderly distribution of property, ensures that children and adults are cared for and supported whenever possible from private rather than public funds, and tracks important epidemiological and demographic data.
>
> Marriage also bestows enormous private and social advantages on those who choose to marry. Civil marriage is at once a deeply personal commitment to another human being and a highly public celebration of the ideals of mutuality, companionship, intimacy, fidelity, and family. . . . Because it fulfills yearnings for security, safe haven, and connection that express our common humanity, civil

marriage is an esteemed institution, and the decision whether and whom to marry is among life's momentous acts of self-definition.[38]

THE LAW AND PUBLIC MEANING OF MARRIAGE

If marriage has a reasonably well understood public meaning, what is added to the symbolic dimension by the *law* of marriage?

The existence of the *legal form* of marriage facilitates the fulfillment of people's serious desire to get married and to *be married* as a matter of common, public knowledge: that is, in the eyes of one's whole society, not just the eyes of one's church or social circle.[39] Marriage is very public: once people know you are married, all sorts of presumptions follow. People know that married spouses have made a special and extensive commitment to one another, typically involving sexual fidelity, sharing a household, and caring for each other. A train of legal entitlements follows as well, many of which we all have some sense of: hospital visitation rights, the right to information from doctors, decision-making authority in the event of absence or incapacitation, and the right to jointly control property. Social invitations will naturally include both spouses. The law of marriage helps make the relationship of marriage socially legible.

The core of the case for a law of civil marriage recognizes, as Ralph Wedgwood notes, that marriage here and now has widely understood social meanings.[40] No other relationship has the same social meaning: domestic partnerships, civil unions, and other options have unclear social meanings, and that could be exacerbated if we introduce a great deal of variety of marital and partnership forms. Status relations are public and defined in advance of our entering into them, and so, by entering, individuals can assume serious commitments of a particular and widely understood sort.

So one benefit of the law of marriage is "informational": if an exclusive dating arrangement is understood to signal a certain level of commitment, marriage signals more. Discussing and committing to marriage furnishes a way for couples to signal their extensive commitment to each other, their family and friends, and the rest of society: getting married signals that commitment in an extremely public way. Those in attendance at marriage ceremonies are frequently asked by whoever is officiating, "Will you help support this couple in their marriage?" or something to that effect. That seems altogether appropriate.

The commitments of marriage, once entered into, become social expectations and bases for moral evaluation: we make judgments about one another that are defined partly by how we inhabit our roles. Spouses are expected to "treat each other affectionately, considerately, and fairly. They should be animated by mutual concern and willing to sacrifice for each other."[41] These understandings form a basis for spouses' mutual expectations, and the expectations of family and friends.

In marriage, the partners agree to limit their freedom of action in some directions by publicly entering into a socially understood commitment. The opportunity to enter into this socially legible bilateral commitment—to assume certain constraints and bear certain obligations, while also enjoying a variety of benefits—is a valuable option and therefore freedom enabling.[42]

Of course, the constraints of marriage may not always be enabling, and that is something we will need to consider later. For those who feel constrained to marry for the sake of securing the basic necessities of life—whether decent housing, health-care benefits, resources needed for child support, or what have you—the decision to marry is not an expression of freedom. Healthy marriages benefit from systems of social provision that help guard against marriage-induced domination by helping people exit abusive or unhappy relationships.

The fact that marriage is a legal institution that requires a formal agreement to enter and leave gives the commitment added seriousness. Before turning to the question of whether the specific legal benefits and obligations associated with marriage are justifiable and appropriate, let us probe more deeply the central good of marital commitment.

MARRIAGE AND THE GOOD OF COMMITMENT

I was slightly taken aback at my partner's parents' fiftieth wedding anniversary when my father-in-all-but-law stood up to say a few words. "The central thing about marriage," he told the sixty or so family and friends gathered, "is commitment." And he hammered that theme home: commitment is what makes marriage work, it is basic. I guess I expected more about love, or something a bit more romantic. But on reflection I think I see his point: the distinctive sort of love that marriage involves is deeply intertwined with the commitment of two people to share their lives in a uniquely comprehensive way, and to work at making the commitment last over the long term.

Marriage is the "committed relationship" par excellence. Many people want to enter into it and, as I have said, to make it known that they are making this commitment. Commitments to particular principles, people, and projects, and carrying those commitments forward over decades, help give our lives structure, narrative unity, and integrity over their course. "The prime virtue of settling," says Robert Goodin, is "to provide you with some fixed points around which to plan your life." "Settling facilitates striving by helping us to stop vacillating—to prevent us from striving in too many different directions at once."[43] Some things need to be taken as settled in order to get on with other aspects of our lives. Settling on, committing to, and settling down with someone else allow us to proceed with common plans and projects, and to pursue them with some measure of common understanding and assurance. Reasonably settled commitments and consistency between those commitments and our actions impart integrity to our character.[44]

The decision to settle down with another person and to commit to sharing one's life for an open-ended future is one of the most consequential and serious undertakings that any of us enter into. Settling on and settling down with another person help give our lives a scaffolding of relatively fixed points that can support and shape one's life as a whole. Given the ways in which so many other aspects of our lives must be made to work around them, marriage commitments are of profound importance to the partners, their children, and also their friends and family.

The institution of marriage facilitates settling by providing an evolved and evolving template for intimate partnership that has proven successful for a great many others. It recognizes and facilitates the desire of the vast number of people to settle down with another person in a socially recognized, committed relationship, and to build a life together in common. By limiting marriage to two, monogamous marriage discourages and stigmatizes polygamous social systems that have, as we will see in part 3, been left behind by developed societies for good reason. Marriage seems to many to unfairly tilt the playing field in a "conservative" direction by discouraging more adventurous and unorthodox domestic relations, but it does not prohibit a wide range of "experiments in living."[45] Here, even more than in other departments of life, it is by no means obvious that having more choices is better. Indeed, because the stakes are so much higher here than with respect to our choice of breakfast cereal or make of car, it is by no means obvious that more choices would make us better off. As Robin West observes, marriage provides some answers to questions that could "otherwise overwhelm us—How should I organize my intimate life? Should I be intimate with one, or a multitude? Should I hope for a monogamous relationship that endures, or will serial monogamy best suit my nature?"[46]

Lifelong and open-ended, marital relationships involve a commitment to flexible mutual adjustments and accommodation to life's many contingencies, unforeseeable events, and the partners' own evolving mutual understandings and needs. Marriage is a commitment to stick with another person in good times and in bad, across all life's contingencies, its fortunes and misfortunes ("for better or worse, in sickness and health"). Like friendship or parenting, marriage must involve a kind of shifting attentiveness to the needs of the other, as Mara Marin argues, and a willingness of both partners to adjust roughly in tandem.[47]

The meanings and purposes that are central to particular marriages will tend to change as couples age together. Sex may matter more early on; children often occupy a dominant place for two decades or more; and relations with extended family and shared friendships may grow in importance over time, along with shifting forms of mutual help and support and a deepening store of shared memories and experiences.

For younger people whose careers are just getting under way, having a partner or spouse offers the prospect of steady support and assistance. And for those couples who wish to begin a family—as do the vast majority of younger married couples—choices will be made concerning paid work and home work. Career plans need to be meshed. When will we have children, and how many? Will both pursue careers, or only one? In marriage, "one commits oneself to seeing one's life always with the other in view. One commits to pursuing one's major projects, even when alone, always in a kind of implicit conjunction with the other." As Eric Schwitzgebel puts it, "One's life becomes a co-authored work."

This conjunction and mutual commitment is the essence of "conjugal love," according to Schwitzgebel, not the intense feeling of passion, which is sometimes identified with romantic love. The love that is at the core of marriage "is something actively built"; it is "a way of structuring one's values, goals, and reactions," always, if implicitly, in conjunction with one's spouse.[48]

Formalized public commitments, backed by sanctions, facilitate interpersonal reliance and cooperation by permitting participants to make credible commitments: to seal their bargains. Penalties can include alimony, child support, the division of marital property and assets, and the less formal sanctions of disrupted social networks and the social disapproval that may follow from the violation of established norms. Marriage is "easy to enter but hard to exit," as William N. Eskridge puts it.[49]

As already mentioned, the norms that surround marital commitment and the sanctions of disapproval that support them have not disappeared, though they have weakened, and changes in the law have contributed to their weakening. The existence of penalties and sanctions contingent on making good or being true to our commitments facilitates mutual reliance and allows spouses to rely more deeply on one another. The costs and difficulties associated with divorce can often induce couples experiencing marital difficulties to take a sober second look before ending the marriage. These costs make it more likely that those who have committed to try to make their marriage work will in fact do so.[50]

Individuals could still make commitments to each other without the law of marriage. They could still publicize their commitment to their friends and try to inform the world at large by posting about it on social media and in other ways. The law of marriage furnishes resources that individuals and private associations never could. It codifies a public understanding of what is for most people life's single most important relationship. It offers a widely understood set of marital default rules, subject to the parties' revisions, which others have found useful and advantageous in the past. The public and personal nature of the marital commitment is meant to help create what Andrew J. Cherlin calls "enforceable trust." Cohabiting is likely to involve only private commitments and undertakings. But the public nature of marital commitment should lower "the risk that your partner will renege on promises to act in ways that would benefit you and your children. It allows you to put time, effort, and money into family life with less fear of abandonment by your partner."[51]

Marital commitments are obviously fraught with risk, but so is settling down with another without getting married, or forgoing commitment altogether. In chapter 6 we will consider the suggestion that, by making divorce too easy, the law has undermined the capacity of marriage to signal and reinforce commitment.

*****

But is the idea of marital commitment passé, given the high divorce rate and the easy availability of divorce without the need to find or assign fault? Marriage involves a series of entanglements and dependencies, typically, that make separation and divorce costly. There is also a perfectly reasonable discussion to be had about whether divorce should be harder: whether it should involve mandatory waiting periods and counseling, for example. I will say a bit more about this in the discussion of marriage reforms in the next chapter.

Let us here consider just one area where marital norms appear to remain quite robust: with respect to adultery. For decades, pollsters have asked Americans, "What is your opinion about a married person having sexual relations with someone other than the marriage partner—is it always wrong, almost always wrong, or not wrong at all?" The percentage answering "always wrong" increased from 70 percent in 1973 to 82 percent in 2004.[52] The rates of disapproval have trended *upward* for all groups, and especially among the better educated, even while Americans have become more accepting of divorce and same-sex sexual relations.[53] I take it that the core moral problem with adultery is infidelity: not being true to the vows one has made to one's spouse. These numbers suggest that fidelity is still normative, considerable hypocrisy notwithstanding. Public revelations of secretive marital infidelity, from Bill Clinton to Anthony Weiner, are met with grave embarrassment and other costs to the offender's reputation.

So important norms and expectations continue to surround marriage. The law allows contracts to be breached with the payment of an appropriate penalty, and contract theory even regards "efficient breaches" as wealth maximizing. But it is not so with marriage: "when we marry, we are obligated unconditionally," says Robin West, "and the moral approbation that would be our due should we breach that promise, is very much central to its meaning."[54] The common expectations and norms are typically also valuable: they help sustain individuals' commitment to their marriages.

The marital commitment and the greater assurance that it provides, when successful, give structure and support to us over the long arc of our lives. Marriage is a great good when it is reasonably happy and stable; with that hope in mind, it is sought by the vast majority even while the pitfalls of divorce are well known. West puts the point well when she observes:

> Civil marriage, as compared with private commitment ceremonies, unadulterated personal promises, nontraditional family forms, informal cohabitation, or single life, gives us a personal structure, validated by historical and current social norms, within which to mold our own expectations and aspirations for our own and our partner's intimate lives. It gives us confidence that the form we've adapted to—a committed intimate relationship—is a good one.[55]

If the idea of marital commitment and stability seems in some obvious ways anomalous in an era in which the pace of movement and change seems ever quicker and its scale ever broader, that may be part of the point. Fewer and fewer of us are able to maintain close ties to the place we were born, or proximity to parents, siblings, and extended family. The idea of spending an entire career with one company is long gone for most. We make new "friends" by the hundred on Facebook, and most of them we barely know. And yet, for those who enter into marriage under favorable conditions, in which both spouses have a college degree, the partnership that is marriage retains a resilience that is in many ways surprising and may be all the more important.

Andrew Sullivan captured an important truth way back in 1989, in his oft-quoted and seminal essay, "Here Comes the Groom":

> Marriage provides an anchor, if an arbitrary and weak one, in the chaos of sex and relationships to which we are all prone. It provides a mechanism for emotional stability, economic security, and the healthy rearing of the next generation. We rig the law in its favor not because we disparage all forms of relationship other than the nuclear family, but because we recognize that not to promote marriage would be to ask too much of human virtue.[56]

CONCLUSION

This chapter has explored the public meaning of marriage, especially its symbolic dimension and social meaning. In the next chapter, I consider, albeit briefly, the legal "incidents" of marriage: the rights and responsibilities that marriage entails, which are supposed to recognize and support the distinctive relationship that marriage is.

The law of marriage and the social meanings and expectations that it helps support shape people's most personal aspirations, helping to create common aims, and placing certain options out of bounds. In these ways, marriage helps people mesh their goals and plans while making other options less readily available. Obviously, marriage is not perfectly neutral with respect to the variety of preferences that people have concerning the shape of their lives and our common social world. But if marriage is not ethically neutral, neither is the desire to eliminate marriage in law: it could make it harder for two people to enter into the sort of public commitment that very many want to enter.

And in spite of its being a "weaker" institution than it once was, in a variety of ways, marriage remains an extremely successful institution for those who are lucky enough to enter into it under favorable circumstances. As we will see below, marriage is not only desired but worth desiring. Marriage facilitates a certain kind of "pair bond" while leaving couples or groups free to fashion other kinds of living arrangements and commitments to one side of marriage.

We need not understand the social meanings that a law of marriage helps to sustain as constituting public endorsement of a problematically "special" moral ideal or status, though this argument is not yet fully made. We need only suppose that people want to be married and want it to be publicly known that they are married; that desire is intelligible, and the benefits sought are supported by independent evidence. The fulfillment of this desire is something that the law can facilitate, without harming others. Marriage does not require, and I doubt that it benefits from, any social stigma being attached to those who are single or couples who choose not to marry.

How much difference the *law of marriage* makes to this more general culture of meanings, norms, and expectations is hard to say, and we will return to this issue later, when we discuss marriage's many benefits for health and happiness. The community's law is uniquely capable of making our commitments a matter of common knowledge among all, and it provides a way of anticipating and providing for risks that couples entering upon a relationship may not foresee. The law of marriage itself may make a difference by strengthening couples' ability to assure each other of the seriousness of their mutual commitment, and this can be enormously valuable for psychological health and general well-being.

Marriage has in general become more fluid and less long lasting, many are waiting longer to marry, and there has been some decline in the desire to marry among the young. But marriage still matters, and the vast majority of people marry at some time in their lives.[57] Moreover, as we will see in the next chapter, reports of marriage's general decline mask its continuing health among those who enter it prepared and with the good fortune of favorable economic circumstances.

CHAPTER 5

MARRIAGE: OBLIGATIONS, BENEFITS, AND ACCESS

So far we have focused on the *symbolic dimension* of marriage as a distinctive form of commitment. The symbolism of marriage has been most central to the very public political debates over same-sex marriage, which is understandable. Focusing only on the symbolic meaning provides only a partial picture of the institution. This chapter fills in the picture by furnishing an overview of three important subjects.

I first describe the specific benefits, responsibilities, obligations, and protections that are associated with marriage by law. These are complex but extremely important. This overview of the various legal implications of marriage will help make clear that marriage as it exists today is well suited to same-sex couples and their relationships. The way for same-sex couples has been cleared by the women's movement and sex equality in marriage. Entering into marriage does not, however, involve simply the acquisition of special marital benefits, as critics of marriage often argue. Wedlock also brings with it a variety of "special" marital obligations and restrictions. This balance of rights and responsibilities is crucial to the fairness of the institution: marriage is not simply a "reward" or an honorific. The law is designed to recognize, facilitate, and assure (to some degree) the fulfillment of the distinctively marital commitment, and that involves the assumption of special responsibilities as well as benefits.

The second task of this chapter is to summarize the benefits that flow to spouses, children, and the wider society as a consequence of marriage. This is highly controversial terrain but an important part of what is at stake in today's debates.

The third task is to uncover the huge class divide that has opened with respect to access to marriage, its importance for parenting, children's well-being, and the future. Strikingly diverging patterns have emerged between better-educated and more economically secure Americans and those with relatively low levels of education and more insecure economic prospects. This class-based marriage divide, not same-sex marriage, is the greatest problem facing us.

THE FUNCTIONS AND GOALS OF MARRIAGE LAW

The specific legal dimensions of marriage—the various legal incidents as they are called—are defined by large bodies of state law that vary and are constantly being revised and updated in response to Americans' changing behavior and expectations, or sometimes in the hope of shaping that behavior. Over a thousand federal laws also refer to marriage and shape marital obligations and benefits. While this complex terrain is often bypassed in theoretical discussions of marriage fairness and reform, it is not ignored by those courts (and law professors) who well understand its importance.[1]

Carl E. Schneider usefully defined five broad functions of marriage law.[2] The law has, as we have already seen, an *expressive* function, providing a language for spouses to communicate their commitment to one another and to the rest of society. Second, the law plays a *facilitative* role by providing a legal form for couples' general marital commitment and any additional specific agreements that they want to enter into. Marriage law provides a set of default rules that can be taken off the shelf as a package, but couples can also enter into prenuptial or postnuptial agreements. Third, the law plays a *protective* role by specifically prohibiting spousal and child abuse, and protecting spouses and children against certain kinds of economic and psychological injury. By singling out these crimes, the law helps signal the special vulnerabilities involved in marital and family relations. Fourth, law plays an *arbitral* role to settle serious disagreements between spouses, especially via the law of divorce, which adjudicates conflicting claims to marital property and future earnings.

Finally, Schneider described marriage as having a *channeling* function, which we discussed in chapter 3, where it was argued only that this is not a reasonable basis for excluding gay and lesbian couples from marriage. Even with gays included, it can be argued that the law seeks to channel people into marriage for the sake of promoting relationships that are healthy, stable, and good for spouses, children, and society.[3] We need to consider just how powerful this channeling function is, and how legitimate it is in a free society.

*****

Thinking of marriage law in terms of these broad functions is useful, but they do not get us very far. A former colleague of Schneider's at the University of Michigan Law School, David L. Chambers, published an influential article in 1996 asking whether marriage law suits the needs of gay and lesbian couples. In doing so, Chambers provided a nice overview of the broad purposes of the various legal dimensions of marriage and argued that "marriage as a legal institution is highly likely to retain useful advantages for same-sex couples." He affirmed, moreover, that "nearly all the legal consequences of marriage have a sound application to the position of long-term lesbian and gay couples."[4] Indeed, he went further and argued that property rules within marriage, "will, in general, serve gay and lesbian couples who choose to marry *better* than they serve opposite sex couples today."[5]

Chambers suggested that the various legal "incidents" help support couples' marital relationships in three broad ways. Marriage law helps, first, to recognize and sustain couples' "affective or *emotional bonds*." In addition, marriage law helps create "an environment that is especially promising or appropriate for the *raising of children*." And finally, marriage laws recognize and support the fact that a married couple is liable to conjoin their *finances and property*.[6] Let us consider these in turn.

Emotional bonds. Law helps recognize and support married couples' emotional closeness by authorizing spouses to make emergency medical decisions for each other, to act as guardian for an incapacitated spouse, and to assert the rights of next of kin to claim human remains and make other decisions concerning a deceased spouse. Spouses become legal representative should one's spouse die without a will. These rights are important protections for couples: they recognize that one's spouse is one's most trusted confidante and the person best placed, in general, to understand and act on behalf of one's interests. In doing so, they help protect the married couple against unwanted interference, for example, by disapproving parents or siblings. Such protections are important for all married couples but may be especially important for gay and lesbian partners, as William N. Eskridge emphasizes.[7]

Federal laws grant spouses and family members preferential immigration and naturalization privileges. This helps married couples and family members maintain physical closeness to one another and recognizes that individuals and society typically benefit from being able to maintain relations with family members.

Also important for recognizing and sustaining relations of care is the eligibility provided for by the Family and Medical Leave Act of 1993, which requires employers with fifty or more employees to provide unpaid leave of up to twelve weeks per year to eligible employees to care for a spouse with a "serious health condition."[8]

The right to assert evidentiary privilege for marital communication—to refuse to testify about marital communications—helps maintain the preconditions of trustful communication. And, should that fail, spouses enjoy the right to visit one's incarcerated or furloughed spouse, which allows for ongoing communication and assistance.[9]

Marriage also brings certain constraints, obligations, and expectations. Spouses generally enjoy what are called "homestead rights and protections" that limit one spouse's ability to throw the other out of the shared household without proof of violence or some other threat, or to deny the other spouse support or maintenance, and a fair share of marital property in the event of one's death or divorce. Guardianship and support obligations help make marriage a form of social insurance. There are variations across states.[10]

Other restrictions sometimes imposed specifically on spouses reflecting the emotional closeness of spouses include antinepotism rules that prohibit employees from participating in decisions to hire or otherwise benefit their spouses.

Another constraint that couples take on in marrying is fidelity, as I discussed previously. Adultery remains a crime in twenty-three states, though it is rarely (essentially never) enforced. It may figure in divorce proceedings, but it seldom does so unless it has had a financial impact.[11] Nevertheless, infidelity remains subject to social disapproval and embarrassment, as we have seen, and the law may help bolster that.

Economic interdependence. A second category of marital benefits and obligations recognizes the couple's likely economic dependence on each other: their sharing of a household, their cooperation in balancing paid and unpaid work, and their joint relationship to the state. The tax code provides some specific benefits for married couples and also some special burdens, reflecting typical married couples' interdependence and the advantages they reap from marrying and establishing a joint household. So the gift and estate taxes do not apply to transfers of property between spouses, and the federal income tax includes a system of joint returns for married couples treating them as a single economic entity. If one spouse earns most of the income, the couple is liable to benefit by joint filing because the law presumes that two are sharing the one income. But if both spouses earn similar incomes, they are likely to pay more than if they filed separately as individuals. Chambers suggests a justification: couples can live more cheaply than two single individuals living separately, so it is fair for them to pay more.[12]

I leave aside the difficult question of the ultimate justifiability of these or other aspects of marriage law. One important point is that this "marriage penalty" in the income tax is one of the most obvious burdens faced by married couples, balancing their "special benefits,"[13] and this is especially likely to fall on same-sex couples, who are less likely than opposite-sex couples to embrace traditional gender roles. Another point is that, here as elsewhere, the specific features of marriage law typically have a plausible rationale. This particular feature is, like many others, subject to ongoing reexamination: it may needlessly discourage some couples from marrying, or it may discourage one spouse in a married couple from working.

Similarly, poorer couples' eligibility for certain kinds of assistance, such as Medicaid, is determined by household income. Many poorer couples may find that they qualify for higher benefits if they remain single. This welfare penalty deserves attention: it argues for more universal assistance programs, though this terrain is obviously especially complicated.[14]

Marriage law also recognizes couples' economic interdependence via special obligations and benefits, some of which have been touched on as also supporting emotional closeness. Spouses are obliged to provide support to each other, and, if separation or divorce should occur, an equitable division of property and possibly the payment of alimony can be required. In the nine community property states (which include California and Texas), spouses are responsible for each other's debts.[15] They are also entitled to receive veterans' and Social Security survivors' benefits.

The final issue that I will discuss concerning how the law recognizes typical married couples' economic dependence on each other concerns the division of marital property at divorce. The nine community property states regard all property acquired during marriage as jointly owned. The remaining common law states allow property that the spouses acquire to be owned jointly or separately. Regardless of who holds title, principles of "equitable division" of marital assets have come to play a prominent role in divorces. That is, judges will consider the length of the marriage, and also whether one of the spouses has significantly increased his or her future earning capacity by, for example, the acquisition of a professional degree, with the support of the other spouse. Only New York State formally regards such a degree as a "property subject to division," but judges in other jurisdictions generally take this into account in considering what is fair.[16] This is a vexed and controversial area of law, but marriage laws do at least seek to address the question of whether spouses' proposed division of assets, or property settlement, is fair as part of the divorce settlement.

Parenting. The third and final broad category of benefits and obligations associated with marriage concerns parenting. In general, the obligations of parents to care for their children do not depend on those parents being married. This is a big change from the past, when the law regarded an "illegitimate" child, born outside of marriage, as "the child of no one."[17]

One important aspect of heterosexual marriage will not apply in the same way to gay and lesbian couples, and that is the presumption of paternity for children born within the marriage. States need not accord any parental rights to a man who has an affair with a married woman who later gives birth, though some states do so. Many states have sought to protect the integrity of the family against what may be the unwanted claims of the biological parent in such a case, and the Supreme Court has said that they are free to do so.[18]

An important set of parenting rights for same-sex as well as many heterosexual couples concerns adoption rights, the stepparent relationship, and rights associated with artificial insemination, sperm donation, and surrogacy. Marriage provides important benefits for those couples raising children together, whether opposite sex or same sex. Marriage makes it much easier for a couple to adopt a child jointly, and those children benefit from the greater security afforded by having two committed parents. Unmarried same-sex partners can petition for joint adoption, but the process is cumbersome and would be eased by access to marriage. Marriage would give lesbian couples easier access to regulated sperm banks that often automatically register joint parenthood by the spouses; this would assure their children of the support of both parents. Children being raised by unmarried partners are ineligible for the full assistance of the Family and Medical Leave Act—which permits employees up to twelve weeks of leave for a sick child or stepchild—and also for Social Security survivor benefits.

The law traditionally accorded few rights either to same-sex partners who are also coparents or to similar opposite-sex stepparents who marry a custodial parent. In both cases, irrespective of the extent of the partner's role in parenting and contributions to the support of the child, both same-sex partners and heterosexual stepparents had, in the past, few rights at divorce concerning visitation or joint custody: the absent biological parent remained, irrespective of family history, financially liable and second in line for custody.[19] In recent decades, however, legislatures and courts have allowed for greater rights for stepparents married to a custodial parent, especially when they come to play an important role in the lives of children. States have expanded stepparents' ability to become a child's full legal parent through adoption, including, in some circumstances, "over the objection of the absent biological parent."[20]

For gay male couples, conceiving a child with a surrogate mother raises additional questions concerning the rights of the biological mother, given her physical and, often, emotional investment in the child she carries to term. Whatever arrangements are made available to heterosexual couples ought to be available to gay couples as well.[21]

Greater flexibility has also been introduced in recent years concerning the "rule of two," which has held that, from birth, a child has two and only two legal parents. Courts in the Canadian province of Ontario and in Pennsylvania have allowed that, under certain circumstances, some parental rights might be parceled out among three parents. Both of these cases concerned a lesbian couple who had been raising a child with ongoing contributions from the sperm donor, who was also a friend. In Pennsylvania, when the lesbian couple split up, the question was whether all three had support obligations, and the court held that they did.[22] In Ontario, the case similarly involved a lesbian couple who conceived a child with a sperm donor whom they also wanted involved in the child's life. The law recognized the biological parents as legal parents, but a judge allowed the lesbian partner who was not the birth mother to become a third parent.[23]

These cases raise concerns among some observers. Does parceling rights among three parents make it easier for each to shirk? Are children harmed by an arrangement that could have greater potential for conflict or instability? I will not enter into a discussion of such questions, which are, however, interesting and important. Courts seek to discern which arrangements are in the best interests of the child, given what have been highly unconventional arrangements but will likely become more common. It is worth observing, however, that courts and marriage law are already moving, in some jurisdictions at least, to introduce greater flexibility in ways that could benefit children and adults.[24]

*****

The various benefits and obligations of marriage, while far from perfect and constantly undergoing debate and revision, are as well suited to same-sex as well as opposite-sex spouses. As Chambers says, "Most of the rules may be seen as facilitative, in the sense that they enable a couple to live a life they define as satisfactory to themselves." And the various benefits and obligations constitute a reasonable package, which couples are free to take "off the shelf," that is, as a given package, but which they may alter in various ways, or reject in favor of an alternative type of relationship. And since same-sex couples are less likely than opposite-sex ones to take on traditional gender roles, they are less likely to be rendered vulnerable to some dire consequences of marital breakup, such as the impoverishment of the stay-at-home spouse.

While marriage opponents sometimes emphasize the unfairness of giving married couples "special benefits" not enjoyed by others in close personal relationships, these benefits are balanced by special constraints and obligations. If marriage were only a matter of receiving legal benefits, more couples would likely marry. However, married couples make a distinctively comprehensive and open-ended commitment to care for each other in sickness as well as health, in vigor and old age. The law of marriage both signals and supports the distinctive and extensive mutual commitment and responsibilities that are central to its public meaning and role in people's lives.

Some of the benefits of marriage are reasonable compensation for the special mutual burdens that married couples undertake.[25] By undertaking to care for one another in sickness, and to be responsible for joint debts, marriage helps relieve third parties, including the political community, of the need to provide certain forms of assistance. On the other hand, reasonable reliance on this arrangement for pooling risks and insuring against the infirmities of old age ought not to be an excuse for failing in our social welfare obligations as a political community, as we do in the United States. I will return to this later (but will only note now that getting rid of marriage would not, by any direct route, get us a Swedish welfare state).

The overall package of marital benefits and obligations seems reasonably appropriate and fair, given the kind of relationship that married couples enter into and the benefits of marriage to them, their children, and society. These should be, and are, subject to ongoing reconsideration in light of families' changing needs and fairness to those inside and outside of marriage.

*****

Here we can consider briefly the controversy and confusion surrounding the idea of "common law marriage." One obvious reason for resisting *imputing* marital commitments to people who have not publicly and explicitly made them is the principle that individuals should be free *not to marry* and thereby to avoid assuming the obligations of marriage.

Couples who cohabit without getting married may undertake particular obligations to "take care of" each other, and, if the relationship ends, this may lead to a "palimony" suit, as in the famous case involving the actor Lee Marvin.[26] But such suits are typically hard to prove and are rarely successful, especially when the promise was implied rather than explicit.[27] Ascribing marital benefits and obligations to couples who have merely lived together in a "marriage-like" relation for some period of time is properly controversial, though it may help protect the vulnerable and guard against unfair exploitation.

Common law marriages are, in contrast, bona fide marriages, and they must meet higher standards of explicitness and publicity than are typically involved in "palimony" suits. In a common law marriage, couples enter a private agreement to be married: they not only cohabit but present themselves to others as married. Marriage does not arise from cohabitation alone.[28]

*****

Obviously, many of the rights and entitlements associated with marriage could be created by legal contract, but we all tend to be myopic, and most of us would rather not dwell on the unpleasant but inevitable facts of eventual incapacitation and death. Having access to a package of legal "default rules" that have been found useful by others is enormously beneficial to many couples.

Equally obviously, little about marriage is set in stone. Its various aspects are under constant critical scrutiny and are tested daily in the changing lives of millions of people. My claim is only that the legal incidents of marriage taken in their broad contours seem reasonably well designed to recognize, facilitate, and protect the marital relationship and its distinctively extensive mutual commitments. Everything that I have discussed is and ought to be subject to ongoing deliberation and democratic reform. The point of the law of marriage, and the key to whatever success it has, is that it facilitates and makes possible a relationship that many people want to enter, and whose terms they find useful and agreeable as they go about their lives.

We need, finally, to undertake the difficult task of considering which benefits are appropriately limited to the marital relation (given the kind of relation it is, and the personal and social goods that flow from it), and which should be available to persons in nonmarital relationships, or on an individual basis. That is a complicated agenda whose importance I can only flag, but I will say a few things about it at the end.

THE BENEFICIAL CONSEQUENCES
OF MARRIAGE IN THE UNITED STATES

Having addressed, in the previous chapter and earlier sections of this chapter, the symbolic and expressive dimensions of marriage as well as the specific legal rights and obligations it entails, it now seems appropriate to say something about the benefits of marriage for individuals and society. This will help round out the case for marriage in law. In the next chapter I will consider a variety of reform proposals advanced by moral and political theorists and policy reformers.

My discussion in what follows summarizes some of the main claims advanced by marriage defenders. We confront one large problem in describing what are generally regarded as the benefits of marriage. Critics of marriage will charge that many of the comparative benefits of married life in our society are a consequence of other features of American life that are unjust and that call out for reform. If marriage reduces psychological stress, for example, perhaps it is partly or largely because social welfare policy in this country fails to provide adequately for the stresses and uncertainties that afflict all but the wealthiest Americans. Marriage, in other words, would matter less in a *more just* social context.

Fair enough. I tend to agree, and I certainly believe that justice requires much more substantial forms of public provision than exist in the United States. Countries like Denmark and Sweden are far more just and happier places than the United States. However, this book is about marriage in the United States. I plead guilty to taking much in American life for granted for the sake of this discussion. The relative importance that Americans assign to marriage as compared with Scandinavians may help explain our inadequate and their more satisfactory social welfare systems. It seems doubtful, however, that marriage is the main thing hindering our pursuit of social justice. The United States is, as compared with Europe and Canada, a large and racially, ethnically, and religiously diverse society: we have a harder time generating social trust and public goods generally.[29] We have, moreover, a strong cultural legacy of individualism, an ethos of personal responsibility, and a federal system that makes centralized provision more difficult.[30] If a genie appeared and offered to stably institutionalize the Danish social welfare state in the United States, but only if we got rid of civil marriage, I would likely take that deal, but it is not on offer.

*****

William A. Galston has observed that "a mountain of evidence" supports marriage's contributions to individual well-being.[31] Beginning with adults, on average, married people are happier, are healthier, enjoy better sex and social lives, live longer, and are more financially secure. The health and happiness advantages include higher self-reports of subjective well-being, or how people say they experience their lives, and also less subjective measures. Married people have lower rates of depression and are less likely to use controlled substances, they also experience less chronic disease and greater longevity. They tend also to have sexual relations more frequently, experience less violence inside and outside the home, and have "better adjusted children."[32] The family income of married couples is higher, and they experience less economic stress. The benefits of marriage are often especially pronounced for men, and seem to depend less (than in the case of women) on social context.[33] And it is important to emphasize that the advantages of marriage in the United States are in comparison with cohabitation, and not only being single.

Evidence indicates that participating in a stable committed relationship contributes to greater happiness and satisfaction for gay male, lesbian, and heterosexual couples, whereas couples in sexually open and less committed relationships experience greater tension and less satisfaction.[34]

It is not easy to isolate the effects of a complex institution such as marriage, or to control for what are known as "selection effects": does marriage make people happier and healthier, or, rather, are happier and healthier people more likely to get married? It is probably some of both, but studies of identical twins provide evidence that marriage itself has a significant positive impact on happiness and health.[35] These studies help control for differences that are not easily measured across individuals, including the quality of parenting and other childhood experiences. Scholars are generally convinced that marriage itself makes a difference in producing the favorable outcomes for spouses mentioned above, but questions of course remain concerning how much difference marriage itself makes to spouses' well-being.

The advantages of marriage are all on average. Marriage does not guarantee good outcomes. Some married people are unhappy, unhealthy, violence prone, substance abusing, and economically unstable. And plenty of single people are extraordinary, accomplished, happy, healthy, and wonderfully admirable. But on average, the benefits of marriage are "pervasive" according to marriage scholars.[36]

And what about marriage's benefits for children? Here we move onto especially sensitive ground. The sensitivity is understandable. Single mothers are, along with other caregivers, among society's greatest unsung heroes, sacrificing and laboring long hours, in very difficult and poorly paid jobs, for the sake of their children. The literature on out-of-wedlock births is full of critical accounts of fathers who fail to take responsibility and provide support for their children and the mothers of those children. Marriage and fatherhood are fragile, but motherhood remains robust in the sense that the maternal bond is, as Offer puts it, still taken to be lifelong.[37] Single mothers typically work hard and try to do their best for their children, often in the face of public policies that are bound to seem punitive.

While there is controversy in this area, a wide range of family scholars would agree with McLanahan and Garfinkel that out-of-wedlock births are a matter of public concern for four broad reasons: unmarried parents have fewer resources, their relationships are less stable, their investments in children are lower, and their children do less well in a wide variety of respects. The percentage of children born to unmarried parents has risen from around 4 percent in 1940 to over 40 percent today. Much of the recent increase in nonmarital childbearing has involved couples who are cohabiting but not married when their child is born.[38]

Evidence suggests that unmarried parents are "very optimistic about the future of their relationship" at the time of their child's birth: more than 90 percent of these cohabiting parents rate the chances of marrying their partner at "fifty/fifty" or better. However, these cohabiting relationships are much less stable than marriages. Five years after the birth of their child, 80 percent of married couples are still living together compared with only about 35 percent of unmarried couples (and of those only about half are married).[39] And as unmarried fathers move out of the house, their levels of financial support and contact also decline precipitously: half of nonresident fathers see their child at least monthly in the first year after a child's birth, but only 35 percent do so after five years. Financial contributions from nonresident fathers are even rarer: a quarter make regular cash payments during the first year, but only 14 percent do so by the fifth year.[40]

A high percentage of unmarried American mothers assert that a single mother can raise a child just as well as a married mother, and that is true, but unmarried mothers face special challenges. Single mothers in the United States experience high rates of poverty, and they also have less time and attention to give to their children, who do less well across a wide range of social indicators. The children of single mothers also face stresses related to the fact that single mothers often seek out and move in and out of new relationships. As already mentioned, two-thirds of unmarried parents have separated by the time the child is age five. McLanahan and Garfinkel report that "more than half of the mothers who are unmarried at their child's birth go on to date or live with a new partner by the time their child is age five." Financial challenges and the greater demands on their time make it harder for single mothers to focus on good parenting. As a consequence, they engage in fewer literacy activities, their household routines tend to be less regular, and they more frequently engage in harsh discipline such as yelling and spanking.[41]

As mothers form new relationships they also often give birth to children with their new partners. For existing children, the entry of these new half-siblings creates additional stresses, tending to reduce the involvement and contributions of their fathers, and also their fathers' families, and increasing children's behavioral problems.[42]

For all these reasons, children of single mothers tend to do less well in terms of physical and psychological health, educational attainment, and economic success, and their own eventual family lives tend to be less stable.[43] Children whose parents cohabit rather than marry are more like to be physically and sexually abused. Evidence also suggests that boys raised in single-parent homes may experience special challenges more frequently than girls.[44]

Divorce also puts children at elevated risk of emotional and other problems. Here again, while most children adapt to the changes to their lives wrought by divorce, about 20–25 percent of young people experience serious problems subsequent to divorce, as compared with 10 percent from families with intact marriages. Galston observes that "this two-fold increase in risk is larger than the association between smoking and cancer." Young peoples' rates of suicide and attempted suicide rise with increasing divorce rates and children living in homes with an absent biological parent.[45] In addition, many men as a consequence of divorce experience loneliness and other problems and do so more often than women.[46]

We should also not exaggerate the magnitude of these effects. Most children who grow up in single-parent homes do fine, and many do extraordinarily well. Barack Obama shows that a child of a single mother can not only thrive but excel to the highest degree; no doubt having loving extended family members can be a great boon, as his maternal grandparents were for Barack Obama.[47] Being raised by two parents in an intact marriage is no guarantee of success. One study found that in cohabiting families only 16 percent of 6–11-year-olds "experienced serious emotional problems" while 84 percent did not. At the same time, in "families headed by married biological or adoptive parents," only 4 percent of children experienced serious emotional problems.[48] As a general matter, a child's vulnerabilities are lower when he or she grows up in an intact two-parent home. Other things being equal, an intact two-parent marriage that is reasonably low in conflict is the best bet for a child's happiness and success.[49]

MARRIAGE, CLASS, AND OUR "DIVERGING DESTINIES"

If marriage is such a good deal for spouses and their children, one might ask, why aren't more people marrying and, especially, marrying before having children? Scholars call this the "marriage paradox."[50]

Some general trends contributed to a weakening of the marriage culture in the 1960s and 1970s. Easier access to contraception and abortion gave women more control over their sexual lives: sexual activity was no longer confined to marriage and a brief window preceding marriage. Young women had more sex and fewer babies and began to attend college in much greater numbers, eventually surpassing men in college attendance. Their participation in the paid workforce also increased enormously, reducing their economic dependence on men and marriage. The stigma previously strongly associated with out-of-wedlock births, or "illegitimacy," disappeared. "Shotgun weddings," once common, became a thing of the past.[51] States also liberalized their divorce laws and the rates of divorce, cohabitation without marriage, and single parenting increased for all groups. In the 1990s, divorce rates leveled off for the country as a whole, and teen pregnancy declined. As women gained greater reproductive and economic independence, they also delayed marriage: women's median age at their first marriage is now 27.[52]

It would be wrong to characterize all this as "the decline of marriage." Marriage is less common and more fragile, but it is also much fairer. Most divorces are initiated by women not men, and when the divorce rate rose, the rate of suicide among women declined. Those "picture-perfect" marriages of yore no doubt sometimes masked the kinds of "quiet desperation" among women especially that Martha Nussbaum has described.[53]

The overall trends described above are reasonably well known. Less well known is the extent to which marital stability has come to differ greatly among different *segments* of the American population. Here we confront the great class divide in American life that continues to unfold before our eyes. Sarah McLanahan famously calls this our "diverging destinies."[54] The prevalence of "fragile families" among the less well off is both a cause and a consequence of widening economic inequality, which has come to be closely associated with educational attainment.

The great divide, both economically and in terms of family patterns and marital stability, is between those with college degrees and those with only a high school education. Among married couples at the top—where both spouses have college degrees—divorce rates have declined to the levels of the mid-1960s. Among the most highly educated fifth of Americans, the median age of motherhood increased from 26 to 32 between 1970 and 2000. Those in this top cohort typically finish college or even a graduate degree, begin a career, and then get married before having children. A high percentage of these mothers now work outside the home, while also lavishing attention on their children. While only 18 percent of mothers in the top quarter worked outside the home in 1970, by 2000 it was 65 percent. And on average, these mothers still spend as much time reading and playing with their children as the nonworking mothers of old, and the fathers are more involved with their children as well.[55]

For the rest, and especially for the least educated and least economically secure, and African Americans especially, divorce rates remain high, as do rates of cohabitation and single motherhood.[56] There has always been a class gap with respect to marriage, but it has widened dramatically. In 1960, 14 percent of mothers in the bottom quarter and 4.5 percent of mothers in the top quarter, in terms of educational attainment, were unmarried, a gap of 9.5 percent. By 2000, 43 percent of the less-educated mothers and 7 percent of the more educated were unmarried, a gap of 36 percent.[57] Among African American women who are high school dropouts, 96 percent of the births are to single mothers.[58]

The college educated have seen their wages rise over the past forty years, while the real wages of male high school dropouts declined by 30 percent from 1973 to 1997.[59] High school–educated women have seen steadier wages over time, and married couples still enjoy improved economic well-being and security at any level of income and education. William A. Galston observed some time ago that those who finish high school and marry after age 20 and only then have a child face only an 8 percent chance of being poor, while among those who do not do these three things, nearly 80 percent will be poor.[60] But the evidence suggests that young men without "steady jobs and decent pay" are often regarded as unattractive marriage partners. Young adults in precarious economic circumstances are increasingly choosing to cohabit rather than marry.[61] Among the least well off, contraceptive use is irregular and often unreliable, and access to abortion is often difficult and/or disapproved. A strikingly high number of pregnancies among less-well-educated single mothers are unplanned or not fully planned.[62] Many less-educated women drift into childbirth, becoming mothers at an earlier age than the better educated, and, in many if not most cases, before they really want to.[63]

The result is that at the top, the norm and practice of having children within marriage are strong, and marriages are stable. Children born to the most advantaged parents—in terms of years of schooling and income (which are closely related)—are the beneficiaries of greater financial resources and also intensive and high-quality parenting. Among less-advantaged parents, those with only a high school degree, and even more so among high school dropouts, childbirth much more commonly takes place outside of marriage in fluid cohabiting relationships, which are stressful for both children and their mothers and more challenging financially, and in many other ways, as described above. It is for these reasons that Richard V. Reeves declares, with only some hyperbole, "Matrimony is flourishing among the rich but floundering among the poor."[64]

The causes of these divergent experiences are complex and uncertain: economic changes, cultural divergences, and public policies seem to all play a role. The disappearance of well-paying and secure factory jobs for men with only a high school education and the decline of private-sector labor unions, have undermined the solid economic foundation on which so many stable, working-class marriages of the past were built. The transformation of the American economy has also undermined the stable communities in which those families raised their children.[65] Women now make up more than half of the workforce and are the main breadwinners in 40 percent of families. As already mentioned, many men seem now like less attractive marriage partners to women, and, here as elsewhere, economic and cultural factors interact. Americans with less formal schooling (and more economic challenges) tend to have more traditional expectations about gender roles in marriage: both women and men in this group are more likely to expect the husband to play the breadwinner role. As Reeves observes, the men who most want to be breadwinners are now "very often the ones least able to fulfill the role."[66] Such attitudes contribute to these couples' reluctance to marry, *even though they would benefit economically and in other ways from marrying.*

Meanwhile, marriages are becoming more equal, with fathers spending considerably more time on housework and child care than they did in the mid-1960s, though still not nearly as much as mothers.[67] And while in the 1970s the amount of time spent on parenting did not vary much by class, Robert D. Putnam has shown that fathers "with college degrees now spend twice as much time with their children as the least-educated fathers."[68]

There are other differences among groups within the population that suggest that culture and values play an important role in explaining the differences. Divorce rates are lower among recent Hispanic immigrants.[69] Marriage rates are lower and divorce rates higher among African Americans, which may be at least partly attributable to the historic assault on the black family associated with slavery.[70] On the other hand, divorce rates are lower among the "actively religious": those who regularly attend church.[71]

This is not the place to enter into a comprehensive assessment of marriage trends and their causes. My purpose in the last two sections has been to make two points: First, evidence suggests that marriage confers benefits on adults, as compared with being single, and on children, as compared with being raised in a single-parent home. None of this is surprising, and it should not be taken as a criticism of single mothers making phenomenal efforts to raise happy and healthy children.

Second, a striking class divide has emerged with respect to marriage. Because marriage does confer benefits on children, financially, emotionally, and in terms of cognitive development, this class divide within marriage suggests that class divisions in our society will grow worse in the decades ahead.

For Americans lucky enough to be entering marriage under what we may consider favorable—though by no means idealized—circumstances, marriage appears to be generally healthy and robust. The marriages of spouses both of whom have college degrees are fairer than marriages in the past, and different in other ways as well. Marriage among better-off Americans generally works well. Among Americans whose socioeconomic status is much less favorable, those with only a high school degree, or only some high school, who are generally much less economically secure, stable marriages have become the exception.

This large class divide, and not same-sex marriage, is the great challenge concerning the future of marriage in America. An important part of the marriage divide seems to be explained by culture, values, and social norms: even among the economically challenged, those who wait to marry first and then have a child will be better off.

THE GOOD OF COMMITMENT AND THE CHANNELING FUNCTION REVISITED

Same-sex marriage opponents have argued that including gay and lesbian couples in marriage does nothing to advance and could undermine the channeling function of marriage as applied to heterosexual couples. The claim has been that the state has a special interest in channeling sexually active heterosexual couples into marriage on account of their propensity to procreate by accident. That's a silly reason for excluding gays and a poor account of why we should encourage young people to appreciate the advantages of marriage.

In some ways, marriage does have a "special status" in our society: it is a widely valued aspiration, a lavishly celebrated turning point in the lives of a couple and their families. The law is far from being responsible for much of the brouhaha that surrounds marriage: the elaborate invitations, the fancy clothes, the gifts, and the expectation of an elaborate meal served to extravagant numbers of close friends and distant relatives, and, of course, the "open bar." The civil law requires none of these things, and they may distract us from marriage's purposes and importance.

The law facilitates peoples' desire to marry by packaging the legal underpinnings of the marriage relation. The law also helps to make this status relation meaningful, consequential, and widely understood. Should the law go further and not only facilitate but encourage people to get married?

I emphasize the facilitative nature of civil marriage because the vast majority of eligible Americans, who are past the age of consent and not yet married, would like to be married. Marriage is a very popular institution. But we should go further.

Jonathan Rauch, in his widely and deservedly praised book on same-sex marriage, argues in favor of a social expectation that people ought to get married: marriage ought to be a social expectation, a kind of rite of maturity, which it is to a great extent.[72] The failure to get married ought to raise eyebrows and occasion comment; marriage should be encouraged. And to support that expectation, he argues against "marriage lite," as it might be called, domestic partnerships or civil unions with some of the same benefits as marriage, but without the public meaning and the social expectations that surround marriage.

I sympathize with Rauch's concerns. Advocates of same-sex marriage frequently judge that gay males in particular need the stabilizing influences of marriage, more than lesbians and more than heterosexual couples, owing to what appears to be a greater propensity of males to engage in frequent and sometimes risky sexual exploits. I join Rauch and others in thinking that the "channeling function" of marriage would do many gay males a lot of good.

Schneider describes the channeling function as working by "rewarding participation" and "disfavoring competing institutions." The "disfavoring" part was once done by stigmatizing illegitimacy and, for example, denying welfare benefits to single mothers. Few favor a return to such policies, including those who believe the law should strengthen marital commitment.

Even when Schneider wrote in 1992, he allowed that the channeling pressures exerted by the law of marriage and by social norms were generally quite gentle; they are even gentler now. In 1992 Schneider could still write that the law supported marriage and punished alternatives by outlawing "sodomy, bigamy, adultery, and prostitution."[73] Sodomy is now part of constitutionally protected liberty, and prosecutions for adultery have been unheard of for decades. Schneider observes that the channeling function does not, in any case, "primarily use direct legal coercion": it "relies centrally but not exclusively on social approval of the institution, on social rewards for its use, and on social disfavor of its alternatives."[74] And these social rewards and sanctions still operate with respect to marital fidelity, spousal and child abuse, and other features of marriage. Indeed, marriage retains its currency as the preferred form of family life including for gays, single mothers, and others who are excluded from marriage or unable to participate in it. It exerts its influence partly by offering a social language of aspiration and success in life that Americans imbibe from infancy.

Marriage matters here, but we should exaggerate neither the pressures to marry nor the constraints that are created by entering into marriage. The status of being married permits a great deal of flexibility in living and working arrangements. Even if marriage still carries with it the outlines of a certain socially defined "script," spouses are, as Mary Ann Case argues, free not to follow it. Spouses are not required to live together, have children, love each other, be sexually exclusive, and so on. These and other common features of marriage are expected, to be sure, but none is legally required. Exit is common if not costless, and the terms of particular marriages can be personalized via pre- and postnuptial agreements, which I discuss in the following chapter.[75] Unmarried couples can do many of the things that married couples do, without marrying.

Nevertheless, public policy could and should do more to encourage young people to recognize the benefits of marriage and commitment. This is especially important for those contemplating, or risking, having a child. We should also, as Cherlin, Sawhill, and others have argued, help young people to postpone having children until they are ready and able, by improving sex education in schools and making sure effective contraceptives are available.[76]

Indeed, as we will see in the next chapter, there is a case to be made that the law has undermined marital commitment and deprived spouses of the possibility of entering into deeper commitments by making divorce too easy.

CONCLUSION

This chapter has provided a brief overview of the legal aspects of marriage, and it has described some of the main benefits of marriage for spouses and families. This chapter, along with chapter 4, helped provide a provisional defense of marriage as a public and private good for people.

This chapter also sketched the wide gulf that has opened between the upper and lower ends of the socioeconomic spectrum with respect to marriage and parenting. For those who enter it under favorable circumstances, marriage is surprisingly successful and stable. But for far too many Americans who face challenging and insecure economic circumstances, marriage seems out of reach and they have turned away from it. More needs to be done, I argue in later chapters, to help make marriage more accessible to the less well off, to encourage them to make choices that better advance their own goals, and to provide greater assistance to those living outside of marriage.

We next consider, in chapter 6, a variety of reform agendas for marriage. These include various proposals to increase the contractual aspects of marriage, to further distinguish and separate the civil and religious dimensions of marriage, and to introduce greater choice, personalization, and deliberate design. In addition, we consider a variety of even more radical reforms that aim to replace marriage, as we know it, with an alternative status focused on the broad good of care. I take up these various proposals and consider their virtues as compared with marriage as a status relation defined in advance by law.

CHAPTER 6

REFORM PROPOSALS AND ALTERNATIVES TO MARRIAGE

The institution of civil marriage is constantly evolving in response to the changing lives of spouses, children, and the wider society. America's federal system provides fifty laboratories within which experimentation can take place. There are, in addition, innumerable proposals for the reform or replacement of marriage, and we take up some of these in this chapter.

I will focus on reform proposals that seem to go to the core of marriage as a unique default status defined for all in a very public way by law and shared traditions. Some reforms seek to introduce greater choice and personalization by abolishing civil marriage and encouraging couples to self-consciously design their own *contractual* legal forms for marriage. In place of a common status relation defined by law, the contractual approach encourages prospective spouses to enter into explicit understanding and agreements on the terms of their marriages. Prenuptial agreements are already allowed across the United States, and some reformers argue that they ought to be more widely utilized. Introducing a greater degree of personalization and choice could make the law more ethically neutral, and more open to personal preferences and social diversity.

Some claim that a related benefit of a more contractual regime is that the word "marriage" could be left to churches and other groups in civil society. The newly minted contractual regime could be constructed under the rubric of "civil unions," domestic partnerships, or something similar. This would have the benefit of more sharply distinguishing marriage as a civil and legal arrangement, and the meaning of "marriage" in various faith communities.

Yet others argue that the newly designated legal arrangements would help distinguish the law of the future from the gender inequality and patriarchy of the past.

In addition, this chapter takes up the suggestions of those who argue that the public's interests should be reconstituted so as to support a broader array of caring and caregiving relationships than can be accommodated in marriage as it exists today. It is a mistake, argue these critics of marriage, to bundle together into marriage the goods of care and caregiving with amorous love and sexual intimacy: the public's interest should be with facilitating everyone's access to caring relationships, in whatever form they may take.

This chapter elaborates a point previously made: that marriage is already a reasonably flexible arrangement. Encouraging couples to articulate their expectations and understandings about the kind of marriage they want can certainly improve communication and mutual understanding. There are some reasons to think, however, that introducing greater personalization by explicitly specifying and limiting marital commitments may undermine distinctively marital commitments. I seek to show that current arrangements and practices that might at first seem strange, such as the rarity of prenuptial agreements in first marriages, actually make a great deal of sense.

I endorse the concern to widen the public's recognition and support for caring and caregiving relationships but argue that this should be done by building on the success of marriage rather than by eliminating it.

ABOLISH CIVIL MARRIAGE?

In a chapter of their widely read book *Nudge*, published in 2008, economist Richard N. Thaler and law professor and political theorist (and former U.S. regulatory czar) Cass R. Sunstein offer a comprehensive brief for marriage reform. They urge that we drop the word "marriage" from all civil laws and substitute the less morally freighted "civil union" to designate legally recognized domestic partnerships. For this "highly libertarian" proposal, as they describe it, they offer a variety of arguments.

It would, they argue, be a way of expanding freedom, especially religious freedom. "Many religious groups, strongly object to same-sex marriage," and they "insist on their right to decide for themselves which unions they are willing to recognize, with attention to gender, religion, age, and other factors." Marriages, under Thaler and Sunstein's proposal, "would be strictly private matters, performed by religious and other private organizations." Instead of the "same one-size-fits all arrangement of state marriage, couples could choose the marriage-granting organization" that suits them (assuming it is willing).[1]

As thing stand, marriage bundles together an enormous array of benefits. And the state monopoly on conferring the status of an "official marriage" gives public authorities the sole power to confer "official legitimacy, a stamp of approval" of "immense importance." It is an anomaly and an anachronism that the state retains such power, say Thaler and Sunstein, and that a "couple that is married within a religious or other private tradition, but not with the authority of the state, lacks an important kind of validation."[2]

In addition to questioning whether many of the legal "incidents" associated with marriage ought to be made available to persons in other, nonmarital relationships, Thaler and Sunstein argue that "official marriage licenses" divide the "world into the status of those who are 'married' and those who are 'single.'" But people might be interested in entering into any of a great variety of private relationships, intimate or otherwise, structured in many different ways. The "simple dichotomy between 'single' and 'married' does not do justice to what people might choose."[3] Moreover, "the institution of state-run marriage has a highly discriminatory past, enmeshed as it has been in both sexual and racial inequality." That past, say Thaler and Sunstein, "cannot be entirely severed from the current version of the institution of marriage."[4]

Finally, these reformers argue that civil marriage produces "unnecessary polarization" in our politics, as conservative religious groups and advocates for same-sex marriage grapple "over fundamental issues and definitions." Their reform proposal, the authors assert, "simultaneously satisfies both of these opposing factions" and allows for a "wide range of experiments— increasing freedom for individuals and religious organizations alike while at the same time reducing the unnecessary and sometimes ugly intensity of current public debates." All it takes is a "simple declaration that *marriage* should be for private institutions, not for the state, and religious organizations" may set their own rules "regarding who could marry."[5]

Thaler and Sunstein offer, in these ways, a comprehensive critique of marriage as a status relation defined for all by law. They do so in the name of values that have great appeal on the political left, right, and center: greater religious freedom and individual choice, respect for a wider range of diversity, and concern for the equal status of those marginalized by a major social institution. They explicitly leave aside the issue of polygamy, which we have also done so far.

There would, however, at the current historical juncture, be one obvious cost to ceding the word "marriage" to churches and civil society groups. Gays and lesbians have been fighting for decades for marriage equality, and the symbolism of the word itself is of enormous importance, both to same-sex marriage supporters and opponents. To drop the term now from the civil law would be a form of "leveling down": it would achieve equality in a degraded or devalued currency. Admittedly Thaler and Sunstein first published their proposal in 2008, when it might more reasonably have been seen as a step forward for gays. Michael Kinsley published a similar proposal in 2003, largely on the ground that he expected the marriage debate to be deadlocked: a stalemate like the controversies over abortion and affirmative action.[6] Who, in 2003, could have guessed the issue would swing as decisively as it has? Nevertheless, these proposals now remind one of those cities that, when they were required to integrate municipal swimming pools and golf courses on the basis of race, instead discovered the virtues of privatization. That was another form of racial insult.

As Evan Wolfson, among others, has argued, what gay and lesbian couples have sought is not "gay marriage" or "same-sex marriage," and certainly not "same-sex partnership," but rather simply *marriage*, "with the same duties, dignity, security, and expression of love and equality" as is enjoyed by straight couples.[7] Marriage equality is rightly seen as essential to securing the equal status and standing of gay people in America.

If the prospect of equal rights for gays had become the occasion for a compromise of the sort Thaler and Sunstein advocated, this important debate might have been moved prematurely from near the center of American consciousness. Gay rights in America could, moreover, have been permanently associated with the degradation of the status of marriage in American law. And, finally, the public retains an important and legitimate interest in marriage, which is to say, in the general shape of citizens' personal lives, notwithstanding the fact that this thought makes many liberals uncomfortable.

Let us leave the equality issue to one side for now and consider the other reform proposals advanced by Thaler and Sunstein. These authors raise important questions that will persist after same-sex marriage is widely accepted in America.

*****

There are pluses and minuses to the idea of further "contractualizing" marriage. Thaler and Sunstein note that, while prenups are easy to obtain, few are executed. They also observe that in those few states where alternatives to the current marriage model, such as covenant marriage, are available, very few people choose them. They suggest that the reason is that couples entering upon marriage are grossly overoptimistic about their prospects for permanence, even while they seem to correctly perceive the general vulnerability of marriage to dissolution. Couples entering upon marriage, evidence suggests, are also generally unaware of the economic and other consequences of divorce.[8]

These are useful observations concerning the unpreparedness of many couples for marriage. As we saw above, however, cohabiting couples about to have a child are also generally far too optimistic about the stability of their relationships, while those who enter marriage under favorable conditions—which is to say, the well educated, mature, and financially reasonably secure—have *good reasons for optimism*.

In general, while Thaler and Sunstein are alert to the downsides to the current regime of marriage as status in law, they pay little attention to the dangers of the contractual alternatives.[9] We can see this by looking more closely at prenuptial agreements, and the question of divorce reform. We first consider two charges against marriage involving its religious dimension, for many, and the charge that it retains the taint of past gender discrimination.

CURING THE CONFUSION OF RELIGIOUS AND CIVIL STATUS?

Perhaps some people are confused, as Thaler and Sunstein argue, by the fact that the same word "marriage" is used to denote a legally defined status and also a religiously sanctified relationship. Many gay marriage opponents invoke the notion of "biblical marriage" ("What God has joined, let no man put asunder"). And we have the further apparent anomaly that most civil marriages in the United States are performed by clergy.[10] So the use of the word "marriage" to denote both a religious and a civil status defined by law can be a source of confusion.[11] Does it present a weighty reason for reforms of the sort Thaler and Sunstein, among others, propose?

According to one poll, over a third of Americans say clergy should "no longer be involved in the state's licensing of marriage," and around half say that "religious weddings should not be connected to the state's definition and recognition of marriage."[12] I do not share these views, which in any case may be weakly held.

The civil law defines who can be married in the eyes of the state and political community, and the legal implications of entering into that status. As a political community, we ought to deliberate together on the shape of the civil law of marriage in the currency of public reasons and accessible evidence. Religious communities are free to define for themselves who is married in the eyes of their church and to recognize religious marriages on their own terms.

When it comes to the issue of confusing religious and civil statuses, Mary Ann Case suggests that it may depend on whether the religious group in question has taken the trouble to define a religious law of marriage. Catholics and Jews have done so, making it clear what the terms of marriage are within those religions. Protestant denominations have done less to elaborate a religious law of marriage, relying more heavily on civil authorities.[13] They are free to do that but can hardly complain when the civil law of marriage follows civil imperatives.

There really is no good excuse for not understanding the difference between marriage as a legal relation and as a relation defined and recognized by particular faith communities. Most people know that divorce and remarriage raise distinctive issues for Catholics, and that, in other ways as well, the public meaning of marriage as a legal institution is distinct from marriage within particular religious and other nonpublic communities. This is crucial. As we saw in part 1, there are many on the right (and, in truth, many on the left as well) who seek to define civil marriage in line with their sectarian philosophical and/or religious traditions. Marriage as a public, civil institution must answer to reasons that appeal to citizens' common sense, and evidence that stands up to public scrutiny. There is a reasonable public justification for same-sex marriage, for marriage as a status institution in law, and, as we shall shortly see, for monogamy. This important institution is subject to ongoing democratic deliberation in the political community, in light of our recognition of the basic freedom and equality of all citizens and our reasonable public purposes.

Religious communities, in contrast, can decide on the contours of the religious institution of marriage in the manner they are accustomed to decide such matters for themselves. There is no guarantee that religious communities will embrace our public understanding: it may yet be many years before the Catholic Church and the Southern Baptist Convention accept same-sex marriage. Refusing to recognize the religious validity of same-sex marriages is an essential aspect of religious freedom.

The very fact that religious communities may define marriage in a way that seems problematic from a public point of view gives the political community a serious interest in keeping its grip on so consequential a public category as marriage. We have a public interest in controlling the legally enforceable terms of marriage, and also in influencing citizens' social understanding of marriage and marital norms. This will become vivid in the case of polygamy. Even if, as we shall see, consenting adults have a right to enter into a plural religious marriage, there may sometimes or often be concerns about the social pressures and expectations generated by these religious marriages. Addressing those is likely to depend on mustering social norms, and not only on imposing legal restrictions.

HISTORICAL BAGGAGE AND GENDER INEQUALITY?

Thaler, Sunstein, and others argue that marriage continues to carry historical baggage associated with past discrimination. And many want to reject the historical baggage that they believe the term "marriage" continues to carry. Many feminists have long viewed traditional marriage as irretrievably mired in gender hierarchy, symbolized by many traditional marriage rituals: the bride being "given away" by her father, taking her husband's name, and being carried by him over the threshold of their new house (how many grooms still do that?).

When Lucy Stine married Henry Brown Blackwell in May 1855, she read a "protest" at their wedding, which he signed. Among its complaints were these:

> We protest especially against laws which give to the husband:
>
> 1. The custody of the wife's person.
> 2. The exclusive control and guardianship of their children.
> 3. The sole ownership and use of her personal real estate, unless previously settled upon, or placed in the hands of trustees, as in the case of minors, lunatics, and idiots.
> 4. The absolute right to the product of her industry.
> 5. Also against laws which give to the widower so much larger and more permanent an interest in the property of his deceased wife, than they give to the widow in that of the deceased husband.
> 6. Finally, against the whole system by which "the legal existence of the wife is suspended during marriage," so that in most States, she neither has a legal part in the choice of her residence, nor can she make a will, nor sue or be sued in her own name, nor inherit property.[14]

None of these inequalities now exists, and couples are free to dispense with the symbolic gendered traditions mentioned above. Nevertheless, even while couples are free to describe themselves as "partners," like Harriett and Joseph, maintaining the institution of marriage is thought by some to help sustain gender inequality and its exploitive tendencies, and other forms of inequality and oppression as well.[15]

The complaint about gender inequality is dated. Thanks to the long struggle for women's equal rights, marriage is no longer essentially gendered, and opponents of same-sex marriage warn precisely that it puts the last nail in the coffin of "gendered marriage." Nan Hunter argued in 1991 that "legalizing lesbian and gay marriage would have enormous potential to destabilize the gendered definition of marriage."[16] That was certainly true in the past. "Off the shelf marriage" is now "ready to wear" for same-sex couples, as we saw above (while plural marriage, in contrast, creates a host of new complications in law). And if marriage is not essentially gendered, then it is not essentially a device for perpetuating gender hierarchy.

As Judge Vaughn Walker observed in the California's Proposition 8 litigation, "Gender no longer forms an essential part of marriage; marriage under law is a union of equals." In that same case, historian Nancy Cott pointed out that "through the 20th century and into our era, the sexual division of labor is no longer necessary for the kinds of work people do in the world." It is not surprising that *Ms. Magazine* has repeatedly celebrated advances in same-sex marriage equality as advances for women generally.[17] Many Americans hope and some fear, and not without reason, that same-sex marriage will help to further break down persistent stereotypes that place responsibility for child care and housework disproportionately on the shoulders of women, and that stigmatize women in the workplace who struggle to balance career and child care.[18]

The enormous changes in marriage brought about by the women's movement—the great advances of gender justice—ought to be *further entrenched by same-sex marriage*. That is one way in which same-sex marriage changes marriage for all, and for the better. And it is one way in which marriage privatization, at this juncture, would derail an important part of the process of entrenching gender equality.

PRENUPS: PROMOTING MORE DELIBERATE AND PERSONALIZED COMMITMENTS?

In 1972 Harriett Mary Cody and Harvey Joseph Sadis wrote up a detailed marriage contract that has been reprinted by *Ms. Magazine* and more widely.[19] They affirmed a number of points of agreement: they would keep their own names (now quite a common practice) and be known as "partners" in the relationship. They promised to give each other plenty of time to make friends outside the marriage and declared "that invitations extended to one of them will not be assumed to have automatically been extended to the other." "The parties freely" acknowledged, however, "their insecurities about sexual relationships beyond the partnership" and so agreed "to maintain sexual fidelity to each other." In the context of the sexual revolution of the late 1960s and early 1970s, this stipulation may have been important. Some of what Harriet and Joseph agreed to seem like the sorts of things that could improve many marriages, including the commitment to share housework equally. They also stipulated things that one might expect at least be up for ongoing discussion, such as "A decision by one party to be sterilized will be supported emotionally and financially by the other." The "contract" specified detailed terms involving control of income and property, including separate bank accounts and individual control of prior assets and future earnings; it was agreed that those terms would govern in the event of a divorce. The agreement also declared a commitment to ongoing communication and negotiation of differences. Harriett and Joseph's marriage declaration exudes the spirit of early 1970s egalitarianism. And indeed, proponents of moving in a more contractual direction often argue that greater choice and personalization will make marriage more equal.

Couples might do well to follow Harriett and Joseph: vowing to honor and cherish each other "according to the terms we set out below." Their declared commitments may well have worked like a written constitution to improve their subsequent relationship. And just as many Americans read the Declaration of Independence aloud on July 4, it is reported that "the couple celebrated each anniversary with a review of the contract for the first 12 to 15 years," though "now they gather as a family on New Year's."[20] It apparently worked well for Harriett and Joseph: at last report, in 2001, they had been happily married for twenty-nine years. Couples entering upon marriage ought to know that agreements of this sort are an option.

Much of what Harriet and Joseph agreed to seems in the spirit of a broad statement of principles, along with some specifics. An agreement of this sort, and periodic review of the "state of the union," seem potentially useful devices for facilitating frank and ongoing communication between spouses about the meaning of their marriage, and for renewing their mutual understanding and dedication to it. It is important for two people entering into marriage to ascertain that their values and their vision of their lives together is compatible, for the essence of marriage is the "collaborative construction of a joint life."[21]

Encouraging people to enter prenuptial agreements might or might not improve people's marriages: there is little or no systematic evidence, and some prenuptial agreements seem to reflect a self-protective mind-set that may undermine the open-endedness and flexibility of marital commitment. Most of the controversy focuses on agreements relating to divorce. Even then, prenups can serve important and legitimate purposes, including in a second marriage and when there are children or a partner from previous relationships with interests to be protected. But when they are entered into in a self-protective spirit, they seem likely to be prone to certain pathologies.

In many prenuptial agreements, prospective spouses seek to anticipate the dissolution of their marriage by specifying some the terms of the divorce settlement. It was long thought that such advance planning would encourage divorce, and, until the 1970s, the law refused to recognize and enforce them. Then in the 1970s, as with so many other matters, people rejected the traditional view. Laws were changed, and no jurisdiction in the United States now treats such agreements as invalid in general or as such.[22] Prenups controlling the spouses' financial obligations to each other are more likely than in the past to be recognized as valid, though the law defines the limits of contractualization, and courts will typically not honor prenups that are "unconscionable," unfair, or otherwise contrary to public policy (such as a bargain that leaves one spouse impoverished).[23]

Prenups in the sense I have described are distinguished from post-nuptial agreements (or "postnups"), which can take the form of reconciliation or separation agreements. Agreements can provide a basis for reconciliation by imposing conditions on marital property or any future postdivorce settlement, perhaps to reassure an aggrieved spouse. Separation agreements, on the other hand, are entered when a divorce or separation is imminent; these must be approved by courts to ensure the terms are reasonably fair to both parties. In child custody agreements, courts seek to provide for the best interests of the child.[24]

Thaler and Sunstein, among others, suggest that the availability of an off-the-shelf legal form can discourage couples from thinking through what they want out of their marriage. True, but there are downsides to certain kinds of legal stipulations that are worth highlighting, especially those that seek to limit the open-ended and unconditioned nature of the marital commitment. The difficulties and risks of anticipation via prenups help to clarify the case for using law to define the broad terms of marriage in advance.

One family law attorney reports that, in her experience, prenups are "almost always coercive" and one-sided, involving the exercise of power by the stronger (and wealthier) over the weaker party. "The less-moneyed spouse generally gives away most of her marital rights as provided by law to the moneyed spouse. . . . In addition, prenups are often 'sprung' on the less-moneyed spouse, if not after the engagement has been set, often after the invitations are sent." She concludes that prenups are typically a contract to defeat the relative fairness that the law of marriage requires in dividing property in the event of a divorce: "the laws were written and interpreted over a long period of time by very knowledgeable people applying fairness and thoughtfulness to real life experiences and situations."[25]

The contract model invites bargaining, and bargaining can disadvantage the weaker or less calculating party. Whatever present or prospective inequalities the parties bring to the table will help shape the bargain they arrive at. Setting the terms of marriage by contractual bargaining may be especially problematic when it takes place under the potentially blinding influence of romantic love, the glare of which may also be distributed unevenly. Therefore the benefits of status may be most important for the weaker and less calculating party, and a common template for marriage may offer unique benefits, precisely because it does not admit, or at least encourage, a great deal of bargaining.

Scholar W. Bradford Wilcox argues that the mindset behind prenups is more appropriate for cohabitation, commenting that

> couples who embrace a generous orientation toward their marriage, as well as those who take a dim view of divorce, are significantly more likely to be happy in their marriages. A National Center for Family and Marriage Research study finds that couples who share joint bank accounts are less likely to get divorced. In fact, married couples who do not pool their income are 145 percent more likely to end up in divorce court, compared to couples who share a bank account.[26]

Here, as elsewhere, there is bound to be a "selection effect": the separate bank accounts and lack of "generous orientation" to marriage may be symptoms of marital problems rather than their causes. Nevertheless, things like a joint bank account may also signal greater mutual dedication to making the relationship work.

The marital commitment is open-ended. The wedding vows—to love and to care for one another "for better or worse, in sickness and in health, 'til death"—express mutual commitment without conditions. Trying to specify and fix the terms of marriage at the outset seems to defy this open-endedness. Attorney Laurie Israel argues that the dynamic set in motion by prenups is antithetical to the distinctive marital commitment: "The more mutually supportive the spouses are (in all ways, not just financial) the stronger and more enduring the marriage."[27] Contracts require disclosure in advance, whereas the current marriage model encourages partners to accept and get used to the other's faults, up to a point.[28] As Fred Hirsch put it, "The more that is in the contracts, the less can be expected without them; the more you write it down, the less is taken—or expected—on trust."[29] Treating marriage as a contract may thus degrade the open-endedness or unconditionality of commitment to which marriages aspire.

Elizabeth Anderson worries that introducing a contractual model more appropriate to business partnerships could "undermine the goods of commitment and intimacy proper to marriage. For the realization of these goods depends on each partner's carrying out the projects constitutive of his shared life in a spirit of trust and love rather than of the piecemeal calculation of individual advantage." As she argues, "Giving and receiving in a spirit of trust is itself one of the goods of marriage. The point of marriage in realizing shared goods is obscured by tending to the terms of an explicit marriage contract, which evaluates the marriage in terms of the distinct advantages accruing to each party."[30] Trying to specify and fix the terms of the marriage bargain in advance "undermines the responsiveness of the marriage to the changed needs of the partners, as well as the promise it holds out for deepening their commitment in light of a more articulate," or simply more sensitive, "understanding of their shared project."[31]

The two positive aspects of prenups concern their capacity to protect the interests of a partner or children from a previous relationship, and their possible usefulness as a device for spouses to think through what they want out of their marriage together, to ensure that there is real commonality. The downside is that prenups may amount in effect to a "set of contingency plans" that anticipate the marriage's failure. All human arrangements (including commitments) are contingent, but "to dwell on their conditionality" is, as Eric Scwitzgebel observes, "already to depart from the project of jointly fabricating a life and to begin to develop a set of individual goals and values opposing those of the partner."[32]

Let me acknowledge: this discussion has been brief, and I have emphasized the downsides of contract to make the case for the reasonableness of status. It is, at least, not obvious that we should prefer the model of marriage as contract. Concerns about marital equality, protection of the vulnerable, and the distinctive nature and value of the marital relationship all furnish reasons for maintaining marriage as a status relation. These values can, moreover, all be understood and defended in the currency of broadly public goods. They will not, of course, be equally powerful in all circumstances.

Two other aspects of the critique of marriage offered by Thaler and Sunstein can be addressed more briefly.

REFORMING DIVORCE AND STRENGTHENING MARRIAGE?

William N. Eskridge has proposed a "smorgasbord" approach to marriage, with a menu of standard options.[33] Perhaps couples, both opposite- and same-sex, should be free to call the relation they are entering a "civil union" instead of a "marriage," if they wish. In truth, of course, they can already call their marriage whatever they want, and describe it to others in the way that suits them. Many now dispense with the terms "husband" and "wife" in favor of "spouse" or "partner." This is a reasonable hybrid suggestion that is certainly worth exploring.

Others have described the current law of marriage with "no-fault" divorce as "marriage lite." Prior to the divorce reforms of the late 1960s and 1970s, obtaining a legal divorce required a prolonged separation, of perhaps two years, or showing that one of the spouses had broken the marriage vows and was at fault. It was widely thought that the old regime encouraged married couples who wished to divorce to collude to deceive courts concerning fault, and that the fault standard sowed unnecessary rancor, poisoning future cooperation. The new regime allows for speedy and unilateral divorce when either spouse is no longer fulfilled by the relationship.

Conservatives and others now often argue that unhappy spouses are apt to give too little weight to the negative impact that divorce can have on children. Working to keep a marriage together that is not especially happy, but in which spouses manage to avoid a great deal of open conflict, is often best for children.[34]

Arkansas, Louisiana, and Arizona have sought to provide and encourage the option of beefed-up marital commitment under the rubric of "covenant marriages." In Arkansas, such marriages require couples to undergo premarital counseling, and additional marriage counseling in the event either spouse seeks a divorce. Couples also agree that neither spouse can obtain a speedy divorce based on the "no-fault" standard that prevails elsewhere, according to which a sense of incompatibility is sufficient. An immediate divorce is available only if one or both spouses commit a serious marital transgression, such as adultery or physical abuse. In all other cases, the spouses must wait at least two years for it.[35]

The idea of curtailing no-fault divorce and strengthening marital commitment is often associated with conservatives and especially the

religious right.[36] Elisabeth S. Scott makes an interesting case for covenant marriage from a broadly liberal point of view. Marriage is supposed
to enable couples to signal their serious commitment to each other and to
society, and it is supposed to strengthen their ability to make good on the
commitment by raising the costs of exit. This is crucial, she emphasizes,
to marriage's precommitment function: by agreeing to an arrangement
that raises the costs of acting on what may well be a transient dissatisfaction with the relationship, marriage enables couples to weather the
inevitable storms of conflict and temporary malaise and disappointment.
The costliness of exit increases the spouses' mutual assurances about each
other's commitment, enabling a deeper investment in the relationship.
Insofar as divorce "no longer carries serious costs," those who "aspire
to life-long marriage are less able to signal accurately their own intentions" by agreeing to marry.[37] As people with shallower commitments are
encouraged to marry, and marital norms and expectations weaken, the
reinforcing power of social expectations also weakens. "Marital failure
may result for some couples whose marriages might have weathered hard
times if legal enforcement of commitment norms had been available to
deter defection."[38]

Scott's proposals are liberal and not paternalistic because her aim is
to use law to facilitate the making of serious long-term commitments
for those who wish to enter into them. Entering into commitments that
include costs for reneging can be important mechanisms that help us
to overcome the common human tendency to mistakenly favor short-
term satisfactions over long-term projects and the satisfactions that go
with them. Scott suggests that when it comes to marriage, divorce reform
has weakened the commitment function. She suggests strengthening it
not by reintroducing divorce for fault, which tends to involve too much
acrimony. Rather, she proposes mandatory waiting periods of the sort
contained in the covenant marriage laws, possibly combined with mandatory counseling, to help ensure that the decision to end a marriage is
undertaken deliberately and on due consideration.[39]

The "slow down" approach that Scott recommends is consistent with
the central recommendations of Andrew J. Cherlin's aptly titled *The
Marriage-Go-Round*. Cherlin shows that Americans' personal relationships are characterized by far greater churn and flux than those of citizens
of other countries, and evidence suggests that this is stressful for adults
and children. He makes a well-informed case for encouraging Americans
to slow down when it comes to decisions to cohabit, marry, divorce, and
remarry. More counseling and thoughtful communication before, during,
and after marriage seem like good ideas.[40]

And yet, while many commentators argue that no-fault divorce has done great damage to marriage, there is no widespread public movement to end or reform it; no campaign with anything like the public profile of the movement opposed to same-sex marriage. And where covenant marriage is available as an option, very few chose it: less than 1 percent of Arkansans in the first few years it was available. The promarriage policies of the George W. Bush administration also appear to have been ineffective.[41] We should not exaggerate the capacity of law and policy to alter people's behavior in this sphere, though I agree with those commentators such as Galston, Cherlin, and Scott who argue that we should seek ways to educate young people about the values and benefits of marriage and marital commitment.

SUPPORTING CARE AND MARRIAGE ALTERNATIVES

Many family scholars and policy experts argue for the need for greater public support for people's basic needs, including those concerned with child care and the care of dependent adults. They argue that we should encourage greater recognition and support for good parenting in a diversity of forms, and also for adult care and caregiving outside of the marital relation, and outside of any sexual relationship. I agree. Marriage is distinctive and, for those entering it under favorable circumstances, very often successful, but it should not be the exclusive focus of our attention when it comes to parenting and caregiving.[42]

What I disagree with are proposals to eliminate marriage in favor of some newly minted form of relationship invented by theorists, or to radically remake marriage into something unrecognizable. We should build on the success of marriage. To see why, let's consider the more radical proposals put forward by Elizabeth Brake and Tamara Metz.

Brake has developed an intriguing line of thought under the rubric "minimal marriage" in an important article and book. Metz and Martha Fineman, among others, offer related proposals. Brake argues that our law is unfairly biased in favor of "amorous dyads" because it conceives of marriage as "a cohabiting, financially entangled, sexually monogamous, exclusive, romantic, central relationship." Marriage so understood is biased against many "relationship types," including various kinds of nonsexual friendship networks. Feminists and queer theorists have for decades branded traditional marriage as "heteronormative," charging that it makes "heterosexist" values normative for all. Brake goes them one better, calling marriage "amatonormative," meaning that marriage unfairly elevates and celebrates the values associated with romantic "dyads." The law of marriage contributes to the general expectation that a happy life involves settling down with a loving partner, but for many, that expectation can be oppressive, argues Brake.

Brake would redefine and broaden the state's interest in marital relationships by using marriage to recognize and support everyone's basic interest in caring and caregiving relationships. Brake draws on social scientific evidence to support the proposition that caring relationships matter a great deal to people's well-being.[43] She argues that such relationships are a "primary good," and that our political institutions should secure for all the "social bases" of this good of care. This yields a thinner understanding of marriage, as including all nondependent caregiving relations between or among adults of *any number and gender*. She argues that the law of marriage should recognize and support caregiving relationships of all sorts, including those that do not involve sexual intimacy. Marriage should not, she argues, be understood as a comprehensive or lifelong mutual commitment: particular people might exchange only a small subset of the "incidents" or aspects normally associated with legal marriage. The exchanges need not be reciprocal, and they might involve a complex network of partial exchanges. That, suggests Brake, is an advantage of her proposal: instead of putting all of one's eggs in the one basket of monogamy, the minimal marriage regime facilitates the forming of far more diverse caregiving networks, and the distribution of "minimal marriage rights" across different persons in one's network. Brake invites us to consider the following example:

> Rose lives with Octavian, sharing household expenses. To facilitate this ménage, Rose and Octavian form a legal entity for certain purposes—jointly owned property, bank account access, homeowner and car insurance, and so on. The arrangement is long term but not permanent. . . . Rose's only living relative, Aunt Alice, lives nearby . . . in genteel poverty, and Rose feels a filial responsibility toward her. . . . Alice needs access to good healthcare and . . . could use the pension that would go to Rose's spouse if she had one. . . . [M]inimal marriage would allow Rose to transfer the eligibility for these entitlements to Alice.
>
> While Rose enjoys Octavian's company and has affection for Alice, only Marcel truly understands her.[44]

And so it goes on. Because she and Marcel are such close friends who spend a lot of time together, it would be nice if he qualified as Rose's family member for some purposes: perhaps for a "family rate" at the local gym. And we might imagine Rose sharing custody of a child with

George, and being in actual love with Stella. Brake's "minimal marriages" would allow traditionalists to "exchange their complete sets of marriage rights reciprocally, while Rose and others like her distribute and receive marital rights as needed and desired with several or many others.[45]

So the legitimate public interest in marriage is broadened and redefined as participation in caregiving relationships of all sorts: any richer and narrower definition in law (involving romantic connection, for example) violates liberal neutrality by failing to respect the diversity of people's preferences concerning their lives and relationships, selecting out and privileging some caregiving relationships over others. "Minimal marriage, and no more extensive or restrictive law, is consistent with political liberalism."[46]

Brake would limit state involvement to securing for all the social bases for enjoying caring and caregiving relationships, irrespective of number, gender, and the presence or absence of sexual or romantic love, or other features. Greatly broadening our understanding of marriage in this way could, as feminists have long sought, help break down the gendered norms that surround (and are sustained by) traditional marriage. We would attempt in this way to retain but change the meaning of marriage. Doing so could, suggests Brake, undermine our unhelpful fetishization of one particular caring relationship to the exclusion and detriment of others.

In response: Brake and others are right that we should recognize the value of many caregiving relationships and support and promote them through appropriate legal forms and public policies. This is required by the sort of pluralistic promotionism that I described earlier and is a condition of just marriage. However, these wider forms of care can be given their due without calling them "marriage." Public policy should recognize and promote caring and caregiving relations in addition to, but not as, "marriage."[47]

Indeed, applying the label of "marriage" to nonmarital forms of caring relationship could powerfully deter many people who might otherwise consider entering such relationships. Consider, for example, relationships involving mutual commitments between younger adults and their elderly relatives, or friends. Allowing a grandson and grandmother to enter into a formal relationship involving the exchange of power of attorney, inheritance, caregiving responsibilities, could be a very good thing. But no one wants to say, "I am marrying my grandmother." Not even minimally.

We do far better to provide appropriate recognition and support to these other nonmarital caregiving relations while also preserving marriage as a particular and well understood relationship of two people who are in love and who make mutual commitments of a uniquely extensive sort.

*****

Tamara Metz advances a distinctive analysis and an alternative proposal. Like Brake, she argues that the institution of "marriage" as currently configured transgresses the limits of liberalism as a political doctrine. Citing Judith Shklar, she insists that liberalism must not be a "philosophy of life." The liberal state must respect the vast religious and ethical diversity of modern states by "drawing a line between public and political on one side and private and non-political life on the other." From this perspective, the law of civil marriage is an anomaly: through it the law shapes the most intimate aspects of our lives, even forming our deepest desires and aspirations by channeling them in certain directions (toward monogamy, for example). "With its border-crossing tendencies, marriage poses an obvious challenge to a political theory that relies heavily on distinctions between public and private life." Marriage is a "formal, comprehensive social institution (FCSI). With its peculiar mix of extralegal character, scope, method, and purpose, marriage, on this account, is more like a religion than other institutions and legal statuses such as civil unions, business partnerships, motherhood, or even funerals, to which it is often compared."[48] By its sponsorship of "marriage" in law, the liberal state improperly assumes the role of ethical authority, and it draws on "the reservoir of meaning" attached to marriage by nonpublic authorities, such as churches.[49]

Metz proposes to disestablish marriage in the same way we have disestablished religion. The central interests of the state in this realm are in recognizing and supporting intimate and dependent caregiving, and also in ensuring that those who engage in these vital tasks and relationships are not made vulnerable thereby. Status relations defined in law can help protect caregivers and those who receive care from domination and oppression, by helping to signal the nature of their relationship and sustain protective social norms. So she would have us create a new social status: Intimate Caregiving Union, or ICGU. This new status "would be expressly tailored to protecting intimate care in its various forms." It would "reflect assumptions of longevity and resource sharing," for example, and, "to protect the norms of unmonitored reciprocity and to protect caregivers, property would be divided upon dissolution in order to achieve substantive post dissolution equality." "Caregiving creates its own vulnerability," so "the state must recognize and regulate intimate caregiving unions to insure against the inherent risks of care," and to help preserve reciprocity and equality.[50]

*****

Progressive scholars and policy experts argue convincingly that the political community should do more to recognize and support nonmarital caring and caregiving relationships. Just over 50 percent of Americans over 16 were unmarried in 2014, a much higher figure than a few decades earlier.[51] Devising useful, appropriate, and feasible supplements to marriage is a matter for careful collective deliberation, as has been recommended in an insightful report by the Law Commission of Canada.[52] This is an important issue of public policy and justice in which we all have an interest.

However, nonmarital caring and caregiving relationships are typically quite different from marriage. While marriage is far from perfect, we should build on its relative success rather than further weakening it. Robin West argues that while "ending marriage might expose the problems of uncompensated care work . . . it is not at all clear that it would end it, rather than exacerbate it." Many single mothers already do "all the caregiving and all the income earning, and suffer hugely because of it." But ending "marriage" as a status relation in law might, argues West, make it harder for "women who want to enter into long-term or for-life committed relationships with their partners"; it might only increase the number of single mothers and "legitimate nonsupport."[53]

Deleting the word "marriage" from the federal register of laws in favor of an arguably more neutral and less ethically freighted term like civil union or social pact will in itself do nothing to assist caregivers and care receivers in nonmarital relationships.

There is also a more positive reason for retaining marriage as a distinctive status relation in law, and for preserving its position as the legal designator for committed long-term relationship: the liberal democratic state has a legitimate interest in the general shape of people's marital and family lives. This will become even clearer in part 3, when we examine the important reasons of justice and public policy for preferring monogamy and discouraging polygamy. Both Brake and Metz discount these interests. Brake would expand her revised institution of "minimal marriage" to groups or networks of whatever number, and she is unconcerned about whether the exchange of "minimal marriage" rights is symmetrical. Metz specifically complains that under the "current regime . . . citizens can be prosecuted for unsanctioned use of the marital title—as was polygamist Tom Green." An advantage of abolishing "marriage" as category in law, for Metz, is that it would transfer from the political community to nonpublic authorities the ethical authority to define marital norms, which have a deep "constitutive" significance for the shape of our lives. "The 'm' word does matter," says Metz, and we should place "control of this constitutive status in the hands of those best suited to wield it effectively," namely, religious and other nonpublic ethical authorities.[54]

Metz is right that marriage shapes our lives profoundly, both individually and collectively. The historic shift from polygamy to monogamy appears to have pervasive implications for the distribution of opportunities across society, as we will see in part 3. From this, Metz seems to conclude that marriage is too important for the political community to get involved with. I draw the opposite conclusion: marital patterns and norms shape the distribution of power and opportunity in society. Polygamy as a social form gives rise to destructive forms of inequality and higher rates of violence in the family and society. Monogamy helps us to secure everyone's fair opportunity to pursue the great good of family life. As we will see, a liberal democratic political community has important interests in the shape of people's marital and family relations. Even if polygamy should be decriminalized—and no one really argues for vigorous enforcement of the criminal laws in any event—it should not be recognized in law, except insofar as we do so for the limited (but important) purpose of protecting those made vulnerable by it.[55]

Insofar as liberal neutralists seek to widen and diversify the scope of our public concerns, that seems to me all to the good. The place of marriage in our public life ought not to blind us or prejudice us with respect to the importance and value of other kinds of caring and caregiving relations. But it would be ironic if this salutary concern for the diversity of human types and needs led us to adopt a reductive, singular, and homogenizing model of care. We need not respond to the call for inclusion in this way: justice permits a wider variety of alternatives. We would do better to provide fair support for a proliferated variety of caring and caregiving relations, insofar as we can. I agree with Linda McClain, who argues that our strategy should not be to eliminate marriage and hope for something that is better and more inclusive but rather to preserve marriage and add to it.

*****

The question of whether and how to provide a variety of marital options is an important one, which I can only flag here. In addition to the various proposals mentioned above, there are various others. And in many U.S. states, people already have options. Many American states, and countries around the world, enacted domestic partnerships and civil unions, often as an alternative to recognizing same-sex marriage. In many places those have remained on the books and are available to some or all heterosexual as well as gay couples.[56]

Options can have downsides, of course: marriage alternatives could attenuate the public legibility and clarity that is one of the great advantages of having a singular public status that admits of various forms of "personalization," while also trying to ensure (no doubt imperfectly) that such agreements do not create unfairness or exploit vulnerability.

The problem is not only that the language of "civil unions" or "domestic partnerships" is relatively opaque as compared with "marriage"; in addition, such labels do not signal the same level of mutual commitment as marriage. And with the decline of those social meanings would come the decline of the norms and expectations that go with them, which some may experience as constraints, but many others view as enabling and want to embrace. Natural law scholar John Finnis has emphasized the "fundamental simplicity and intelligibility" of marriage as a legal framework, and Andrew Sullivan argued decades ago for the legal and personal benefits of "a clear, common symbol of commitment," as does Jonathan Rauch.[57] I agree with them.

There have been a number of times when I have explained to a bank clerk or insurance agent that I wanted to open an account or policy with my "partner" David, only to be asked what business we were in together and what sort of a commercial account or policy it should be. It can be not only awkward, but demeaning and embarrassing to explain. And obviously there could be much worse situations in hospital waiting rooms and elsewhere. Marriage greatly simplifies our social relations: two people become the mutual default designees for a whole series of important prerogatives involving incapacity, caregiving, and so forth. And it simplifies matters for third parties.[58]

"Off-the-rack" arrangements that contain packages of default rules can have considerable gains in clarity and efficiency.[59] And then too, marriage is designed so as to balance benefits and responsibilities reasonably: designing alternative statuses is a complicated business. We have only scratched the surface of the complexity of marriage law. A law of domestic partnerships would have to work out a roughly comparable range of issues or confine itself to a few matters. Where legal alternatives to marriage exist, as I noted above, few avail themselves of them, at least in the United States. For decades, the vast majority of gay and lesbian Americans have fought for equal access to marriage, not domestic partnerships.

As I have said before, the symbolic dimension of marriage seems to be less weighty in other countries, including in France, where social pacts have proven quite popular, though they seem often to be a stepping-stone to marriage.[60] These are issues worthy of further exploration.

*****

A further important issue is to specify which of the various traditional legal incidents of marriage ought to be untied from the marital bundle and made available to persons in other relationships. Some privileges of marriage may appropriately compensate for the specific commitments that marriage entails. It is clear that some or many of the traditional legal incidents of marriage ought to be made more widely available to persons in nonmarital relationships, in part to support and recognize wider forms of caring and caregiving relationships. This process is already well under way: people are using contractual relations to allocate to persons other than spouses legal powers often associated with marriage, including powers of attorney, hospital visitation rights, next of kin privileges, and so forth.

We should try to make sure that those who do not wish to marry are treated fairly, that we promote their interests. Providing appropriate support and recognition for other caregiving relations should strengthen the case for marriage, and is required by fairness.

CONCLUSION: POLICY REFORM AND DEMOCRATIC DELIBERATION

Carol Sanger has argued that civil marriage "offers a system of sanctioned commitment from which more inventive arrangements may veer but to which they seem to return for certain basics, such things as shared resources, support obligations, and a system for dividing children and property upon dissolution."[61] So the *status* model may have decisive advantages over the *contractual* one, especially given predictable inequalities in bargaining power, and asymmetrical vulnerabilities to exploitation.

For now, I hope that this part has shown the following: marriage is defensible in terms of broadly public values. It enhances the well-being of spouses and their children, as well as the wider society. The vast majority of Americans honor and esteem marriage and wish to be happily married.

The public meaning and associated norms of marriage are resources to which many citizens want access. The institutions of marriage and the family are basic to our social lives. The meaning and the norms associated with marriage are not creations of law alone but of centuries of evolving practice that have deeply shaped our ways of life. Marriage figures prominently in our culture and literature. It gains further meaning and resonance from its parallel recognition in communities of faith.

The civil case for marriage does not depend on one's holding any particular philosophical or religious framework, such as that deployed by New Natural Law. Marriage is not universally valued and is controversial, at least in some circles. But the case for marriage is public in the sense that the various benefits and values associated with marriage are widely appreciated. Marriage is an altogether fit subject for ongoing democratic deliberation. We can describe marriage and its benefits without having to invoke any obscure philosophical claims.

There are many proposals for reforming marriage, and there is an important collective conversation to be had about the fairness of the current benefits associated with marriage: the fairness toward singles and those in nonmarital caring relationships. The case for marriage need not be understood and should not be treated as demeaning those not in marital relations. These are matters for ongoing democratic deliberation, guided by reasonable conceptions of the public good and principles of equality and inclusion.

I turn in part 3 to the issue of plural marriage. Monogamy is central to modern marriage, and one oft-repeated question is whether there is a public case for monogamy in the wake of gay marriage.

PART III

WHY TWO?
MONOGAMY, POLYGAMY,
AND DEMOCRACY

CHAPTER 7

THE CHALLENGE
OF POLYGAMY

The law of marriage, as we saw in part 2, allows two people to make a distinctively extensive commitment to each other: to love and care for each other, raise their children (should they have them), and share their lives and fortunes. The law helps make the general nature of marital commitment well known, and it allows people to make their own marriage a matter of common knowledge. Marriage enhances the well-being of spouses and children, including greater happiness and better health, both mental and physical. The political community has good reasons to take an interest in marriage—to regard it as not only desired but desirable—and to preserve it as a status in law.

The question then arises, why should we—indeed, *may we legitimately*—confine the availability of this relationship to two persons only? For surely there will be some married couples who wish, by mutual consent, to bring a third or even a fourth adult into their marriage. If they wish to establish a household together and commit to love and care for one another, why not? Can we justify prohibiting or denying recognition to polygamous marriages? Ought we to drop restrictions based on numbers and focus on the quality of people's relationships? That could mean seeking to prevent marriages and other intimate relationships, of whatever number, that involve coercion, domination, or abuse of spouses or children.

Like homosexuals, polygamists in the United States have often been subject to hostility and persecution, though this has given way to a policy of de facto tolerance. Does our refusal to recognize plural marriages reflect anything more than animus? On what grounds can nonrecognition and discouragement of polygamy be justified?

These are the questions addressed in this part. While same-sex marriage helps us secure equal basic liberty and fair opportunity for all, substantial evidence suggests that the spread of plural marriage would undermine these same values. Polygamy as a social form is associated with inequality and heightened conflict within the family and in society. There are reasonable grounds for not extending equal recognition to polygamous marriages, and also for discouraging them. At the same time, I allow that many polygamous families appear to be reasonably happy and successful. We should not demonize polygamy.

I also take up, more briefly, the elusive phenomenon known as "polyamory," an egalitarian form of plural relationship that is frequently held to be a harbinger of future forms of complex, networked relationships and new family forms.

David L. Chambers, whom I have already quoted, warns defenders of marriage equality to pause before concluding that, "polygamy deserves to be looked on less favorably than same-sex marriage." Polygamists and homosexuals have been widely demonized, and their lives distorted to mirror the "fears of their opponents." Polygamists have been described, by no less a liberal than William O. Douglas, as notoriously promiscuous, just as gays are. When one actually gets to know them, says Chambers, "the 'homosexual lifestyle' turns out to be nearly as dull as everyone else's."[1] Television shows such as *Sister Wives* suggest the same thing is often true of polygamists, or at least those who embrace fame and exposure.

The nature of the public's interest in monogamy is one of the most important and least examined questions regarding marriage, and it is this that we explore in what follows.

As the fight over same-sex marriage comes to a head, the question is repeatedly asked: if marriage need not involve one man and one woman but may be entered by two men or two women, then why not one man and two women, or other threesomes, foursomes, or what have you? Does discrimination against those in plural relationships have a reasoned basis? Or does it, like discrimination against homosexuals, rest on various forms of prejudice and animus?

On the right, we encounter our old friend: the slippery slope from same-sex marriage to "bigamy, . . . adult incest, prostitution, masturbation, adultery, fornication, bestiality, and obscenity." Justice Antonin Scalia has repeatedly insisted, in *Lawrence*, *Windsor*, and elsewhere, that protections for gay rights render unsustainable state prohibitions on the entire parade of horribles just mentioned.[2] Ryan T. Anderson asserts that "candid and intellectually serious supporters of" same-sex marriage "are willing to scrap, together with sexual complementarity, the limiting of spouses to two in redefining marriage." After all, he asks, "if marriage is fundamentally a sexual-romantic domestic partnership founded on emotional bonding, as opposed to being a conjugal union of man and woman in a partnership ordered to procreation ... then there is absolutely no reason to suppose that marriages are by nature the union of only two persons."[3]

On the political left, many agree with Justice Kennedy that the Constitution "gives substantial protection to adult persons in deciding how to conduct their private lives in matters pertaining to sex."[4] When, in *Lawrence v. Texas* (2003), the Supreme Court extended rights of sexual privacy and autonomy to gays, Justice Kennedy's majority opinion argued, "Our obligation is to define the liberty of all, not to mandate our own moral code."[5] Following Kennedy, Barbara Bennett Woodhouse argues that both same-sex marriage and polygamy gain support from "the freedom to define and redefine the self's most intimate and identifying connections."[6] Chambers, writing in the mid-1990s, agreed with Arkes and Anderson that recognition of same-sex marriage could make the state more receptive to "units of three or more," including those "bound by friendship alone."[7]

Indeed, since polygamy often has the backing of religious faith and may even, as in fundamentalist Mormonism, be regarded as an imperative religious duty, the case for recognizing polygamy might seem stronger than the case for gay marriage. And to this we can add that polygamy is deeply embedded in many cultures around the world, including those of some indigenous people in North America, across most of Africa and the Middle East, in parts of Asia, and elsewhere. Plural marriage may thus claim the imprimatur of multiculturalism.

Many on the left would therefore agree with Andrew March, who argues for a strong "presumption of permissibility" when it comes to matters involving sexual autonomy, personal liberty, and privacy. Liberals must start from the bottom of the slippery slope, he says, and when it comes to plural unions there is no way back up.[8]

There are even a brave few on the left who, confirming Justice Scalia's direst warnings, argue that general prohibitions on incest ought to be relaxed, as we will see later. Chambers wonders whether opposition to incest is much like the "instinctive revulsion" of many conservatives to both polygamy and same-sex marriage.[9]

For decades there has been no shortage of voices on both the political right and the political left arguing that acceptance of polygamous unions is *compelled* by the *same principles* that justify equal rights for gay and lesbian Americans, as we have seen.

These various important claims concerning monogamy, equal liberty, and the public good are too little studied. They are bound to receive more attention in the wake of same-sex marriage, and what follows is a start. I argue that same-sex marriage and polygamy have little in common, aside from being deviations from "traditional" monogamy. The values of equal freedom that undergird gay rights support a wide variety of well-founded worries about polygamy as a social system.

DEFINITIONS AND PRACTICE

Polygamy derives from the Greek *polygamia*, which means the state of being married to many spouses. It is sometimes also referred to as "plural marriage." Strictly speaking, polygamy comes in two different forms. The first and by far the most common is "polygyny," a marriage in which one husband takes multiple wives. This form is so dominant, as a matter of common human practice, that when people use the more general term "polygamy," they are typically referring to polygyny.

The second form of polygamy is "polyandry," in which one wife has multiple husbands. Though not completely unknown, polyandry is rare in the historical record and in current practice. It exists in a few societies in central China and near Tibet today, sometimes taking the form of "brother marriage" that enables male siblings to keep the family farm intact, so that it can support both of them.[10] In conditions of subsistence farming and extreme poverty, a small family farm may simply be unable to support more than one family.[11] Zeitzen reports that, in Asia and Africa, polyandry affords protection to the "wife in a dangerous country when her husband is away. A woman's and her offspring's chances of survival are greater . . . when she has a group of brothers maintaining her."[12] Controlling male jealousy in such marriages is extremely difficult. Among polyandrous Tibetans, says Zeitzen, those who succeed "do not seem to be moved by love either," suggesting that the cost of this suppression is the suspension of all "strong emotional bonds."[13] Societies may be driven to polyandrous arrangements out of necessity, but they appear both rare and fragile. Moreover, it is telling that whereas polyandrous marital arrangements often seem the consequence of desperate circumstances, polygyny has often been an exalted status to which the most successful males aspire.

There are also some rare forms of group marriage that have occurred and seem still to occur among some indigenous tribes in Southeast Asia, in which, for example, two brothers might marry four sisters. An explanation for such marriages seems to be economic security in very poor conditions (as a participant remarked to a curious interviewer, "a large family makes for a big workforce"[14]).

The main focus of this discussion will be on the most familiar alternative to monogamy, which is polygamy in the form of polygyny. There is, however, a third set of alternatives to monogamy within which some want to locate a new form (or forms) of marriage or a relationship form that could substitute for marriage. I will briefly mention these more complex arrangements now and return to them at the end.

This third category is often known as *polyamory* or *polyfidelity*. One scholar terms it "postmodern polygamy."[15] In contrast with polygamy, polyamory is egalitarian and nonhierarchical. Unlike "group marriage" as practiced in some very poor societies, polyamory focuses not on survival but on exploring adult sexuality. Polyamory is not associated with any particular religious tradition or national or ethnic culture. Polyamorists describe their lifestyle as "multipartner relationships unburdened by patriarchal gender roles, heterosexual constraints, or monogamous exclusivity."[16] These adult relationships are often fluid, involving different combinations of genders and a liberated attitude toward sexual restraints.

Polyamory has been called "the culmination of many of the same liberal principles that justify same-sex marriage and flexible gender roles in opposite-sex marriage."[17] When the philosopher Elizabeth Brake endorses relationships involving any number and combination of gendered partners and calls them "minimal marriages," she explicitly affirms polyamory rather than traditional polygyny. It is not at all clear that these really constitute a form of marriage. However, as conservatives never tire of pointing out, many dozens of progressive academics and intellectuals who have signed a public statement called "Beyond Marriage" endorse the spread and legal recognition of a wider array of family forms that include polyamory.[18]

Polyamory raises questions quite different from those associated with polygamy, so I treat it separately in chapter 9, where I also say a few words about incest.

Monogamy is the marital form with which we are most familiar, of course, in which marriage is limited by a "rule of two" spouses per marriage, for many centuries understood to be a husband and wife. When the law of divorce and remarriage allows people easy exit from marriage and entry into a new one, and they take advantage of this, it is sometimes referred to as "serial polygamy": having multiple spouses in sequence, versus all at once. We should not exaggerate this tendency: in America, where marriage, divorce, and remarriage are most frequent, 55 percent over the age of 15 are married, only 12 percent of Americans have been married twice, and 3 percent have been married three or more times.[19]

If we take a wider and longer view, monogamy is far from dominant. Approximately 85 percent of the human societies studied by anthropologists have practiced polygyny and regarded it as the preferred marital form for those with sufficient resources and social standing.[20] This is referred to as "normative polygamy," meaning that it is preferred and even socially expected among the privileged. Polygamy as polygyny, in this sense, was practiced by the Church of the Latter Day Saints (LDS, or Mormons) in the latter half of the nineteenth century, and it is practiced today in fundamentalist Mormon sects scattered across the western United States and Canada. Polygyny is legal and practiced in much of North, West, and Central Africa, in the Middle East, and in Indonesia (but it is banned in Turkey and Tunisia). It continues to exist as "traditional marriage" in South Africa, where it is practiced by President Jacob Zuma, but it is hemmed in by controversy.[21] It is permitted in Islam, in which men may marry up to four wives, so long as they treat them equally; even where it is permitted, most Muslim men do not practice it.[22]

*****

Polygamy as practiced historically is overwhelmingly *polygyny*: a gendered and hierarchical relationship and social system. (I will use polygamy and polygyny interchangeably, as is common.) Studies of early civilizations—from Mesopotamia and Egypt to the Aztec and the Inca, India and China—found elaborate social hierarchies organized around polygamy, with kings and maharajas enjoying hundreds of wives and concubines, and a great number of unmarried lower-status males. Generally, polygamy can be enjoyed by only a small percentage of men in a given society, and it is associated with prestige and high status. It was reserved in imperial China to "emperors and emperor-like men," who made up no more than 10 percent of the population.[23]

Polygamy as *polygyny* is far from ideal under favorable circumstances, as we will see. It can, however, serve valuable social functions in unfavorable circumstances. Nicholas Bala observes that, "In a primitive agrarian or hunting-based society with a high male death rate, especially due to war, and economic support and protection only available to those women and children who lived in a male-headed household," polygamy could enhance women's and children's physical and economic security.[24] And still today, in poor regions of Africa and elsewhere, women may well find it more advantageous to be the second or third wife of a relatively wealthy farmer than the sole spouse of a destitute husband.[25] In China it appears that the old practice of concubinage has reappeared, illegally, as very rich men keep secret households with "second wives," or *ernai*, who gain economic security.[26]

Opposition to polygamy in the United States has often been linked to mainstream Christian hostility to Mormonism as a religion and, more generally, to religious teachings in favor of monogamy. The origins of monogamy are Western but not Christian. Monogamy prevailed among the classical Greeks and the Romans prior to Christianity, though it co-existed with the existence of concubines among the privileged.[27]

Christian missionaries encouraged monogamy in Africa and else-where, and it has spread along with modernizing influences such as hu-man rights and gender equality, often through the agency of local political action.[28] Polygamy was banned in Japan in the 1920s as part of its push to modernize. Mao Zedong and the Communist Party passed a marriage law in 1950 that aimed to destroy the "feudal" family and replace it with monogamy and gender equality, as well as marital freedom (including divorce), but retaining the Confucian idea of reciprocal obligations of care between parents and children (with adult children responsible for caring for their parents).[29] In India, after independence was achieved, the Hindu Marriage Act of 1955 outlawed polygamy among Hindus while permitting it among Muslims only.[30] Polygamy is declining in popularity in Africa; it was recognized but regulated and restricted in South Africa after its independence and the adoption of its constitution. Opposition to polygamy was led by the African National Congress, which has a strong commitment to gender equality. Some countries, such as France, that eased restrictions on polygamy among immigrants from Muslim coun-tries in the late 1960s and 1970s later reinstated tighter controls. In spite of France's 1993 ban, it is estimated that 140,000 people there live in polygamous families.[31] International human rights treaties and women's groups around the world generally call for its restriction and abolition.[32]

*****

All American states outlaw polygamy by criminalizing *bigamy*, which involves entering into a second legal marriage while one of the spouses is already married.[33] Outside of openly polygamous communities, bigamy has often involved deception and fraud. In nineteenth-century Amer-ica, a stranger might arrive in town on business, profess his love for and commitment to a woman, and begin a family with her, keeping secret a previous marriage elsewhere.[34]

In the United States and Canada, general criminalization has long been coupled with a widely understood policy of nonenforcement absent evidence of some other crime, such as having sexual relations with a minor, or tax or welfare fraud. The constitutionality of these prohibitions has recently been challenged in both Canada and the United States, offering two fascinating legal dramas that help to organize the discussion below.

The spectrum of possible reforms concerning polygamy or plural marriage ranges from decriminalization to the extension of equal recognition in law to polygamous marriages. Defenders of extending greater recognition and acceptance to plural marriages point out that these marriages *need not* take the traditional patriarchal form. Nor need plural marriages necessarily involve very young women being pressured into marrying much older men. The hope of many progressive advocates of marital diversity is that polygamy in conditions of well-entrenched gender equality could take new, more egalitarian forms.

In addition, some observe that polygamists often seem highly responsible in comparison with men who father children and then fail to help support those children and their mothers. Kody Brown, star of the TLC reality television show *Sister Wives*, is married to four women, and, as we will see, there are many appealing aspects of this fundamentalist Mormon family. Joe Darger and his three wives have twenty-three children and a book, *Love Times Three*; they provided the inspiration for HBO's *Big Love*. Even these mild patriarchs are clearly the heads and ultimate deciders within their families, but their families seem reassuringly normal.[35]

While recent discussions of polygamy are rare, it attracted furious scrutiny in the United States in the latter half of the nineteenth century, on account of intense and often brutal opposition to Mormon polygamy. As Utah sought a path to statehood, it was insisted that polygamy must be renounced, and so it was, but only after considerable vitriol had been expended in condemning the institution. The attacks on Mormonism were often filled with venom and prejudice, facts that we must keep in mind.

Nevertheless, a substantial case for discouraging polygamy emerges from the study of its practice. Recognizing marriage as a relationship of two and only two persons—opposite sex or same sex—helps to *secure for all persons a "fully adequate scheme of equal basic liberties" and the fair opportunity to pursue the great good of family life*.[36]

We ought not to take monogamy for granted: it is a very particular way of organizing the most important parts of our personal and social lives, with pervasive moral, cultural, and political implications. Institutionalizing monogamy deeply shapes peoples aspirations and partly constitutes the forms of the good life that will flourish in a given society.

My aim here is not to provide a general account of human marital forms and their consequences—a gargantuan task!—but only to suggest that there is a reasoned case backed by substantial, though not uncontroversial, evidence in favor of monogamy as a social form. The basic principles of equal liberty and fair opportunity that undergird the case for same-sex marriage argue against polygamy.

I will begin, in this chapter, with some brief historical background on Mormonism in North America, and then take up, in chapters 8 and 9, the very different ways that courts in British Columbia and Utah have dealt with polygamy. In chapter 8 I summarize both the principled grounds, in law and political morality, for distinguishing polygamy from same-sex marriage, and the evidence, presented in British Columbia and elsewhere, for favoring monogamy and discouraging or even prohibiting polygamy. In chapter 9 I focus on the complexities surrounding the recent litigation over polygamy in Utah involving Kody Brown and his four wives, stars of *Sister Wives*. I conclude that chapter with an examination of polyamory, a supposed egalitarian form of polygamy, and a brief discussion of incest. I hope these discussions put to rest the suggestion that same-sex marriage sets us on various slippery slopes.

NORTH AMERICAN POLYGAMY AND THE TROUBLED LEGACY OF *REYNOLDS V. UNITED STATES*

Polygamy emerged as an issue in the United States in 1852, when, at a special conference called for the purpose, Elder Orson Pratt read aloud the "Revelation on Celestial Marriage" that Joseph Smith said he had received in 1843. In so doing, Pratt made official what had long been rumored: that "the Principle" of plural marriage had become central to the LDS, which had been founded by Joseph Smith in 1830 with the publication of his "new scripture," the Book of Mormon. The 1843 revelation, which Joseph recorded, gave him the power to covenant celestial marriages that "would endure for eternity, governing relations in heaven as in life, and dictating the degree of exaltation achieved in the afterlife."[37] Of those permitted to enter into these marriages, said Joseph, "Then shall they be Gods, because they have no end . . . [and] because they have all power, and [even] the angels are subject to them."[38]

The Mormons were intensely unpopular from early on, for two principal reasons. One was polygamy, obviously, which Joseph Smith began to practice in the early 1830s, secretly, before the doctrine was officially pronounced. It is estimated that he entered into at least forty-seven polygamous unions. Brigham Young, who built the church in Utah, eventually had as many as fifty-five wives, though the exact number is unknown.[39]

Yet only a small percentage of Mormon marriages were polygamous, and in most of those, men had two wives.[40]

Another reason for the LDS's unpopularity was the authoritarian nature of the church, which extended its power broadly over the lives of church members. Mark E. Brandon describes Smith's style of political rule in Nauvoo, Illinois, as "theocratic authoritarianism—evidenced by Joseph's multiple public offices, his armed militia, his use of secret councils for control and governance, the destruction of the press, and the imposition of martial law." Nauvoo is lost to history, but in the early 1840s it was the second largest city in Illinois after Chicago, and its "city militia was the largest armed force in the state." The Prophet, as he was known, was "the city's mayor, its chief justice, lieutenant general of militia, trustee for the local university, real estate agent, publisher of a newspaper, owner of a store, and part owner of a steamboat," besides writing up and publishing his various prophecies. Finding himself with time on his hands, he ran for president of the United States in 1844 as a third-party candidate.[41] Mormons "rejected tolerance for the beliefs of others" and sought political control wherever they settled.[42]

Plural marriage remained a central doctrinal tenet of the LDS Church until 1890. While Islam merely permits the practice of polygamy, LDS beliefs made the practice of polygamy a religious obligation for the elite whose circumstances permitted. Plural marriages were "reserved for the most righteous of men, those most dedicated to the Church and capable of enhancing the power of the Church."[43] Church authorities carefully controlled access to celestial marriage and divorce. Women were understood to be incapable of achieving godhood on their own, but could "only share in their husband's godly power."[44]

Early Mormonism was a highly gendered aristocracy. Today's LDS Church website allows that, "for many who practiced it, plural marriage was a significant sacrifice."[45] Brigham Young famously declared, "My wives have got to do one of two things—either round up their shoulders and endure the afflictions of this world and live their religion, or . . . leave. . . . I will go into heaven alone, rather than have scratching and fighting around me."[46] It was common for Mormon wives to view polygamy as a "temporary purgatory" on earth, according to Terryl L. Givens.[47]

And yet women were unequal all across America, and Mormon women enjoyed rights denied to those living elsewhere, including the vote and the right to divorce, which they initiated with considerable frequency.[48] When their church and way of live were attacked, many Mormon women spoke publicly in defense of their community and way of life. It appears that most plural wives made their family lives work with relative harmony, and most of the children raised in these families had fairly normal experiences with their fathers, their mothers, and their father's other wives.[49]

It is argued nowadays that plural marriage served various practical imperatives on the nineteenth-century western frontier, including the need to populate the sparsely settled territory. This claim is said to be supported by the "near universality of marriage among women and the abundant opportunities for remarriage among previously married women of childbearing age."[50] However, others report that "while Mormon polygamy produced more children per father than did monogamy," it produced fewer children per wife as compared with monogamous marriage.[51]

One defender of Mormon polygamy in the 1950s defended it as more realistic than monogamy. Men will inevitably tend to seek multiple sexual outlets; given that fact, polygamy helps reduce the incidence of adultery and prostitution.[52] Similar claims are advanced nowadays. This defense sits uneasily with the claim that polygamy is motivated by virtue and self-restraint; Brandon also notes the uncomfortable fact that most Mormon wives entered plural marriages "in their late teens, regardless of the age of the husband."[53]

*****

For American republicans, "[S]topping polygyny was understood as the key to thwarting the theocratic ambitions of the Mormon Church and establishing a secular rule of law" in the American West.[54] Congress made polygamy and bigamy federal criminal offenses with its passage of the Morrill Anti-Bigamy Act in 1862.[55] Representative Shelby Collum, defending an antipolygamy bill in the 1870s, fulminated that "polygamy has gone hand [in] hand with murder, idolatry, and every secret abomination"; it is "an institution founded in lustful and unbridled passions of men, devised by Satan himself to destroy purity and authorize whoredom."[56]

George Reynolds, secretary to Mormon leader Brigham Young, was convicted of bigamy under that act in a federal district court for the Utah Territory. His appeal eventually made it to the U.S. Supreme Court and generated an enduringly controversial ruling and opinion, as we will see. Reynolds insisted, among other things, that the Morrill Act infringed on his constitutional right to the free exercise of his religious beliefs. In 1878 a unanimous Supreme Court found that the free exercise clause of the First Amendment deprived Congress "of all legislative power over mere opinion" but left it "free to reach religiously-motivated actions which were in violation of social duties or subversive of good order."[57] Religious reasons and motivation did not provide grounds for carving out an exception to general laws deemed to serve a legitimate public purpose.

The Reynolds case is not particularly notable for its constitutional reasoning or holding, but the rhetoric deployed by Chief Justice Morrison Waite remains deeply alarming: "Polygamy has always been odious among the northern and western nations of Europe, and, until the establishment of the Mormon Church, was almost exclusively a feature of the life of Asiatic and of African people," he declared.[58] Citing legal scholar Frances Lieber, Waite said that "polygamy leads to the patriarchal principle, and which, when applied to large communities, fetters the people in stationary despotism."[59]

Seventy years later, in 1947, the Supreme Court reaffirmed the holding of *Reynolds* in *Cleveland v. United States*, a case involving members of fundamentalist Mormon sects, prosecuted under a federal statute that targeted trafficking in prostitution across state lines. Writing for the Court majority in *Cleveland*, no less a liberal than Justice William O. Douglas characterized polygamy as "a notorious example of promiscuity" and "in the same genus as the other immoral practices covered by the Act," including prostitution. Echoing *Reynolds*, he also called polygamy "a return to barbarism. It is contrary to the spirit of Christianity and of the civilization which Christianity has produced in the Western world."[60] Writing in dissent, Justice Frank Murphy pointed out that *polygyny* is "one of the basic forms of marriage. Historically, its use has far exceeded that of any other form. It was quite common among ancient civilizations and was referred to many times by the writers of the Old Testament."[61]

The *Reynolds* holding was reaffirmed once again, in 1985, by a federal appeals court: "Monogamy is inextricably woven into the fabric of our society. It is the bedrock upon which our culture is built. In light of these fundamental values, the state is justified, by a compelling interest, in upholding and reinforcing its ban on plural marriage."[62]

Both *Reynolds* and *Cleveland* seem to make the *inherent immorality* of polygamy and its odiousness to Christians its central features. So the Court in *Reynolds* emphasizes widespread moral revulsion rather than ill effects ("there never has been a time in any State of the Union when polygamy has not been an offence against society"[63]) and in *Cleveland* links polygamy with "prostitution," "debauchery," and "other immoral purpose[s]."

Nowadays, religious liberty and diversity, multiculturalism, and respect for difference are far more central values in our public life than when Justices Waite and Douglas penned their opinions. In the nineteenth century and the early decades of the twentieth, "scientific racism" bolstered a sense of Western superiority and Eastern inferiority that helped rationalize imperial rule. In a historic December 2013 ruling striking down part of Utah's antipolygamy law, which I explore at length below, Judge Clark Waddoups of the United States District Court in Utah emphasized that "*Reynolds v. United States* displays 'the essence of Orientalism' through its explicit 'distinction between Western superiority and Oriental inferiority.'... For the *Reynolds* Court, the comparison with non-European peoples and their practices is precisely what made the Mormons' practice of polygamy problematic."[64] "What," he asks, "was the 'social harm' identified by the *Reynolds* Court?" It was that "American Mormons were engaging in a practice thought to be characteristic of Asiatic and African peoples who were believed at the time to be civilizationally and racially inferior." The Supreme Court's reasoning in *Reynolds*, he insists, reflects an "orientalist mindset" and is "morally repugnant."[65]

Judge Waddoups is not wrong in these observations, and his determination to draw attention to the moral and intellectual shortcomings exhibited in these cases is salutary, but these lead him, unfortunately, to tell only part of the story. There is a reasoned case to be made against polygamy. The fact that it can be used to rationalize or amplify prejudice should sensitize us to the inevitability of our own biases but not derail balanced inquiry.

CONTEMPORARY FLDS PRACTICE

The Mormons "lifted the command to practice plural marriage" in 1890, as part of Utah's successful effort to gain statehood.[66] Some number of new plural marriages continued to be performed, and Congress voted to exclude a practicing polygamist from being seated as Utah's member of Congress in 1899. The Mormon Church never denied the truth of the "Revelation on Celestial Marriage,"[67] but it suspended the practice in the face of unrelenting hostility. The church issued a more emphatic policy in 1904 that strictly prohibited new plural marriages and urged their cessation, under intense and sustained pressure from the U.S. government. By the 1920s the Latter Day Saints were led by men determined to leave celestial marriage behind. This provoked those who remained committed—perhaps ten to thirty thousand—to break away and form their own churches. Some within the LDS Church, probably a small minority, might welcome the return of celestial marriage.[68]

Monogamous marriage has been the rule across the United States since the Latter Day Saints renounced the practice, but there have been pockets of exception. Fundamentalist offshoots of Mormonism are scattered across the American and Canadian West and northern Mexico. Some Muslim immigrants enter into polygynous marriages, some Hmong refugees from Laos brought the practice with them to the United States, and some migrants from Africa continue their practice of customary plural marriage. Estimates of the number of people living in polygamous families in the United States vary widely, but most put the number of fundamentalist Mormons in the country at well over forty thousand.[69] The largest such group is the Fundamentalist Latter Day Saints (or FLDS), headed for decades by Rulon Jeffs and then his son Warren, now in federal prison.

In the late 1920s, some fundamentalist Mormons began settling in the town of Short Creek, on the Utah and Arizona borders. Law enforcement officials conducted periodic raids on the polygamists in the 1930s, 1940s, and again in 1953.[70] All Short Creek residents were taken into custody, including 36 men, 86 women, and 236 children. The polygamists received favorable publicity: *Life* magazine portrayed them "as harmless, simple folk whose only crime was being different."[71] Despite some evidence of crimes, none of the women would testify against their husbands, and none of the children were found to have been neglected. Televised images of crying children being taken from their mothers fanned public outrage and forced the state to back off. Wary toleration has been the general policy since.[72] Paul Van Dam, the attorney general of Utah, remarked in 1990:

> Every law enforcement officer in Utah knows there are tens of thousands of polygamists in the area, and they are clearly violating the law. Yet if we prosecute these men and women, we know [from experience] that we will produce an incredible social disruption. Thousands of children must be cared for emotionally and otherwise, and that's a terribly expensive proposition.[73]

Utah's first polygamy prosecution in a half century came in 2001, when Tom Green, who had at the time five wives and thirty-one children, was convicted of four counts of bigamy and failure to pay child support.[74] Later, he was also found guilty of child rape for marrying and conceiving a child with a 13-year-old girl. He was sentenced to five years to life in prison. A few years later, Rodney Hans Holm, 32, an FLDS member, "married" his wife's 16-year-old sister in a religious ceremony, had sexual relations with her, and conceived two children with her before her eighteenth birthday.[75] Holm was convicted of both bigamy and having sexual relations with a minor. These cases were the immediate background to Kody Brown's challenge to Utah law, described below.

By 2000 there were more than five thousand fundamentalists residing in two towns that grew out of Short Creek: Colorado City, Arizona, and Hildale, Utah, with others living in Colorado, Texas, South Dakota, and in the towns of Bountiful and Creston in British Columbia. Warren Jeffs emerged as leader of the FLDS in 2002, succeeding his father Rulon. As "President and Prophet, Seer and Revelator," Jeffs is understood by his followers to speak directly for God and has sole authority to assign wives, perform marriages and divorces, and even reassign wives and children of any who disobey. Nearly all the property in Colorado City and Hildale was owned by a church trust controlled by Jeffs.[76] Young men have reported being exiled from the church to prevent their competition with elderly male members of the church for the limited number of marriageable women or girls. Jeffs "took more than 70 women as wives, many of whom had been his father's spouses."[77] After moving his people to the Yearning for Zion compound in Eldorado, Texas, he also served as principal of the FLDS school, where his favorite motto was "Perfect obedience produces perfect faith, which produces perfect people."[78]

Authorities eventually raided the Yearning for Zion compound.[79] Jeffs and seven other men were indicted. A former FLDS bishop, Fredrick Merril Jessop, was found guilty of conducting a marriage ceremony between a 12-year-old girl and the then-50-year-old Jeffs in 2006. Jeffs was eventually convicted on multiple counts: of being an accomplice to rape and also, in 2011, for sexually assaulting a 15-year-old girl as well as the 12-year-old girl he claimed to wed when he was 50.[80] Charges against other adults and an effort to remove the over four hundred children from the sect were unsuccessful.[81]

CONCLUSION

There is obviously a danger of focusing solely on the "problem cases" of polygamy that make it into court. As I have tried to make clear in this brief overview, the experience of families under polygamy varies, as it does under monogamy. The vast majority of polygamists living in North America and Europe have not been charged with crimes. There is a stark contrast between creepy cult leaders like Warren Jeffs and the smiling quasi-normality of *Sister Wives*, as we will see. Life in the isolated enclaves seems most worrisome, for seclusion allows social pressure to be brought to bear against young girls and boys, and it can facilitate and help shroud sexual abuse.

How should we regard polygamy as a form of married life? Ought we to decriminalize and normalize it so as to integrate polygamous families into the mainstream, where any abuses are more liable to be reported and where norms of freedom and gender equality may reshape objectionable practices? Or ought we to go further and regard plural marriage as an acceptable form of diversity and even, perhaps, protected by principles of religious liberty? If same-sex marriage is to be the law of the land, are there good grounds for treating plural marriage differently? Or should we get over the "instinctive revulsion that we feel when we contemplate polygamy,"[82] and even incest, as so many seem to finally have done with respect to gay and lesbian people?

To answer these questions I turn next, in the first part of chapter 8, to the general principled considerations that distinguish polygamy from same-sex marriage. Then I examine the systematic evidence presented to the Supreme Court of British Columbia—the most comprehensive record yet assembled.

CHAPTER 8

POLYGAMY, MONOGAMY, AND MARRIAGE JUSTICE

Polygamy, as we have seen, has frequently been subject to vitriolic condemnation out of proportion to the reasonable concerns that people may have about it as a social form. But what considerations, if any, justify public concern? And what should the attitude of our law be with respect to a practice that has, like homosexuality, often been condemned as morally abhorrent, associated with civilizational backwardness, and deemed inconsistent with the way of life of Christian societies in the West?

In fact, as we will see in this chapter, there are both principled reasons and a substantial body of evidence to support the judgment that any widespread practice of polygamy is a substantial matter for public concern. The considerations that can be advanced against polygamy deal with what it amounts to as a social form and its consequences for participants and the wider society. These considerations are far removed from the moralistic concerns with sexual acts that characterize natural law opposition to equal rights for gays. Whether the arguments against polygamy are sufficient to justify ongoing general criminalization is a more difficult question, which I address in chapter 9.

The argument for concern regarding polygamy is cumulative: there are a number of considerations that add up to a substantial case for discouraging it, or so it seems to me. I argue in what follows that polygamy as a widespread practice, or normative system, appears to be inconsistent with efforts to secure the preconditions of equal liberty and fair opportunity for all. Polygamy should not be regarded as within the scope of our basic liberties.

I begin with the variety of principled reasons for distinguishing polygamy from same-sex marriage and then turn to the evidence that was ably assembled by the Supreme Court of British Columbia in a landmark case decided in December 2012. In chapter 9 we return to polygamy in the United States.

PRINCIPLED GROUNDS DISTINGUISHING POLYGAMY AND SAME-SEX MARRIAGE

Four broad considerations help justify the different treatment that I accord to same-sex and polygamous marriages. These also further bolster the claim that we ought not to recognize plural marriages in law, and we should not count plural marriage among the *equal basic liberties*.

Orientation vs. Preferences

First, preferences for polygamy are not equivalent to same-sex orientations. The history of the struggle for gay rights has demonstrated that a large class of people have deep-seated and stable same-sex orientations. As Andrew Sullivan long ago observed, "Almost everyone seems to accept, even if they find homosexuality morally troublesome, that it occupies a deeper level of human consciousness than a polygamous impulse."[1] In contrast, a desire to enter into polygamous or polyamorous relations is not an equivalently deep-seated and limiting feature of human personality. Any of us might at some point wish to include an additional spouse in our marriage, but there is no class of people who, by nature or deep-seated nurture, have the "orientation" of only falling in love with two or more people at a time. As Justice Bauman put it, "There is no evidence that a predisposition toward polygamous marriage is anything more than how the expert psychologists described it, an advantageous strategy available to those with the inclination and resources to pursue it."[2] Where rich and powerful men rule over others and enjoy special privileges, it is not surprising that marriage will also be arranged to their liking.

This proposition gains support from the fact that in no Western society is there any broad social movement for polygamous or "polyamorous rights" that is equivalent to the decades-long struggle for the rights of gay, lesbian, and transgendered citizens.

These observations are qualified, but only partly, by the fact that some people's sincere religious beliefs—fundamentalist Mormons principally— make polygamy a religious obligation, and so, in those cases, it is not merely a "preference." This presumably deserves some weight in favor of tolerating and permitting the practice.

David L. Chambers goes further and argues that "supporters of gay marriage are simply wrong to claim that gay people's need for a union with another person of the same sex is more compelling than the needs of others who already have a spouse and who want to add a second or a third." He adds, with a refreshing generosity of spirit, "Those of us who favor same-sex marriage need to become more understanding of needs derived from sources other than the libido."[3] Good point. Nevertheless, I am not sure that the point made in the first quotation is correct. The need to find and settle down with and love another person is deep and profound. Same-sex orientation appears to be quite universal and is found in societies that are extremely repressive. On the other hand, people's felt desire for polygamous marriages appears to be highly variable and dependent on prevalent institutions and culture.

As I have already indicated, we need to construct a system or scheme of equal basic rights and opportunities that secures everyone's equal freedom, status, and standing in society. Our concerns with polygamy, in contradistinction to same-sex rights, proceed directly from these basic political values, as we will see.

What about the respect owed to religious liberty specifically? American constitutional jurisprudence holds that when state laws advance important public purposes, are supported by evidence concerning the seriousness of the harm that government seeks to prevent, and are reasonably well designed to address the harm, without unnecessarily infringing protected liberties, then they pass constitutional muster.[4] Monogamy seems to facilitate the realization of equal liberty while polygamy does not. *Brown v. Buhman* makes a reasonable case that "plural cohabitation" among consenting adults should be tolerated, as we will see, but it does not make the case, and never even considers the case, that it deserves equal treatment to monogamous marriage.

Twoness, Reciprocity, and Stability

Another set of considerations that count in favor of the "twoness" of marriage has to do with practical and commonsense aspects of stability and flourishing in human relations. Marriage nowadays is not just an alliance for the pooling of property and other resources; it is unique (or nearly so) in the depth and breadth of its commitments. Two people come to depend on each other deeply and across wide segments of their lives, making each other uniquely and deeply vulnerable to loss and betrayal. Anyone who has been married or in a long-term relationship similar to marriage knows how difficult it is to get to know and accept another person across a wide swath of private and public settings. Life partners and spouses must negotiate ways of living together and planning for the future, coordinating their actions and plans across extensive parts of their lives, from the trivial to the profound: from their preferences for food and drink to their deepest moral and religious beliefs, their choices of occupations and friends, their taste in entertainment and politics (but I repeat myself).

Bringing in a third person—making the dyad a triad—compounds the complexity of all of these negotiations and seems a recipe for conflict. Given the depth and breadth of the mutual commitments associated with marriage, it is hardly surprising that threesomes or larger multiples are more conflictual, at least if they aspire to protect and promote all the spouses' interests equally (where wives are highly dependent on their husband, polygamy can be stable). The classic social theory account of dyads and triads is Georg Simmel's: only in dyads do we get a perfect symmetry of reciprocal dependence.[5] It seems no mystery that the twoness of marriage makes sense in egalitarian societies: with monogamy, each spouse depends equally and reciprocally on the other.

Obviously, when children become part of a family, this complicates the twoness of family life. The important point is that *marriage* remains a fully reciprocal partnership between two spouses.

Marriage Markets and Distributive Justice

A third consideration in favor of one spouse per person is distributive fairness. Marriage is a great good, sought by the vast majority of people. Most men and women strive mightily to find a suitable marriage partner. We should design our social and political institutions, here as elsewhere, to secure the conditions within which this opportunity is available to all on fair terms; that is, so that all people have a fair opportunity for a happy family life.

Evidence suggests that if we grant people in general permission to marry multiple spouses, the opportunity will be taken up unevenly and will tend to be to the advantage of higher-status, more powerful, and wealthier males. As noted above, polygamy may be a reasonable option for women in unfavorable conditions where it is better to be the second or third wife of a well-off farmer than to starve with a poor husband of one's own. But the historical record and other evidence suggest that where circumstances become more favorable, we should welcome the disappearance of polygamy.[6]

Andrew March of Yale has jokingly likened this argument for limiting everyone to one spouse to the Lockean "proviso" that limited an individual's acquisition of property in the state of nature: we must leave "enough and as good in common" for others.[7] A very funny remark. But the evidence I have surveyed supports the general thought. Henrich concludes that "legalizing all forms of polygamy will principally result in an increase in polygynous marriages by wealthy, prestigious men. . . . *Nothing of what we know about our species' evolved psychology or from anthropological diversity indicates that either polyandry or forms of group marriage will spread beyond trivial frequencies.*"[8] Monogamy helps furnish the social basis for a fair distribution of the opportunities for family life.

I should hasten to add that monogamy is far from sufficient to secure a fair distribution of the benefits of social cooperation. In chapter 5 we encountered the astonishing class divide that has now opened with respect to marriage in America. This is one sign among many others of the profound destructiveness of the inequality that has grown so great in America since the 1970s.

Degrading Marital Assurance

An additional consideration suggests the value of regarding monogamous marital norms as locked in place. Look at it this way: it has been argued for decades that same-sex marriage would degrade marriage for heterosexuals, but, as we saw in part 1, it has never been explained how. It is not plausible that, once there is same-sex marriage, heterosexuals will turn gay, or that marriage will be made less desirable to straight people.

Marriage as it has come to exist seems generally well designed for same-sex couples. As we saw in part 2, however, including same-sex couples may work some subtle changes. Same-sex marriage seems to further entrench the norm of spousal equality in marriage. So we might say that same-sex marriage is a double improvement from the standpoint of justice: it extends the institution to a formerly excluded class of people long subject to discrimination, and it makes the character of the institution more just.

There is a much better case for the proposition that acceptance of plural marriage would change the character of marriage for all in a way that would degrade some of its core functions. I emphasized in part 2 that one of the prime virtues of institutionalized commitments such as marriage is that they allow us to join with another person, settle parts of our lives together, and build a joint future on that settled foundation. The building will involve children (typically), home, careers, family, and friends. All the good things in our lives, and all the bad, will now be undertaken jointly and shared in partnership with another. Marital commitment provides some considerable assurance of stability in these foundations. With marriage, we expect the "psychic repose" that comes with the "credible (even if not always reliable) promise of exclusivity in the relationship."[9] Chambers insightfully observes that this "sense of repose," built on trust, is deeply important to many people and worth preserving.

Notice how distant this is from the case of same-sex marriage. Under the old regime of stigma and persecution of homosexuals, many gay men and lesbians entered into heterosexual marriages. As the stigma and prejudice lifted, with great rapidity, in the 1970s, 1980s, and 1990s, some considerable number of mature adults found that a new world had opened before them, and many came out to their spouses and children, and many ended their marriages. In this respect, equal rights of gay and lesbian people did indeed disrupt those marriages, sometimes, no doubt, with real pain. But who would turn back the clock?[10]

Some Mormon fundamentalist and Muslim wives outside the United States enter their marriage knowing that a second and additional wives may be brought into the relationship. But this is not true of the marriages that have been entered into in the United States and other Western nations. Any general accommodation of plural civil marriage would undermine assurances that are central to marriage as we know it, assurances that the law of monogamous marriage has underwritten. It is not silly, indeed, to worry about the corrosive effects of general acceptance of plural *religious* marriages, that is, marriages entered into via a religious ceremony without purporting to be recognized in law. I explore this further in chapter 9.

THE BRITISH COLUMBIA REFERENCE CASE

The best summary of the evidence concerning polygamy was assembled by the Supreme Court of British Columbia, so let us turn to that. As criminal charges were being assembled against the heads of the two polygamous communities in the town of Bountiful in British Columbia, questions were raised concerning the constitutionality of the Canada's criminal ban on polygamy.[11] The provincial government referred the question to the BC Supreme Court, which handed down its ruling in December 2011. Chief Justice Robert J. Bauman wrote the court's decision upholding the province's criminal prohibition, arguing that "The prevention of [the] collective harms associated with polygamy"—to women, children, and society—"is clearly an objective that is pressing and substantial."[12]

The town of Bountiful has been home to several thousand members of FLDS communities closely associated with the communities in Colorado City, Hildale, and elsewhere. Winston Blackmore, formerly FLDS bishop of Bountiful, broke with Jeffs in the early 2000s and has since headed his own less authoritarian community. Blackmore has been at the center of legal conflict over polygamy in Canada for two decades. In public meetings and on various Canadian and American television programs, the garrulous Blackmore has defended the normality of his "lifestyle" and laughed off suggestions of child abuse. In contrast to the reclusive Warren Jeffs, he even welcomed a Canadian television documentary team onto his compound; the half-hour report is well worth watching.[13] He admitted to having 34 wives and 107 children. He had no good answer as to where most of his grown sons—who as children and adolescents worked in his lumber mill—went after reaching the age of maturity. Complaints filed with the BC Human Rights Tribunal included one by the sixth wife of Winston Blackmore's father, who married the elder Blackmore when she was 15 and he was 57. Winston has made several alarming admissions at different times, in public meetings with hundreds present and on CNN with Larry King, including that he has married "several under-aged girls," including one who was 15, under the legal age of consent, and that his son married a 14-year-old.[14]

Reporters like Daphne Bramham have long expressed outrage at the underenforcement of criminal prohibitions in the face of such evidence of child abuse. Blackmore defended himself most recently (as I write), testifying in Salt Lake City in 2014 that while he wed on different occasions three 15-year-old girls, "I never touched anyone before they were 16."[15]

THE EVIDENCE

Bauman drew on an impressive evidentiary record that included firsthand testimony by members of polygamous families and extensive affidavits prepared by leading scholars in a variety of disciplines. Walter Scheidel, chair of Stanford University's classics department, detailed the origins of monogamy and its links with the emergence of democracy and republican government in Greece and Rome. John Witte, Jr., professor of law at Emory University, provided an overview of the history of legal practice and ethical reflection on marriage and religious liberty. Rose McDermott, a distinguished professor of political science at Brown University, summarized existing evidence and her own research concerning the effects of polygamy on women's well-being. And finally, Joseph

Henrich, a leading scholar of evolutionary psychology and anthropology, presented an account of the comparative historical and anthropological records concerning the effects of polygamous as compared with monogamous marital regimes. His research appears to have made the biggest impact.

These materials—drawn from history, anthropology, empirical social science, ethical reflection, and evolutionary biology and psychology—furnish an impressive evidentiary basis for thinking about the characteristic shape of polygamy as a social system. Bauman rightly observed that this was "the most comprehensive judicial record on the subject ever produced." That record demonstrated, in his judgment, "a very strong basis for a reasoned apprehension of harm . . . inherent in the practice of polygamy,"[16] harm "to women, to children, to society and to the institution of monogamous marriage."[17] The record suggests that the harm to women and children would be most acute when polygamy exists in sectarian enclaves, but harm to society would come about wherever polygamy as polygyny became a significant presence, even if fully voluntary and nonoppressive. Bauman found sufficient evidence that significant social and personal harm would be generated *if* polygamy were to become a significant presence in society.

That last observation focuses on a key issue: does decriminalization pose a significant risk of a substantial increase in the incidence of polygamy? That requires some educated speculation, as we will see.

*****

Let's begin with the harm to women and children within the family, and the wider society, along with the general account of why these harms are inherent, though not inevitable, in the practice of polygamy.

Within families, polygyny creates the problem of how to manage cooperation and control *jealousy among plural wives and siblings*. As compared with the families of intact monogamous couples, polygamous households are characterized by greater complexity in the relations and genetic "relatedness" of adults and children. It hardly seems surprising that the opportunities for jealousy, rivalry, factionalism, and conflict would be greatly multiplied in households in which several wives and many half-brothers and sisters cohabit. Zeitzen observes that "studies of polygyny often focus on rivalry, antagonism, and jealousy between cowives."[18] Even accounts sympathetic to polygamy and polyamory argue that these arrangements create special problems of jealousy.[19] Evidence suggests that life in these communities is detrimental to the health and well-being of women and children in a wide variety of ways. McDermott, drawing on a wide range of social scientific evidence and her own comprehensive database of factors related to the health and welfare of women and children around the world, summarizes the evidence thus:

> Women in polygynous communities get married younger, have more children, have higher rates of HIV infection than men, sustain more domestic violence, succumb to more female genital mutilation and sex trafficking, and are more likely to die in childbirth. Their life expectancy is also shorter than that of their monogamous sisters. In addition, their children, both boys and girls, are less likely to receive both primary and secondary education.[20]

Other studies describe the "emotional devastation" caused by the experience, for many women, of sharing their husband with other women.[21]

Economist Gary Becker has speculated that by decreasing the "supply" of women relative to men, polygyny would increase women's "value" to men and their power in the marriage market, thus making the practice of plural marriage advantageous for women. He argues:

> Some oppose polygyny because they believe too many women would be "swept off their feet" by smooth-talking actual or potential polygamists. If that were a great concern, women could be required to be older before they could legally marry into polygamist households, or a "cooling off" period could be mandated before they could do that. Yet isn't it offensively patronizing to women to believe they cannot make their own decisions about whether to enter into marriages that contain other wives? We do not offer men any special protections against the "wiles" of women, so why do women need such protection? Indeed, I believe that in marital decisions women are more thoughtful and far-sighted than men, partly because marriage has meant much more to women than to men.

And he poses these questions: "Why the strong opposition to polygyny if it would be so rare? If modern women are at least as capable as men in deciding whom to marry, why does polygyny continue to be dubbed a 'barbarous' practice?"[22]

Becker is not alone in advancing these reasonable observations, and I take up some of them later. For now let us note that Becker imagines actors moved by rational calculations without accounting for culture, upbringing, and social norms. Most accounts of life in the fundamentalist enclaves suggest that they depend on a set of interlinked practices designed to encourage young women's availability to older, high-status males. Historical, anthropological, and social scientific evidence suggests that in practice, polygamy increases the competition among men for women, and that tends both to reduce the supply of unmarried women and to lower women's age at marriage. Marriages tend to be arranged, and family members pressure young girls into marrying older men.[23] Most of the women who enter plural marriages in FLDS sects appear to do so as teenage girls, and they do so "under considerable religious, familial and community pressure to consent to plural marriages." Young wives typically become pregnant soon after marrying and often begin a "cycle of childbearing" that can make it harder to leave the marriage.[24] Moreover, young women in these communities often receive a minimum of formal education, and they may know few if any people outside the community, so their exit options are highly constrained.

When young women of 17 or 18 who have been raised in polygamous enclaves agree to enter polygamous marriages with much older men, can we consider their consent freely given and autonomous? It is hard to say for sure, but Justice Bauman points to a number of grounds for concern.[25] Strassberg, following anthropological work by Janet Bennion, allows that the choice to enter a plural marriage tends to be free for those who take up the option in their mid-twenties, thirties, or forties; for them, plural marriage may be a reasonable alternative to an unhappy first marriage or being single. But these women constitute a minority of the women entering plural marriages. "Practically speaking," Strassberg argues, "Mormon fundamentalist polygyny is only made possible by the large numbers of community women raised in polygyny who are available as plural wives."[26] Rose McDermott, one of the expert intervenors in the BC Reference Case, summarizes the ample evidence that women, children, and lower-status males fare poorly under polygamy: "polygyny's negative effects are wide-ranging, statistically demonstrated, and independently verified" using a variety of analytic tools.[27]

As I mentioned earlier, even where the coercion and sexual violation of young women is not present, complex households of plural wives and half-brothers and sisters are prone to higher levels of jealousy and violence.[28] And then there is the obvious fact that in polygynous communities, men have the option or privilege of taking on additional spouses, but women are barred from doing the same. (If Becker were right about polygyny increasing women's value, one might expect to see societies dominated by men scheming to establish polyandry!)

It is worth remembering that traditional polygamy is not merely *contingently* but *inherently* unequal: inequality is "woven into the very fabric of the institution."[29] Traditional polygamy (as polygyny), with its "hub and spokes" structure, gains its stability from the unequal rights of the central spouse, as Gregg Strauss nicely puts it.[30] Rivalry, conflict, and jealousy are built into the structure of the relationships, and the historical and empirical record supports this. Vulnerabilities to jealousy are also distributed highly asymmetrically: the husband retains the right to marry additional wives, but not vice versa.[31]

This asymmetry in the relations of the central and peripheral spouses creates an additional and powerful inequality with respect to divorce, whose effects are likely to shape marital relations more broadly. As Thom Brooks points out, peripheral spouses can divorce only the central spouse, whereas the central spouse can divorce any peripheral spouse. Thus the central spouse can single out and remove one spouse while retaining the other spousal relations and an otherwise intact family, reducing the cost of the divorce threat vis-à-vis each wife. Wives, on the other hand, face a much higher cost in threatening divorce, as they thereby lose the only spouse they have, plus whatever familial relations they have formed with the other peripheral spouses.[32]

Indeed, the Quran warns, "You cannot be equitable in a polygamous relationship, no matter how hard you try."[33] While it is often pointed out that the Quran allows polygamy, many interpreters emphasize that what is most notable is the set of restrictions and conditions it imposes on a practice that was already widely practiced, and that was taken to be inevitable.

Inequality is thus inherent in polygyny in a way that distinguishes it from monogamy, which is why human rights conventions describe polygamy as a form of gender discrimination.[34] Inherent inequalities can, obviously, be overcome in particular polygamous families by practices of consultation and deliberative decision making, as portrayed in the polygamous Hendrickson family of *Big Love*. Nevertheless, the evidence surveyed above suggests that people's experiences within polygamous marriages do tend to reflect the inherent power asymmetries, resulting in increased inequality and conflict within families.

*****

Let us next consider children. I will be briefer, because many of the preceding observations about complex households of plural wives, half-brothers, and half-sisters apply here: children in such families are more likely to confront higher levels of jealousy and rivalry, emotional stress and tension, conflict and violence. "Polygamy is associated with poor emotional and educational outcomes for children, and children of different wives are often treated unequally."[35] As Bauman summarized, children "in polygamous families face higher infant mortality, even controlling for economic status and other relevant variables. They tend to suffer more emotional, behavioural and physical problems, as well as lower educational achievement than children in monogamous families.... Children are also at enhanced risk of psychological and physical abuse and neglect."[36]

In addition, polygamy tends to *reduce the average parental investment* per child in a variety of ways. Fathers may be unable to give sufficient affection and disciplinary attention to all their children, and other resources may also be lacking. As compared with monogamy, polygamy allows male heads of household to invest surplus resources in securing additional wives, leaving fewer resources for the education of rising generations. Indeed, studies of Mormon polygamy in the nineteenth century have found that the children of poorer Mormon men tended to enjoy greater health and longevity because their fathers couldn't afford to have multiple wives.[37]

*****

And what, finally, about society as a whole, including the many men who are bound to be excluded from marriage? Evidence suggests that when polygamy as polygyny is a significant presence, societies experience increased "*intrasexual competition*" among men. Even "a small increase in polygyny," argue Henrich, Boyd, and Richerson, "leads to a substantial increase in men without mates," and higher proportions of unmarried men are associated with higher rates of violence, drug and alcohol abuse, and crime.[38]

Robert Frank notes that even if only 10 percent of men in a given society have three wives, 20 percent of men will have no wives.[39] Unmarried "low-status men" are more likely to "discount the future and more readily engage in risky status-elevating and sex-seeking behaviours."[40] The competitive tendencies unleashed among men by plural marriage leads Frank to describe laws against plural marriage "as positional arms control agreements that make life less stressful for men."[41] That seems true enough as far as it goes, but the problems do not only affect men. Polygynous societies experience "higher rates of murder, theft, rape, social disruption, kidnapping (especially of females), sexual slavery and prostitution."[42] The "shortage" of women eligible for marriage in polygamous societies tends to lower the age of women's marriage and increase men's efforts to control women.

As mentioned above, the "cruel arithmetic" of polygamy, to borrow the title of Craig Jones's book, requires that many younger and lower-status males, who are competitors for younger wives, must be expelled from the community or marginalized by older, higher-status men, typically their fathers and uncles.[43] This traumatic experience is deeply psychologically damaging and destructive of the life chances of these boys or young men, who are often called the "lost boys."[44]

Because monogamy, in comparison, both increases the surplus resources available to be invested in children and reduces destructive conflict and competition among men, it appears to be productive of greater social progress. The origins of monogamy are unknown, but it appears that what Walter Scheidel calls "socially imposed universal monogamy" (applying even to the wealthiest and most powerful males) became the rule in ancient Greece and Rome and spread through Rome's influence. The transition to institutionalized monogamy appears to have contributed to more egalitarian social relations, greater social progress, and a fairer distribution of the opportunity to enter into family relations.

WHAT WOULD HAPPEN IF POLYGAMY WERE DECRIMINALIZED?

The inherently inegalitarian structure of polygyny and evidence concerning its practical consequences provide substantial grounds for associating polygamy in its traditional social form with a wide range of personal and social pathologies. But would decriminalization make polygamy significantly more widespread in modern and generally liberal democratic societies such as Canada or the United States? Or would plural marriage, even after decriminalization, remain very rare?

The practical question that the BC Supreme Court faced in the Reference Case was whether there was reasonable ground for retaining criminal prohibitions on polygamy. Decriminalization could affect not only the *incidence* of plural marriage but also its form or *character*. That is, by encouraging polygamists to emerge from the shadows, decriminalization could make it easier to monitor polygamous families and detect abuses. Drawing polygamists into the mainstream could help assimilate them to more conventional and egalitarian social norms, making plural marriages less harmful to participants. However, insofar as polygamy *tended to be polygyny*, plural marriage would contribute to the "cruel arithmetic" of imbalanced sex ratios: increasing the pool of unmarried males. The court focused on this effect because it would tend to be manifest even in those societies in which polygamy as polygyny took its most benign observable form: of the sort represented, as we will see, by the Kody Brown family.

Social scientists argue that fairly small changes in the sex ratios of those seeking marriage can have significant consequences. "In China," as Justice Bauman summarized the evidence, "sex ratios rose markedly between 1988 and 2004 as a consequence of the gradual implementation of China's one-child policy and paternal preference for male children. During the same period, crime rates doubled." Obviously, many things were going on during this period, but "this research showed, after controlling for certain demographic and economic variables, that a 0.01 increase in sex ratio was associated with a 3 percent increase in property and violent crimes." In addition, "Murder rates in India showed similar results. Districts with more males had much higher murder rates than could be predicted purely by an increase in the number of 'average males.' For example, the murder rate in a Uttar Pradesh, which has a male to female ratio of 0.97, was half that of Kerala, which has a male-to-female ratio of 1.12."[45]

The BC court decided that there is a reasonable apprehension of significant social harm resulting from the decriminalization of polygamy. A crucial premise is the prediction that polygamy would, in the future, tend to take the form of polygyny, even in societies in which gender equality is normatively well established. This would, in turn, give rise to the "cruel arithmetic" of some men with several wives, and a larger number of unmarried males.

But why should we anticipate this?

Two claims were particularly important to the BC court in establishing a reasonable apprehension of harm as a result of decriminalizing polygamy. First, Henrich, an eminent evolutionary scientist, defended the view that the *evolved nature* of human beings tugs us in the direction of polygyny. According to much evolutionary biology and psychology, the evolved physical differences among men and women shapes behavior. It appears to be universal that men (especially young men) have a greater tendency to violence and aggression, and this appears linked to higher levels of testosterone. Evolutionary scientists tend also to argue that evolved differences between men and women tend to manifest themselves in different sexual behaviors, or "mating strategies," that persist in some form across different social contexts.[46] Females are limited in the number offspring they can rear to maturity and are "necessarily committed to high levels of investment, at least in the form of providing the egg, gestation and lactation." Males, on the other hand, can with "little investment" "potentially have thousands of offspring that they can decide to invest in, or not," based on the other options that are available to them for obtaining sex and offspring.[47]

The upshot is that familiar gender stereotypes—the wandering promiscuous male and the coy/choosy female—have a basis in human nature, and this helps explain why polygyny is so common across human societies while polyandry is so rare. As Bauman summarized: "Through polygyny, both men and women can effectively follow their evolved mating strategies. Polygyny allows males to form multiple simultaneous pair-bonds, while it also allows more females access to high-status males, as they are not monopolized by a single female."[48]

If polygamy makes sense from the standpoint of powerful, selfish males (and their selfish genes), how, on an evolutionary account, did some human societies come to embrace monogamy? This leads to the second general idea that Henrich advanced concerning the importance of cultural systems and social norms in shaping behavior. Humans are inventive and, in different societies, devise and try out novel moral and cultural codes of conduct that motivate and regulate social relations in new ways. As Judge Bauman summarizes the argument,

> Marriage systems represent collections of these social norms, which include rules about the number and arrangement of partners. These marriage norms do not entirely replace or subvert mating psychology, but they can strongly influence behavioural patterns, both because compliance with these norms is intrinsically rewarding and because third parties are willing to punish norm violators.[49]

Societies compete with one another, in effect, on the basis of differing norms and patterns of behavior, and the more successful will tend to prevail over and be copied by others. Thus a process of "group selection," paralleling natural selection, can help favor more successful forms of social organization, and the values associated with them. Evolutionary theorists refer to "social or cultural evolution."[50] Monogamy reduces destructive conflict among men within a society and helps lay the groundwork for the more cooperative, inclusive, open, and egalitarian social relations that we associate with democracy. Social scientists, such as Josiah Ober, have emphasized that these sorts of societies have, like classical Athens, competitive advantages over their more authoritarian and hierarchical rivals.[51] From the point of view of justice, what is important is that these more egalitarian social relations are not only more productive of power and wealth but more consistent with the equal freedom for all that is at the heart of our understanding of liberal democratic justice.[52]

The upshot is that monogamy has been favored by group or social selection. We can, in addition, endorse this choice on the basis of greater justice: democratic equality is not only "good" for enhancing social cooperation and well-being but also a better approximation to justice.

These more cooperative social relations are rather recent, on an evolutionary time scale, and the *tug of polygyny* remains and could contribute to the spread of polygynous marriage if the social norms against it were relaxed by decriminalization.

*****

Henrich's testimony and supporting evidence, and the predictions they underwrote, were central to Bauman's decision upholding the criminal ban.[53] However, we must tread carefully. In claiming to trace differences among men and women in our society and other societies back to the inner core deposited by evolution, it is extremely difficult, and perhaps impossible, to fully control for the differential effects of culture and up-bringing, including the subtle rewards and signals that boys and girls receive from the moment they are born, and throughout their lives. There are many pitfalls here.

Lori D. Hager argues that those who study human origins tend to "cast females in gender stereotypes of the time and place out of which the researcher came. . . . [M]any models of early hominid life are replete with assumptions about males and females which are based on western views of modern men and women."[54] It has proven notoriously easy, in the past, to attribute to nature differences that we have subsequently learned to understand better as largely shaped by environment and upbringing.

Even if we were confident that we had isolated certain evolved sex differences inherent in human nature, these would only establish some deep tendencies or dispositions. How these manifest themselves in behavior is also dependent on cultural and social norms of all sorts, institutions, and individual choice. Evolved dispositions and differences are neither inevitable nor immutable and are compatible with a wide variety of reasoned and habitual patterns of behavior. Even if we grant Henrich's premises concerning the tendencies of our evolved natures, evolutionary insights do not inform us how powerful and resilient are the restraining and elevating effects of culture, social norms, moral judgments, and the institutions and policies that could be brought to bear to curb gendered polygyny. A pinch of culture may be worth a pound of biology, as Sperling and Beyene have suggested.[55]

So while the weight of professional evidence among evolutionary scientists and psychologists supports the general propositions that Henrich advances, it is hard to be confident that these evolved tendencies would be likely to override social norms, moral judgments, and the effects of consciously designed policies of discouragement. In particular, Henrich's account does not purport to tell us anything about ways in which polygamy might be reasonably and effectively discouraged without resorting to the criminal law.

*****

Here, reasoned judgment becomes a matter of educated guesswork. It strikes me as quite unlikely that many women would tolerate polygynous marriages, outside the cult-like confines of FLDS communities. It is not unreasonable to suppose both that polygamy in its traditional form will remain very rare and that integration into mainstream society will make polygamous communities less able to dominate their members. It is not inconceivable, however, that polygamy could become a more significant presence in some communities; I would worry about the possible behavior of some wealthy men, and their possible influence on others.

The litigation also highlighted worries about immigration: decriminalization could encourage polygamists to migrate to North America. And among the other things that are hard to predict are the reactions of religious and cultural groups. Were polygamy to be decriminalized, might the Mormon Church, or a portion of it, revisit and revise the manifestos renouncing the practice of plural marriage, which were promulgated under duress?[56]

CONCLUSION

The most controversial aspect of Justice Bauman's decision was his judgment that the Canadian Parliament had a reasoned and adequate basis for retaining the criminal sanction:

> Having found a reasoned apprehension that polygamy is associated with numerous harms, it follows that criminalizing the practice is one way of limiting those harms.... The government need only show that "it is reasonable to suppose that the limit [on the right] may further the goal, not that it will do so."... The evidence that the incidence of polygamy would plausibly increase in a non-trivial way if not criminalized certainly makes this point.[57]

A number of scholars joined in support of retaining the regime of "general criminalization" coupled with underenforcement and prosecutorial discretion: absent evidence of child abuse, or some additional problem, law enforcement officials tend to leave these communities alone.[58]

Courts in Canada are often more deferential to legislatures than in America, and more willing to allow rights to be balanced against public interests. To justify a criminal statute such as the one at issue here,

Canadian constitutional jurisprudence requires only a "rational connection" to a "pressing and substantial" purpose, and a choice of means that is "proportionate" given the effects. American constitutional law could, depending on whether a prima facie violation of constitutional rights were found, hold the law to a far more exacting standard.

The case for criminalization is strongest when confronting traditional polygamist patriarchs like Warren Jeffs, and also the sunnier and more open Winston Blackmore. Even there, however, it seems doubtful that general criminalization amounts to anything more than an expression of disapproval. Actual prosecutions require genuine crimes, such as having sexual relations with a minor.

The criminal sanction is much harder to defend, as we will now see, in the face of plural marriages among genuinely consenting and apparently autonomous adults. In these cases the social harm seems quite remote from the choices of individuals. A submission to the BC court put it well: under Canadian law, "everyone who enters into a conjugal union with more than one other person" will be "subject to penal sanction . . . because the gender arrangement of their intimate and personal conjugal union has to some degree skewed the gender ratio among unmarried persons in the rest of the population," making unmarried men "more prone to anti-social behaviour." This amicus brief continues, "The harms alleged are *impossibly remote* from the criminalized act, and the supposed moral gravamen [essence or core] of the crime is entirely indiscernible at the point of its commission."[59]

It is at least clear, at this point, that polygamy raises a host of serious questions that are not present in the context of same-sex marriage, making equal treatment of plural marriages seem like a poor idea. The British Columbia Supreme Court and Chief Justice Bauman deserve applause for providing a substantial scholarly and practical context within which to think about polygamy.

Let us next consider the Kody Brown family and their case. After that we will return to the question of how the law should respond.

CHAPTER 9

POLYGAMY UNBOUND?
THE KODY BROWN FAMILY
AND THE FUTURE OF
PLURAL MARRIAGE

The British Columbia Reference Case was an impressive effort on the part of well-funded and capable legal professionals to come to grips with the phenomenon of polygamy. The Kody Brown case was a rather different matter. In contrast to the voluminous evidence compiled in British Columbia, the county attorney charged with defending the Utah law in the federal district court filed a seven-page memorandum that Judge Waddoups characterizes as lacking in substance. Unlike the extensive expert academic testimony brought to bear in Canada, the Utah County Attorney's Office provided some "academic discussion about the 'social harms'" associated with polygamy in Utah, but this was presented, said Waddoups, outside of the court's briefing schedule, and "no admissible evidence" was submitted.[1]

Because the Brown family and the County Attorney's Office agreed on the basic facts, Judge Waddoups issued a "summary judgment" on the question of whether Utah can, consistent with the U.S. Constitution, criminalize the kind of polygamy practiced by the Browns.[2] Waddoups's opinion is scholarly and clear, but, perhaps because of the absence of an evidentiary record concerning polygamy, it lacks any sense of polygamy as a lived social form.

Most states criminalize only actual legal bigamy: seeking multiple marriage licenses. The Utah statute challenged by Kody Brown and his four wives swept more broadly and held that a "person is guilty of bigamy when, knowing he has a husband or wife or knowing the other person has a husband or wife, the person purports to marry another person or cohabits with another person."[3] The crucial issue is how to construe the phrases "*purports to marry . . . or cohabits*" in the law. Does it apply to polygamists, such as the Browns, who regard themselves as married spiritually and in the eyes of their religious community, but who never sought more than one marriage license?

The Browns are far more sympathetic practitioners of polygamy than the fundamentalist Mormons we encountered earlier. Their show, which airs on the TLC network, turns the premise of HBO's *Big Love* on its head. *Big Love* was all about efforts by the polygamous Hendricksons to hide their plural marriage from the outside world. The real life Kody Browns of *Sister Wives* are "unapologetically open."[4] As the show debuted in 2010, Kody and his first three wives had been married for twenty, seventeen, and sixteen years, respectively. Interestingly, all three marriages took place before any of their children were born, so the thirteen children born to these three wives were all raised with three mothers. As Kody explains, "I'm a polygamist, but we're not the polygamists you think you know. I have three awesome wives—Meri, Janelle, and Christine . . . I like marriage. And I'm a repeat offender. I have adopted a faith that embraces that lifestyle." Kody is a member of the Apostolic United Brethren, a sect that has broken away from Mormonism.[5]

By the end of the first episode, Kody is courting his fourth wife, Robyn, a divorced woman with three children. Christine admits that she "freaked" when she "learned that Kody and Robyn sealed their engagement with a kiss," but the three wives nevertheless express their cautious support, as do the children, "at least while being filmed." In the rest of the episode, the wives talk about the benefits of their division of labor: one can pursue a career, while another can pay more attention to cooking and cleaning, and there are more hands to help with children. The first show also addresses the issue of sex. Each wife and her children have their own "apartment" arrayed around a common area. "Kody is welcome in each of [the three] bedrooms. Alone. That's just how it is. We don't go weird."[6]

On most nights, "Kody picks one family to dine with and one wife to sleep with. At times, the wives admit to feeling jealous of each other." While major decisions involve what Joanna L. Grossman calls "some measure of advice and consent from the sister wives," there is sometimes "clear tension over Kody's role as ultimate decisionmaker."[7] The family, as is their aim, exudes normalcy, aside from the small matters of polygamy and illegality. The tensions that arise from polygamy itself seem, for them, within the bounds of what is typical in the families we are familiar with. None of the Browns has any record of arrests or other legal violations, and there are no allegations of child or sexual abuse.[8]

According to the Browns' complaint, Kody and his family were well known to local law enforcement officials, socially and professionally. The Browns sometimes appeared as spokespersons for plural marriage at public meetings and the occasional university seminar. Christine had participated with local, state, and federal officials, including the U.S. Census Department, on outreach to polygamous families who were less well integrated. State officials have sought, in recent decades, to go beyond merely tolerating polygamous communities but have also sought to break down their isolation and provide counseling and support of various kinds, through a program called Safety Net and others.[9] People are not prosecuted simply for being polygamists, as the Browns also point out in their complaint.[10]

But the first episode of *Sister Wives* was a step too far for law enforcement officials, who acknowledge that it "triggered" the public announcements of investigations; one prosecutor denounced the Browns for "committing crimes every night on television."[11] It appears that it was the Browns' flaunting of their "lifestyle" on national television that provoked law enforcement officials, in turn, to publicly announce investigations and threaten prosecution. Kody and all four of his wives could have faced substantial jail time if convicted—polygamy is a felony in Utah— along with separation from their children.[12] The family felt compelled to move to neighboring Nevada, which has a more narrowly drawn statute. The family's complaint says that wife Meri Brown was fired from her job on account of the adverse publicity.[13]

The county attorney subsequently decided that his office did not wish to prosecute, but the damage was done so far as the Browns and the court were concerned: there was "no guarantee that the Browns will not be prosecuted in the future for polygamy," so the threat of prosecution hung over their heads.[14] The decision struck down part of Utah's law as an unconstitutional violation of the U.S. Constitution's First Amendment protections for the "free exercise of religion." These details are important because the particular circumstances confronted by the Brown family helped justify the court's decision to strike down and narrow parts of Utah's law.

Recall that the Utah statute provided that a "person is guilty of bigamy when, knowing he has a husband or wife or knowing the other person has a husband or wife, the person purports to marry another person or cohabits with another person."[15] The federal district court hearing the

Brown case was bound by the Utah Supreme Court's earlier interpretation of state law, in the Holm case, according to which the law "criminalizes not only privately 'marrying' someone after having legally married, but also merely cohabiting with a second adult partner after having married a first partner."[16] Would it be consistent with the guarantees of the U.S. Constitution to prosecute the Browns under the "purports to marry" or cohabitation provision, so understood?

The prosecutors conceded that the law was not applied to "adultery or mere adulterous cohabitation."[17] The reason is that this sort of behavior is common in Utah, as elsewhere. A Utah prosecutor in the 1990s explained: "If we [were] going after illegal cohabitation we'd have to line them all up—the older people living together, young couples, even homosexual couples living together—all violate the bigamy/cohabitation law. People don't make complaints about polygamists or cohabitation, so we don't investigate, don't file charges."[18]

The prosecutors in the Brown case insisted, however, that in their view it is nevertheless "illegal under the statute to participate in a wedding ceremony between a legally married individual and a person with whom he or she is cohabiting and/or to call that person a wife." This means that the law as applied singles out what the court called "religious cohabitation": cohabitation would not be prosecuted absent the private religious ceremony, which the participants (but not the law) regard as a spiritual marriage.[19]

Both Tom Green and Rodney Hans Holm defended themselves against bigamy charges by insisting, like Kody Brown, that they never sought to engage in more than one legal marriage at a time. Green went so far as to marry each of his five wives in Utah, obtaining a legal divorce from each in Nevada before marrying the next one. He thus claimed, with perfect sincerity, that "in the eyes of the government, I consider myself single. . . . In the eyes of God, I consider myself married." He added: "Linda Green is my wife by my definition all the time, but by the government's definition I don't think she is my wife."[20] In both the Green case (2005) and *Utah v. Holm* (2006), the Utah Supreme Court interpreted "marry" to include "both legally recognized marriages and those that are not state-sanctioned."[21] But of course, both Green and Holm were convicted of having sex with a minor, so the more flexible and expansive interpretation of what it means to "purport to marry" was not needed to prosecute them.

For Judge Waddoups the fatal feature of the Utah law, as applied, was that the Browns could be subject to prosecution when they enacted, privately, "the trappings of a religious marriage ceremony" for which they sought no legal recognition.[22] If they simply cohabited, without the religious ceremony, they would be left in peace by the law.

Other aspects of state practice also suggest prosecutorial selectivity and arbitrariness. Religiously motivated polygamy is not generally prosecuted unless the union involves underage girls, but the state has argued that there are "rampant abuses" in polygamist communities. The state contends that the law's flexibility is needed to allow it to charge religious polygamists when it has "insufficient evidence of other crimes," but this is illogical in light of its general policy of nonprosecution. Here, moreover, prosecution was threatened merely because the Browns "openly discussed their religious cohabitation in the media." In short, the court was unwilling to "let stand a criminal law simply because it enables the state to conduct a fishing expedition for evidence of other crimes"; doing so would allow "apparently limitless prosecutorial discretion."[23] So the "cohabitation" provision of the Utah law was struck down altogether.

The prohibition on purporting to marry someone who is already married was interpreted narrowly to prohibit trying to obtain a second legal marriage license or to solemnize a second marriage in a way that would be *legally recognized*.[24] Kody Brown and his wives did not seek more than one marriage license, so they are not bigamists in the eyes of the law.

These are all powerful points.

The Browns, like Green and Holm, are "members of a religious group that believes polygamy is a core religious practice."[25] Their religious plural "marriage" has no legal effect, so there is no actual bigamy (or polygamy) in the eyes of the law.[26] The tendency of Utah's antibigamy statute to be used to single out religiously solemnized plural relationships and prosecute those as uniquely harmful had no justification, argued Waddoups. It suggests a special animus with regard to religiously sanctioned plural relationships and reflected the "orientalist" mindset of race and civilizational prejudice mentioned earlier.

ORIENTALIST PREJUDICE OR SOCIAL HARM?

Judge Waddoups is right to condemn the "morally repugnant reasoning" exhibited in *Reynolds* and other legal and political sources. But that should not be the end of the analysis. Waddoups insists that the perceived "social harm" of Mormon polygamy "was introducing a practice perceived to be characteristic of non-European people—or non-white races—into American society," a form of "Barbarism" that is "contrary to the spirit of Christianity." Thus he attributes concerns about polygamy to racial prejudice and religious and civilizational chauvinism, relegating to a footnote the acknowledgment of "individualized harm to women who were subjugated as wives."[27]

In *Reynolds* the Supreme Court also observed that "polygamy leads to the patriarchal principle," which, "when applied to large communities, fetters the people in stationary despotism." These remarks are admittedly cryptic and undeveloped, but they are not merely, as Waddoups asserts, just "another racist or orientalist observation about this Mormon practice based in the 'scientific' perspective of the day."[28] Discrimination on the basis of sex is inherent in polygyny, and patriarchy is also strongly associated with it in practice.

Neglecting the public interests that weigh against polygamy may also lead one to mistakenly conclude that support for monogamy is based on an unreasoned preference for the form of marriage favored by Christians and Europeans. The Brown family legal complaint claims that they are victims of "majoritarian Judeo-Christian beliefs." It also suggests that monogamy simply favors the majority's preferred "moral code" and is an "establishment of religion."[29]

This is incorrect: monogamy tends to promote the Constitution's core values of equal individual freedom, and the publicly justified interests of families and society. If the preference for monogamy were explained by Western chauvinism, it would be ironic indeed that large, proud, and independent Asian nations such as China, India, and Turkey embraced monogamy in the twentieth century as part of their efforts to modernize.

Entering this fraught terrain does indeed call for the sort of sympathetic openness to diversity that Judge Waddoups exhibits, but it also requires a searching inquiry into social consequences of the sort undertaken by the Supreme Court of British Columbia. Reasonable people will still come to different conclusions, but it should be on the basis of the full picture.

HOW SHOULD THE LAW TREAT POLYGAMY?

But should polygamy continue to be branded in law as a criminal offense? Do justice and due regard for individual rights and autonomy permit this?

Several important considerations argue for decriminalization. First, giving local prosecutors discretion to charge people with criminal offenses creates opportunities for arbitrariness of the sort on display in Utah. Second, it seems doubtful that, outside certain religious enclaves, large numbers of people would enter into polygamous relationships.

Third, it would likely be easier to regulate abusive practices were polygamy brought "above ground," and criminalization may have the effect of driving polygamy underground. On the other hand, prosecutions for polygamy alone have been so rare that one might question its effect. Polygamists like the Brown family have not had much of a reason to hide, and they have not; those who really separate themselves, like the Jeffs and their ilk, may continue to do so.

Patriarchal FLDS enclaves do raise grave concerns.[30] But if polygamy is to be prosecuted only when there is child abuse or fraud, why not simply enforce those criminal laws?[31] Detection and prevention of genuine abuses would be easier if polygamous communities were drawn out of their insularity. And of course, there may be better ways to discourage polygamy.[32]

Prosecution of polygamy has been abandoned by law enforcement officials, apparently for good reason. It is too draconian to disrupt families and inflict the trauma of removing children from their parents in the absence of evidence of a serious crime, such as child abuse (as was the case with *Green* and *Holm*). Maintaining a general *unenforced* criminal prohibition on polygamy could be of value expressively: as a way of signaling that polygamy is socially undesirable. But we then provide prosecutors and police with a license for arbitrariness, while counting on their wisdom and good judgment, and this would appear to presume too much.

The state of Utah in effect renounced the general criminalization of polygamy as such, by its well-known record of nonenforcement and its sensible efforts to engage polygamists and draw them out of their insular enclaves, so it might as well admit as much. It seems intolerable as well as irrational for the state to seek to draw polygamists out of their isolation while also hanging over their heads the threat of arbitrary criminal prosecution for being polygamists.

As the Browns' complaint also argues, it cannot possibly be appropriate for police and prosecutors to undertake highly public investigations and threaten prosecutions simply because people are going on television to talk about or argue in favor of what they are otherwise free to do. I might prefer that polygamists keep quiet about their way of life, but I cannot think it reasonable to threaten criminal prosecution if they exercise their rights to free speech.[33]

*****

On the other hand, the evidence assembled by the Supreme Court of British Columbia furnishes ample grounds, it seems to me, for denying equal recognition and the status of "marriage" to polygamous unions. The experience of polygamy and monogamy both vary. But where polygamy as polygyny exists as a social and *normative system*, rather than as a scattered collection of unusual instances, it seems, as compared with monogamy, inherently *unequal* for the women involved and for men generally; prone to *conflict*, on account of family complexity; and inclined to *domination*, on account of the structurally central role of the husband.

It is admirable that patriarchs like Kody Brown and Bill Hendrickson in the fictional *Big Love* make considerable efforts to consult and be reasonable. Nevertheless, these sympathetic TV polygamous marriages—one fictional, one real—are of the traditional "hub and spoke" form. The "real-life" Kody Browns seem fairly normal: that of course is part of the appeal of the television show. His successive marriages are not characterized by wide disparities in age.[34] But Kody is the center of authority, the head of household, and the ultimate decider. Only he has the right to marry additional spouses, and he, apparently, feels entitled to arrive at what was, in the case of his fourth wife, at least a provisional engagement before consulting his other wives and children. The show might have been called *Father Knows Best*. The Brown household "believes in patriarchy," as Grossman and Friedman put it, "and practices it as part of its faith."[35] Theirs is a mild form of patriarchy, and the intense publicity surrounding their family provides assurance against gross abuses of power. But the glare of television lights is not generally present in polygamous homes. The Browns appear to present a best-case scenario for plural marriage, and in that respect they may be very unrepresentative of the typical polygamists in the United States.

Obviously, in spite of its greater inherent proneness to inequality, many polygamous families fashion reasonably healthy family lives. It was not uncommon in Mormon polygamous households for first wives to have a great deal of say in the choice of the second wife, and in most polygamous families there were only two wives. Many or most Mormon men's treatment of their wives was shaped by religious strictures that made it incumbent on them to treat all their wives and children equally.[36]

Chambers observes that non-Mormon women in plural marriages might be "worse off if non-Mormon men who married second and third wives failed to accept the obligation, apparently instilled" by Mormon communities, to "treat their wives equally." For precisely this reason, a polygamous Mormon man in Canada, when interviewed in 1992, doubted the wisdom of legalizing polygamy as a general matter: "If plural marriage is legal, the nonrighteous could take numerous wives without heeding God's laws."[37] That seems, after all, to concede the point—also evident in the Quranic verse quoted above—that plural marriages create special stresses that make them prone to domination in the absence of special virtue.

While polygamy does not necessarily involve direct harm to particular others, such as the coercion or domination of women or the abuse of children, and criminal prosecution of nonabusive polygamists seems wrong, as most people have concluded, the discussion above suggests that we have good grounds for regarding polygamy as a social form inherently prone to a variety of abuses, and tending to produce general social harms, as compared with monogamy. In the contemporary world, monogamy is at least *structurally egalitarian*: the spousal roles are no longer defined and differentiated on the basis of gender, at least formally, though practice too frequently lags. Gender roles are not defined in law, and only the act of procreation—the old-fashioned way—necessarily requires distinctive contributions of man and woman. Husbands and wives have equal rights over common property, equal obligations to the other party, equal rights to sue for divorce. In principle, if frequently not in practice, monogamy today is equal for the spouses and the norms that surround it are increasingly egalitarian.

Monogamy helps secure everyone's fair opportunity to pursue the great good of family life and thereby bolsters our basic constitutional commitments to securing the freedom and equality of all. Everything we know about human history suggests that plural marriage is strongly and inherently associated with a host of pathologies within the family and in the larger society. The actual practice of plural marriage in our own society, where it exists, reflects these very same pathologies. The law of monogamy, including the criminal prohibition on plural marriage, would seem to play an important educative and formative role in our society: buttressing important social norms that encourage people to form marital commitments that are at least formally reciprocal, equal, and available to all.

The evidence produced in British Columbia furnishes a reasoned basis for concern about the spread of polygamous families. The political community should refuse to extend the right to marry beyond the "rule of two." Those who engage in plural marriages are fringe characters, and we have reason to hope they remain such.

*****

The courts should tread carefully and resist the impulse, evident in the Kody Brown case, to engage in sweeping pronouncements in the absence of thorough investigation. But, a critic might reply, is not the same true of same-sex marriage? Opponents say that it is also an untested social experiment about which we have little reliable information.

The difference is that in 2015 we have decades of information about gay and lesbian Americans and their relationships. Judges across the country have, for decades, placed children for adoption in the homes of lesbian and gay couples based on their judgments about the best interests of the child. Those placements were banned by the legislatures of many states in the 1990s and 2000s as part of the more general mobilization against gay rights; the bans were not supported by social scientific studies challenging the quality of parenting in those households.[38] I argue for caution and incremental change, not for the kind of feverish reaction against polygamy that many on the right mounted against same-sex rights from the 1970s through 2008. I have no doubt that we should and will learn more about marital forms in the decades ahead.

PLURAL MARRIAGE, SINGLE MOTHERS, AND "LESSER EVILS"

Defenders of decriminalization and greater acceptance of polygamy, especially in the case of a man like Kody Brown, draw a pertinent comparison. Consider the man who sleeps with various women, fathers children with them, and fails to help support them. The law will come after such a man for child support, but he will not be prosecuted for the underlying behavior. In contrast, the polygamist who solemnizes his various relationships in a religious ceremony that involves *pledges of support and commitment* could be criminally prosecuted under the old Utah law. The crime that led to Kody Brown's prosecution (and Tom Green's before him) was, as columnist Steve Chapman observed, going on television and proclaiming, "These are my five wives," rather than "These are my five girlfriends."[39]

Are we to criminalize, in this way, the use of words "wife," "husband," and "marriage" in order to protect the civil institution of marriage and to deter the various social harms that the British Columbia court identified? I am all for protecting and enhancing the civil institution, but I must allow that the term and concept "marriage" is shared by the civil law and religious communities (along with other private parties who wish to appropriate the concept). I argued in chapter 5 that we have good reason not to cede the language of marriage to religious communities, but I doubt that we have the authority to deny them the right to use these terms in their own ways.

The comparison above is important. Whereas polygamy is a fringe phenomenon in our society, out-of-wedlock births are not. And, as we saw in chapter 5, a large percentage of these births are unplanned or not fully planned. Moreover, many of the women giving birth believe that their relationship with the father will last, and probably in many instances the father has made some assurances along those lines. Certainly, many men fail to act responsibly toward the women they sleep with and the children conceived as a result, doing great and long-lasting harm. Kody Brown is innocent of that kind of irresponsibility.

Some go further and advance a "modest proposal" for responding to the shortage of responsible fathers. In a pair of provocative essays, Adrien K. Wing has suggested that "African Americans today face conditions in which de facto polygamy can flourish." The reason, says Wing, herself an African American professor of law, is that a "disproportionate number of our men are unavailable for marriage—due to early death, imprisonment, high unemployment, and [racial] intermarriage."[40] Black women, she observes, surpass black men in higher education and employment, and so a large number "of well employed and educated Black women seek a small pool of 'suitable' men." In 2010 less than 30 percent of African American women over 15 were married compared with 51 percent of white women.[41] And in 2012 among non-Hispanic blacks, 72 percent of births were to single mothers as compared with less than 30 percent to non-Hispanic whites.[42]

"In the U.S. Constitution," Wing pointedly concludes, "Blacks were counted as three-fifths of a person for representation purposes. Today, some lonely women remain ready to have a much smaller piece than three-fifths of a man."[43] She further notes the examples of prominent and successful African American men—including Johnny Cochran and Jesse Jackson—who have been revealed to have secret families.[44] Wing's aim is only to "initiate a discussion within the American legal academy on polygamy."[45]

Some defenses of polygamy begin with the premise that men will stray. We should be "realistic" and take men as they are and make the best (or the least worst) of it. Polygamy's great advantage, in this view, is that it provides for the women and children in the man's secondary and tertiary relationships, who are apt to be the "losers" under monogamy. We saw such an argument advanced above in defense of older Mormon marital practices, and it is also advanced in defense of polygamy in Islam. Dr. Bilal Philips declares, "Males in general continue to be protected by monogamy, while prostitutes, call girls, mistresses, secretaries, models, actresses, store clerks, waitresses and girl friends remain their playground." Polygamy, asserts Philips, would "force" men "to fidelity."[46] He argues that polygamy would strengthen the family structure, presumably by increasing the attractiveness of marriage for some men.[47]

Philips is right to draw attention to the plight of single women and their children, whose interests are sadly neglected by irresponsible men and our wider society.

It seems to me fantastic to suppose that we could introduce plural marriage into the United States in the way that is imagined in order to address the real problems associated with out-of-wedlock births. As we saw in chapter 5, part of the problem is that many Americans living in challenging economic circumstances are reluctant to marry. Telling them they can have multiple spouses would not solve the problem! Nor are wealthier men lining up to marry poorer single mothers. Justice requires that we do far more than at present to help create the conditions within which more Americans are enabled to support a family and commit to *one* marriage.

*****

Even if we have good reasons for discouraging polygamy, we owe certain protections to those who live within such relationships. We already recognize polygamy in law for some purposes. Janelle Brown applied for emergency Medicaid when she was out of work and a child became sick. State officials inquired and ascertained from the Browns that they were in a "polygamous relationship," and on that basis "all of Kody's income was applied against Janelle and her children," to deny her coverage.[48] So the state is already, in this and other ways, giving legal effect to Kody's polygamous relationship, without regarding it as a marriage.

Suppose that, after decades of marriage to all his first three wives, Kody should die without a will. Were there a dispute within the family, it would seem unfair and unacceptable for a court not to acknowledge some claims to inheritance on the part of all the wives and their children.

In immigration and asylum proceedings as well, limited forms of recognition of plural relationships may be necessary. Under current U.S. immigration law, it appears that a husband in a polygamous marriage can immigrate to the United States with one of his wives and all the children—from all his wives—if he so chooses, leaving the less favored wives deprived of their children and fending for themselves. Sarah Eichenberger argues persuasively that the United States can learn from Canadian and British reforms that facilitate entry of immigrant women in polygamous unions, on humanitarian grounds, without endorsing plural marriage.[49] In these and other ways, the law needs to recognize polygamous family relations as having legal effects, even if they are not recognized as marriages and even if they are discouraged.

If we ought to tolerate plural relationships, such as that of the Browns, we ought also to seek to educate the public about the dangers of plural unions and to protect members of polygamous households against abuse. In 1999 the Utah legislature raised the minimum age for marriage from 14 to 16: that certainly seems long overdue.[50] Utah also criminalizes sexual relations with 16- or 17-year-olds when the partner is more than 10 years older. Holm violated this criminal prohibition when he "married" his wife's younger sister. More such protections could and should be written into the law to recognize the vulnerabilities and protect the autonomy of young adults.

The law may need to take account of polygamous religious "marriages" in other ways as well. Recall Winston Blackmore's chilling assertion that, while he wed on different occasions three 15-year-old girls, "I never touched anyone before they were 16."[51] Separation of church and state notwithstanding, the law should prohibit efforts by older men to bind underage women in this way.

BUT IS MONOGAMY JUST AS BAD?

It could be argued that much of the foregoing has focused on the problems generated by polygamous relations, without acknowledging many problems that also plague monogamous marriage today.

High rates of divorce and remarriage have been called "serial polygamy," and there are many famous examples: Zsa Zsa Gabor married nine times; Elizabeth Taylor and Mickey Rooney eight times each; Larry King, Jerry Lee Lewis, and others more than six times. (Rooney famously advised, "Always get married early in the morning. That way, if it doesn't work out, you haven't wasted a whole day."[52]) Rich and powerful men and women frequently marry much younger people after divorce: Newt Gingrich has married a series of younger women, as did Johnny Carson and many others.[53] So is the "serial polygamy" currently on offer just as bad as, or worse than, polygamy?

The "one spouse at a time" rule is a serious and reasonable constraint, given the justifiability of divorce and remarriage, and it also addresses worries about imbalanced sex ratios of the sort emphasized by Judge Bauman. In addition, as mentioned earlier, only 3 percent of Americans over the age of 15 have been married more than twice, so the issue of "serial polygamy" is easy to exaggerate.

Finally, as we saw in chapter 5, marriages that are nowadays entered into under favorable circumstances are actually quite stable.

THE IMPORTANCE OF THE
INTERNATIONAL CONTEXT

We ought to consider the possible impact of our decisions on evolving global human rights norms including, in the present context, history's great unfinished sweep in the direction of gender equality, which has both contributed to and benefited from the decline of polygamy. Nowhere in the developed world where women are equal is there any widespread social movement in favor of plural marriage. And where plural marriage exists but women are becoming empowered, polygamy is typically viewed as an obstacle to greater equality.

As I mentioned above, polygamy was outlawed in the twentieth century in Asian countries such as China and India, as well as Turkey. While Western missionaries may have played a role in suggesting the superiority of monogamy, it was Communist leader Mao Zedong who imposed monogamy in China in 1950 as part of the official commitment to gender equality, under the rubric of "state feminism." Kemal Ataturk, the "Father of Modern Turkey," outlawed polygamy as part of his modernizing efforts in 1926. In postindependence India, polygamy was banned for Hindus, though the practice was accommodated among the Muslim minority.[54]

In many of the countries where polygamy is currently permitted, it is surrounded by increasing embarrassment and disapproval. In Africa, for example, twenty-eight nations have ratified the African Union's protocol on women's rights, which calls for an end to all forms of discrimination against women, insists that "women and men enjoy equal rights and are regarded as equal partners in marriage," and holds that "monogamy is encouraged as the preferred form of marriage."[55]

The post-Apartheid South African Constitution of 1996 bans unfair discrimination on a wide variety of grounds that include not only race, ethnicity, and religion but also, "gender, sex, pregnancy, marital status," and "sexual orientation." It also seeks to protect traditional African culture, within the bounds of these and other guarantees, creating some uneasy tensions. The Recognition of Customary Marriages Act, passed by parliament in 1998, recognizes polygamy for black South Africans only as a form of "customary marriage" but subjects the practice to the nondiscrimination clauses of the constitution. This was a compromise between feminists in the African National Congress and traditional tribal leaders, who sought to immunize customary marriage from the reach of gender equality.[56]

Judith Stacey, a progressive feminist who is also sympathetic to cultural and marital pluralism, draws attention to the oddness, in South Africa, of a racially and culturally exclusive accommodation for polygamy. There is, moreover, no provision for polyandry, which would outrage the patriarchal champions of tradition. Stacey underlines the widespread belief that polygamy "will continue to erode as society modernizes."[57] Public opinion polls suggest that a large majority of South Africans disapprove of polygamy, though a significant minority of black men favor it (with black women overwhelmingly opposed).[58] And this notwithstanding the fact that current president Jacob Zuma is father of at least twenty-one children by ten different women.[59]

Negotiating the deep tensions between egalitarian constitutional principles and persisting traditional attitudes and expectations is an ongoing challenge. Sarah Song has noted that, in South Africa, before taking a second wife a husband must enter into a written contract with his existing wife that fairly divides marital property accrued to that point, and he must persuade a family court judge that the contract is fair to all involved.[60] The requirement of a written contract and division of property at the time of a second marriage amounts to a partial divorce and property settlement: it permits the husband to enter a new marriage without completely terminating the old one, if that is what he and his first wife wish. This would seem a sensible way of protecting the interests of first wives. However, many of the customary marriages never get registered, so the protections are not operative.[61] Countries like South Africa have to negotiate their own way forward in light of their constitution's democratic aspirations and the need to sometimes accommodate traditional ways of life.

The practice of concubinage has apparently resurfaced in China, as some few amass great wealth while others remain poor. Some estimate that several hundred thousand men have "second wives," or *ernai*. The arrangement, which is illegal and generally secret, is typically long-term and allows a poor women to secure an apartment (usually in her own name) and support from a wealthy older married man, which can be a boon to her and her family. Growing inequality along with persistent poverty may play a role in encouraging a resurgence of polygamy elsewhere in Asia as well.[62] We live in an interconnected world in which, happily, human rights and norms of democratic legitimacy continue to spread, if haltingly and unevenly. Courts and other public institutions learn from one another. We have reason to worry that any recognition amounting to endorsement of polygamy in the United States, Canada, and other Western countries could be detrimental to human rights norms, and especially to gender equality.

When it comes to polygamy, our public interests can be stated in the language of justice itself. As an experienced rather than imagined form of life, plural marriage is inconsistent with securing equal liberty and fair opportunity for all. John Rawls speaks not of a *general right to liberty* but rather of the centrality to justice of a "fully adequate scheme of equal basic liberties," whose enjoyment by some is fully compatible with the equal enjoyment by others.[63] That sort of locution seems to me on the mark. We need to define a system of basic rights and liberties as fundamental parts of a wider scheme of institutions that help secure everyone's equal standing and fair opportunity to pursue a good and successful life. Libertarian impulses to the contrary should be resisted. The case of incest shows clearly that certain claims of individual autonomy can be overridden by our need to protect an important social institution.

INCEST AND TABOO, MORALISM AND EQUAL LIBERTY

So what of incest, one of the greatest and most universal of taboos, but not one to which much serious thought has been given. Sonu Bedi argues that just as state nonrecognition of same-sex marriage "rests on the intrinsic moral superiority of one set of couplings," so, "in a similar fashion, limitations on adult incestuous or plural marriage privilege one conception of the good—a two, non-blood related union—over another—a three person or a blood-related union." He argues that the state should avoid taking "sides in a very personal decision about what constitutes the good life."[64] And of course, as the reader well knows, all such arguments echo back, mockingly, from the right; so, Maggie Gallagher, "If not sex for babies, why not sisters? . . . Why just two?"[65]

So what about incest? If adult incestuous couples have no plans—or, let us say, lack the capacity—to conceive children prone to genetic defects, why not permit them to marry?[66] To sharpen the issue and test our intuition, Bedi suggests we imagine adult incestuous *same-sex* couples. Or indeed we could imagine sexual relations involving stepparent and adult stepchild, whether opposite-sex or same-sex (stepparent and stepchild have, in legal parlance, relations of family "affinity," not of "consanguinity," nor of blood or genetic relatedness). Why not allow them to conceive children? Why, when there is not the clear and present danger of genetic deformity, should the law interfere with the free choices of consenting adults concerning the most intimate aspects of our lives?

Luckily, we have more available to us here than taboo or sheer moralism. An obvious harm of incest is that the distinctive goods of family life depend on strong norms against sexual relations among immediate family members.[67] The distinctive forms of love and trust that characterize healthy family relations, and the commitment of family members to care for one another and support one another physically and emotionally, depend on the exclusion of sexual relations. For siblings or parents and children to consider each other as eligible sexual partners *prospectively* is inherently corrupting of norms that sustain healthy and valuable family relations, and these are vital to human well-being. Relaxing the incest taboo would give rise to far too many possibilities for abuse, manipulation, and exploitation.

And so far as the wider family is concerned, how could sexual relations possibly take place among particular immediate family members without giving rise to feelings of betrayal and jealousy, leading to possible violence and other forms of conflict?

I suppose the intuition that supports the more libertarian conclusion is the idea that, once people are grown and mature adults, and assuming they rule out conceiving children, what is the great harm if a mature brother and a sister, or two brothers or two sisters, wish to live together romantically? Their free choice of these two people to become romantically involved, considered in isolation, might seem in itself innocent.

The problem with the libertarian suggestion is that we could not accept the propriety of brother-sister or child-parent sexual relations among particular people at any stage of life without revising and relaxing the very strong general prohibition on sexual relations among immediate family members. If we were to announce permission for adult siblings, or parents and their adult children, past a certain age to have sexual relations, this would reshape the way that siblings and parents and children regard one another generally, including from the time children are very young. I see no way for the consequences to be limited to those truly voluntarily agreeing in the later stages of life. Adult relationships provide models for children and young adults, imagining their future.

Once the idea becomes socially acceptable, it becomes a prospective possibility available to all, shaping (or eligible to shape) the imaginations of the young and older family members. It becomes thinkable for parents to consider raising their children to be prospective sexual partners, but of course, only at the proper age. How could we trust, if ever this happened, that the parent had not manipulated and subverted the education for independence and equal freedom that every child is owed (like Humbert Humbert's rearing of Lolita)? The central parental responsibility is to bring their necessarily needy and vulnerable children to healthy maturity and prepare them to lead their own independent lives, and that responsibility is breached radically by incest. Our collective moral culture and particular social institutions are shaped by constitutive social norms, and in this case it would seem right to say that we all have a moral duty to uphold them.

And it bears repeating that evidence supports the widespread conviction that sexual abuse of children, especially by an immediate family member, tends to produce deep and lasting psychological scars. First-cousin marriage is a more complicated question, and it is permitted in many U.S. states. In some societies, worries about the political power and social consequences of large, clannish families may, when first-cousin marriage is frequent, provide good grounds for deterring it.[68]

There can, of course, be highly unusual circumstances—perhaps involving siblings separated early in life who meet later, fall in love, and only subsequently realize that they are blood siblings. That sort of bizarre scenario seems ripe for an episode of *Law and Order* but too strange to worry much about. There are, however, repeat sperm and egg donors who may contribute to the genetic makeup of many members of the community; disclosure laws might then be necessary to avoid unintended genetic problems.[69]

There is good reason to think that the distinctive goods of family life depend on certain constitutive prohibitions on sexual activity within the immediate family. We should not focus on the individual point of view to the exclusion of a reasonable concern with the norms that underlie the important social institutions on which we all depend. We all benefit from reasonable constraints that enable the good of family life and other social goods. Prohibitions on incest leave everyone with an ample range of alternative sexual partners. Happily, there is no actual public controversy here. But this does tell us something important about the moral resources needed to sustain a healthy liberal and democratic society. Here as elsewhere, fundamental principles of liberal democratic political morality reach into the most private aspects of our lives, ruling out some conceptions of the good life and imparting a distinctive shape to those that remain.[70]

Those conservatives who argue that gay marriage changes marriage for everyone are right. Gay marriage further entrenches gender equality; in that respect and others, it changes the public meaning of marriage for everyone for the better. Extending privacy and marriage rights to gay and lesbian Americans in no way undermines the moral norms against sexual activity among close family members. Incest is obviously not in the realm of our equal basic liberties: a right to incest is not required to accord any class of people a fully adequate scheme of equal basic liberties. The categorical prohibitions on sexual relations among immediate (nonspouse) family members, for the sake of preserving trusting and loving family relationships, apply not only to heterosexual parents and their biological children but also to family members by adoption, and to same-sex parents and their children and siblings.[71] Society's legitimate concerns here are by no means limited to the birth of children with genetic defects.

Does this mean that liberal democratic states, justifying disfavored treatment for polygamy or incest, must sometimes invoke, as Bedi suggests, the "intrinsic moral superiority" of particular relationships or ways of life? No. In the first instance, as I have said, the claim is that certain institutional forms help us realize and sustain a regime of equal liberty and fair opportunity for all.

WHAT OF POLYAMORY AND EGALITARIAN GROUP MARRIAGES?

The foregoing discussion refers mainly to the past and to poor traditional societies that face pressures that more developed modern societies have largely left behind. Our values, norms, and religious convictions have changed. The power of male dominance and tradition has waned.

Under these more egalitarian conditions, plural marriage in the future could take on new forms, such as the more complex and egalitarian arrangements known as polyamory or polyfidelity: horizontal, nondominating network relations involving multiple partners of various genders, in which all the participating spouses have equal and reciprocal rights.[72] Bringing in an additional spouse would require the agreement of all. Columbia University law professor Elizabeth F. Emens describes this new form of plural marriage as "ethical nonmonogamy" and insists that it "bears serious consideration."[73]

Here again, the historical record is useful, and it suggests that there are more problems here than meet the eye. Polyamory can claim various historical antecedents, including the utopian Oneida Community of upstate New York, founded in 1848 by Yale theologian John Humphrey Noyes, who advocated what he called "complex marriage": a highly regulated version of "free love," according to which all the men were married to all the women of the community. It is reported that after the first generation of founding members, "many of the younger communitarians desired to enter into exclusive, traditional marriages." The community dissolved in 1881, leaving, as a legacy to mankind, a company that makes excellent silverware.[74]

It is certainly true that polyamory and polyfidelity, as described, are radically different from traditional polygamy. First there is the formal equality of rights, and the more general egalitarian ethos. In addition, polyamory is not closely associated with any particular religious community, and polyamorists nowadays have no tendency to break off from mainstream society and live in isolated enclaves according to their own laws. They do not depend on pressuring teenagers into marriage and have no orientation toward having large numbers of children; they focus on the happiness of adults. So it seems right to say that the moral pathologies inherent to polygamy are not inherent in polyamory and polyfidelity.[75]

However, an additional important fact about polyamory and polyfidelity is that they seem to mark a set of unstable social arrangements that have proven too fleeting to yield any reliable account. We know very little about polyamory as a stable social form. Polyamorous households appear now to exist as a scattering of fringe and fleeting "experiments in living." The British Columbia court said it had scant information about polyamorous households: as best it could tell, there may be 120 such households in Canada.[76]

How many polyamorists are there in the United States? Conservatives, such as Girgis, Anderson, and George, and some progressives cite claims that there are 500,000 polyamorous households in the United States.[77] The source for that large number appears to be a *Time* magazine article that cites as its source Deborah Taj Anapol, author of *Polyamory in the 21st Century*. Anapol "guesses," according to *Time*, that the percentage of polyamorists in the United States is 0.5 percent to 3.5 percent of the population.[78] *Newsweek*, without supplying any evidence, has described polyamory as experiencing "growing pains."[79]

Anapol's website is called "Love without Limits." Her online biography at International School of Temple Arts describes her as "an explorer of the spaces where sex, spirit, sustainability, love and ecology meet. Her Tantric journey through inner and outer space is an ongoing process of discovery." She is a kind of spiritual sex therapist, operating out of California (naturally). She advocates "pelvic heart integration."[80] I wish her the best of luck with that. But she provides no scientific evidence in support of her claims.

If polyamory is so rare, why does it register so prominently in these debates? There several possible reasons. Stories about the supposed dawning of the age of polyamory may sell magazines. Conservatives have an obvious reason for crediting the spread of polyamory: it plays into their narrative of sexual chaos following same-sex marriage. "This group is really rising up from the underground, emboldened by the success of the gay-marriage movement," opines Glenn Stanton, the director of family studies for Focus on the Family, a conservative and evangelical Christian group. "And while there's part of me that says, 'Oh, my goodness, I don't think I could see them make grounds,' there's another part of me that says, 'Well, just watch them.'"[81] Girgis, Anderson, and George point to polyamory as a possible consequence of same-sex marriage.

One of the best-known pieces of scholarship defending greater legal recognition of polyamory is "Monogamy's Law," by Elizabeth F. Emens. This is an interesting and provocative exploratory piece, but its basis in evidence consists mainly of four vignettes about people involved in complicated relationships that wound up in court or in portrayals in the popular media, such as in the magazine *Redbook*, or in *Loving More*, a polyamorist publication. One of her examples involved a polyandrous threesome and a disapproving grandmother who found out about the trio after they appeared in a documentary on polyamory that aired on MTV. The grandmother filed for removal of the child and custody in a Tennessee juvenile court in 1999. Court-appointed experts testified that the three-year-old child was not harmed by the relationship, but the judge rejected their findings and removed the child from her mother's home, citing his responsibility for the "moral upbringing of the child" and the mother's attitude that "I can have my cake and eat it too."[82]

Another of Emens's examples is a foursome that includes a heterosexual woman (monogamously inclined, but very open minded), her legal husband who announced after their marriage that he is bisexual and wanted to have relationships with men, and two other men, one of whom is also bisexual, and the other of whom is either bisexual or gay (it isn't clear from the description). The men sleep with one another in various combinations, and also with outsiders. They report that their main problem is coordinating their schedules.[83]

Third is a fundamentalist Mormon husband in Utah with nine wives, who founded his own church. The twist on the usual story is that eight of the wives have careers, and they describe the marriage as highly functional for the modern career women. Plus, they report some "group sex" in which various combinations of women have participated; that's spicier than the Mormon fundamentalist norm. More in line with tradition, the wives regard their husband as "a god."[84]

The fourth example is a profile of people who have conflicting and unsettled views about the virtues of monogamy; the two central figures wrote a book together called *The Ethical Slut: A Guide to Infinite Sexual Possibilities* (1997).

To her credit, Emens allows that agreements to have open sexual relations beyond the bounds of monogamy have a strong tendency to be undone by jealousy.[85] The article leaves one with the same impression one gets from surfing "reality" television programs: it's a big world and there are a lot of unusual people out there. And as I said, stories about complicated romantic relationships sell magazines and draw viewers to television shows. None of this furnishes sound reasons to suppose that a new form of family life is in the offing!

Elizabeth Brake, whose work on "minimal marriage" provides a variation on marriage privatization and pluralization, also argues for recognizing polyamorous marriages. To muster some evidence about polyamory, Brake cites Emens frequently, and Sasha Cagen, a writer and entrepreneur (a "life coach for quirky types. Wondering how I can help? Set up a time for an introductory chat") and founder of the "quirkyalone movement" (the quirkyalone Facebook page has more than thirteen hundred "likes").[86]

Brake also draws on Ethan Watters's thoughtful, nonacademic book, *Urban Tribes,* and she adapts the term "urban tribalists" to denote what she supposes is an emerging form of egalitarian polyamory.[87] But Watters's book does not support Brake. *Urban Tribes* is an account of the household Watters shared in San Francisco for several years after college with a shifting group of 20- and 30-somethings. His current web biography describes the book as "an examination of the mores of affluent 'never marrieds.'"[88] They lived in a communal setting and hung out. They became "like family" in important respects, as friends are liable to do. Brake takes all this as a harbinger of a new form of family life, and a possible model for a new form of egalitarian and fluid poly-union not (necessarily) involving sexual intimacy among participants. The fly in the ointment is that Watters eventually settled down and got married. He looks back on his experience as a stage of life: a sort of extended young adulthood. His website reports that nowadays, "He lives in San Francisco with his wife and children."

So what should we make of polyamory? Conservatives urge us to see it as a stage on the slippery slope from same-sex marriage to sexual anarchy. For progressives, polyamory heralds a new egalitarian vision of nonmonogamous households and loving adult networks. It seems to me, however, that we have no basis for concluding anything. There are zero scientific studies of polyamorous households. Experts on polyamory include people with names like "Pepper Mint" and "Cunning Minx."[89]

What we know is largely a miscellany of anecdote, speculation, free-love advocacy, and fantasy.

Some progressives suggest that legal recognition is called for: Brake would open her reformed "minimal marriage" to people of any number and gender combination, whether or not they are romantically involved.[90] I would agree that the law should support some familiar nonmarital caring relationships, and certainly, when polyamorous relations wind up in court, judges need sympathy and creativity. But there is nothing stable or definite here that bears any resemblance to the decades-old struggle for the recognition of same-sex marriage. When it comes to polyamory, it appears that there may be more people writing about it than doing it.

CONCLUSION: RESPECT FOR DEMOCRACY AND SOCIAL LEARNING

Older criticisms of polygamy in our public records and case law are marked by a decided moralism and superficiality: vehement rejection without much clarity concerning the nature of the public interest. Nevertheless, nineteenth-century discussions of polygamy in cases such as *Reynolds* also associate the practice with patriarchy, status hierarchies, and comparative social stagnation, while observing that monogamy is more conducive to democracy. Those observations still seem correct.[91] Normative monogamy best secures citizens' equal basic liberties, equal status and standing, and fair opportunities to pursue the good of family life. When it comes to polygamy, we need not rely on sheer moralism. Liberal and democratic justice supports efforts to discourage polygamy.

To summarize: preferences for polygamy are not equivalent to same-sex orientations; there is no class of people who, by nature or deep-seated nurture, are "oriented" toward only loving multiple persons (no one has the "orientation" of only falling in love with two or more people at a time). Normative polygamy as a social system is strongly associated in the historical record with women's inequality and subordination, higher crime rates and rates of violence in the home, and less investment in the education and human capital of children. For reasons I explain, these do not appear to be simply matters of historical and cultural contingency. An additional set of considerations in favor of the twoness of marriage has to do with practical aspects of stability and flourishing in the type of relation that marriage is. An important fact about oft-mentioned non-traditional "polyamorous" relationships is that we know virtually nothing about them as a social form. And finally, it is worth remembering that vast numbers of people in our society have invested in and built their lives around monogamous marriages; the option of legally recognized plural unions cannot simply be layered on top of those commitments. Legitimizing the "poly" option within marriage undermines the good of marital commitment as currently understood because so many married persons would find this a deeply unwelcome option.

But *how should we justly discourage polygamy?* How can we do that without engaging in gratuitous persecution of consenting adults who do not directly harm others? These are important questions that I cannot claim to have adequately answered. The arbitrary exercise of prosecutorial discretion, as in Utah, is deeply troubling. I also sympathize with the sober assessment of the harms described by experts and the court in British Columbia.

This is not an area ripe for sweeping judicial pronouncements, at least not ones that would enact radical changes to the status quo. We need to learn more, as a society, about the various existing forms of plural relationships before we revise the legal frameworks within which people shape and structure their lives.

In this respect it is striking that, as I observed above, there are no broad social movements for polygamy or polyamory in advanced Western societies. The situation is in sharp contrast with gay, lesbian, and even transgender rights, where broad social movements have now existed for decades, drawing in people from all walks of life and segments of society. Through a complex set of political campaigns and court cases, and innumerable conversations in the media, at work, at the dinner table, and elsewhere, LGBT rights have made astonishing progress in the scant twenty-eight years since *Bowers v. Hardwick*.[92] Advocates of LGBT rights have advanced impressive bodies of scholarly and empirical work, contested by their opponents at every step of the way. Through political advances and reversals, there has been a halting but steady winning over of the public mind. Progress has been made in virtually every forum and department of American life, beginning with the arts and culture and the academy and spreading finally to military service and marriage.

There is simply no equivalent with respect to polyamory. My guess is that our evolved human nature means that twoness makes sense for marital and marriage-like commitments. Jealousy is an extremely powerful human passion and one that, I reckon, makes polyamory a nonstarter for loving relations that are committed and reciprocal, at least for the vast majority. But in any event, polyamory registers as a kind of hypothetical of interest in academic debates but not possessing the weight of popular support that would make it of consequence in democratic lawmaking.

When I speak to students about this, they express dissatisfaction. The conversation always begins with their saying, "I know someone who...." It never begins, "There's a new study on polyamory out of the University of Michigan." We have little reliable social knowledge here: little by way of a basis for collective judgment about a social form or forms with a settled or definable shape. If lawmaking on polyamory would be premature, consenting adults are of course free to engage in "experiments in living." Sexually open egalitarian communities have been tried before, and no doubt they will be tried again. My skepticism may turn out to be misplaced.[93]

From a global perspective, same-sex marriage and polygamy are on entirely different historical trajectories. Indeed, same-sex marriage is closely associated—historically, sociologically, and ethically—with norms of gender equality that preclude institutionalized polygamy in its common forms. Charles Krauthammer has observed that, "as gay marriage is gaining acceptance, the resistance to polygamy is much more powerful."[94] Polygamy as widely practiced is a form of *hypertraditional marriage*: gendered and patriarchal.

Democracy matters: as people fashion lives in conditions of freedom over time, we should learn more about what are the reasonable, stable, and healthy forms of human relationship. Decisions about complex matters of law and public policy around which millions of individuals construct their lives ought to be based on socially reliable knowledge: reasons and evidence that are widely accessible and that form an appropriate basis for lawmaking. As citizens acting on behalf of our common interests in a large and complex political community, we are entitled to judge the likely consequences of extending marriage beyond monogamy on the basis of the best evidence we have. What we know about polygamy as a stable social form suggests we are well-off to have left it behind. We should respect the ongoing progress of democratic deliberation and social learning.

CONCLUSION

HAPPILY EVER AFTER

Same-sex marriage, marriage, and monogamy: all three make sense here and now, given what we know about the stable and successful forms of life to which the vast majority of Americans aspire. There is, if I am right, no slippery slope from same-sex wedlock to marriage abolition, polygamy, or certain other radical reforms. The case for marriage preservation remains strong, though justice also requires that we attend more effectively to the needs of those outside of marriage and also put in place policies that allow more people to fulfill their aspirations to marry.

In this conclusion I recap and develop some of the main points of the argument. I begin with same-sex marriage and monogamy, briefly reconsidering how same-sex marriage might change marriage for all. I then say a bit more about what marriage tells us about the ideal of an ethically neutral state and liberalism as a public philosophy.

SAME-SEX MARRIAGE AND MONOGAMY

What is most astonishing about same-sex marriage is how much ground it has gained and how quickly. The Supreme Court took its first short step in this direction in *Romer v. Evans* (1996), and now, less than twenty years on, we have arrived. Support for legalizing same-sex sexual relations actually declined during most of the 1980s. Support for gay marriage was roughly constant from the 1980s to the early 2000s, but since then it has increased rapidly. Young people are more tolerant, but people of all ages have also changed their minds.[1] Why? No doubt the driving force has been the sudden revelation, or slowly dawning realization, that Aunt Marge, Jimmy from church, my niece Suzie, and that nice weatherman on TV are all gay.

We should also give due credit to our collective quest for justifying reasons and evidence. The courts have played a lead role, but so have legislators, journalists, activists, academics, members of the clergy, and ordinary citizens on both sides of the political spectrum.

Exclusion of gay and lesbian Americans from marriage is, like their exclusion from the military, invidious: a badge of inferiority and second-class status that perpetuates harmful stereotypes and stigma that are bound to be especially damaging to children and young adults. And like the exclusion from military service, keeping gays from marrying accomplishes nothing for the greater good. To the contrary, I agree with those who have long argued that marriage equality holds out to gay and lesbian couples the opportunity to solemnize and stabilize their commitments, and this should be especially appealing to conservatives.

The question of how same-sex marriage changes marriage is an interesting one, and I sought to draw a contrast in this regard (in chapter 8) with polygamy. Same-sex marriage entrenches a norm of marital equality and seems likely to encourage other changes occurring in heterosexual marriage including more equal parenting.

We considered the possibility, in chapter 3, that the somewhat more open attitudes of some same-sex couples to outside sexual involvements, in the form of "consensual nonmonogamy," could weaken norms of marital fidelity. However, the form of infidelity that is most clearly morally troubling involves faithlessness in the form of betrayal and deception of one's spouse or partner. The accounts of greater sexual openness in same-sex relationships also suggest that there is greater frankness, honesty, and agreement.

I am skeptical that "open" relationships are consistent with stable commitment. However, couples' private, consensual sexual lives are generally their own business. Edward Stein has recently pointed out that consensual nonmonogamy seems to be associated with safer sex practices and reduced jealousy along with greater honesty.[2] Consensual nonmonogamy seems far less objectionable than the covert and deceptive kind. If both partners are really fine with it, they practice safe sex, and it does not hurt and maybe helps their relationship, is there a ground for public concern about discreet swinging?

Consensual nonmonogamy raises policy questions that need more attention. As Stein points out, in those states that consider adultery a factor in divorce settlements (in the decision whether to award alimony for example), courts do not generally give effect to spouses' nonmonogamy agreements because they regard such agreements as contrary to public policy. That seems anomalous.

The obvious ethical concern is that honesty and consent are not suffi-cient. Sexual virtue, self-control, and the stable integration of sexual activ-ity into loving and committed relationships all require, or at least benefit greatly from, social norms that frown on and discourage nonmonogamy in general. On this view, we might say that the wedding vows pronounced in public involve not only the spouses but the larger community: nonmonog-amy breaks faith with one's fellow citizens and weakens the social norms on which we all depend.

It seems true that a norm of sexual exclusivity is part of the consti-tutive meaning and good of marriage for most Americans. They have reason to be concerned about how the sexual adventures of nonmonog-amous married couples could undermine expectations and norms at the heart of marital commitment as generally understood. Nevertheless, con-cerns about consensual nonmonogamy, whether same-sex or opposite-sex, seem to me largely matters of personal-ethical and social-moral judgment, rather than of public policy and law. The behavior in question is, like premarital sex and cohabitation, within the realm of protected liberty. Absent as well is good evidence of the sort of serious harms we saw with polygamy.

Here we confront the old question of the boundary between what John Stuart Mill termed the "self-regarding" conduct that affects others only indirectly or because of their own free choices, which ought to be governed by the principle of individual liberty, and the "other-regarding" conduct that affects our "distinct and assignable" obligations to others, or that otherwise fall within the sphere of social regulation.[3] The boundary, in practice, is not quite as sharp as Mill's theory suggests.

With respect to the matters at hand, I have suggested that polygamy falls within the realm of public concern, even if not the criminal law. No doubt the social harms associated with polygamy in its best forms—consensual and apparently nondominating forms of polygyny, such as is practiced by the Kody Browns—are "downstream" of the conduct itself. Nevertheless, it seems to me that the arguments for recognizing same-sex marriage and not recognizing plural marriage in civil law are clear and substantial. Monogamy secures a variety of important public values and goods, partly because the alternative, polygamy as polygyny, is asso-ciated with so many pathologies including greater conflict in family and society, lower investment in rising generations, and the domination by higher-status males of women and lower-status males.

The most basic principles of our constitutional order—liberty, equality, and fair opportunity for all—make the extension of marriage to same-sex couples a requirement of justice. Those principles also argue in favor of monogamy, and for the continued discouragement of polygamy while leaving open the question of "how."

The negative judgment concerning polygamy is distinguished from conservative opposition to gay marriage by being, to use a distinction suggested by Ronald Dworkin, "impersonally" rather than "personally" judgmental.[4] My claim was not that the polygamous marriages are inherently perverted or morally abhorrent, but rather that the state of affairs to which they tend to give rise is fraught with problems: greater conflict and violence; poorer health among women, children, and lower-status males; and greater inequality with regard to the opportunity to achieve some of life's most highly valued and valuable relationships.

I have no doubt that we will learn more about all of these matters, and I am confident that nothing written here is the "last word" on anything. My main complaint, which applies to those I have criticized on the left as much as on the right, is the hastiness of suggesting that gay rights or same-sex marriage leads inexorably or automatically to this or that. Polygamy is quite distinct from same-sex marriage and worthy of scrutiny on its own. The same is true of consensual nonmonogamy.

MARRIAGE AND THE ETHICALLY NEUTRAL STATE

Progressive critics of civil marriage allow that, so long as it exists, same-sex couples should have equal access. But should it continue to exist as a status relationship in law? Can the special place of marriage and monogamy in our law and our lives be sustained in the face of America's growing diversity, the declining interest in marriage among some, and the fact that many disadvantaged Americans regard the dream of married life as beyond their reach?

Marriage, as we saw in part 2, can be defended without reference to special philosophical principles or ethical ideals. Marriage makes available to couples a wide range of highly valued benefits and opportunities. The "goods" invoked in defense of marriage are standard components of public policy. Marriage seems to promote better health for spouses and longer, happier lives. Children do better in stable, reasonably low-conflict marriages: they have fewer psychological problems, do better in school, and generally tend to be more successful. On average of course! Most children of single mothers do fine, and many of those children excel and do extraordinary things, like becoming president.

Same-sex marriage leaves unaddressed the massive and widening class divide over marriage that policy analysts have been warning about for over a decade. People's economic prospects and security are nowadays highly correlated with their relative level of education, and these have also become highly predictive of women's likelihood of marrying before having children. Overall marriage rates have declined, and the rate of out-of-wedlock births has increased, but those general trends mask huge differences associated with class, race, and ethnicity.

Radical critics of marriage, including some feminists, queer theorists, and others, are liable to pounce and reiterate their oft-stated point that marriage equality has always had greater appeal to the relatively privileged and successful. I have argued, however, that we should do more to address the difficult circumstances of poorer and less economically secure Americans. Support for marriage should not be a substitute for just forms of social provision, and, indeed, greater economic security for working Americans could help assure many that they are ready for marriage. Greater support should be provided for singles and for those engaged in the important work of caring for others.

All this may be important, but none of it gets at the specific complaint that proceeds from the idea of an ethically neutral state.

The "liberal state should get out of the 'marriage business,'" says Andrew March, "by leveling down to a universal status of 'civil union' neutral as to the gender and affective purpose of domestic partnerships."[5] Sonu Bedi, Elizabeth Brake, Clare Chambers, Tamara Metz, and many others agree that monogamous marriage is unfairly biased.[6] They urge that government should support a wide variety of caring and caregiving relationships under the aegis of a new law of marriage, or under an altogether new designation—such as Metz's Intimate Caregiving Unions—which will take the place of marriage in our law.

The key theme of this neutralist chorus is that monogamous civil marriage unfairly favors some conceptions of the good life over others. Lack of ethical neutrality, in this context, signals bias or unfair favoritism on the part of the state and our law in favor of some conceptions of the good life and against others.

The charge of unfairness as favoritism is partly addressed by what I have said about providing appropriate recognition and assistance to those in caring and caregiving relationships that are not marital. Furthermore, if there are serious proposals for addressing the unmet needs of singles, and doing so would also promote greater fairness, then we should do that as well. I think we do better to proceed by addition rather than subtraction, building on and around marriage and not trying to create a catch-all substitute for it.

We might further respond by pointing out that, in actual practice, democratic publics do not narrowly limit their governments to providing public goods strictly defined. Public (and quasi-public) agencies routinely promote appreciation for and access to natural beauty of many different kinds via the national park system, local parks, and public gardens and arboretums. We preserve against commercial development unspoiled areas of natural beauty, buildings, places, and neighborhoods that are aesthetically and historically significant. We promote excellence in and access to the fine arts, broadly conceived, via the National Endowment for the Arts (an independent agency of the federal government), and state and local arts organizations and museums that are partially publicly funded and often publicly encouraged. The National Medal of Arts is awarded by the president of the United States to individuals or groups who "are deserving of special recognition by reason of their outstanding contributions to the excellence, growth, support and availability of the arts in the United States."[7] Our governments have long supported intellectual endeavor and inquiry in a wide variety of fields, artistic endeavor in a profuse array of art forms, athletic achievement in sporting activities of every description, and recreation in a dizzying variety of forms.

In each case controversial judgments must be made about which works of art are most worth purchasing, which places of great natural beauty are worth preserving. The relevant judgments in each case cannot be said to be "neutral" among conceptions of the good life: there will always be some taxpayers who simply do not care about this or that agency or institution, let alone the particular exhibitions or programs they sponsor. Nevertheless, the overall systems of modest subsidy and encouragement are made fully legitimate by several considerations.

First, we acknowledge and respect pluralism with regard to the human good: the great variety of human types and the many forms of excellence that free people pursue.[8] We seek not to favor some people's preferred activities and endeavors over those of others but rather to ensure that a deep and significant array of valuable alternatives remains available, and that the opportunities for human flourishing are not narrowed and degraded by brute social forces such as those generated by economic markets, whose aggregate consequences we may reject for good reason. Deliberative democratic political institutions may be better at expressing certain kinds of valuations than market institutions, as many others have observed.[9] As citizens we may be readier and better able to act as custodians of natural and cultural treasures than we would be as consumers.

In addition, we take seriously subjective valuing as well as objective value. The aim is to enrich the experience of freedom by preserving and enhancing the array of significant options and experiences available to people, especially those options that humans have found and continue to find deeply satisfying, for good reason.

A rich, deep, and complex cultural landscape enhances the value of personal autonomy, since it keeps alive the rich and complex traditions that stimulate and exercise our critical and creative intellectual and aesthetic powers, and not only economic and technical innovation. And importantly, it enhances the value of everyone's autonomy by ensuring they do have options available, even if they decide not to pursue them. By acting as custodians of the wide repertoire of human achievement, we also enhance the opportunities and options available to our children and future generations.

A similar argument applies to marriage: if it were not generally available to people, the richness of the options available to us would be diminished. Indeed, Ronald Dworkin, whose work is often relied on by proponents of the ethically neutral state, described marriage as utterly "unique" and a "distinct mode of association and commitment that carries centuries and volumes of social and personal meaning." He continued:

> We can no more create an alternative mode of commitment carrying a parallel intensity of meaning than we can create a substitute for poetry or love. The status of marriage is therefore a social resource of irreplaceable value to those to whom it is offered; it enables to people together to create value in their lives that they could not create if that institution had never existed.[10]

Critics may here point out that there is a big difference between the institution of marriage and those various cultural and natural resources, such as art museums and national parks, discussed above. Public goods of the latter sort preserve valued resources and enrich our options but do not, in any direct way, imprint a distinctive pattern on the most personal aspects of our lives, our aspirations, and society as a whole. Marriage goes much deeper, and it extends its influence over every aspect of our lives. It is architectonic, giving a distinct structure to our life plans.

James Fleming and Linda McClain argue that marriage offers to many "the most productive and individually fulfilling relationship that one can enjoy in the course of a lifetime"; it is central to the happiness of a great many.[11] The law of marriage recognizes marriage's special place, facilitates it, and even in some ways rewards it. It does so by furnishing an elaborate system of law that facilitates couples' entry into a widely understood status, furnished with safeguards in the forms of rights and responsibilities that others have found useful and that have been worked out over centuries.

But not everyone values the institution of marriage, and defenses of it are controversial on ethical grounds. Critics advance the plausible charge that marriage favors particular patterns of life over others. Monogamous marriage is so fabled in our culture and so important in many people's lives that it is bound to shape our plans and aspirations from an early age, making it harder to imagine and undertake alternative forms of relations, such as the networks of care imagined by Metz, Brake, and many others.

I have argued that, from the standpoint of justice, monogamous marriage helps imprint the DNA of equal liberty onto the very fiber of family and sexual intimacy. From the standpoint of goodness, however, critics might argue that there are other ways of securing equal liberty that do not privilege lifelong commitment. The distinctiveness of marriage as a plan of life goes beyond its role in securing justice. One can certainly imagine alternative ways of life that are consistent with liberal democratic values but that are less dependent on monogamous commitment, including the nonoppressive networks of caring imagined by Brake. Lifelong monogamous marital commitment is a distinctive plan of life. As I asked in the introduction: what business has the state in encouraging, or facilitating, this form of coupling?

Society is a going concern, and many generations have built their lives around this particular institution. No doubt its widespread success partly feeds its success: through the law of monogamous marriage, vast numbers of people spread across diverse regions are able to coordinate their expectations and mesh their plans. Two people can meet and fall in love and have available a flexible template that nevertheless sets out some of the main contours of a joint plan of life.

The particular way of life involving monogamous marriage is one that large numbers of people have converged on over the course of generations. Alternatives are now readily available, but many people continue to aspire to marriage, and people have not coalesced around alternative arrangements that have a definite shape. The costs of transitioning to a new model for committed relationships (of the sort proposed by Brake or Metz) could be enormous, and the payoffs are speculative. Theorists and social critics play a salutary role in proposing alternatives, but radical reform should not be imposed in a top-down manner in the absence of clear injustices. It is relatively easy to fashion a personal philosophy of life, but it is not at all easy to bring about a new social philosophy that others will readily embrace.[12]

NOTES

INTRODUCTION

1. The 95 percent figure is from Frank Newport and Joy Wilke, "Most in U.S. Want Marriage, but Its Importance Has Dropped: Young Adults More Likely Not to Want to Get Married," Gallup online, http://www.gallup.com/poll/163802/marriage-importance-dropped.aspx. See also Mark Mather and Diana Lavery, "In U.S., Proportion Married at Lowest Recorded Levels," Population Reference Bureau, http://www.prb.org/Publications/Articles/2010/usmarriagedecline.aspx; Joanna L. Grossman and Lawrence M. Friedman, *Inside the Castle: Law and the Family in 20th Century America* (Princeton: Princeton University Press, 2011), 53; and Andrew J. Cherlin, *The Marriage-Go-Round: The State of Marriage and the Family in America Today* (New York: Vintage, 2010), 7. Stephanie Coontz points out that the "percentage married" considers all Americans over the age of 15 as eligible, so as people wait longer to marry, that percentage automatically drops. See "The Disestablishment of Marriage," *New York Times*, June 22, 2013.

2. Newport and Wilke, "Most in U.S. Want Marriage."

3. Anemona Hartocollis, "Jacques Beaumont and Richard Townsend," *New York Times*, August 14, 2011, 13.

4. By adding to the California Constitution the words "only marriage between a man and a woman is valid or recognized in California."

5. David Boies and Theodore B. Olson, *Redeeming the Dream: The Case for Marriage Equality* (New York: Penguin, 2014), 199.

6. Perry v. Schwarzenegger, 704 F. Supp. 2d 921-Dist. Court, ND California 2010, J. Walker quoting transcript, 154:20–23, 172:8–12.

7. U.S. Supreme Court, United States v. Windsor, 133 S. Ct. 2675 (2013), 2693. The Court here invokes oft-quoted language from

a previous case, USDA v. Moreno, 413 US 528 (1973), in which the unpopular group was hippies.

8.   United States v. Windsor, 2695.

9.   Ibid., 2696–97.

10.   U.S. Supreme Court, Hollingsworth v. Perry, 133 S. Ct. 2652 (2013).

11.   Opinion of Judge Jeffrey Sutton, DeBoer v. Snyder 14–1341, 6th Circuit Court of Appeals of the United States, November 6, 2014.

12.   Defense of Marriage Act: Hearing on H.R. 3396 before the Subcommittee on the Constitution of the House Committee on the Judiciary, 104th Cong. 88 (1996). See also Hadley Arkes, "The Closet Straight," *National Review*, July 5, 1993, reprinted in part in *Same-Sex Marriage: Pro and Con*, ed. Andrew Sullivan (New York: Vintage, 2004), 158: "once the arrangement is opened simply to 'consenting adults,' on what ground would we object to the mature couplings of aunts and nephews, or even fathers and daughters—couplings that show a remarkable persistence in our own age, even against the barriers of law and sentiment that have been cast up over centuries?"

13.   I owe these and the preceding quotations to David L. Chambers, "Polygamy and Same-Sex Marriage," *Hofstra Law Review* 26 (1997): 57–58n20, 58nn21, 25. The sources are William Bennett, "Leave Marriage Alone," *Newsweek*, June 3, 1996, 27; Jennifer Harper, "Bork Envisions Gay 'Marriages' Winning in Courts," *Washington Times*, September 21, 1996, A5; Gary Bauer, president of Family Research Council, testimony on Defense of Marriage Act: Hearing on S. 1740 before the Senate Committee on the Judiciary, 104th Cong. 22 (1996), 142 Cong. Rec. H7443 (daily ed., July 11, 1996).

14.   Sean Loughlin, "Santorum under Fire for Comments on Homosexuality," April 22, 2003, http://www.cnn.com/2003/ALL POLITICS/04/22/santorum.gays/index.html.

15.   U.S. Supreme Court, Lawrence v. Texas, 123 S. Ct. 2472 (2003), 2490 (J. Scalia dissenting).

16.   See Boies and Olson, *Redeeming the Dream*, 89, 139, 146–47.

17.   Ryan T. Anderson, "The Roe of Marriage: Traditionalists Should Defend Their Conception of the Truth," *National Review*, August 2014, https://www.nationalreview.com/nrd/articles/383581/roe-marriage.

18.   Mark Joseph Stern, "Judge Upholds Puerto Rico's Gay Marriage Ban in a Comically Inane Opinion," *Slate*, http://www.slate.com /blogs/outward/2014/10/22/puerto_rico_gay_marriage_ban_upheld _by_federal_judge_in_inane_opinion.html.

19. Judge Martin C. Feldman, Robicheaux v. Caldwell (2:13-cv-05090-MLCF-ALC (E.D. La.)), September 3, 2014, 28.

20. John Finnis, "The Profound Injustice of Judge Posner on Marriage," *Public Discourse*, October 9, 2014, http://www.thepublicdiscourse.com/2014/10/13896/.

21. Chambers, "Polygamy," 59.

22. U.S. Supreme Court, Planned Parenthood v. Casey, 505 US 833 (1992).

23. See the discussion in chapter 4.

24. Shannon Gilreath, "Rebuttal: Arguing Against Arguing for Marriage," in Nelson Tebbe, Deborah Widiss, and Shannon Gilreath, "Debate, The Argument for Same-Sex Marriage," *University of Pennsylvania Law Review* 159, PENNumbra (2010): 30, 34, http://www.pennlawreview.com/online/159-U-Pa-L-Rev-PENNumbra-21.pdf.

25. Gillian Calder, "Penguins and Polyamory: Using Law and Film to Explore the Essence of Marriage in Canadian Family Law," *Canadian Journal of Women and the Law* 21, 1 (2009): 83.

26. See the discussion in chapter 6.

27. Elizabeth Brake, *Minimizing Marriage: Marriage, Morality, and the Law* (Oxford: Oxford University Press, 2012), 144.

28. Ibid., 160–66.

29. Sonu Bedi, *Beyond Race, Sex, and Sexual Orientation: Legal Equality without Identity* (Cambridge: Cambridge University Press, 2013), 221.

30. See, for example, the remarks of former British Columbia Attorney General Wally Oppal, quoted in Rebecca Johnson, "Reflecting on Polygamy: What's the Harm," *Polygamy's Rights and Wrongs: Perspectives on Harm, Family, and Law*, ed. Gillian Calder and Lori G. Beaman (Vancouver: University of British Columbia Press, 2014), 112.

31. Edward Collins Vacek, "Acting More Humanely: Accepting Gays into the Priesthood," *America: the National Catholic Review*, December 16, 2002, http://americamagazine.org/issue/416/article/acting-more-humanelyaccepting-gays-priesthood.

32. See chapter 5.

33. Bedi, *Beyond Race*, 240.

34. For an excellent account, see James E. Fleming and Linda C. McClain, *Ordered Liberty: Rights, Responsibilities, and Virtues* (Cambridge, MA: Harvard University Press, 2013). See also Stephen Macedo, *Liberal Virtues: Citizenship, Virtue, and Community in Liberal Constitutionalism* (Oxford: Clarendon Press, 1990), and *Diversity and Distrust:*

Civic Education in a Multicultural Democracy (Cambridge, MA: Harvard University Press, 2000).

35. Although I would align myself with the sorts of claims made for the priority of justice and basic rights advanced by John Rawls, *A Theory of Justice*, rev. ed. (Cambridge, MA: Harvard University Press, 1999), and Ronald Dworkin, *Taking Rights Seriously* (Cambridge, MA: Harvard University Press, 1977), an inquiry into law and policy in this area requires in addition some appreciation of the social meaning of marriage and family in a particular place, as Michael Walzer argues for in *Spheres of Justice: A Defense of Pluralism and Equality* (New York: Basic Books, 1984).

36. See Olson in Boies and Olson, *Redeeming the Dream*, 26–27.

37. J. Alito, *Windsor* dissent, 8, 13–14. See also remarks of Timothy Samuelson, assistant attorney general of Wisconsin, in Wolf v. Walker, oral argument, http://media.ca7.uscourts.gov/sound/2014/rt .2.14–2526_08_26_2014.mp3.

CHAPTER 1

1. Karlyn Bowman, Andrew Rugg, and Jennifer K. Marsico, *Polls on Attitudes on Homosexuality and Gay Marriage*, AEI Public Opinion Studies (Washington, DC: American Enterprise Institute, updated March 2013), citing NORC/GSS poll, 32, http://www.aei.org /publication/polls-on-attitudes-on-homosexuality-gay-marriage -march-2013/.

2. Tom W. Smith, "Public Attitudes toward Homosexuality," NORC/University of Chicago, September 2011, http://www.norc.org/ PDFs/2011%20GSS%20Reports/GSS_Public%20Attitudes%20 Toward%20Homosexuality_Sept2011.pdf; and see Andrew R. Flores, "National Trends in Public Opinion on LGBT Rights in the United States," Williams Institute, University of California, Los Angeles, School of Law (November 2014), http://williamsinstitute.law.ucla.edu /wp-content/uploads/POP-natl-trends-nov-2014.pdf.

3. Bowman, Rugg, and Marsico, *Polls on Attitudes*, 32–45.

4. Ibid., 33.

5. Tom W. Smith and Jaesok Son, "Trends in Public Attitudes about Sexual Morality," Final Report NORC/GSS, April 2013, http:// www.norc.org/PDFs/sexmoralfinal_06–21_FINAL.PDF. See also Bowman, Rugg, and Marsico, *Polls on Attitudes*, 4.

6. Pew Research Global Attitudes Project, "The Global Divide on Homosexuality: Greater Acceptance in More Secular and Affluent

Countries," June 4, 2013, http://www.pewglobal.org/2013/06/04/the
-global-divide-on-homosexuality/.

7. See D. M. Cutler, E. L. Glaeser, and K. E. Norberg, "Explaining
the Rise in Youth Suicide," in *Risky Behavior among Youths: An Economic
Analysis*, ed. Jonathan Gruber (Chicago: University of Chicago press,
2001); also the discussion in Avner Offer, *The Challenge of Affluence:
Self-Control and Well-Being in the United States and Britain since 1950*
(Oxford: Oxford University Press, 2007), 350.

8. "Divorce rates . . . are highly correlated with youth-suicide
rates." See Cutler, Glaeser, and Norberg, "Youth Suicide," 224, 246–
50; and Offer, *Challenge of Affluence*, 346–57. Other factors offset the
effects of divorce and single parenting on suicide rates, including the
amount of time spent with mothers and absent fathers. I return to this
below.

9. I was once scolded by a winner of the Nobel Prize in Economics
for raising the issue at a conference ostensibly concerned with the moral
foundations of the free society.

10. Various, "Sex and God in American Politics: A Symposium,"
Policy Review (Spring 1984): 25.

11. Ibid., 26

12. Ibid., 24.

13. Ibid., 23.

14. Ibid., 25.

15. Comments of Rabbi Gerald Siegel, Congressman Jack Kemp,
and Senator Orrin Hatch, in ibid., 24, 25, 26.

16. Ibid., 25.

17. Ibid., 26.

18. Harry V. Jaffa, *Original Intent and the Framers of the Constitution: A Disputed Question* (Washington, DC: Regnery, 1993), 255–56,
263. I draw here on my "Homosexuality and the Conservative Mind,"
Georgetown Law Journal 84 (1995): 261–300.

19. Harry V. Jaffa, "Sodomy and the Academy: The Assault on the
Family and Morality by 'Liberation' Ethics," in Jaffa, *American Conser-
vatism and the American Founding* (Claremont, CA: Claremont Institute
Press, 1984, reprint 2002), 263, 276–77. See also Jaffa, "Humanizing
Certitudes and Impoverishing Doubts," *Interpretation: A Journal of
Political Philosophy* 16, 1 (Fall 1998): 111.

20. Jaffa, *Original Intent*, 380, 383, 257. Similar comments by Jaffa
can be found at http://www.tfp.org/current-campaigns/traditional
-marriage-crusade/morality-is-absolute-equal-protection-clause-has
-nothing-to-do-with-same-sex-marriage.html.

21. Harvey C. Mansfield, "Saving Liberalism from Liberals," *Harvard Crimson*, November 8, 1993, 2.

22. Ibid.

23. Ibid.

24. In fairness to Mansfield, these remarks are all taken from an opinion piece he wrote for the *Harvard Crimson* in response to a colleague's provocation. He has not written much on the topic, and his much later book *Manliness* (New Haven: Yale University Press, 2006) avoids it. In fairness to me, shortly before penning these remarks he gave expert testimony on these matters in a court of law.

25. "This case does not require a judgment on whether laws against sodomy between consenting adults in general, or between homosexuals in particular, are wise or desirable." Bowers v. Hardwick, 478 US 186 (1986), opinion of J. White, 190.

26. Griswold v. Connecticut, 381 US 479 (1965).

27. Eisenstadt v. Baird, 405 US 438 (1972); Stanley v. Georgia, 394 US 557 (1969).

28. Roe v. Wade, 410 US 113 (1973).

29. White, in *Bowers,* 196.

30. Patrick Devlin, *The Enforcement of Morals* (Oxford: Oxford University Press, 1965), 2.

31. Ibid., viii, 15. For an excellent account of some of the weaknesses of Devlin's view, see Robert P. George, *Making Men Moral: Civil Liberties and Public Morality* (Oxford: Oxford University Press, 1993), intro. and chap. 1.

32. Devlin, *Enforcement of Morals,* 89, quoting Justice Felix Frankfurter in Minersville School Board v. Gobitis, 310 U.S. 586 (1940): 596, which upheld the constitutionality of a Pennsylvania law that permitted the expulsion of schoolchildren who refused to salute the flag or say the Pledge of Allegiance, in this case, Jehovah's Witness schoolchildren who refused, on religious grounds, to salute the American flag. The Supreme Court reversed itself in West Virginia State Board of Education v. Barnette, 319 US 624, 63 S. Ct. 1178, 87 L. Ed. 1628 (1943), overturning a West Virginia law that compelled students in public schools to salute the flag and recite the Pledge of Allegiance.

33. Discriminatory laws may rest on nothing more than "habitual dislike for, or ignorance about, ... [a] disfavored group," as Justice Stevens remarked. *Bowers,* 219.

34. Blackmun, in ibid., 199. The quoted remarks from Blackmun's dissenting opinion are taken from Oliver Wendell Holmes, "The Path of the Law," *Harvard Law Review* 10 (1897): 469.

35. Blackmun, in *Bowers*, 200. Blackmun further noted that the brief submitted by the state of Georgia invoked, in support of its criminal law, "Leviticus, Romans, St. Thomas Aquinas, and sodomy's heretical status during the Middle Ages." That "certain, but by no means all, religious groups condemn the behavior at issue gives the State no license to impose their judgments on the entire citizenry.... A State can no more punish private behavior because of religious intolerance than it can punish such behavior because of racial animus," 211–12.

36. Ibid., 211, emphasis added.

37. See the discussion in Michael J. Klarman, *From the Closet to the Altar: Courts, Backlash, and the Struggle for Same-Sex Marriage* (New York: Oxford University Press, 2013), 37–39; and see William N. Eskridge, Jr., *Equality Practice: Civil Unions and the Future of Gay Rights* (New York: Routledge, 2002), 17.

38. This has been a central challenge for participants in this debate for decades and certainly since *Bowers*. I address the issue in "In Defense of Liberal Public Reason: Are Abortion and Slavery Hard Cases?," *American Journal of Jurisprudence* 42 (1997): 1–29.

39. Baehr v. Lewin, 74 Haw. 530, 852 P.2d 44 (1993). See Klarman, *Closet to Altar*, 48. The gay community itself "remained deeply divided over whether to pursue gay marriage." See more at http://family.findlaw.com/marriage/1993-the-hawaii-case-of-baehr-v-lewin.html#sthash.DbY0yEUX.dpuf.

40. See Klarman's excellent account, *Closet to Altar*, 59.

41. U.S. House of Representatives, House debate on Defense of Marriage Act, May 30, 1996, excerpted in Sullivan, *Same-Sex Marriage*, 225.

42. See the discussion in Robert D. Putnam and David E. Campbell, *American Grace: How Religion Divides and Unites Us* (New York: Simon and Schuster, 2010), 396–99; and Klarman, *Closet to Altar*, 111–13.

43. Space does not permit attention to the shift in public attitudes, and the long campaign waged on many fronts, but there are excellent accounts available: see David K. Johnson, *The Lavender Scare: The Cold War Persecution of Gays and Lesbians in the Federal Government* (Chicago: University of Chicago Press, 2004); John D'Emilio and Estelle B. Freedman, *Intimate Matters: A History of Sexuality in America*, 3rd ed. (Chicago: University of Chicago Press, 2012); and William N. Eskridge, Jr., *Gaylaw: Challenging the Apartheid of the Closet* (Cambridge, MA: Harvard University Press, 1999).

44. Richard Posner, "Homosexual Marriage," *Becker-Posner blog*, May 13, 2012, http://www.becker-posner-blog.com/2012/05/homosexual-marriageposner.html.

45.   Judge Richard Posner, opinion in Baskin v. Bogan and Wolf v. Walker, United States Court of Appeals for the Seventh Circuit, Case: 14–2386, Decided September 4, 2014, 9; citing Gregory M. Herek et al., "Demographic, Psychological, and Social Characteristics of Self-Identified Lesbian, Gay, and Bisexual Adults in a US Probability Sample," *Sexuality Research and Social Policy* 7 (2010): 188. See also APA, "Answers to Your Questions: For a Better Understanding of Sexual Orientation & Homosexuality" 2 (2008), http://www.apa.org/topics/lgbt/orientation.pdf.

46.   Perry v. Schwarzenegger, U.S. Court of Appeals for the Ninth Circuit, 2012, opinion of Judge Vaughn Walker, 6.

47.   Robicheaux v. Caldwell, 5. Judge Feldman characterizes same-sex marriage as "personal, genuine, and sincere lifestyle choices recognition."

48.   Edmund White, "I Do, I Do," *New York Review of Books*, August 14, 2014, 26.

49.   Ngram Viewer, https://books.google.com/ngrams/graph ?content=sexual+preference%2Csexual+orientation&year_start=1960 &year_end=2008&corpus=15&smoothing=2&share=&direct_url=t1% 3B%2Csexual%20preference%3B%2Cc0%3B.t1%3B%2Csexual%20 orientation%3B%2Cc0. See Dudley Clendinen and Adam Nagourney, *Out for Good: The Struggle to Build a Gay Rights Movement in America* (New York: Simon and Schuster, 1999), 265.

50.   See the compilation of national poll results in *Polls on Attitudes on Homosexuality and Gay Marriage, AEI Public Opinion Studies* (updated March 2013).

51.   The figures are from Klarman, *Closet to Altar*, 197; and see Judge Sutton's opinion in DeBoer v. Snyder, at 34.

52.   See Robert Beachy, *Gay Berlin: Birthplace of a Modern Identity* (New York: Knopf, 2014).

53.   See, for example, Frontiero v. Richardson, 411 US 677 (1973), opinion of Justice Brennan.

54.   Romer v. Evans, 517 US 620 (1996).

55.   Ibid., J. Kennedy, 623, quoting from the dissent of Justice Harlan in Plessy v. Ferguson, 163 US 537 (1896), 559.

56.   Ibid., 624.

57.   Ibid., 632, 633.

58.   Klarman, *Closet to Altar*, 69–70.

59.   J. Scalia, in Romer v. Evans, 644, 648.

60.   Various, "The End of Democracy: The Judicial Usurpation of Politics," *First Things*, November 1996, http://www.firstthings.com

/article/1996/11/001-the-end-of-democracy-the-judicial-usurpation
-of-politics. This symposium issue was provoked by Romer v. Evans,
plus the Supreme Court decision requiring the Virginia Military
Institute to admit qualified women, United States v. Virginia, 518 U.S.
515 (1996), and a lower federal court decision establishing a constitutional right of terminally ill patients to doctor-assisted suicide (unanimously overturned by the Supreme Court the next year in Washington
v. Glucksberg, 521 US 702 [1997], leaving the states free to prohibit
doctor-assisted suicide).

61. Lawrence v. Texas, 539 US 558 (2003), 572, 567.

62. Ibid., 578.

63. Ibid., 583.

64. U.S. Constitution, Fourteenth Amendment.

65. Arkes, "A Culture Corrupted," in Symposium, *First Things*.

66. Lawrence v. Texas, 604.

67. The reference is a bit oblique; it occurs when he asks, rhetorically, at the end of his dissent, "what justification could there possibly be
for denying the benefits of marriage to homosexual couples exercising
'[t]he liberty protected by the Constitution'? Surely not the encouragement of procreation, since the sterile and the elderly are allowed to
marry." Ibid., Scalia dissent, 605. As we will see below, critics of natural
law have for decades held up its inclusion of sterile and elderly couples
within marriage as an inconsistency.

68. Scalia dissenting, *Lawrence*, 599; *Romer*, 644.

69. Scalia dissenting, *Lawrence*, 599.

70. Devlin, *Enforcement of Morals*, 128, 138.

71. For the Declaration, see http://www.archives.gov/exhibits
/charters/declaration_transcript.html. For *Federalist* #1, see http://
thomas.loc.gov/home/histdox/fedpapers.html.

72. For a classic account, see John Hart Ely, *Democracy and Distrust:
A Theory of Judicial Review* (Cambridge, MA: Harvard University Press,
1980).

73. See Judge Posner's opinion in *Baskin*, 3.

74. "A Culture Corrupted," in Symposium, *First Things*. Roy S.
Moore, Chief Justice, Alabama Supreme Court, Letter to Hon. Robert
Bentley, Governor of Alabama, January 27, 2015, http://media.al.com
/news_impact/other/Read%20Chief%20Justice%20Moore%20letter
.pdf.

75. See Fleming and McClain, *Ordered Liberty*, 195, describing the
California litigation.

76. Judge Vaughn Walker, in Perry v. Schwarzenegger, 102, 106.

77. See Boies and Olson, *Redeeming the Dream*, 144–45.

78. Pew Research Religion and Public Life Project, "Religious Beliefs Underpin Opposition to Homosexuality," http://www.pewforum.org/files/2003/11/religion-homosexuality.pdf.

79. Fleming and McClain, *Ordered Liberty*, 205n144.

80. Ibid., 199.

81. Ruben Diaz, quoted in ibid., 200.

82. Michelle Kim, "Bronx Senator, Granddaughter Battle over Gay Marriage: Sen. Diaz Holds Rally against Same-Sex Marriage; Gay Granddaughter Condemns Stance," *NBC New York*, May 16, 2011, http://www.nbcnewyork.com/news/local/Bronx-Senator-Granddaughter-in-Battle-Over-Gay-Marriage-121865914.html.

83. Nathan Black, "Grisanti Defends Switch to 'Yes' on NY Gay Marriage," *Christian Post*, June 28, 2011.

84. Assembly Member Deborah Glick, quoted in Fleming and McClain, *Ordered Liberty*, 202, 203.

85. Assembly Member Daniel O'Donnell, quoted in ibid., 203. I am indebted here to the excellent discussion in ibid., 199–206.

86. Kennedy, in *Lawrence*, 571.

87. David Moats, "Civil Unions in Vermont: Public Reason Improvised," *Perspectives on Politics* 1, 1 (March 2003): 131–35.

CHAPTER 2

1. Federal Defense of Marriage Act, sec. 3: "In determining the meaning of any Act of Congress, or of any ruling, regulation, or interpretation of the various administrative bureaus and agencies of the United States, the word 'marriage' means only a legal union between one man and one woman as husband and wife, and the word 'spouse' refers only to a person of the opposite sex who is a husband or a wife." http://www.gpo.gov/fdsys/pkg/BILLS-104hr3396enr/pdf/BILLS-104hr3396enr.pdf. Proposition 8: "Only marriage between a man and a woman is valid or recognized in California." See Perry v. Schwarzenegger.

2. John Finnis, "Is Natural Law Theory Compatible with Limited Government?," in *Natural Law, Liberalism, and Morality: Contemporary Essays*, ed. Robert P. George (New York: Oxford University Press, 1996), 12.

3. George, *Making Men Moral*, 5.

4. Anderson, "The Roe of Marriage."

5. Sherif Girgis, Ryan T. Anderson, and Robert P. George, *What Is Marriage? Man and Woman: A Defense* (New York: Encounter Books, 2012), 27.

6. Ibid. For a shorter version, see "What Is Marriage?" *Harvard Journal of Law and Public Policy* 34, 1 (2011): 245–87.

7. In the natural law view, our understanding of law and morality of sex should take its bearings from the "specific, intrinsic perfection" of relations between man and woman found in marriage: "marriage realizes the potentiality of man and woman for unqualified, mutual self-giving." Germain Grisez, *Way of the Lord Jesus*, vol. 2: *Living a Christian Life* (Quincy, IL: Franciscan Press, 1993), 569–70, 634–35, http://www.twotlj.org/G-2-V-2.html.

8. For a general introduction see Mark Murphy, "The Natural Law Tradition in Ethics," in *The Stanford Encyclopedia of Philosophy* (Winter 2011), ed. Edward N. Zalta, http://plato.stanford.edu/archives/win2011/entries/natural-law-ethics/.

9. Girgis, Anderson, and George, *What Is Marriage?*, 6, 24.

10. Ibid., 44–46.

11. See Institute for American Values, *Why Marriage Matters*, 3rd ed., citing Kristi Williams, "Has the Future of Marriage Arrived? A Contemporary Examination of the Effects of Marital Status and Marital Quality on the Psychological Well-Being of Women and Men," *Journal of Health and Social Behavior* 44, 4 (December 2003): 470–87. See also the evidence in Cherlin, *Marriage-Go-Round*, on the detrimental effects of marriages with a good deal of open conflict; and Linda C. McClain, *The Place of Families: Fostering Capacity, Equality, and Responsibility* (Cambridge, MA: Harvard University Press, 2006), 129–30.

12. Girgis, Anderson, and George, *What Is Marriage?*, 25.

13. Many accounts of marriage contain these elements; see, e.g., Cherlin, *Marriage-Go-Round*, 26.

14. Girgis, Anderson, and George, *What Is Marriage?*, 36.

15. Ibid., 30.

16. "This generative kind of act physically embodies their specific marital commitment." Ibid., 36. None of these arguments is new. *What Is Marriage?* is a restatement of a now familiar position; see Robert P. George and Gerard V. Bradley, "Marriage and the Liberal Imagination," *Georgetown Law Journal* 84 (1995): 301–20.

17. Patrick Lee and Robert P. George, "What Sex Can Be: Self-Alienation, Illusion, or One-Flesh Union," *American Journal of Jurisprudence* 42, 1, art. 5 (1997): 144, http://scholarship.law.nd.edu/ajj/vol42/iss1/5?utm_source=scholarship.law.nd.edu%2Fajj%2Fvol42%2Fiss1%2F5&utm_medium=PDF&utm_campaign=PDFCoverPages.

18. "[N]o same-sex or group relationship will include organic bodily union, or find its *inherent* fulfillment in procreation, or require, *quite apart from the partners' personal preferences*, what these two features

demand: permanent and exclusive commitment" (emphasis added). Girgis, Anderson, and George, *What Is Marriage?*, 87.

19.   George, Finnis, and others espousing New Natural Law have frequently expressed their debt to Grisez: "we present a natural law argument for the proposition that sexual acts are morally right only within marriage, an argument first developed in detail by Germain Grisez." Lee and George, "What Sex Can Be," 136. As another philosopher, who attained higher office, has put it: "Conjugal love involves a totality, in which all the elements of the person enter—appeal of the body and instinct, power of feeling and affectivity, aspiration of the spirit and of the will. It aims at a deeply personal unity, a unity that, beyond union in one flesh, leads to forming one heart and soul; it demands *indissolubility* and *faithfulness* in definitive mutual giving; and it is open to *fertility* (*Familiaris consortio*, no. 13)." Pope John Paul II, quoted in W. Bradford Wilcox, "Seeking a Soulmate: A Social Scientific View of the Relationship between Commitment and Authentic Intimacy," for *Promoting and Sustaining Marriage as a Community of Life and Love*, Colloquium of Social Scientists and Theologians, October 24–25, 2005, http://old.usccb.org/laity/marriage/Wilcox.pdf.

20.   Girgis, Anderson, and George, "What Is Marriage?," 267–68. "Of course, a true friendship of two men or two women is also valuable in itself. But lacking the capacity for *organic bodily union*, it cannot be valuable specifically as a marriage: it cannot be the comprehensive union on which *aptness for procreation* and distinctively marital norms depend." The authors conclude that "whatever the state says, in other words, no same-sex marriage or group relationship will include organic bodily union, or find its inherent fulfillment in procreation, or require, quite apart from the partners' preferences, what these two features demand: permanent and exclusive commitment. Nor can sheer legislative will make these differences meaningless, or make disregarding them harmless to the common good." Girgis, Anderson, and George, *What Is Marriage?*, 87.

21.   For a similar observation, see Robin West, *Marriage, Sexuality and Gender* (St. Paul: Paradigm, 2007), 62.

22.   Gallagher in John Corvino and Maggie Gallagher, *Debating Same-Sex Marriage* (New York: Oxford University Press, 2012), 177; and Girgis, Anderson, and George, *What Is Marriage?*, 27, 6. Also see George & Bradley, "Marriage and the Liberal Imagination," 301, for the phrase "two-in-one-flesh communion."

23.   Girgis, Anderson, and George, *What Is Marriage?*, 33. The rest of the quote is also useful: "If bodily union is essential to marriage, we

can understand why marriage, like the union of organs into one healthy whole, should be total and lasting for the life of the parts ('till death do us part'). Being organically united—as 'one flesh'—spouses should have, by commitment, the exclusive and lifelong unity that the parts of a healthy organic body have by nature." That's a big "if."

24. Ibid., 27n.

25. Mark Joseph Stern, "The Sexual Fetish of Gay Marriage Opponents: Defenders of DOMA and Proposition 8 Say Marriage Isn't about Love or Parenting. It's about Coitus," *Slate*, http://www.slate.com /articles/news_and_politics/jurisprudence/2013/03/gay_marriage_and _sex_why_do_defenders_of_doma_and_prop_8_worship_coitus.html.

26. Grisez, *Way of Lord Jesus*, 573; Finnis, "Profound Injustice of Judge Posner."

27. See Patrick Lee and Robert P. George, *Body-Self Dualism in Contemporary Ethics and Politics* (Cambridge: Cambridge University Press, 2008), 180, and see generally chap. 6, "Sex and the Body," 176–217.

28. Scalia dissent in Romer v. Evans, 644.

29. Including the idea that pleasure is not a reason for action, and the claim that all nonmarital sexual acts involve a destructive "mind-body dualism."

30. Grisez, *Way of Lord Jesus*, 672.

31. Stephen J. Pope, "The Magisterium's Arguments against 'Same-Sex Marriage': An Ethical Analysis and Critique," *Theological Studies* 65 (2004): 539.

32. Associated Press, "Pope Strongly Defends Church Teaching against Contraception," *New York Post*, January 16, 2015, http://nypost .com/2015/01/16/pope-strongly-defends-church-teaching-against -contraception/.

33. Grisez, *Way of the Lord Jesus*, 648–56 (claiming that nonmarital sexual acts are wrong). See also Finnis, "Law, Morality, and 'Sexual Orientation,'" *Notre Dame Law Review* 69 (1994): 1066–68.

34. George and Bradley, "Marriage and the Liberal Imagination," 302.

35. Grisez, *Way of Lord Jesus*, 684.

36. Ibid., 685–86. The last claim is a quotation from John Paul II, *Familiaris consortio*, 32, AAS 74 (1982) 120, OR, December 21–28, 1981, 7.

37. George has argued at length that the police powers of the state ought to be mobilized to express disapproval of sexual immorality in general, and this would include overturning Bowers v. Hardwick so that states can criminalize gay sex, including in the privacy of the home.

See Robert P. George, "The Concept of Public Morality," in *The Clash of Orthodoxies: Law, Morality, and Religion in Crisis* (Washington, DC: Intercollegiate Studies Institute Press, 2001), 107. See also Robert P. George and William L. Saunders, "Romer v. Evans: The Supreme Court's Assault on Popular Sovereignty," *Civil Rights Practice Group Newsletter* 1, 1 (Fall 1996), http://www.fed-soc.org/publications/detail /romer-v-evans-the-supreme-courts-assault-on-popular-sovereignty.

38. Finnis, "Law, Morality, and 'Sexual Orientation,'" 1066–67.

39. Lee and George, *Body-Self Dualism*, 186; they add that acts performed "for the sole immediate purpose of pleasure . . . constitute mere masturbation, either solitary or mutual," and "masturbatory sex is objectively morally wrong." Defenders of New Natural Law frequently ascribe a self-"disintegrating" mind-body dualism to all nonprocreative sex acts as intrinsically immoral, and they further argue that pleasure is not a reason for action. See ibid., 216–17: "To engage in sex merely for pleasure uses a person's animal sexuality as a mere extrinsic tool for gratification, thus depersonalizing the body-as-sexual, treating it as a subpersonal object. Moreover, sexual acts aimed at expressing affection or love but outside marriage are choices of an illusory experience, since" there can be no real "personal communion" of the sort there is when sex is procreative (uncontracepted) and in a marriage involving a man and a woman.

40. Weithman, "Natural Law, Morality, and Sexual Complementarity," in *Sex, Preference, and Family: Essays on Law and Nature*, ed. David M. Estlund and Martha C. Nussbaum (New York: Oxford University Press, 1997), 237, 241.

41. Pope, "Magisterium and 'Same-Sex Marriage,'" 544–45.

42. Rachel K. Jones and Joerg Dreweke, "Countering Conventional Wisdom: New Evidence on Religion and Contraceptive Use," Guttmacher Institute, April 2011, http://www.guttmacher.org/pubs //Religion-and-Contraceptive-Use.pdf. According to UN Reports, over 75 percent of American women ages 18–49 who are married currently use contraceptives. Undoubtedly, many of the rest are not having intercourse or have already reached menopause.

43. "New Harris Poll Finds Different Religious Groups Have Very Different Attitudes to Some Health Policies and Programs," Harris Poll 78, October 20, 2005, http://www.harrisinteractive.com/harris_poll /index.asp?PID=608.

44. Lawrence B. Finer, "Trends in Premarital Sex in the United States, 1954–2003," *Public Health Report* 122, 1 (January–February 2007): 73–78, http://www.ncbi.nlm.nih.gov/pmc/articles/PMC1802 108/pdf/phr122000073.pdf.

45. These observations shift the focus away from the *form* of sex acts performed by partners to the partners' intentions and orientation vis-à-vis the raising of children.

46. Girgis, Anderson, and George, *What Is Marriage?*, 26–27.

47. Alec Baldwin, "Why Childless Straight Couples Make the Case for Gay Marriage," blogpost, May 25, 2011, http://www.huffingtonpost .com/alec-baldwin/why-childless-straight-co_b_208457.html.

48. See the discussion in chapter 3. For evidence on the effects of marriage on spousal health and well-being, see Richard G. Wight, Allen J. LeBlanc, and M.V. Lee Badgett, "Same-Sex Legal Marriage and Psychological Well-Being: Findings from the California Health Interview Survey" (2013), http://ajph.aphapublications.org/doi/full/10.2105 /AJPH.2012.301113.

49. Goodridge v. Dept. of Public Health, 798 N.E. 2d 941 (Mass. 2003), Ch. J. Margaret Marshall, 331–33.

50. Lynn D. Wardle, "Image, Analysis, and the Nature of Relationships," in *Marriage and Same-Sex Unions: A Debate*, ed. Lynn D. Wardle et al. (Westport, CT: Greenwood, 2003), 115.

51. Girgis, Anderson, and George, *What Is Marriage?*, 7, 17, describe the revisionist or companionate conception of marriage as "emotional union" that features friendship plus sex. Only coitus *"unifies* sex and other features of marriage as one good"* (18).

52. Ibid., 49.

53. Ibid., 28–29.

54. Gallagher, in Corvino and Gallagher, *Debating*, 177.

55. Leon R. Kass, "The Other War on Poverty," *National Affairs* 12 (Summer 2012): 8–9.

56. Baker v. Vermont, 744 A.2d 864 (Vt. 1999); see also the discussion in David Moats, *Civil Wars: The Battle for Gay Marriage* (Boston: Houghton Mifflin, Harcourt, 2004), 5–6.

57. Boies and Olson, *Redeeming the Dream*, 127.

58. Ibid., 135–36.

59. I am indebted to Rob Katz for this formulation and many others here.

60. See John Corvino's very useful discussion in Corvino and Gallagher, *Debating Same-Sex Marriage*. For discussion of related issues see John Bowlin, *Contingency and Fortune in Aquinas's Ethics* (New York: Cambridge University Press, 2010).

61. Edward Collins Vacek, "The Meaning of Marriage: Of Two Minds," *Commonweal* 130, 18 (October 24, 2003): 17–19; which cites and discusses Congregation for the Doctrine of the Faith,

"Considerations Regarding Proposals to Give Legal Recognition to Unions between Homosexual Persons," *Origins* 33 (August 14, 2003): 177–82, http://www.vatican.va/roman_curia/congregations/cfaith /documents/c_con_cfaith_doc_20030731_homosexual-unions_en.html.

62. Boies and Olson, *Redeeming the Dream*, 76, 87, 90.

63. Ibid., 83.

64. Girgis, Anderson, and George, *What Is Marriage?*, 27.

65. Mansfield, *Manliness*, 203

66. Paul J. Griffiths, "Legalize Same-Sex Marriage: Why Law and Morality Can Part Company," *Commonweal*, June 28, 2004, https:// www.commonwealmagazine.org/legalize-same-sex-marriage-0.

67. Jonah Goldberg, "Abortion and Gay Marriage: Separate Issues; America Has Become More Pro-Life, More Pro-Gun, and More Pro-Gay," *National Review* http://www.nationalreview.com/articles/343636 /abortion-and-gay-marriage-separate-issues-jonah-goldberg.

68. Grisez, *Way of Lord Jesus*, 608.

69. John Finnis, "Profound Injustice of Judge Posner."

70. Boies and Olson, *Redeeming the Dream*, 84–85.

71. Official Transcript, U.S. Supreme Court, Dennis Hollingsworth, et al., v. Kristin Perry, et al., No. 12–144, Washington, DC, March 26, 2013: 24–25, http://www.supremecourt.gov/oral_arguments/argument _transcripts/12–144a.pdf.

72. Thurmond was governor of South Carolina, presidential candidate for the segregationist Dixiecrats in 1948, and, for forty-eight years, U.S. senator from South Carolina. He fathered four children in advanced middle age, beginning when he was 68 and his second wife was 25. Shortly after his death in 2003 at age 100, it was revealed that he had, at age 22, impregnated a 16-year-old daughter of the family's African American maid, who subsequently bore a child, Essie Mae Washington-Williams. In the wake of all these revelations, she stepped forward and was acknowledged by the Thurmond family.

73. Klarman, *Closet to Altar*, 197. See also "New Numbers, and Geography, for Gay Couples," *New York Times*, August 25, 2011.

74. See Michael Paulson, "Pastor Led Son's Gay Wedding, Revealing Fault Line in Church," *New York Times*, July 13, 2014; and Sarah Pulliam Bailey, "Conservative United Methodists Say Divide over Sexuality Is 'Irreconcilable,'" Religion News Service, May 23, 2014, http:// www.religionnews.com/2014/05/23/amid-sexuality-debates-80-pastors -threaten-possible-division-within-united-methodist-church/.

75. http://www.nationaljournal.com/columns/on-the-trail/will -grace-and-a-decade-of-change-on-gay-rights-20130626. Similar speculation is in Putnam and Campbell, *American Grace*, 404.

CHAPTER 3

1. See George Gilder, *Men and Marriage* (revised and expanded edition of *Sexual Suicide*) (Gretna: Pelican, 1992); and, more subtly, Roger Scruton, *Sexual Desire: A Philosophical Investigation* (London: Weidenfeld and Nicholson, 1986), 305–11.

2. See, e.g., Robert Wright, *The Moral Animal*, 100–101; and the sources discussed in Mansfield, *Manliness*, chap. 2.

3. Gilder is clearest, drawing on the work of Margaret Mead and others, *Men and Marriage*, 29 and chap. 3.

4. James Q. Wilson, *The Marriage Problem: How Our Culture Has Weakened Families* (New York: HarperCollins, 2003); David Blankenhorn, *Fatherless America: Confronting Our Most Urgent Social Problem* (New York: Basic Books, 1995); for an interesting account of the empirical evidence see Eleanor E. Maccoby, *The Two Sexes: Growing Up Apart, Coming Together* (Cambridge, MA: Harvard University Press, 1998). I do not discount the idea of a special "male problematic" but rather the ways that conservatives often seek to address it. On the unruliness of male sexual desire from a gay male perspective, see Marshall Kirk and Hunter Madsen, *After the Ball: How America Will Conquer Its Fear and Hatred of Gays in the 90's* (New York: Doubleday, 1989).

5. Finnis, "Profound Injustice of Judge Posner."

6. Rose McDermott, Dominic Johnson, Jonathan Cowden, and Stephen Rosen, "Testosterone and Aggression in a Simulated Crisis Game," *ANNALS of the American Academy of Political and Social Science* 614, 1 (2007): 15–33.

7. See Steven E. Rhoads, *Taking Sex Differences Seriously* (San Francisco: Encounter Books, 2004), 10–12; and Mansfield, *Manliness*, 7–8.

8. McClain, *The Place of Families*, 140.

9. Blankenhorn, *Fatherless*, 102.

10. Ibid., 122.

11. McClain, *The Place of Families*, 147.

12. Blankenhorn, *Fatherless*, 119, 122, 123.

13. McClain, *The Place of Families*, 149.

14. Ibid.

15. http://www.theatlantic.com/magazine/print/2012/07/why-women-still-cant-have-it-all/309020/.

16. *Congressional Record* (hereafter *CR*), July 9–14, 2004 (Washington, DC: Government Printing Office, 2004), July 9, 2004; speeches of Senators Orrin Hatch and John Cornyn. I draw here on Frederick Liu and Stephen Macedo, "The Federal Marriage Amendment and the

Strange Evolution of the Conservative Case against Gay Marriage," *PS: Political Science and Politics* 38, 2 (April 2005): 211–15.

17. Stanley Kurtz, "The End of Marriage in Scandinavia," *Weekly Standard*, February 2, 2004, 29; and Stanley Kurtz, "Going Dutch?," *Weekly Standard*, May 31, 2004, 26.

18. *CR*, July 14, 2004.

19. *CR*, July 13, 2004.

20. Denmark repealed its joint adoption prohibition in 1999; Sweden followed in 2003. See William N. Eskridge, Darren R. Spedale, and Hans Ytterberg, "Nordic Bliss? Scandinavian Registered Partnerships and the Same-Sex Marriage Debate," *Issues in Legal Scholarship, Single-Sex Marriage*, article 4 (2004): 3, http://www.bepress.com/ils/iss5/art4; William N. Eskridge, Jr., and Darren R. Spedale, *Gay Marriage: For Better or for Worse? What We've Learned from the Empirical Evidence* (New York: Oxford University Press, 2006), 169–202.

21. Perry v. Schwarzenegger, opinion of Judge Walker, 10.

22. Ibid., 17–19.

23. Walker, in Perry v. Schwarzenegger, 24.

24. Bipartisan Legal Advisory Group (BLAG) of the U.S. House of Representatives, Brief, 42, http://www.clearinghouse.net/chDocs/public/PB-NY-0017–0015.pdf.

25. For an overview of his findings, see Mark Regnerus, "Queers as Folk: Does It Really Make No Difference If Your Parents Are Straight or Gay?," *Slate*, June 11, 2012, http://www.slate.com/articles/double_x/doublex/2012/06/gay_parents_are_they_really_no_different_html; and for the study itself, Mark Regnerus, "How Different Are the Adult Children of Parents Who Have Same-Sex Relationships? Findings from the New Family Structures Study," *Social Science Research* 41 (2012): 752–70. Note the quoted remarks on 757: "'States and large metropolitan areas with relatively low concentrations of gay and lesbian couples in the population tend to be areas where same-sex couples are more likely to have children in the household.' A recent updated brief by Gates (2011, F3) reinforces this: 'Geographically, same-sex couples are most likely to have children in many of the most socially conservative parts of the country.' Moreover, Gates notes that racial minorities are disproportionately more likely (among same-sex households) to report having children; whites, on the other hand, are disproportionately less likely to have children." Regnerus is quoting from Gary J. Gates and Jason Ost, *The Gay and Lesbian Atlas* (Washington, DC: Urban Institute Press, 2004), 47; and Gary J. Gates, *National Council of Family Relations Report* 56, 4 (2011): F1–F3.

26. William Saletan, "Back in the Gay: Does a New Study Indict Gay Parenthood or Make a Case for Gay Marriage?" *Slate*, June 11, 2012, http://www.slate.com/articles/health_and_science/human_nature /2012/06/new_family_structures_study_is_gay_parenthood_bad_or_is _gay_marriage_good_.html.

27. American Academy of Pediatrics, "Promoting the Well-Being of Children Whose Parents Are Gay or Lesbian," http:// http:// pediatrics.aappublications.org/search?fulltext=promoting+the+well -being+of+children&submit=yes&x=0&y=0; from the abstract, p. 1. See also the Cambridge University report on same sex adoptions, http:// www.cambridge-news.co.uk/News/Children-as-happy-with-gay -adopted-parents-says-report-05032013.htm.

28. Saletan, "Back in the Gay."

29. Carl E. Schneider, "The Channeling Function in Family Law," *Hofstra Law Review* 20 (Spring 1992): 495.

30. BLAG, Brief on the Merits, in U.S. v. Windsor, no. 12–307; filed January 22, 2013, http://www.supremecourt.gov/docket/pdfs/12 –307_brief_on_the_merits_for_respondent.pdf, 44, 45. Oddly, the BLAG brief adds: "Particularly in an earlier era when employment opportunities for women were at best limited, the prospect that un- intended children produced by opposite-sex relationships and raised out-of-wedlock would pose a burden on society was a substantial gov- ernment concern" (44–45). Proponents of Proposition 8 in federal court had previously highlighted the channeling argument in the brief to Judge Walker: the "central purpose of marriage, in California and every- where else, . . . to promote naturally procreative sexual relationships and to channel them into stable, enduring unions for the sake of producing and raising the next generation." Doc. no. 172–1, 21, Walker opinion, 8–9. Also Hernandez v. Robles, 855 N.E. 2d 1 (N.Y. 2006).

31. BLAG brief, 18.

32. As Judge Feldman pointed out, to contrast the same-sex mar- riage ban with *Lawrence*. See *Robicheaux*, 24.

33. J. Mitchell, "AG Greg Abbott: Texas Opposes Gay Marriage Because the State Has an Interest in Procreation?," *dallasnews.com*, July 30, 2014, http://dallasmorningviewsblog.dallasnews.com/2014/07 /ag-greg-abbott-texas-opposes-gay-marriage-because-the-state-has-an -interest-in-procreation.html/.

34. *Robicheaux*, 15.

35. See, e.g., the majority opinion of Judge Jeffrey Sutton, which begins by conceding the apparent inevitability of gay marriage, in DeBoer v. Snyder, 14–1341, November 6, 2014.

36. Posner, *Baskin*, 15.

37. Marcus Dillender, "The Death of Marriage? The Effects of New Forms of Legal Recognition on Marriage Rates in the United States," *Demography* 51 (2014): 563–85.

38. Posner, *Baskin*, 19–20.

39. See chapter 1.

40. Posner, *Baskin*, 18.

41. Ibid., 18–19.

42. As Judge Feldman suggested in *Robicheaux* (17n11), "the application of a finding of animus generally requires some structural aberration in the law at issue, like the imposition of wide-ranging and novel deprivations upon the disfavored group," citing Judge Holmes's concurrence in Bishop v. Smith, nos. 14–5003 and 14–5006, 2014 US App. LEXIS 13733, 93–133 (10th Cir., July 18, 2014), 106.

43. Posner, *Baskin*, 11.

44. Ibid., 20–21, citing Gary J. Gates, "LGBT Parenting in the United States" (Williams Institute, UCLA School of Law, February 2013), 3, http://williamsinstitute.law.ucla.edu/wp-content/uploads/lgbt -parenting.pdf.

45. Posner, *Baskin*, 22–23.

46. Centers for Disease Control, Press Release, "More than Half of Young HIV-Infected Americans Are Not Aware of Their Status," http://www.cdc.gov/media/releases/2012/p1127_young_HIV.html; Chuck Colbert, "HIV Rates Rise in Youth," *Bay Area Reporter*, December 6, 2012, http://www.ebar.com/news/article.php?sec=news&article =68309%20%20.

47. See the citations in David L. Chambers, "What If? The Legal Consequences of Marriage and the Legal Needs of Lesbian and Gay Male Couples," *Michigan Law Review* 95, 2 (1996): 460n51, citing studies from the early 1980s.

48. Dan Savage, *The Commitment: Love, Sex, Marriage, and My Family* (New York: Penguin, 2005), 130–33.

49. Scott James, "Many Successful Gay Marriages Share an Open Secret," *New York Times*, January 29, 2010, http://www.nytimes.com/2010 /01/29/us/29sfmetro.html?_r=0&pagewanted=print.

50. "SL Letter of the Day: Do Monogamous Gay Couples Exist?," posted by Dan Savage, June 20, 2012, *The Stranger*, http://slog.the stranger.com/slog/archives/2012/06/20/sl-letter-of-the-day-do -monogamous-gay-couples-exist.

51. For more on this, see Jonathan Rauch, *Gay Marriage: Why It Is Good for Gays, Good for Straights, and Good for America* (New York: Henry Holt, 2004).

52. Jonathan Katz, executive coordinator of the Larry Kramer Initiative for Gay and Lesbian Studies at Yale, quoted in Savage, *The Commitment*, 130.

53. Directed by Paul Mazursky.

54. Plato, *The Republic*, http://classics.mit.edu/Plato/republic.html. On Oneida and other utopian communities with "group marriage," see Nancy L. Rosenblum, "Democratic Sex," in *Membership and Morals: The Personal Uses of Pluralism in America* (Princeton: Princeton University Press, 1998); and Mark E. Brandon, *States of Union: Family and Change in the American Constitutional Order* (Lawrence: University Press of Kansas, 2013).

55. Alex Williams, "Open Marriage's New 15 Minutes," *New York Times*, February 3, 2012, http://mobile.nytimes.com/2012/02/05/fashion/open-marriages-new-15-minutes.html?_r=0.

56. Jenifer L. Bratter and Rosalind B. King, "'But Will It Last?': Marital Instability among Interracial and Same-Race Couples," *Family Relations* 57 (April 2008): 168.

57. Loving v. Virginia 388 US 1 (1967), 12.

58. Turner v. Safley 482 US 78 (1987); Zablocki v. Redhail, 434 US 374 (1978).

59. Lawrence v. Texas 574.

60. David Blankenhorn, "How My View on Gay Marriage Changed," *New York Times*, June 22, 2012, http://www.nytimes.com/2012/06/23/opinion/how-my-view-on-gay-marriage-changed.html.

61. A point recognized by many, including Offer, *Challenge of Affluence*, 316.

CHAPTER 4

1. Brake, *Minimizing Marriage*, 135–39; see also Tamara Metz, *Untying the Knot: Marriage, the State, and the Case for Their Divorce* (Princeton: Princeton University Press, 2010); Andrew F. March, "Is There a Right to Polygamy? Marriage, Equality and Subsidizing Families in Liberal Public Justification," *Journal of Moral Philosophy* 8 (2011): 246–72; Bedi, *Beyond Race*; David M. Estlund and Martha C. Nussbaum, *Sex, Preference, and Family: Essays on Law and Nature* (New York: Oxford University Press, 1997).

2. Bedi, *Beyond Race*, 210, referring to Brake.

3. Ibid., 27.

4. Lawrence G. Torcello, "Is the State Endorsement of Any Marriage Justifiable? Same-Sex Marriage, Civil Unions, and the Marriage Privatization Model," *Public Affairs Quarterly* 22, 1 (January 2008): 43–61.

5. Metz, *Untying the Knot*, 114–15.
6. March, "Is There a Right to Polygamy?," 246.
7. Brake, *Minimizing Marriage*, 144.
8. Among those who have explored the topics of political liberalism, ethical neutrality, and marriage reform are Adrian Alex Wellington, "Why Liberals Should Support Same Sex Marriage," *Journal of Social Philosophy* 26 (1995): 5–32; Kory Schaff, "Kant, Political Liberalism, and the Ethics of Same-Sex Relations," *Journal of Social Philosophy* 32 (2001): 446–62, and "Equal Protection and Same-Sex Marriage," *Journal of Social Philosophy* 35 (2004): 133–47; and a related argument in Nicholas Buccola, "Finding Room for Same-Sex Marriage: Toward a More Inclusive Understanding of a Cultural Institution," *Journal of Social Philosophy* 36 (2005): 331–43. On polygamy, see Cheshire Calhoun, "Who's Afraid of Polygamous Marriage? Lessons for Same-Sex Marriage Advocacy from the History of Polygamy," *San Diego Law Review* 42 (2005): 1023–42; and Jeremy Waldron, "Autonomy and Perfectionism in Raz's Morality of Freedom," *Southern California Law Review* 62 (1988–89): 1097–1152. I am indebted here to Brake, "Minimal Marriage." I take up these issues at greater length in the conclusion.
9. Paula L. Ettelbrick, "Since When Is Marriage a Path to Liberation?" *Outlook: National Gay and Lesbian Quarterly* 6 (Fall 1989): 9, 14–17.
10. Bedi, *Beyond Race*, 240.
11. Bella DePaulo, *Singlism: What It Is, Why It Matters, and How to Stop It* (Np: DoubleDoor Books, 2011).
12. Point made to me by Jeffrey Tulis; for discussion, see Mary Ann Case, "Why Evangelical Protestants Are Right When They Claim That State Recognition of Same-Sex Marriage Threatens Their Marriages and What the Law Should Do about It," working paper presented at Princeton University History Department, May 2013.
13. See, for an influential discussion, Martha Albertson Fineman, *The Autonomy Myth: A Theory of Dependency* (New York: New Press, 2004); Metz, *Untying the Knot*; Brake, *Minimizing Marriage*.
14. Metz, *Untying the Knot*, 43; Brake, *Minimizing Marriage*, 143; Bedi, *Beyond Race*, chap. 6.
15. See Rawls's discussion of "broadly based properties" as related to the good applied to persons, in *Theory of Justice*, sect. 66.
16. Fleming and McClain, *Ordered Liberty*, 190.
17. Bedi, *Beyond Race*, 208–51; Brake, *Minimizing Marriage*, 82.
18. Metz, *Untying the Knot*, 33.
19. Paul Taylor, executive vice president of Pew Research Center, talks about what we can learn about the state of marriage by looking at

who gets hitched, particularly when it comes to money and class. *Brian Lehrer Show*, WNYC, July 10, 2013.

20. See Klarman, *Closet to Altar*.

21. Lewis v. Harris, 188 NJ 415, at 458; 908 A.2d. 196 at 221. See Harry D. Krause and David D. Meyer, *Family Law in a Nutshell*, 5th ed. (St. Paul: Thompson/West, 2007).

22. Andrew J. Cherlin, "The Growing Diversity of Two-Parent Families: Challenges for Family Law," in *Marriage at the Crossroads: Law, Policy, and the Brave New World of Twenty-First-Century Families*, ed. Marsha Garrison and Elizabeth S. Scott (New York: Cambridge University Press, 2012), 295.

23. Robert E. Emery, Erin E. Horn, and Christopher R. Beam, "Marriage and Improved Well-Being: Using Twins to Parse the Correlation, Asking How Marriage Helps, and Wondering Why More People Don't Buy a Bargain," in Garrison and Scott, *Crossroads*, 137, citing *Child Trends*, 2009.

24. Henry Maine, *Ancient Law* (New York: Dutton, Republished Classics, 2013), chap. 9, 115.

25. Krause and Meyer, *Family Law*, 79.

26. Maynard v. Hill, 125 US 190 (1888); Krause and Meyer, *Family Law*, 79; see also In re Marriage of Walton, 28 Cal. App. 3d 108, 104 Cal. Rptr. 472, 476 (1972), in ibid., 80.

27. Goodridge v. Dept. of Public Health, 321.

28. https://globaljusticeinitiative.files.wordpress.com/2011/12/united-states-age-of-consent-table11.pdf.

29. Bix, *Family Law*, 135–69. See also Joanna L. Grossman and Lawrence M. Friedman, *Inside the Castle: Law and Family in 20th Century America* (Princeton: Princeton University Press, 2011), 209–13; Krause and Meyer, *Family Law*, 81–85.

30. Reported by Laura Petrecca, *USA Today*, March 11, 2010, http://usatoday30.usatoday.com/money/perfi/basics/2010–03–08-prenups08_CV_N.htm. Bix suggests that there are no reliable data on prenups, *Family Law*, 138. Also see Krause and Meyer, *Family Law*.

31. See Marty Blase, "Funny Wedding Vows, Wedding Vows Inspired by Dr. Seuss," http://weddings.about.com/od/yourwedding ceremony/a/SeussFunnyVows.htm.

32. See Stephanie Coontz, *Marriage, a History: How Love Conquered Marriage* (New York: Penguin, 2006).

33. *Meet the Press*, with David Gregory, May 6, 2012, http://www.nbcnews.com/id/47311900/ns/meet_the_press-transcripts/t/may-joe-biden-kelly-ayotte-diane-swonk-tom-brokaw-chuck-todd/#.VMWk7FoyCS0.

34. For a similar account, see Judge Walker's opinion in *Perry*, 111. See also Brenda Cossman, *Sexual Citizens: The Legal and Cultural Regulation of Sex and Belonging* (Stanford: Stanford University Press, 2007), and the notion of marriage as involving "self-disciplining." See also the insightful brief statement by Professor Eric Schwitzgebel, "Thoughts on Conjugal Love," June 4, 2003, on his website at the Philosophy Department, University of California, Riverside, http://www.faculty.ucr.edu /~eschwitz/SchwitzAbs/ConjugalLove.htm.

35. Goodridge v. Department of Public Health, 322.

36. Suzanne B. Goldberg, "Why Marriage?" in Garrison and Scott, *Crossroads*, 234.

37. Some, like John Witte, Jr., *From Sacrament to Contract: Marriage, Religion, and Law in the Western Tradition*, 2nd ed. (Louisville: John Knox Press, 2012), describe the current reality as "post-companionate" and focused on individual satisfaction.

38. Goodridge v. Department of Public Health, 322.

39. Ralph Wedgwood, "The Fundamental Argument for Same Sex Marriage," *Journal of Moral Philosophy* 8 (2011): 225–42. My discussion is much indebted to this important article.

40. Ibid., 232.

41. Schneider, "Channeling Function," 501.

42. I have benefited greatly from Jonathan Rauch's discussion in *Same-Sex Marriage*.

43. Robert E. Goodin, *On Settling* (Princeton: Princeton University Press, 2012), 40.

44. See ibid., 38–40.

45. John Stuart Mill, *On Liberty* (1869), http://www.bartleby.com /130/.

46. West, *Marriage*, 76.

47. See Mara Marin, "Care, Oppression, and Marriage," *Hypatia* 29, 2 (Spring 2014): 337–54.

48. Schwitzgebel, "Thoughts on Conjugal Love." Notice that Schwitzgebel nowhere insists on the need for coitus.

49. Eskridge, *Same-Sex Marriage*, 71.

50. Goodin, *Settling*, 39–44.

51. Cherlin, *Marriage-Go-Round*, 138.

52. Ibid., 26.

53. John Sides, "Americans Have Become More Opposed to Adultery. Why?" blogpost, July 27, 2011, *Monkey Cage*, http://themonkey cage.org/2011/07/27/americans-have-become-more-opposed-to -adultery-why/.

54. West, *Marriage,* 98.

55. Ibid., 76.

56. Reprinted in *Slate* magazine, http://www.slate.com/articles /news_and_politics/politics/2012/11/gay_marriage_votes_and_andrew _sullivan_his_landmark_1989_essay_making_a.single.html.

57. The percentage of American adults currently married declined from 72 percent in 1960 to 52 percent in 2008. But nearly all Americans get married at some point in their lives (the percentage of women "ever married" by ages 50–54 was 95 percent in 1975 and remained at that same level in 1990). See Grossman and Friedman, *Inside the Castle,* 53–54.

CHAPTER 5

1. I draw here upon William N. Eskridge, Jr., *The Case for Same-Sex Marriage: From Sexualized Liberty to Civilized Commitment* (New York: Free Press, 1996), 66–71. I have benefited a great deal from this book, and from Eskridge's other important work on this subject.

2. Schneider, "Channeling Function."

3. Ibid., 497–500.

4. Chambers, "What If?," 487, 488.

5. Ibid., 483, emphasis added.

6. Ibid., 453. The various legal incidents under one state's law are also usefully summarized in Baker v. State of Vermont (98–032); 170 Vt. 194 (1998).

7. See Eskridge's discussion in *Same-Sex Marriage,* 67–70.

8. Chambers, "What If?," 458–59, citing 29 U.S.C. sections 2611–54, 2612(a)(1)(C) (1994).

9. For a critical discussion, see Law Commission of Canada, *Beyond Conjugality: Recognizing and Supporting Close Personal Adult Relationships* (Ottawa: Law Commission of Canada, 2001): 52–57, http:// www.samesexmarriage.ca/docs/beyond_conjugality.pdf.

10. Some of this depends on whether the state has a "community property" regime, in which there is a presumption that property acquired during marriage is held jointly. Bix, *Family Law,* 159–64.

11. See ibid., 163–64.

12. Chambers, "What If?," 472–73.

13. Ibid., 472–75.

14. For a discussion and some recommendations, see Sara S. McLanahan and Irwin Garfinkle, "Fragile Families: Debates, Facts, Solutions," in Garrison and Scott, *Crossroads,* 142–69.

15. At least absent a pre- or postnuptial agreement. See http://www.nolo.com/legal-encyclopedia/debt-marriage-owe-spouse-debts-29572.html.

16. Bix. *Family Law*, 163.

17. Ibid., 59–60.

18. Ibid., 62–64; also see Michael H. vs. Gerald D., 491 US 110 (1989).

19. Chambers, "What If?," 463.

20. Ibid., 464.

21. Ibid., 468–69.

22. Bix, *Family Law*, 71, discussing Jacob v. Shultz-Jacob, 923 A2d. 473 (Pa. Super. 2007).

23. Ibid., 71–72, discussing A.A. v. B.B. OR 3d 561 (2007) (Court of Appeal of Ontario).

24. Again, see the useful general discussion in Bix, *Family Law*, 71–78.

25. A point made in discussion by Alan Patten.

26. Marvin v. Marvin 557 P.2d 106 (Cal. 1976).

27. Bix, *Family Law*, 52–53.

28. Ibid., 51. For a massive and very useful resource on this form of marriage, see Göran Lind, *Common Law Marriage: A Legal Institution for Cohabitation* (Oxford: Oxford University Press, 2008).

29. For an insightful exploration, see Robert D. Putnam, "E Pluribus Unum: Diversity and Community in the Twenty-First Century," 2006 Johan Skytte Prize Lecture, *Scandinavian Political Studies* 30, 2 (June 2007): 137–74.

30. On personal responsibility, see Roland Benabou and Jean Tirole, "Belief in a Just World and Redistributive Politics," *Quarterly Journal of Economics* 121, 2 (2006): 699–746.

31. William A. Galston, *Liberal Purposes: Goods, Virtues, and Diversity in the Liberal State* (New York: Cambridge University Press, 1991).

32. I lift this summary from Emery, Horn, and Beam, "Marriage and Improved Well-Being," 126. A general survey of the evidence is in Linda J. Waite and Maggie Gallagher, *The Case for Marriage: Why Married People are Happier, Healthier, and Better Off Financially* (New York: Broadway Books, 2000). The various benefits are summarized in Institute for American Values, *Why Marriage Matters: Thirty Conclusions from the Social Sciences*, 3rd ed. (New York: Institute for American Values, 2011).

33. On the importance of social context for marital happiness, see Kristen Schultz Lee and Hiroshi Ono, "Marriage, Cohabitation, and

Happiness: A Cross-National Analysis of 27 Countries," *Journal of Marriage and Family* 74 (October 2012): 953–72.

34. Alan P. Bell and Martin A. Weinberg, *Homosexualities: A Study in Diversity among Men and Women* (New York: Simon and Schuster, 1978); and see the sources cited and discussed in Eskridge, *Same-Sex Marriage*, 237nn87, 88.

35. See Emery, Horn, and Beam, "Marriage and Improved Well-being," 126–41.

36. Ibid., 126.

37. Offer, *Challenge of Affluence*, 339.

38. McLanahan and Garfinkel, "Fragile Families," 142; and see Rachel M. Shattuck and Rose M. Kreider, "Social and Economic Characteristics of Currently Unmarried Women with a Recent Birth: 2011," United States Census Bureau (May 2013), http://www.census.gov/prod /2013pubs/acs-21.pdf.

39. McLanahan and Garfinkel, "Fragile Families," 146–47.

40. Ibid., 148.

41. Ibid., 157, 152–53.

42. That, at least, is how I interpret ibid., 153–54.

43. Ibid., 148–49; McLanahan, "Diverging Destinies," 610–11; see also Sara McLanahan and Gary Sandefur, *Growing Up with a Single Parent: What Hurts, What Helps* (Cambridge, MA: Harvard University Press, 1994).

44. Overall, children raised by married parents are 44 percent more likely to go to college, according to W. Bradford Wilcox, "Marriage Makes Our Children Richer—Here's Why," *Atlantic Monthly* (October 2014), http://www.theatlantic.com/business/print/2013/10/marriage -makes-our-children-richer-heres-why/280930/. See also Richard V. Reeves, "How to Save Marriage in America," *Atlantic Monthly* (February 2014), http://www.theatlantic.com/business/print/2014/02/how-to -save-marriage-in-america/283732/.

45. Cutler, Glaesar, and Norberg, "Rise in Youth Suicides," 246, 248, 250, 254, 260, 265; also Scottye J. Cash, and Jeffrey A. Bridge, "Epidemiology of Youth Suicide and Suicidal Behavior," *Current Opinion in Pediatrics* 21, 5 (October 2009): 613–19.

46. William A. Galston, "What about the Children?" *Blueprint Magazine*, May 21, 2002, http://www.dlc.org/print2f98.html?contentid =250506.

47. See Barack Obama, *Dreams from My Father: A Story of Race and Inheritance* (New York: Broadway Books, 2004).

48. McLanahan and Garfinkel, "Diverging Destinies."

49.   The research concerning the many benefits of marriage has been usefully summarized by scholars associated with the Center for Marriage and Families at the Institute for American Values, which includes McLanahan, Cherlin, and Amato. Their "fundamental conclusions" are that, first, "children are most likely to thrive—economically, socially, and psychologically" in "intact, biological, married" families; second, "Marriage is an important public good, associated with a range of economic, health, educational, and safety benefits that help local, state, and federal governments serve the common good"; and, finally, "The benefits of marriage extend to poor, working-class, and minority communities, despite the fact that marriage has weakened in these communities in the last four decades." Institute for American Values, "Why Marriage Matters," Executive Summary, 5, http://www.americanvalues.org /catalog/pdfs/wmm3es.pdf.

50.   E.g., Emery, Horn, and Beam, "Marriage and Improved Well-Being," 136–39.

51.   On the marriage culture generally and its interaction with other factors, see Wilson, *Marriage Problem.*

52.   June Carbone and Naomi Cahn, "Red v. Blue Marriage," in Garrison and Scott, *Crossroads*, 13–14.

53.   Galston, "What about the Children?"; Martha C. Nussbaum, "Women in the Sixties," in *Reassessing the Sixties: Debating the Cultural and Political Legacy*, ed. Stephen Macedo (New York: Norton, 1997).

54.   Sara McLanahan, "Diverging Destinies: How Children Are Faring under the Second Demographic Transition," *Demography* 41, 4 (November 2004): 607–27.

55.   Ibid., 609–11. For a lucid overview and analysis, see June Carbone and Naomi Cahn, *Marriage Markets: How Inequality is Remaking the American Family* (New York: Oxford University Press, 2014).

56.   Carbone and Cahn, "Red v. Blue Marriages," 16–17.

57.   Andrew J. Cherlin, "American Marriage in the Early Twenty-First Century," *The Future of Children* 15, 2 (Fall 2005): 33–55, 38.

58.   Carbone and Cahn, "Red v. Blue Marriages," 10.

59.   Ibid., 15.

60.   Cited in James Q. Wilson, "Why We Don't Marry," *City Journal* (Winter 2002), http://www.city-journal.org/html/12_1_why_we.html.

61.   Ibid.

62.   See in particular Isabel V. Sawhill, *Generation Unbound: Drifting into Sex and Parenthood without Marriage* (Washington, DC: Brookings, 2014); and W. Bradford Wilcox et al., *Knot Yet: The Benefits and Costs of Delayed Marriage in America*, Report of the National Marriage Project,

University of Virginia, http://nationalmarriageproject.org/. See also
Amy L. Wax, "Engines of Inequality: Class, Race, and Family Structure," Faculty Scholarship Paper 205 (2008), http://scholarship.law
.upenn.edu/faculty_scholarship/205

63. See Sawhill, *Generation Unbound.*

64. Reeves, "How to Save Marriage."

65. On these profound changes, see Robert D. Putnam, *Our Kids:
The American Dream in Crisis* (New York: Simon and Schuster, 2015).

66. Reeves, "How to Save Marriage."

67. Ibid., 7, citing Kim Parker and Wendy Wang, *Parenthood: Roles
of Moms and Dads Converge as They Balance Work and Family* (Pew,
2013).

68. Reeves, "How to Save Marriage," 6, citing Putnam, "Requiem
for the American Dream? Unequal Opportunity in America," Aspen
Ideas Festival, June 29, 2012, Aspen, Colorado, http://www.aspenideas
.org/session/requiem-american-dream-unequal-opportunity-america.

69. See Putnam, *Our Kids.*

70. For some interesting reflections, see Katherine Franke, "The
Curious Relationship of Marriage and Freedom," in Garrison and Scott,
Crossroads, 87–104. See also Wilson, *Marriage Problem,* and "Why We
Don't Marry."

71. W. Bradford Wilcox and Elizabeth Williamson, "The Cultural
Contradictions of Mainline Family Ideology and Practice," in *American
Religions and the Family,* ed. Don S. Browning and David A. Clairmont
(New York: Columbia University Press, 2007), 50.

72. Rauch, *Same-Sex Marriage.*

73. Schneider, "Channeling Function," 503.

74. Ibid., 504.

75. As the Massachusetts Supreme Court pointed out in *Goodridge,*
946, a married couple need not "mingle their finances or actually depend on one another for support," nor "even see each other on a regular
basis." In contrast, it has been common for civil or domestic partnership
laws to pry more deeply into couples' personal lives, imposing conditions for receipt of benefits; New Jersey requires joint financial arrangements, and, with California, a common residence. Case, "Marriage
Licenses," 1773. Case puts it nicely: "Which is the greater restriction
on my ability freely to structure my life with my partner—the requirement that I must marry that partner and on rare occasions produce the
marriage license to third parties, or the requirement that we must reside
together, be sexually faithful to one another, comingle our finances . . .
provide to third parties the details of how we live our lives, as domestic

partnership ordinances . . . often require?" She concludes that "marriage today . . . has the potential to be far more flexible, liberatory, and egalitarian than most available alternatives," while allowing that "societal expectations and traditions" exert some additional constraints on married couples, Ibid., 1774; see also Mary Ann Case, "Couples and Coupling in the Public Sphere: A Comment on the Legal History of Litigating for Lesbian and Gay Rights," *Virginia Law Review* 79 (1993): 1643–94.

76. See Cherlin, *Marriage-Go-Round*; and Sawhill, *Generation Unbound*.

CHAPTER 6

1. Richard H. Thaler and Cass R. Sunstein, *Nudge: Improving Decisions about Health, Wealth, and Happiness*, rev. ed. (New York: Penguin, 2009), 217–18.

2. Ibid., 219–20.

3. Ibid., 222.

4. Ibid., 220–21.

5. Ibid., 225, 226.

6. Michael Kinsley, "Abolish Marriage," *Slate*, July, 2 2003, http://www.slate.com/articles/news_and_politics/readme/2003/07/abolish_marriage.html.

7. Evan Wolfson, *Why Marriage Matters: America, Equality, and Gay People's Right to Marry* (New York: Simon and Schuster, 2004), 17.

8. Thaler and Sunstein, *Nudge*, 226, citing Heather Mahar, "Why Are There So Few Prenuptial Agreements?" Olin Center for Law and Economics Report, Harvard University.

9. See Carol Sanger, "A Case for Civil Marriage," *Cardozo Law Review* 27 (January 2006): 1311–23.

10. Cathy Lynn Grossman, "Should Clergy Be Involved With Civil Marriage? 1 In 3 Americans Say No: Survey," Religion News Service, December 7, 2014, *HuffPost*, January 26, 2015, http://www.huffington post.com/2014/12/07/clergy-civil-marriage_n_6257774.html.

11. Thaler and Sunstein, *Nudge*, 218. Thaler and Sunstein "duck the question of whether civil unions can involve more than two people." Polygamy, as we shall see in chapter 7, raises a variety of interesting problems. Traditionally, if a man or woman entered into a bigamous or polygamous second marriage, recognized in the eyes of their church, that would not protect them from the civil consequences, at least in those jurisdictions with common law marriage. In that sense, and in those states at least, there has been no "religious exemption" to the laws

banning polygamy. But the situation is now in flux, though not for reasons that have anything to do with same sex marriage, as we will see in the next chapter.

12. Grossman, "Should Clergy Be Involved."

13. Mary Ann Case, "Why Evangelical Protestants Are Right When They Claim That State Recognition of Same-Sex Marriage Threatens Their Marriages and What the Law Should Do about It," working paper, presented at Princeton University History Department, May 2013.

14. Marriage Protest of Lucy Stone and Henry B. Blackwell, May 1, 1855, http://www.historyisaweapon.com/defcon1/stoneblack wellmarriageprotest.html; *Women's Rights in the United States: A Comprehensive Encyclopedia of Issues, Events, and People*, vol. 1, ed. Tiffany K. Wayne (Santa Barbara: ABC/Clio, 2015), 271–72, http://www.seattle lwv.org/files/ celebrating_women's_history2001.pdf.

15. I draw on Case, "Marriage Licenses," 1780.

16. Nan D. Hunter, "Marrriage, Law, and Gender: A Feminist Inquiry," *Law & Sexuality* 1 (1991): 12.

17. Audrey Bilger, "Marriage Equality Is a Feminist Issue," *Ms. Magazine Blog*, December 11, 2012, http://msmagazine.com/blog/2012 /12/11/marriage-equality-is-a-feminist-issue/.

18. See the excellent discussion in Anne-Marie Slaughter, "Why Women Still Can't Have It All," *Atlantic Monthly* (July/August 2012), http://www.theatlantic.com/magazine/archive/2012/07/why-women -still-cant-have-it-all/309020/.

19. Reprinted in "Celebrating Women's History" (Seattle, 2001), http://www.seattlelwv.org/files/celebrating_women's_history2001.pdf, which reports that "the contract has been printed in textbooks for schools of sociology and law and in various periodicals," including *Ms. Magazine*, which published it in its spring 2008 issue. See http://www.msmagazine .com/marriagecontract/.

20. "Celebrating Women's History," S-15.

21. Schwitzgebel, "Thoughts on Conjugal Love."

22. See Brian Bix, "Bargaining in the Shadow of Love: The Enforcement of Premarital Agreements and How We Think about Marriage," *William & Mary Law Review* 40 (1998): 153–54; and Brian Bix, "Domestic Agreements," *Hofstra Law Review* 35, 4 (2007): 1765, http://scholarlycommons.law.hofstra.edu/hlr/vol35/iss4/5.

23. Grossman and Friedman, *Inside the Castle*, 209–13. Those who feel they have been burned by an unhappy first marriage may be unwilling to enter into a second marriage except with the reassurance of a prenuptial agreement. Krause and Meyer, *Family Law*, 81–85.

24. Bix, *Family Law*, 143–50.

25. Laurie Israel, "Ten Things I Hate about Prenuptial Agreements," http://www.ivkdlaw.com/the-firm/our-articles/prenuptial
-agreements-and-lawyering/ten-things-i-hate-about-prenuptial
-agreements/. See also Laurie Israel, "Bad for Marital Health," http://
www.nytimes.com/roomfordebate/2013/03/21/the-power-of-the
-prenup/prenups-can-be-bad-for-marital-health. The "stealth prenups"
described by another attorney seem an especially egregious example of
spousal deception and self-protection. See Thomas J. Handler, "Do Your
Research, and Be Stealthy," http://www.nytimes.com/roomfordebate
/2013/03/21/the-power-of-the-prenup/a-stealthy-prenup-can-help
-protect-assets.

26. W. Bradford Wilcox, "If You Want a Prenup, You Don't Want
Marriage," http://www.nytimes.com/roomfordebate/2013/03/21/the
-power-of-the-prenup/if-you-want-a-prenup-you-dont-want-marriage.
Also see http://nationalmarriageproject.org/ and http://twentysome
thingmarriage.org/in-brief//.

27. Israel, "Ten Things." See also Laurie Israel, "Bad for Marital
Health," http://www.nytimes.com/roomfordebate/2013/03/21/the
-power-of-the-prenup/prenups-can-be-bad-for-marital-health.

28. Sanger, "For Civil Marriage."

29. Fred Hirsch, *The Social Limits to Growth* (London: Routledge &
Kegan Paul, 1978), 88.

30. Elizabeth Anderson, *Value in Ethics and Economics* (Cambridge,
MA: Harvard University Press, 1993), 157.

31. Ibid.

32. Schwitzgebel, "Thoughts on Conjugal Love."

33. William N. Eskridge, *Equality Practice: Civil Unions and the
Future of Gay Rights* (New York: Routledge, 2002), 210–29.

34. Wilson, *Marriage Problem*; Cherlin, *Marriage-Go-Round*;
Galston, "What about the Children?"; Offer, *Challenge of Affluence*,
chaps. 13 and 14.

35. My account is indebted to Cherlin, *Marriage-Go-Round*, 13.
For Louisiana, see http://new.dhh.louisiana.gov/index.cfm/page/695.

36. Governor Mike Huckabee advocated the reform in Arkansas.
See Cherlin, *Marriage-Go-Round*.

37. Elizabeth S. Scott, "Marital Commitment and the Legal Regulation of Divorce," in *The Law and Economics of Marriage and Divorce*,
ed. Antony W. Dnes and Robert Rowtham (Cambridge: Cambridge
University Press, 2010), 45.

38. Scott, "Marital Commitment," 46; and see the parallel argument
in Offer, *Challenge of Affluence*, chap. 13.

39. Scott, "Marital Commitment," 48–51.

40. Andre J. Cherlin, *Marriage-Go-Round*, chap. 8.

41. See Ron Haskins, "Marriage, Parenthood, and Public Policy," *National Journal* (Spring 2014): 64–66.

42. Martha Albertson Fineman, *The Autonomy Myth: A Theory of Dependency* (New York: New Press, 2004): 284–91, and passim; Maxine Eichner, *The Supportive State: Families, Government, and America's Political Ideals* (New York: Oxford University Press, 2010), chaps. 3 and 4.

43. Elizabeth Brake, "Minimal Marriage: What Political Liberalism Implies for Marriage Law," *Ethics* 120 (January 2010): 329n87.

44. Ibid., 311.

45. Ibid., 311–12.

46. Ibid.

47. See McClain, *The Place of Families*, and others.

48. Metz, *Untying the Knot*, 9.

49. Ibid., 7, 9, 130.

50. Ibid., 135, 13.

51. Rich Miller, "Is Everybody Single? More than Half the U.S. Now, Up from 37% in '76," *Bloomberg*, September 9, 2014, http://www.bloomberg.com/news/2014-09-09/single-americans-now-comprise-more-than-half-the-u-s-population.html.

52. Law Commission of Canada, *Beyond Conjugality: Recognizing and Supporting Close Personal Adult Relationships* (Ottawa: Law Commission of Canada, 2001), http://www.samesexmarriage.ca/docs/beyond_conjugality.pdf.

53. West, *Marriage, Sexuality, and Gender*, 138, 202.

54. Metz, *Untying the Knot*, 141–43.

55. Or for related purposes, such as preventing serious unfairness or exploitation.

56. Eskridge, *Equality Practice*, 227–29.

57. Finnis, "Profound Injustice of Judge Posner"; Andrew Sullivan, "Here Comes the Groom," *New Republic*, August 28, 1989, http://www.newrepublic.com/article/79054/here-comes-the-groom; Rauch, *Same-Sex Marriage*.

58. Case, "Marriage Licenses," 1783.

59. Thanks to Andy Koppelman and Rob Katz for emphasizing this point.

60. See Marion Leturcq, "Competing Marital Contracts? The Marriage after Civil Union in France," June 2011, https://ideas.repec.org/f/ple448.html or https://halshs.archives-ouvertes.fr/halshs-00655585/document.

61. Sanger, "For Civil Marriage."

CHAPTER 7

1. Chambers, "Polygamy and Same-Sex Marriage," 69, 76–77.

2. J. Scalia dissent in *Lawrence*, 2490; see Romer v. Evans, 1644, 1648–51. See also *Goodridge*, 2495.

3. Ryan T. Anderson, "North Carolina, Biden, and Same-Sex Marriage," *National Review*, May 8, 2012. http://m.nationalreview.com /corner/299394/north-carolina-biden-and-same-sex-marriage-ryan-t -anderson/page/0/1.

4. Lawrence v. Texas, 2480, referring to the liberty protected by the Fourteenth Amendment. I benefit here from Samantha Slark, "Are Anti-Polygamy Laws an Unconstitutional Infringement on the Liberty Interests of Consenting Adults?" *Journal of Law and Family Studies* 6 (2004): 451–60 generally, and 457.

5. 539 U.S., 571.

6. Barbara Bennett Woodhouse, "'It All Depends on What You Mean by Home': Toward a Communitarian Theory of the 'Nontraditional' Family," *Utah Law Review* (1996): 570.

7. Chambers, "What If?," 491; and see David L. Chambers, "Polygamy and Same-Sex Marriage," *Hofstra Law Review* 26 (1997): 81–83.

8. March, "Is There a Right to Polygamy?," 256.

9. Chambers, "Polygamy and Same-Sex Marriage," 60; see also Bedi, *Beyond Race*.

10. Numerous accounts confirm the rarity of polyandry. See Joseph Henrich, Affidavit no. 1, Sworn July 15, 2010, no. S-097767, Vancouver Registry, in the Supreme Court of British Columbia, in the Matter of The Constitutional Question Act, R.S.B.C. 1996, C.68, etc., http:// stoppolygamy.com/court-documents-2/affadavits-witnesses/dr-joseph -henrichs-affidavit-1/. This contains a comprehensive overview of the evidence, also surveyed in Joseph Henrich, Robert Boyd, and Peter J. Richerson, "The Puzzle of Monogamous Marriage," *Philosophical Transactions of the Royal Society B* 376, 1589 (March 2012): 657–69, http://rstb.royalsocietypublishing.org/content/367/1589/657.abstract; Nicholas Bala, "Why Canada's Prohibition of Polygamy Is Constitutionally Valid and Sound Social Policy," *Canadian Journal of Family Law* 25 (2009): 182: "polygyny is the only form of polygamy that is widely practiced." An invaluable source is the thorough account of the expert testimony offered in the Reference Case on polygamy in British Columbia, *Reference re: Section 293 of the Criminal Code of Canada*, 2011 BCSC 1588; and see Craig Jones, *A Cruel Arithmetic: Inside the*

Case against Polygamy (Toronto: Irwin Law, 2012). Even Judith Stacey, who advocates acceptance and recognition of a wide range of family forms, says "modern polyandry is scarcely thinkable." *Unhitched: Love, Marriage, and Family Values from West Hollywood to Western China* (New York: New York University Press, 2012), 150.

11. Henrich, Affidavit no. 1, 60.

12. Miriam Koktvedgaard Zeitzen, *Polygamy: A Cross-Cultural Analysis* (Oxford: Berg, 2008), 111 and passim. "Family loyalty is essential in keeping the family's property united and ensuring its economic survival."

13. Ibid., 117, 120.

14. The example is from a documentary, discussing an offshoot of the Ni-See tribal minority near Szechuan, China, which could involve four brothers marrying two sisters. See the documentary, http://www.youtube.com/watch?v=FHR9F4G0kvc, at 17 minutes.

15. Maura I. Strassberg, "The Challenge of Post-Modern Polygamy: Considering Polyamory," *Capital University Law Review* 31 (2003): 439.

16. Maura Strassberg, "The Crime of Polygamy," *Temple Political and Civil Rights Law Review* 12 (Spring 2003): 355.

17. Jaime M. Gher, "Polygamy and Same-Sex Marriage—Allies or Adversaries within the Same-Sex Marriage Movement," *William & Mary Journal of Women & Law* 14 (2008): 559–603, http://scholarship.law.wm.edu/wmjowl/vol14/iss3/4Gher; Strassberg, "Considering Polyamory."

18. See http://www.beyondmarriage.org/signatories.html.

19. United States Census Bureau, "Census Bureau Reports 55 Percent Have Married One Time," News Release, May 18, 2011, http://www.census.gov/newsroom/releases/archives/marital_status_living_arrangements/cb11–90.html.

20. Henrich, Affidavit no. 1, discussed below; Henrich's evidence and my discussion here are consistent with the claims advanced in Edward Westermarck's *The History of Marriage* (London: Macmillan, 1891), still widely cited and useful.

21. See James Fenske, "African Polygamy: Past and Present," CSAE [Centre for the Study of African Economies] Working Paper WPS/2012–20, 17, fig. 1, http://www.csae.ox.ac.uk/workingpapers/pdfs/csae-wps-2012–20.pdf.

22. Imani Jaafar-Mohammad and Charlie Lehmann, "Women's Rights in Islam Regarding Marriage and Divorce," *William Mitchell Journal of Law & Practice*, 4, 3 (April 11, 2011), http://wmlawandpractice.com/2011/04/11/women's-rights-in-islam-regarding-marriage-and-divorce/.

23. Quotation from Keith McMahon, "The Institution of Polygamy in the Chinese Imperial Palace," *Journal of Asian Studies* 72 (November 2013): 924. An authoritative source is Westermarck's *The History of Marriage*. See also Henrich, Affidavit no. 1.

24. Bala, "Prohibition of Polygamy," 179.

25. See E. E. Evans-Pritchard, *Kinship and Marriage among the Nuer* (Oxford: Clarendon Press, 1990).

26. Qi Wang, "Sex, Money, Social Status—Chinese Men and Women in the Whirlwind of Modernization and Market Economy," *NIAS Nytt* (Nordic Institute of Asia Studies) (June 2008): 12–14, http://nias.ku.dk/sites/default/files/files/NIASnytt_1_08_web.pdf; James Palmer, "Kept Women: Mistresses Are Big Business in China, Where No Official Is a Real Man without His Own *Ernai*. What's in It for the Girls?," *Aeon Magazine*, October 10, 2013, http://aeon.co /magazine/living-together/why-young-women-in-rural-china-become -the-mistresses-of-wealthy-older-men/.

27. For an exploration, see Walter Scheidel, "Monogamy and Polygyny in Greece, Rome, and World History," Princeton/Stanford Working Papers in Classics, June 2008, http://www.princeton.edu /~pswpc/pdfs/scheidel/060807.pdf.

28. See Douglas J. Falen, "Polygyny and Christian Marriage in Africa: The Case of Benin," *African Studies Review* 51, 2 (September 2008): 51–75. International human rights treaties have established the Committee on the Eradication of Discrimination against Women (CEDAW) and the Human Rights Committee (HRC), both of which describe polygamy as a form of discrimination against women; note that in no case does "customary marriage" in Africa sanction polyandry. General Comment No. 28, of the Human Rights Committee, adopted March 29, 2000, "The equality of rights between men and women," holds that "equality of treatment with regard to the right to marry implies that polygamy is incompatible with this principle. Polygamy violates the dignity of women. It is an inadmissible discrimination against women. Consequently, it should be definitely abolished wherever it continues to exist." See the official websites of each: http://www.un.org /womenwatch/daw/cedaw/; http://tbinternet.ohchr.org/Treaties/ CCPR/Shared%20Documents/1_Global/CCPR_C_21_Rev-1_Add -10_6619_E.pdf.

29. Akiko Hashimoto and Charlotte Ikels, "Filial Piety in Changing Asian Societies," *The Cambridge Handbook of Age and Ageing*, ed. Malcolm L. Johnson (Cambridge: Cambridge University Press, 2005), 440.

30. http://bokakhat.gov.in/pdf/The_hindu_marriage_act.pdf. For a general account, see the BC Reference Case.

31. Zeitzen, *Polygamy*, 166–67; Rose McDermott, "Polygamy: More Common than You Think," *Wall Street Journal*, April 1, 2011, http://online.wsj.com/article/SB1000142405274870380630457623455159632690.html.

32. See Stacey, *Unhitched*, 121; Adrien Katherine Wing, "Polygamy from Southern Africa to Black Britannia to Black America: Global Critical Race Feminism as Legal Reform for the Twenty-first Century," *Journal of Contemporary Legal Issues* 11 (2001): 853.

33. The Utah antibigamy statute reads in part that a "person is guilty of bigamy when, knowing he has a husband or wife or knowing the other person has a husband or wife, the person purports to marry another person or cohabits with another person." Utah Code Ann. § 76–7-101(1) (2013). "Cohabitation is not typically a requisite element of the offense. Merely entering into a second marriage with knowledge that one is currently married to another living person will support an indictment for polygamy." "Under certain statutes it is not considered polygamous for an individual to remarry after a certain period of time has elapsed during which the former spouse was absent and thought to be dead. For example, California exempts from its law "any person by reason of any former marriage whose husband or wife by such marriage has been absent for five successive years without being known to such person within that time to be living." Cal. Pen. Code § 282. See http://legal-dictionary.thefreedictionary.com/Bigamy+(in+Civil+Law).

34. See the important study by Hendrik Hartog, *Man and Wife in America: A History* (Cambridge, MA: Harvard University Press, 2002).

35. Kody Brown et al., *Becoming Sister Wives: The Story of an Unconventional Marriage* (New York: Gallery Books, 2012); Joe Darger et al., *Love Times Three: Our True Story of a Polygamous Marriage* (New York: HarperOne, 2011).

36. John Rawls, *Political Liberalism* (New York: Columbia University Press, 1993), 331–34.

37. Mark E. Brandon, *States of Union: Family and Change in the American Constitutional Order* (Lawrence: University Press of Kansas, 2013), 195; Sally Barringer Gordon, *The Mormon Question: Polygamy and Constitutional Conflict in Nineteenth-Century America* (Chapel Hill: University of North Carolina Press, 2002), 22. I draw in this paragraph from 20–29.

38. Revelation received at Nauvoo, Illinois, on July 12, 1843, in Marquardt, *The Joseph Smith Revelations*, 323–28, quoted in Brandon, *States of Union*, 195.

39. Brandon, *States of Union*, 198.

40.   Jessie L. Embry, *Mormon Polygamous Families: Life in the Principle* (Draper, UT: Greg Kofford Books, 2008), 34; see also Chambers, "Polygamy," 62.

41.   See the illuminating account in Brandon, *States of Union*, 191–94, 198.

42.   Klaus J. Hansen, *Mormonism and the American Experience* (Chicago: University of Chicago Press, 1981); see also Chambers, "Polygamy."

43.   Strassberg, "Crime of Polygamy," 361.

44.   Maura I. Strassberg, "Distinctions of Form or Substance: Monogamy, Polygamy and Same Sex Marriage," *North Carolina Law Review* 75 (1997): 1579–80; see also Strassberg, "Crime of Polygamy," 359.

45.   "Plural Marriage and Families in Early Utah," LDS.org, https://www.lds.org/topics/plural-marriage-and-families-in-early-utah ?lang=eng.

46.   Gordon, *Mormon Question*, 173. Elsewhere he said that women's "counsel and wisdom (although there are many good women) don't weigh as much as a fly turd. . . . It is not a woman's place to counsel her husband." Brandon, *States of Union*, quoting Embry, *Polygamous Families*, 45–49.

47.   Terryl L. Givens, *Wrestling the Angel* (New York: Oxford University Press, 2015), 187.

48.   See Chambers, "Polygamy," 66, discussing Embry, *Polygamous Families*, 176–77.

49.   Chambers, "Polygamy," 66–67, discussing Gustave O. Larson, "The 'Americanization' of Utah for Statehood," 67–69, 133, 225–26; and Embry, *Polygamous Families*, 134–40, 157–61. It would be a mistake to discount women's agency or to regard them simply as hapless pawns in all cases.

50.   "Plural Marriage and Families in Early Utah," n6, https://www .lds.org/topics/plural-marriage-and-families-in-early-utah?lang=eng, citing L. L. Bean and G. P. Mineau, "The Polygyny-Fertility Hypothesis: A Re-evaluation," *Population Studies* 40 (1986): 67–81; Zeitzen, *Polygamy*, 62–63.

51.   Embry, *Polygamous Families*, 39–45; see also Brandon, *States of Union*, 201.

52.   Orson Pratt offered this justification in 1952; see Brandon, *States of Union*, 201. It is offered nowadays on behalf of plural marriage in Islam.

53.   Embry, *Polygamous Families*, 45–47; see also Brandon, *States of Union*, 201.

54.   Strassberg, "Crime of Polygamy," 363. None of this, I should emphasize, is meant to justify the persecutions that were inflicted on

members of the LDS Church in the nineteenth century, which included the murder of Joseph Smith and the Extermination order issued by Missouri governor Lilburn Boggs in 1838, Hansen, *Mormonism*, 138. See http://en.wikipedia.org/wiki/Missouri_Executive_Order_44.

55. The act held in part: "Be it enacted by the Senate and House of Representatives of the United States of America in Congress assembled, That every person having a husband or wife living, who shall marry any other person, whether married or single, in a Territory of the United States, or other place over which the United States have exclusive jurisdiction, shall, except in the cases specified in the proviso to this section, be adjudged guilty of bigamy, and, upon conviction thereof, shall be punished by a fine not exceeding five hundred dollars, and by imprisonment for a term not exceeding five years" (37th Congress. sess. II. chap. 126). See also Slark, "Anti-Polygamy Laws," 452–55.

56. *Great Debates in American History: Civil Rights*, part 2, ed. Marion Mills Miller (Current Literature Publishing, 1913); 443, http://books.google.com/books/about/Great_Debates_in_American_History_Civil.html?id=3hYOAAAAIAAJ. Also see Chambers, "Polygamy," 64.

57. Reynolds v. United States, 98 US 145 (1878), 164.

58. Ibid.

59. "The only question which remains is, whether those who make polygamy a part of their religion are excepted from the operation of the statute. If they are, then those who do not make polygamy a part of their religious belief may be found guilty and punished, while those who do, must be acquitted and go free." Ibid., 166. The Court further insisted that neither human sacrifice nor the Indian practice of sutee, or widow burning, ought to be exempted from criminal prohibitions on grounds of religious liberty. "To permit this would be to make the professed doctrines of religious belief superior to the law of the land, and in effect to permit every citizen to become a law unto himself. Government could exist only in name under such circumstances." Ibid., 167.

60. Cleveland v. United States, 329 US 14 (1946), 19.

61. Ibid., 26.

62. Potter v. Murray City 760 F.2d 1065 (10th Cir. 1985). Thanks to Paul Baumgardner for comments.

63. *Reynolds*, 165.

64. Kody Brown et al., v. Jeffrey R. Buhman, Case 2:11-cv-00652-CW-BCW Document 78 Filed 12/13/13, Opinion of Judge Clark Waddoups, 14, http://libertasutah.org/drop/bigamy.pdf.

65. Ibid., 11, 21.

66. From the LDS website, "Plural Marriage and Families in Early Utah," http://www.lds.org/topics/plural-marriage-and-families-in-early -utah?lang=eng . See also Brown v. Buhman, 9–10n7; and Nancy Rosenblum, "Democratic Sex," in *Sex, Preference, and Family: Essays on Law and Nature*, ed. David M. Estlund and Martha C. Nussbaum (New York: Oxford University Press, 1997), 77.

67. Gordon, *The Mormon Question*, 236

68. In response to poll questions, only 11 percent of Americans say polygamy is morally acceptable, but a quarter of people in Utah say it is not morally wrong, with another 15 percent saying they are unsure. See http://libertasutah.org/survey/public-opinion-poll-utah-voters-opine -on-the-nsa-alcohol-policy-and-polygamy/; http://www.economist .com/blogs/democracyinamerica/2011/05/family_values_0. See also Givens, *Wrestling the Angel*, 279–90.

69. See Strassberg, "Considering Polyamory." On the United States, see Bala, "Prohibition of Polygamy," quoting M. Kopala, "Bountiful Is a Detour on the Road to Same-Sex Marriage," *Ottawa Citizen*, January 29, 2005, B6. On the Hmong, see Zeitzen, *Polygamy*, 166–67.

70. See Neil J. Young, "Short Creek's Long Legacy: How a Failed 1953 Raid Shaped the Relationship between Polygamists and the Government, *Slate*, April 16 2008, http://www.slate.com/articles/life/faith based/2008/04/short_creeks_long_legacy.single.html.

71. Jones, *Cruel Arithmetic*, 71–72.

72. Martha Sonntag Bradley, "A Repeat of History," in *Modern Polygamy in the United States*, ed. Cardell K. Jacobson and Lara Burton (New York: Oxford University Press, 2010), 31, 33.

73. Quoted in Arkes, *First Things* Symposium.

74. State of Utah v. Green, 99 P.3d 820 (Utah 2004).

75. State v. Holm 137 P.3d 726 (Utah 2006), par. 2.

76. See Wade Goodwyn, Howard Berkes, and Amy Walters, "Warren Jeffs and the FLDS," *NPR*, May 3, 2005, http://www.npr.org /templates/story/story.php?storyId=4629320.

77. Young, "Short Creek's Legacy."

78. Bradley, "Repeat," 28.

79. Young, "Short Creek's Legacy." See also Martha Sonntag Bradley, *Kidnapped from That Land: The Government Raids on the Short Creek Polygamists* (Salt Lake City: University of Utah Press, 1993); and Carolyn Jessop, *Escape* (New York: Broadway Books, 2007).

80. Matthew Waller, "Jessop Given Maximum: 10 Years in Prison, $10,000 Fine," *San Angelo Standard-Times*, November 8, 2011, http:// www.gosanangelo.com/news/2011/nov/08/jessop-performed-15-under age-marriage-ceremonies/.

81.   Sam Brower, *Prophet's Prey: My Seven-Year Investigation into Warren Jeffs and the Fundamentalist Church of Latter-Day Saints* (New York: Bloomsbury, 2012), 277–80.

82.   Chambers, "Polygamy and Same-Sex Marriage," 60.

CHAPTER 8

1.   Andrew Sullivan, "Three's a Crowd," *New Republic*, June 17, 1996, 10; see also Jonathan Rauch, "Marrying Somebody," in Andrew Sullivan, *Same-Sex Marriage: Pro and Con* (New York: Vintage, 2004), 285, 286. Justice Scalia has referred, perhaps facetiously, to those with "polygamous 'orientations'"; see Romer v. Evans, 648.

2.   Justice Bauman, Reference Case, par. 1258.

3.   Chambers, "Polygamy," 79.

4.   See City of Boerne v. Flores, 521 US 507 (1997).

5.   Georg Simmel, "The Number of Members as Determining the Sociological Form of the Group. I," *American Journal of Sociology* 8, 1 (July 1902): 1–46.

6.   George Gilder says, "Monogamy is egalitarianism in the realm of love." *Men and Marriage*, 58.

7.   Andrew F. March, "Is There a Right to Polygamy? Marriage, Equality and Subsidizing Families in Liberal Public Justification," *Journal of Moral Philosophy* 8 (2011): 246–72.

8.   Henrich, Affidavit no. 1, 59; my emphasis.

9.   Chambers, "Polygamy," 82–83.

10.   It would be overly hasty to answer, "no one." See the brief discussion of Finnis's remarks on "opportunistic lesbianism" in the conclusion.

11.   The language of the Canadian criminal statute is indeed sweeping. Reference Case, par. 17, sect. 293, provides:

> 293(1) Everyone who
> (a) practises or enters into or in any manner agrees or consents to practise or enter into
> (i) any form of polygamy, or
> (ii) any kind of conjugal union with more than one person at the same time,
> whether or not it is by law recognized as a binding form of marriage; or
> (b) celebrates, assists or is a party to a rite, ceremony, contract or consent that purports to sanction a relationship mentioned in subparagraph (a)(i) or (ii),

is guilty of an indictable offence and liable to imprisonment for a term not exceeding five years.

(2) Where an accused is charged with an offence under this section, no averment or proof of the method by which the alleged relationship was entered into, agreed to or consented to is necessary in the indictment or upon the trial of the accused, nor is it necessary on the trial to prove that the persons who are alleged to have entered into the relationship had or intended to have sexual intercourse.

12.   *Reference re: Section 293 of the Criminal Code of Canada*, 2011 BCSC 1588. For a good discussion, see Nicholas Bala, "Polygamy in Canada: Justifiably Not Tolerated," *Jurist*—Forum, December 3, 2011, http://jurist.org/forum/2011/12/nicholas-bala-canada-polygamy.php.

13.   http://www.youtube.com/watch?v=UixdcBdOjNM.

14.   Daphne Bramham, *The Secret Lives of Saints: Child Brides and Lost Boys in Canada's Polygamous Mormon Sect* (Toronto: Vintage Canada, 2008), 351–53; "B.C. Supreme Court Rules Polygamy Ban Is Constitutional, but Flawed," *Postmedia News*, November 23, 2011, http://news.nationalpost.com/2011/11/23/b-c-supreme-court-rules -polygamy-law-is-constitutional/.

15.   Quoted in Brian Hutchinson, "Charges Laid against Bountiful Leader Winston Blackmore after Judge Rules Charter Should Not Protect Polygamists," *National Post*, August 14, 2014, http://news.national post.com/2014/08/14/na0815-polygamy/#__federated=1.

16.   Reference Case, par. 6.

17.   Ibid., par. 181.

18.   Zeitzen, *Polygamy*, 128.

19.   "Both fundamentalist Mormons and polyamorists argue that having several partners requires people to be more loving and generous and to learn to overcome jealousy." Belinda Luscombe, "I Do, I Do, I Do, I Do," *Time Magazine*, August 6, 2012, http://www.time.com/time /magazine/article/0,9171,2120495,00.html.

20.   See Rose McDermott, "Polygamy: More Common than You Think," *Wall Street Journal*, April 1, 2011, http://online.wsj.com/article /SB10001424052748703806304576234551596322690.html; the quoted paragraph is similar to paragraph 154 of "Expert Report Prepared for the Attorney General of Canada," in the British Columbia Reference Case, submitted July 15, 2010, https://stoppolygamyincanada .files.wordpress.com/2011/04/mcdermott-report.pdf.

21.   Tracy, *Secret Story*, 124.

22.   Gary Becker, "Is There a Case for Legalizing Polygamy?" *Becker-Posner blog*, October 22, 2006, http://www.becker-posner-blog.com /2006/10/is-there-a-case-for-legalizing-polygamy-becker.html. See also Robert Wright, *The Moral Animal*, 97–101.

23.   Henrich, Boyd, and Richerson, "The Puzzle of Monogamous Marriage," 660–61. See also Bauman, Reference Case, par. 10: "Early marriage for girls is common, frequently to significantly older men. The resultant early sexual activity, pregnancies and childbirth have negative health implications for girls, and also significantly limit their socio-economic development. Shortened inter-birth intervals pose a heightened risk of various problems for both mother and child." See also McDermott, "Expert Report," pars. 25–31.

24.   Strassberg, "Crime of Polygamy," 389, 384. See also the excellent collection of research papers, Angela Campbell et al., *Polygamy in Canada: Legal and Social Implications for Women and Children: A Collection of Policy Research Reports*, Alberta Civil Liberties Research Centre (Ottawa: Status of Women Canada, 2005), http://www.crilf.ca /Documents/Polygamy%20in%20Canada%20-%20Nov%202005.pdf; see especially "Separate and Unequal: The Women and Children of Polygamy," by Alberta Civil Liberties Research Centre, principal authors Melissa Luhtanen, Linda McKay-Panos, and Brian Seaman.

25.   Bauman, Reference Case, par. 8: "Women in polygamous relationships . . . tend to have less autonomy, and report higher rates of marital dissatisfaction and lower levels of self-esteem. They also fare worse economically, as resources may be inequitably divided or simply insufficient."

26.   Strassberg, "Crime of Polygamy," 393.

27.   McDermott, "Expert Report," pars. 25–28, 96, 98, 101, 106, 116, 121, 137–58.

28.   Bauman, Reference Case, par. 8: "Women in polygamous relationships are at an elevated risk of physical and psychological harm. They face higher rates of domestic violence and abuse, including sexual abuse. Competition for material and emotional access to a shared husband can lead to fractious co-wife relationships. These factors contribute to the higher rates of depressive disorders and other mental health issues that women in polygamous relationships face."

29.   Zeitzen, *Polygamy*, 131.

30.   Gregg Strauss, "Is Polygamy Inherently Unequal?" *Ethics* 122 (April 2012): 516–44.

31.   Strauss, "Polygamy," 527–29.

32.   Thom Brooks, "The Problem with Polygamy," *Philosophical Topics* 37, 2 (2009): 109–22, sec. 5. See also Strauss, "Polygamy," n23.

33.   4:129; quoted in Bala, "Polygamy Prohibition," 179. A variety of translations can be found on the website Islam Awakened, including this which it says is literal: "And never will you be able to deal justly between [the] women even if you desired, but (do) not incline (with) all the inclination and leave her (the other) like the suspended one. And if you reconcile and fear (Allah) then indeed, Allah is Oft-Forgiving, Most Merciful"; see http://www.islamawakened.com/quran/4/129/.

34.   See Convention on the Elimination of All Forms of Discrimination against Women (CEDAW), which calls on states to "eliminate all forms of discrimination against women with a view to achieving women's de jure and de facto equality with men in the enjoyment of their human rights and fundamental freedoms," General Recommendation 25, article 4, par. 1, of the Convention (temporary special measures), UN CEDAWOR, 30th Sess., UN Doc. HRI/GEN/1/Rev. 7 (2004), 282, par. 4; see http://www.un.org/womenwatch/daw/cedaw/.

35.   Bala, "Polygamy Prohibition," 190. Bauman, Reference Case, par. 13: "Polygamy has negative impacts on society flowing from the high fertility rates, large family size and poverty associated with the practice. It generates a class of largely poor, unmarried men who are statistically predisposed to violence and other anti-social behaviour. Polygamy also institutionalizes gender inequality. Patriarchal hierarchy and authoritarian control are common features of polygamous communities. Individuals in polygynous societies tend to have fewer civil liberties than their counterparts in societies which prohibit the practice."

36.   Bauman, Reference Case, par. 9.

37.   Henrich, Boyd, and Richerson, "Puzzle of Monogamous Marriage," 661, 662; and Zeitzen, *Polygamy*, 89–107.

38.   See Henrich, Affidavit no. 1; and Henrich, Boyd, and Richerson, "Puzzle of Monogamous Marriage."

39.   Robert H. Frank, "Polygamy and the Marriage Market: Who Would Have the Upper Hand?" *New York Times*, March 16, 2006, http://www.nytimes.com/2006/03/16/business/16scene.html?_ . . . 1of 211/18/131:28PMMarch16&_r=0.

40.   Henrich, Boyd, and Richerson, "Puzzle of Monogamous Marriage," 661: "imagine a society of 40 adults consisting of 20 males and 20 females. . . . 12 men with the highest status marry 12 of the 20 women in monogamous marriages. Then, the top five men (top 25% status) all take a second wife, and the top two (10%) take a third wife . . . [and] top guy takes a fourth wife. Now, 58 per cent of marriages are monogamous. Only men in the top 10 per cent of status married more than two women. The most wives that anyone has is four. . . . [T]his degree of polygyny is not extreme historically, [but] it creates

a pool of 40 per cent of the male population who are shut out of the marriage market. To enter the marriage market, a man has to be in the top 60 per cent of male status."

41.   Frank, "Polygamy and the Marriage Market."

42.   Henrich, Boyd, and Richerson, "Puzzle of Monogamous Marriage." See also Bauman, Reference Case, par. 14: "Polygamy's harm to society includes the critical fact that a great many of its individual harms are not specific to any particular religious, cultural or regional context. They can be generalized and expected to occur wherever polygamy exists."

43.   John M. Glionna, "After Fleeing Polygamist Sect, Boys Face a New World," *Los Angeles Times*, May 8, 2013, http://www.latimes.com /great-reads/la-na-utah-lost-boys-20130508-dto,0,2143256.htmlstory #axzz2qbeEgock. See also http://childbrides.org/boys.html; and the excellent Canadian news report by Carolyn Jarvis, "Inside Bountiful: Polygamy Investigation" *16x9*, http://watchdocumentary.org/watch/16x9 -inside-bountiful-polygamy-investigation-video_335e94162.html.

44.   Bauman, Reference Case, par. 11, "The sex ratio imbalance inherent in polygamy means that young men are forced out of polygamous communities to sustain the ability of senior men to accumulate more wives. These young men and boys often receive limited education as a result and must navigate their way outside their communities with few life skills and social support." See also Daphne Bramham, *Secret Lives of the Saints*.

45.   Bauman, Reference Case, par. 514–16.

46.   Ibid., par. 500.

47.   Women do not "generally benefit from establishing simultaneous pair-bonds with multiple males," because women can have only one pregnancy at a time, and males are apt to be especially jealous of one another on account of uncertainties connected with paternity (and "paternal confidence increases paternal investment"). See Henrich, Affidavit no. 1, 22, quoted in Bauman, Reference Case, par. 500. See also Wright, *Moral Animal*, 89–102. Currently, women appear to be four or five times more likely to marry older men than the reverse, though the disparity seems to be declining somewhat. U.S. Census Bureau, Current Population Survey, 2013 Annual Social and Economic Supplement, table FG3. Married Couple Family Groups, by Presence of Own Children under 18, and Age, Earnings, Education, and Race and Hispanic Origin of Both Spouses: 2013. See http://www.census.gov/hhes /families/files/cps2013/tabFG3-all.xls.

48.   Bauman, Reference Case, par. 501. Of course, evolutionary theory may seem superfluous here: all we need to understand are the

biological differences involved in procreation to know that prudence dictates greater caution on the part of women.

49. Ibid., par. 502.

50. Jones, *Cruel Arithmetic*, 59–62. On monogamy and democracy, see Walter Scheidel, "Monogamy and Polygyny in Greece, Rome, and World History," *Princeton/Stanford Working Papers in Classics*, June 2008, http://www.princeton.edu/~pswpc/pdfs/scheidel/060807.pdf. For a broader account of monogamy, democracy, and progress, see Wright, *Moral Animal*, 92–99; and William Tucker, *Marriage and Civilization: How Monogamy Made Us Human* (Washington, DC: Regnery, 2014).

51. Josiah L. Ober, *Knowledge and Democracy: Innovation and Learning in Classical Athens* (Princeton: Princeton University Press, 2010).

52. For a historian's appropriation and deployment of similar ideas, see Ian Morris, *Why the West Rules—for Now: The Patterns of History, and What They Reveal about the Future* (New York: Farrar, Straus & Giroux, 2010); and *Foragers, Farmers and Fossil Fuels: How Human Values Evolve*, ed. Stephen Macedo (Princeton: Princeton University Press, 2015). See also Scheidel, affidavit.

53. For an account of the evidence, see Jones, *Cruel Arithmetic*, 54–56; and for very able and readable overviews of the evidence and theory concerning evolution's influence on society and culture, see Robert Wright, *The Moral Animal: Why We Are, the Way We Are: The New Science of Evolutionary Psychology* (New York: Vintage, 1994); Stephen Pinker, *How the Mind Works* (New York: Norton, 1997).

54. Lori D. Hager, "Sex and Gender in Paleoanthropology," in *Women in Human Evolution*, ed. Lori D. Hager (London: Routledge, 1997), 1–3.

55. See Susan Sperling and Yewoubdar Beyne, "A Pound of Biology and a Pinch of Culture or a Pinch of Biology and a Pound of Culture? The Necessity of Integrating Biology and Culture in Reproductive Studies," in Hager, *Women in Human Evolution*, chap. 7.

56. Part of my point is that phenomena such as polygamy need to be examined in their particulars, and not merely as abstract propositions. Were polygamy to be legally recognized, or merely decriminalized, it would be practiced not by autonomous individuals in the abstract but by members of particular communities informed by particular religious and cultural traditions.

57. BC Ref pars. 1335–36, quoting Alberta v. Hutterian Brethren of Wilson Colony 2009 SCC 37, [2009] 2 S.C.R. 567, par. 48.

58. Bala, "Polygamy in Canada"; and Strassberg, "Crime of Polygamy."

59. See Bauman, Reference Case, par. 1282.

CHAPTER 9

1. Waddoups, Brown v. Buhman, 3.

2. I have benefited from Joanna L. Grossman and Lawrence M. Friedman, "Kody's Big Score in the Challenge to Polygamy Law," December 24, 2013, http://verdict.justia.com/2013/12/24/kodys-big-score -challenge-polygamy-laws.

3. Utah Code Ann. § 76–7-101(1) (2013). The quoted sentence in the code ends, "or cohabits with another person." But there was no suggestion in *Brown* and the earlier case on which the decision drew, *State of Utah v. Holm*, 2006 UT 31, 137 P.3d 726, that the Browns were being prosecuted for (or being regarded as married because of) cohabitation. Such a prosecution would also appear to violate U.S. constitutional guarantees of individual liberty and sexual autonomy; see Lawrence v. Texas.

4. The characterization is from Joanna L. Grossman and Lawrence M. Friedman, "'Sister Wives': Will Reality Show Stars Face Prosecution for Polygamy in Utah?" *Findlaw*, October 4, 2010, http://writ.news .findlaw.com/grossman/20101004.html. I draw in what follows from three of the online postings.

5. Ibid. See also Joanna L. Grossman, "The Reality Show Sister Wives: Will Its Stars Prevail in Their Civil Rights Lawsuit?," *Verdict: Legal Analysis and Commentary from Justicia*, July 18, 2011, http://verdict .justia.com/2011/07/18/the-reality-show-sister-wives.

6. Quotations from Grossman and Friedman, "Sister Wives"; and Grossman, "Reality Show."

7. Grossman, "Reality Show."

8. Brown v. Buhman, 8.

9. http://www.safetynetutah.org/index.html. See also Brown v. Buhman, 6, "Factual Background," pt. 7. See "The Primer: A Guidebook for Law Enforcement and Human Services Agencies Who Offer Assistance to Fundamentalist Mormon Families." This primer is authored by the Utah Attorney General's Office, the Arizona AG Office, other Utah domestic relations agencies, and several professional associations and nonprofits. See http://attorneygeneral.utah.gov/cmsdocuments/The _Primer.pdf, 4. My thanks to Paul Baumgardner for his insights on this issue, and others treated in this chapter.

10. Civil Rights Complaint files in the United States District Court, District of Utah, Central Division, website of Jonathan Turley, attorney for the Browns as plaintiffs, http://jonathanturley.files.word press.com/2011/07/brown-complaint.pdf.

11. Brown v. Buhman, factual stipulations, 6. See also the various news reports, including "'Sister Wives' Family under Investigation

Following TV Debut," September 27, 2010, http://www.ksl.com/?nid =148&sid=12603468.

12. Utah Code Sect. 76–7-101(1) (2013); Brown v. Buhman, 25.

13. Brown Complaint, 176–77.

14. Brown v. Buhman, 7.

15. Utah Code Ann. § 76–7-101(1) (2013).

16. Brown v. Buhman, 27.

17. Ibid., 8, "undisputed fact" no. 22.

18. Chambers, "Polygamy," 71, quoting Irwin Altman and Joseph Ginat, *Polygamous Families in Contemporary Society* (New York: Cambridge University Press, 1996), 58. Regarding bigamy in particular, see Ralph Slovenko, "The De Facto Decriminalization of Bigamy," *Journal of Family Law* 17, 2 (1978–79), 297–308.

19. Brown v. Buhman, 8; passim. The *Holm* majority, upholding his conviction for bigamy, held that "an unlicensed solemnized marriage can serve as a subsequent marriage that violates the bigamy statute," 25; quoted in Brown v. Buhman, 82. Interestingly, the Court specifically puts aside Lawrence v. Texas as a ground for striking down the polygamy law; see p. 43, end of 2.B.b.

20. Quoted in Ryan D. Tenney, "Tom Green, Common-law Marriage, and the Illegality of Putative Polygamy," *Brigham Young University Law Journal* 17, 1 (2003): 141, 145.

21. State of Utah v. Holm, par. 18, 137 P.3d, 733.

22. Brown v. Buhman, 65.

23. Ibid., 63–65, quoting Chief Justice Durham's dissent in *Holm*.

24. Ibid., 65.

25. Ibid., 5.

26. To regard whatever religious ceremony the Browns may have engaged in as having the legal effect of marriage violates, the Court asserted, the free exercise clause. The antipolygamy statute—on its face and as applied to the Browns—is "operationally non-neutral" with respect to their religious beliefs, see ibid. For an interesting wrinkle, see ibid., 49–50, especially nn53–55, in which Waddoups engages in a lengthy critique of the Utah Supreme Court's decisions in *Green* and *Holm* for ascribing bigamous marriages based on common law marriage.

27. Ibid., 20 and n28.

28. Ibid., 18, citing *Reynolds*, 98 US 166.

29. See Jonathan Turley and Adam Alba, Complaint for Declaratory, Injunctive, and Other Relief, in Brown v. Buhman, 37–38, pars. 224–29, "Sixth Ground for Complaint: Establishment of Religion." From website of Jonathan Turley.

30. Strassberg argues that even consensual polygamous families within the typical FLDS sectarian communities make a contribution to sustaining "insular and theocratically governed communities" that constitute distinct political and economic units in which leaders wield great power at odds with democratic equality. This is a point that Nancy Rosenblum also emphasizes; see "Democratic Sex." Strassberg, "Crime of Polygamy," 409–11.

31. The worry is that decriminalization could encourage more polygamy by removing the deterrent effects exerted by the criminal law's expressive disapproval. I do not know how to substantiate or measure these risks.

32. As Corey Brettschneider and others have argued, the government has a variety of ways of seeking to bolster particular value judgments, aside from criminalization. See *When the Government Speaks, What Should it Say? How Democracies Can Protect Expression and Promote Equality* (Princeton: Princeton University Press, 2012).

33. See Turley and Alba, Brown Family Complaint.

34. http://en.wikipedia.org/wiki/Sister_Wives. And see Kody Brown, Meri Brown, Janelle Brown, Christine Brown, and Robyn Brown, *Becoming Sister Wives: The Story of an Unconventional Marriage* (New York: Gallery Books, 2012).

35. Grossman and Friedman, "Kody's Big Score."

36. Embry, *Polygamous Families*, 34 and passim.

37. Chambers, "Polygamy," 83; and, "Canada Court: Polygamy Ban Is Invalid," *Salt Lake Tribune*, June 16, 1992, A4, quoted in Chambers, "Polygamy," 83n176.

38. For an overview of some controversies and a set of sensible recommendations, see Barbara Bennett Woodhouse, "Children's Rights in Gay and Lesbian Families: A Child-Centered Perspective," in *Child, Family, and State: NOMOS XLIV*, ed. Stephen Macedo and Iris Marion Young (New York: New York University Press, 2003).

39. Steve Chapman, "It's Not Our Place to Persecute Polygamists," *Baltimore Sun*, September 4, 2001, 13A; quoted in Tenney, "Putative Polygamy," 158.

40. Adrien Katherine Wing, "Polygamy from Southern Africa to Black Britannia to Black America: Global Critical Race Feminism as Legal Reform for the Twenty-first Century," *Journal of Contemporary Legal Issues* 11 (2001): 862.

41. http://blackdemographics.com/households/marriage-in-black -america/.

42. "Births: Preliminary Data for 2012," *National Vital Statistics* 62, 3, http://www.cdc.gov/nchs/data/nvsr/nvsr62/nvsr62_03.pdf.

43. Wing, "Polygamy," 858.

44. Ibid., 859.

45. Ibid., 858.

46. Bilal Philips, "Monogamy and Polygamy," http://www.islams women.com/marriage/monogamy_and_polygamy.php.

47. Laurie Shrage, a Western feminist philosopher, has defended a variation on the Islamic practice of "temporary marriage."

48. See Complaint for Declaratory relief, 23, pt. 26.

49. Sarah L. Eichenberger, "When for Better Is for Worse: Immigration Law's Gendered Impact on Foreign Polygamous Marriage," *Duke Law Journal* 61, 5 (2012): 1104–07.

50. In most states the minimum age for marriage is 16, and children under 18 seeking to marry must have parental permission, but there is a lot of variation. In Alabama, children 14 and up can marry with parental permission.

51. Quoted in Brian Hutchinson, "Charges Laid against Bountiful Leader Winston Blackmore after Judge Rules Charter Should Not Protect Polygamists," *National Post*, August 14, 2014, http://news.national post.com/2014/08/14/na0815-polygamy/#__federated=1.

52. http://www.accesshollywood.com/i-do-again-access-top-10 -most-marrying-celebs_gallery_2571#PREmMJHwsJrhVVYG.99.

53. Wright, *Moral Animal*, 101–2.

54. See Zeitzen, *Polygamy*, chap. 6 and 165–68.

55. Protocol to the African Charter on Human and Peoples' Rights on the Rights of Women in Africa, article 6, http://www.achpr.org/files /instruments/women-protocol/achpr_instr_proto_women_eng.pdf.

56. Stacey, *Unhitched*, 96. The act specifically "does not include marriages concluded in accordance with Hindu, Muslim, or other religious rites." See also David L. Chambers, "Civilizing the Natives: Marriage in Post-Apartheid South Africa," *Daedalus* 129, 4 (Fall 2000): 101–24.

57. Stacey, *Unhitched*, 99.

58. The *Economist* reports that "in a 2005 survey on marriage, 87% of South Africans favored lifelong monogamy, whereas 25% of black men and 15% of white ones preferred polygamy. Women of all colours were a lot less keen." By 2003 fewer than 4% of South Africans were in polygamous relationships. "South Africa and Polygamy, Swimming against the Tide, President Jacob Zuma Happily Bucks the Trend towards Monogamy," April 28, 2012, Johannesburg, http://www.economist.com/node /21553461. See also "Polygamy and the President: Survey Taps Opinion," *TheSouthAfrican.com*, March 30, 2009, http://www.thesouthafrican.com /polygamy-and-the-president-survey-taps-opinion/.

59. Ibid.; Traditionalists frequently, like President Jacob Zuma, regard same-sex marriage as disgraceful, see Stacey, *Unhitched*, 104–6.

60. Sarah Song, *Justice, Gender, and the Politics of Multiculturalism* (Cambridge: Cambridge University Press, 2007), 164.

61. See Stacey, *Unhitched*.

62. Zeitzen, *Polygamy*, 5; Wang, "Sex, Money, Social Status." In Kazakhstan it has been reported that while a large majority opposed polygamy in the past, including a majority of Muslims, more have lately become sympathetic. The reason, say some, is growing inequality due to the country's oil wealth. "Becoming a tokal [second wife] would be a fairy tale," said one woman from southern Kazakhstan. A presidential candidate advocated polygamy as a way of "marrying off Kazakhstan's single women." See Roberto A. Ferdman, "In Kazakhstan, Inequality and Polygamy May Go Hand-in-Hand," http://qz.com/153316/in-kazakhstan-inequality-and-polygamy-may-go-hand-in-hand/.

63. Rawls, *Political Liberalism*, 331–34.

64. Bedi, *Beyond Race*, 210.

65. Gallagher, in Corvino and Gallagher, *Debating Same Sex Marriage*, 147.

66. Krause and Meyer argue that "the historical fact that incest is an all-but-universal taboo" is unlikely to be regarded by the U.S. Supreme Court as a "sufficient justification" in light of *Lawrence*. See Krause and Meyer, *Family Law*, 48 and 46. In fact, state courts continue to uphold criminal prohibitions on incest as reasonably related to legitimate state interests in protecting families against "destabilizing or exploitive influences." Though, in one surprising post-*Lawrence* development, an appeals court in Connecticut overturned the conviction of a putative stepfather for sexual assault in the third degree, citing as partial grounds (in addition to doubts that he was related as stepparent to the victim) the equal protection of the laws: this because the Connecticut law in question seemed to reach only heterosexual but not homosexual incest. State v. John M., 94 Conn. App. 667, 894 A.2d 376 (2006), review granted, 278 Conn. 916, 889 A.2d 622 (2006).

67. Jonathan Rauch also makes this point in Sullivan, ed., *Same Sex Marriage: Pro and Con*, 287–88.

68. See the discussion in Posner, *Sex and Reason*, 199–201, 395–402; and also Jack Goody, *The Development of the Family and Marriage in Europe* (Cambridge: Cambridge University Press, 1990), chap. 4 and passim.

69. Naomi Cahn, "Accidental Incest: Drawing the Line—or the Curtain—for Reproductive Technology," *Harvard Journal of Gender and the Law* 109 (2009): 67–107.

70. For a fuller discussion in the context of debates surrounding religious liberty and diversity, see Macedo, *Diversity and Distrust.*

71. For some interesting observations on *agape* and *eros,* see Pope Benedict XVI, *Deus Caritas Est,* Encyclical Letter, http://www.vatican.va/holy_father/benedict_xvi/encyclicals/documents/hf_ben-xvi_enc_20051225_deus-caritas-est_en.html.

72. Strauss, "Polygamy," also calls this "molecular marriage," 540–44.

73. Elizabeth F. Emens, "Monogamy's Law: Compulsory Monogamy and Polyamorous Existence," *New York University Review of Law & Social Change* 29, 2 (2004): 283, crediting Lana Tibbetts for that first phrase.

74. See the discussions in Nancy Rosenblum, "Democratic Sex," in *Membership and Morals;* and Mark Brandon, *States of Union.*

75. See Strassberg, "Crime of Polygamy." This form is similar to the third model of marriage, or the one Strauss calls "molecular."

76. Strassberg observes a small "polyfidelity" movement. See "Postmodern Polygamy," 440.

77. Girgis, Anderson, and George, *What is Marriage?,* 51.

78. Luscombe, "I Do, I Do, I Do, I Do." The author of the article characterizes this as "a guess."

79. Jessica Bennett, "Only You. And You. And You. Polyamory—Relationships with Multiple, Mutually Consenting Partners—Has a Coming-Out Party," *Newsweek,* July 28, 2009.

80. See http://www.lovewithoutlimits.com/workshops.html and http://schooloftemplearts.org/deborahtajanapol.

81. Quoted in Bennett, "Only You."

82. Emens, "Monogamy's Law," 311.

83. Ibid., 313–14.

84. Ibid., 317.

85. Ibid.

86. Sasha Cagen, *Quirkyalone: A Manifesto for Uncompromising Romantics* (San Francisco: Harper San Francisco, 2004).

87. Ethan Watters, *Urban Tribes: A Generation Redefines Friendship, Family, and Commitment* (New York: Bloomsbury, 2003).

88. http://crazylikeus.com/AUTHOR_BIO.html.

89. For the former, see http://www.pepperminty.com and https://freaksexual.wordpress.com. For the latter, see http://polyweekly.com/tag/cunning-minx/.

90. Brake, *Minimizing Marriage,* 158–88; see also "Beyond Same-Sex Marriage."

91.   See Wright, *Moral Animal,* offering the "Darwinian" view that "monogamy is a straightforward expression of political equality among men," 99.

92.   See Klarman, *Closet to Altar,* for an excellent account.

93.   See the valuable discussion by Nancy Rosenblum, "Democratic Sex," in *Membership and Morals.*

94.   Charles Krauthammer, "Pandora and Polygamy," *Washington Post,* March 17, 2006, http://www.washingtonpost.com/wp-dyn/content /article/2006/03/16/AR2006031601312.html.

CONCLUSION

1.   Flores, "Public Opinion on LGBT Rights."

2.   Edward Stein, "Same-Sex Couples, the Future of Marriage, and Consensual Non-Monogamy," paper presentation at American Association of Law Schools annual meeting, January 4–6, 2015; Powerpoint slides on file with the author. My thanks to Professor Stein, of the Cardozo School of Law, and also to Linda McClain.

3.   Mill, *On Liberty,* 99.

4.   Dworkin, *Is Democracy Possible Here?,* 70–71.

5.   March, "Right to Polygamy?"; see abstract, 246.

6.   Brake *Minimizing Marriage,* 135–39; see also the general discussion and citations in chapter 4 of this volume.

7.   http://www.nea.gov/honors/medals/.

8.   For a valuable exploration, see Galston, *Liberal Purposes.*

9.   For interesting observations along these lines, see Mark Sagoff, *The Economy of the Earth: Philosophy, Law, and the Environment,* 2nd ed. (New York: Cambridge University Press, 2008), 48. It is important to remember that market institutions themselves are "not neutral amongst competing ideas of the good life." Dworkin, "Liberalism," in *A Matter of Principle,* 202.

10.   Ronald Dworkin, *Is Democracy Possible Here? Principles for a New Political Debate* (Princeton: Princeton University Press, 2008), 86.

11.   Fleming and McClain, *Ordered Liberty,* 195.

12.   I believe this paraphrases something I have read, but I cannot remember where.

BIBLIOGRAPHY

African Union. Protocol to the African Charter on Human and Peoples' Rights on the Rights of Women in Africa, adopted 11 July, 2003, http://www.achpr.org/files/instruments/women-protocol/achpr_instr _proto_women_eng.pdf.

Al-Krenawi, Alean. *Psychosocial Impact of Polygamy in the Middle East.* New York: Springer, 2014.

Altman, Irwin, and Joseph Ginat. *Polygamous Families in Contemporary Society.* New York: Cambridge University Press, 1996.

American Academy of Pediatrics. "Promoting the Well-Being of Children Whose Parents Are Gay or Lesbian," pediatrics.aapublications .org/content/131/4/e1374.full.pdf.

American Enterprise Institute (AEI). *Public Opinion Studies. Polls on Attitudes on Homosexuality & Gay Marriage* (updated March 2013). Compiled by Karlyn Bowman, Andrew Rugg, and Jennifer Marsico, citing NORC/GSS 32, http://www.aei.org/publication/polls-on -attitudes-on-homosexuality-gay-marriage-march-2013/.

Anderson, Elizabeth. *Value in Ethics and Economics.* Cambridge, MA: Harvard University Press, 1993.

Anderson, Ryan T. "North Carolina, Biden, and Same-Sex Marriage." *National Review*, May 8, 2012, http://m.nationalreview.com/corner /299394/north-carolina-biden-and-same-sex-marriage-ryan-t -anderson/page/0/1.

———. "The Roe of Marriage: Traditionalists Should Defend Their Conception of the Truth." *National Review*, August 2014, https:// www.nationalreview.com/nrd/articles/383581/roe-marriage.

Associated Press. "Pope Strongly Defends Church Teaching against Contraception." *New York Post*, January 16, 2015, http://nypost.com /2015/01/16/pope-strongly-defends-church-teaching-against -contraception/.

Bailey, Sarah Pulliam. "Conservative United Methodists Say Divide over Sexuality Is 'Irreconcilable.'" *Religion News Service*, May 23, 2014, http://www.religionnews.com/2014/05/23/amid-sexuality -debates-80-pastors-threaten-possible-division-within-united -methodist-church/.

Bala, Nicholas. "Polygamy in Canada: Justifiably Not Tolerated." *Jurist*—Forum, December 3, 2011, http://jurist.org/forum/2011/12 /nicholas-bala-canada-polygamy.php.

———. "Why Canada's Prohibition of Polygamy Is Constitutionally Valid and Sound Social Policy." *Canadian Journal of Family Law* 25 (2009): 165–221.

Baldwin, Alec. "Why Childless Straight Couples Make the Case for Gay Marriage." *Huffington Post*, May 25, 2011, http://www.huffingtonpost .com/alec-baldwin/why-childless-straight-co_b_208457.html.

Banks, Ralph Richard. *Is Marriage for White People? How the African American Marriage Decline Affects Everyone*. New York: Plume, 2012.

Beachy, Robert. *Gay Berlin: Birthplace of a Modern Identity*. New York: Knopf, 2014.

Bean, L. L., and G. P. Mineau. "The Polygyny–Fertility Hypothesis: A Re-evaluation." *Population Studies* 40 (1986): 67–81.

Becker, Gary. "Is There a Case for Legalizing Polygamy?" *Becker-Posner blog*, October 22, 2006, http://www.becker-posner-blog.com/2006 /10/is-there-a-case-for-legalizing-polygamy-becker.html.

Bedi, Sonu. *Beyond Race, Sex, and Sexual Orientation: Legal Equality without Identity*. Cambridge: Cambridge University Press, 2013.

Benabou, Roland, and Jean Tirole. "Belief in a Just World and Re-distributive Politics." *Quarterly Journal of Economics* 121, 2 (2006): 699–746.

Benedict XVI, Pope. *Deus Caritas Est*, Encyclical Letter, http://w2 .vatican.va/content/benedict-xvi/en/encyclicals/documents/hf_ben -xvi_enc_20051225_deus-caritas-est.html.

Bennett, Jessica. "Only You. And You. And You. Polyamory— Relationships with Multiple, Mutually Consenting Partners—Has a Coming-Out Party." *Newsweek*, July 28, 2009.

Bennion, Janet. *Women of Principle: Female Networking in Contemporary Mormon Polygyny*. New York: Oxford University Press, 1998.

"Beyond Same-Sex Marriage: A New Strategic Vision for All Our Families & Relationships," July 26, 2006, http://www.beyond marriage.org.

Bilger, Audrey. "Marriage Equality Is a Feminist Issue," *Ms. Magazine blog*, December 11, 2012, http://msmagazine.com/blog/2012/12/11 /marriage-equality-is-a-feminist-issue/.

Bipartisan Legal Advisory Group (BLAG) of the U.S. House of Representatives, *Brief on the Merits, in US vs. Windsor*, No. 12–307, filed January 22, 2013, http://www.supremecourt.gov/docket/pdfs/12–307_brief_on_the_merits_for_respondent.pdf.

Bix, Brian. "Bargaining in the Shadow of Love: The Enforcement of Premarital Agreements and How We Think about Marriage." *William & Mary Law Review* 40 (1998): 145–207.

———. "Domestic Agreements," *Hofstra Law Review* 35, 4 (2007): 1753–71, http://scholarlycommons.law.hofstra.edu/hlr/vol35/iss4/5.

———. *Family Law.* New York: Oxford University Press, 2013.

Black, Nathan. "Grisanti Defends Switch to 'Yes' on NY Gay Marriage." *Christian Post*, June 28, 2011, http://www.christianpost.com/news/grisanti-defends-switch-to-yes-on-ny-gay-marriage-51647/.

Blankenhorn, David. *Fatherless America: Confronting Our Most Urgent Social Problem.* New York: Basic Books, 1995.

———. "How My View on Gay Marriage Changed." *New York Times*, June 22, 2012, http://www.nytimes.com/2012/06/23/opinion/how-my-view-on-gay-marriage-changed.html.

Blase, Marty. "Funny Wedding Vows, Wedding Vows Inspired by Dr. Seuss," http://weddings.about.com/od/yourweddingceremony/a/SeussFunnyVows.htm.

Boies, David, and Theodore B. Olson. *Redeeming the Dream: The Case for Marriage Equality.* New York: Penguin, 2014.

Bowlin, John. *Contingency and Fortune in Aquinas's Ethics.* New York: Cambridge University Press, 2010.

Bowman, Karlyn, Andrew Rugg, and Jennifer K. Marsico. *Polls on Attitudes on Homosexuality and Gay Marriage*, AEI Public Opinion Studies. Washington, DC: American Enterprise Institute, updated March 2013, http://www.aei.org/publication/polls-on-attitudes-on-homosexuality-gay-marriage-march-2013/.

Bradley, Martha Sonntag. *Kidnapped from That Land: The Government Raids on the Short Creek Polygamists.* Salt Lake City: University of Utah Press, 1993.

Brake, Elizabeth. "Minimal Marriage: What Political Liberalism Implies for Marriage Law." *Ethics* 120 (January 2010): 302–37.

———. *Minimizing Marriage: Marriage, Morality, and the Law.* Oxford: Oxford University Press, 2012.

Bramham, Daphne. *The Secret Lives of Saints: Child Brides and Lost Boys in Canada's Polygamous Mormon Sect.* Toronto: Vintage Canada, 2008.

Brandon, Mark E. *States of Union: Family and Change in the American Constitutional Order.* Lawrence: University Press of Kansas, 2013.

Bratter, Jenifer L., and Rosalind B. King. "'But Will It Last?': Marital Instability among Interracial and Same-Race Couples." *Family Relations* 57 (April 2008): 160–71.

Brettschneider, Corey. *When the Government Speaks, What Should It Say? How Democracies Can Protect Expression and Promote Equality.* Princeton: Princeton University Press, 2012.

Brooks, Thom. "The Problem with Polygamy." *Philosophical Topics* 37, 2 (2009): 109–22.

Brower, Sam. *Prophet's Prey: My Seven-Year Investigation into Warren Jeffs and the Fundamentalist Church of Latter-Day Saints.* London: Bloomsbury, 2012.

Brown, Kody, Meri Brown, Janelle Brown, Christine Brown, and Robyn Brown. *Becoming Sister Wives: The Story of an Unconventional Marriage.* New York: Gallery Books, 2012.

Buccola, Nicholas. "Finding Room for Same-Sex Marriage: Toward a More Inclusive Understanding of a Cultural Institution." *Journal of Social Philosophy* 36 (2005): 331–43.

Buss, David M. *The Dangerous Passion: Why Jealousy Is as Necessary as Love and Sex.* New York: Free Press, 2000.

———. *The Evolution of Desire: Strategies of Human Mating.* Rev. ed. New York: Basic Books, 2003.

Cagen, Sasha. *Quirkyalone: A Manifesto for Uncompromising Romantics.* San Francisco: Harper San Francisco, 2004.

Cahn, Naomi. "Accidental Incest: Drawing the Line—or the Curtain—for Reproductive Technology." *Harvard Journal of Gender and the Law* 109 (2009): 67–107.

Cahn, Naomi, and June Carbone. *Red Families v. Blue Families: Legal Polarization and the Creation of Culture.* New York: Oxford University Press, 2011.

Calder, Gillian. "Penguins and Polyamory: Using Law and Film to Explore the Essence of Marriage in Canadian Family Law." *Canadian Journal of Women and the Law* 21, 1 (2009): 55–89.

Calhoun, Cheshire. "Who's Afraid of Polygamous Marriage? Lessons for Same-Sex Marriage Advocacy from the History of Polygamy." *San Diego Law Review* 42 (2005): 1023–42.

Campbell, Angela, Nicholas Bala, Katherine Duvall-Antonacopoulos, Leslie MacRae, Joanne J. Paetsch, Martha Bailey, Beverley Baines, Bita Amani, and Amy Kaufman. *Polygamy in Canada: Legal and Social Implications for Women and Children: A Collection of Policy Research Reports.* Alberta Civil Liberties Research Centre. Ottawa: Status of Women Canada, 2005, http://www.crilf.ca/Documents/Polygamy%20in%20Canada%20-%20Nov%202005.pdf.

Carbone, June, and Naomi Cahn. *Marriage Markets: How Inequality Is Remaking the American Family*. New York: Oxford University Press, 2014.

———. "Red v. Blue Marriage." In *Marriage at the Crossroads: Law, Policy, and the Brave New World of Twenty-First-Century Families*. Edited by Marsha Garrison and Elizabeth S. Scott. New York: Cambridge University Press, 2012.

Carpenter, Dale. *Flagrant Conduct: The Story of Lawrence v. Texas*. New York: Norton, 2012.

Carter, Sarah. *The Importance of Being Monogamous: Marriage and Nation Building in Western Canada to 1915*. Edmonton and Athabasca: University of Alberta Press and AU Press, Athabasca University, 2008.

Case, Mary Ann. "Couples and Coupling in the Public Sphere: A Comment on the Legal History of Litigating for Lesbian and Gay Rights." *Virginia Law Review* 79 (1993): 1643–94.

———. "Marriage Licenses," *Minnesota Law Review* 89 (2005): 1758, http://www.law.uchicago.edu/files/files/case-marriagelicenses.pdf.

———. "Why Evangelical Protestants Are Right When They Claim That State Recognition of Same-Sex Marriage Threatens Their Marriages and What the Law Should Do about It," working paper presented at Princeton University History Department, May 2013.

Cash, Scottye J., and Jeffrey A. Bridge. "Epidemiology of Youth Suicide and Suicidal Behavior." *Current Opinion in Pediatrics* 21, 5 (October 2009): 613–19.

Centers for Disease Control. Press Release. "More Than Half of Young HIV-Infected Americans Are Not Aware of Their Status," http://www.cdc.gov/media/releases/2012/p1127_young_HIV.html.

Chambers, Clare. "The Marriage-Free State." *Proceedings of the Aristotelian Society* 103, part 2 (2013): 123–43.

Chambers, David L. "Civilizing the Natives: Marriage in Post-Apartheid South Africa." *Daedalus* 129, 4 (Fall 2000): 101–24.

———. "Polygamy and Same-Sex Marriage." *Hofstra Law Review* 26 (1997): 53–83.

———. "What If? The Legal Consequences of Marriage and the Legal Needs of Lesbian and Gay Male Couples." *Michigan Law Review* 95, 2 (1996): 447–91.

Cherlin, Andrew J. "American Marriage in the Early Twenty-First Century." *The Future of Children* 15, 2 (Fall 2005): 33–55.

———. *Labor's Love Lost: The Rise and Fall of the Working-Class Family in America*. New York: Russell Sage Foundation, 2014.

———. *The Marriage-Go-Round: The State of Marriage and the Family in America Today*. New York: Vintage, 2010.

Clendinen, Dudley, and Adam Nagourney. *Out For Good: The Struggle to Build a Gay Rights Movement in America*. New York: Simon and Schuster, 1999.

Colbert, Chuck. "HIV Rates Rise in Youth." *Bay Area Reporter*, December 6, 2012, http://www.ebar.com/news/article.php?sec=news& article=68309%20%20.

Condon, Patrick. "Jack Baker and Michael McConnell, Couple in 1971 Minnesota Gay Marriage Case, Still United." Associated Press, December 10, 2012, *HuffPost*, http://www.huffingtonpost.com/2012/12 /10/jack-baker-michael-mcconnell-minnesota-gay-marriage_n _2271573.html.

Congregation for the Doctrine of the Faith. "Considerations Regarding Proposals to Give Legal Recognition to Unions between Homosexual Persons." *Origins* 33 (August 14, 2003): 177–82, http://www.vatican .va/roman_curia/congregations/cfaith/documents/rc_con_cfaith_doc _20030731_homosexual-unions_en.html.

Congressional Record, July 9–14, 2004. Washington, DC: Government Printing Office, 2004.

Connolly, Brian. *Domestic Intimacies: Incest and the Liberal Subject in Nineteenth-Century America*. Philadelphia: University of Pennsylvania Press, 2014.

Coontz, Stephanie. "The Disestablishment of Marriage." *New York Times*, June 22, 2013.

———. *Marriage, a History: How Love Conquered Marriage*. New York: Penguin, 2006.

Corvino, John, and Maggie Gallagher. *Debating Same-Sex Marriage*. New York: Oxford University Press, 2012.

Cossman, Brenda. *Sexual Citizens: The Legal and Cultural Regulation of Sex and Belonging*. Stanford: Stanford University Press, 2007.

Cutler, D. M., E. L. Glaeser, and K. E. Norberg. "Explaining the Rise in Youth Suicide." In *Risky Behavior among Youths: An Economic Analysis*. Edited by Jonathan Gruber. Chicago: University of Chicago Press, 2001.

Darger, Joe, Alina Darger, Vicki Darger, and Valerie Darger, with Brooke Adams. *Love Times Three: Our True Story of a Polygamous Marriage*. New York: HarperOne, 2011.

D'Emilio, John. *Sexual Politics, Sexual Communities: The Making of a Homosexual Minority in the United States, 1940–1970*. 2nd ed. Chicago: University of Chicago Press, 1998.

D'Emilio, John, and Estelle B. Freedman. *Intimate Matters: A History of Sexuality in America*. 3rd ed. Chicago: University of Chicago Press, 2012.

Den Otter, Ronald C. *In Defence of Plural Marriage*. New York: Cambridge University Press, 2015.

DePaulo, Bella. *Singlism: What It Is, Why It Matters, and How to Stop It*. Np: DoubleDoor Books, 2011.

Devlin, Patrick. *The Enforcement of Morals*. Oxford: Oxford University Press, 1965.

Dnes, Antony W., and Robert Rowtham, eds. *The Law and Economics of Marriage and Divorce*. Cambridge: Cambridge University Press, 2010.

Dworkin, Ronald. *Is Democracy Possible Here? Principles for a New Political Debate*. Princeton: Princeton University Press, 2008.

———. *A Matter of Principle*. Cambridge, MA: Harvard University Press, 1985.

———. *Taking Rights Seriously*. Cambridge, MA: Harvard University Press, 1977.

Easton, Dossie, and Janet W. Hardy. *The Ethical Slut: A Practical Guide to Polyamory, Open Relationships, and Other Adventures*. 2nd exp. ed. Berkeley: Celestial Arts, 2009.

Edin, Kathryn, and Maria Kefalas. *Promises I Can Keep: Why Poor Women Put Motherhood before Marriage*. Berkeley: University of California Press, 2011.

Edin, Kathryn, and Timothy J. Nelson. *Doing the Best I Can: Fatherhood in the Inner City*. Berkeley: University of California Press, 2013.

Eichenberger, Sarah L. "When for Better Is for Worse: Immigration Law's Gendered Impact on Foreign Polygamous Marriage." *Duke Law Journal* 61, 5 (2012): 1067–1110.

Eichner, Maxine. *The Supportive State: Families, Government, and America's Political Ideals*. New York: Oxford University Press, 2013.

Ely, John Hart. *Democracy and Distrust: A Theory of Judicial Review*. Cambridge, MA: Harvard University Press, 1980.

Embry, Jessie L. *Mormon Polygamous Families: Life in the Principle*. Draper, UT: Greg Kofford Books, 2008.

Emens, Elizabeth F. "Monogamy's Law: Compulsory Monogamy and Polyamorous Existence." *New York University Review of Law & Social Change* 29, 2 (2004): 277–376.

Emery, Robert E., Erin E. Horn, and Christopher R. Beam, "Marriage and Improved Well-Being: Using Twins to Parse the Correlation, Asking How Marriage Helps, and Wondering Why More People Don't Buy a Bargain." In *Marriage at the Crossroads: Law, Policy, and the Brave New World of Twenty-First-Century Families*. Edited by Marsha Garrison and Elizabeth S. Scott. New York: Cambridge University Press, 2012.

Eskridge, William N., Jr. *The Case for Same-Sex Marriage: From Sexual Liberty to Civilized Commitment*. New York: Free Press, 1996.

———. *Equality Practice: Civil Unions and the Future of Gay Rights*. New York: Routledge, 2002.

———. *Gaylaw: Challenging the Apartheid of the Closet*. Cambridge, MA: Harvard University Press, 1999.

Eskridge, William N., Jr., and Darren R. Spedale. *Gay Marriage: For Better or for Worse? What We've Learned from the Empirical Evidence*. New York: Oxford University Press, 2006.

Eskridge, William N., Jr., Darren R. Spedale, and Hans Ytterberg. "Nordic Bliss? Scandinavian Registered Partnerships and the Same-Sex Marriage Debate." *Issues in Legal Scholarship, Single-Sex Marriage* 4 (2004): 3, http://www.bepress.com/ils/iss5/art4.

Estlund, David M. "Shaping and Sex: Commentary on Parts I and II." In *Sex, Preference, and Family: Essays on Law and Nature*. By David M. Estlund and Martha C. Nussbaum, 148–70. New York: Oxford University Press, 1997.

Estlund, David M., and Martha C. Nussbaum. *Sex, Preference, and Family: Essays on Law and Nature*. New York: Oxford University Press, 1997.

Ettelbrick, Paula L. "Since When Is Marriage a Path to Liberation?" *Outlook: National Gay and Lesbian Quarterly* 6 (Fall 1989): 9, 14–17.

Evans-Pritchard, E. E. *Kinship and Marriage among the Nuer*. Oxford: Clarendon Press, 1990.

Falen, Douglas J. "Polygyny and Christian Marriage in Africa: The Case of Benin." *African Studies Review* 51, 2 (September 2008): 51–75.

Fenske, James. "African Polygamy: Past and Present." *CSAE [Centre for the Study of African Economies] Working Paper* WPS/2012–20, 17, fig.1. http://www.csae.ox.ac.uk/workingpapers/pdfs/csae-wps-2012–20.pdf.

Ferdman, Roberto A. "In Kazakhstan, Inequality and Polygamy May Go Hand-in-Hand," http://qz.com/153316/in-kazakhstan-inequality -and-polygamy-may-go-hand-in-hand/.

Fineman, Martha Albertson. *The Autonomy Myth: A Theory of Dependency*. New York: New Press, 2004.

Finer, Lawrence B. "Trends in Premarital Sex in the United States, 1954–2003." *Public Health Report* 122, 1 (January–February 2007): 73–78, http://www.ncbi.nlm.nih.gov/pmc/articles/PMC1802108 /pdf/phr122000073.pdf.

Finnis, John. "Is Natural Law Theory Compatible with Limited Government?" In *Natural Law, Liberalism, and Morality: Contemporary Essays*. Edited by Robert P. George. New York: Oxford University Press, 1996.

———. "Law, Morality, and 'Sexual Orientation'." *Notre Dame Law Review* 69 (1994): 1049–76.

———. "The Profound Injustice of Judge Posner on Marriage." *Public Discourse*, October 9, 2014, http://www.thepublicdiscourse.com/2014 /10/13896/.

Fleming, James E., and Linda C. McClain. *Ordered Liberty: Rights, Responsibilities, and Virtues.* Cambridge, MA: Harvard University Press, 2013.

Flores, Andrew R. "National Trends in Public Opinion on LGBT Rights in the United States." Williams Institute, University of California, Los Angeles, School of Law, November 2014, http://williams institute.law.ucla.edu/wp-content/uploads/POP-natl-trends-nov -2014.pdf.

Frank, Robert H. "Polygamy and the Marriage Market: Who Would Have the Upper Hand?" *New York Times*, March 16, 2006, http:// www.nytimes.com/2006/03/16/business/16scene.html?_ . . . 1of211 /18/131:28PMMarch16&_r=0.

Franke, Katherine. "The Curious Relationship of Marriage and Freedom." In *Marriage at the Crossroads: Law, Policy, and the Brave New World of Twenty-First-Century Families.* Edited by Marsha Garrison and Elizabeth S. Scott. New York: Cambridge University Press, 2012.

Gagnon, Robert A. J. *The Bible and Homosexual Practice: Texts and Hermeneutics.* Nashville: Abingdon Press, 2001.

Galston, William A. *Liberal Purposes: Goods, Virtues, and Diversity in the Liberal State.* New York: Cambridge University Press, 1991.

———. "What about the Children?" *Blueprint Magazine*, May 21, 2002, http://www.dlc.org/print2f98.html?contentid=250506.

Garrison, Marsha, and Elizabeth S. Scott, eds. *Marriage at the Crossroads: Law, Policy, and the Brave New World of Twenty-First-Century Families.* New York: Cambridge University Press, 2012.

Gates, Gary J. "LGBT Parenting in the United States." Williams Institute, UCLA School of Law, February 2013, http://williamsinstitute .law.ucla.edu/wp-content/uploads/lgbt-parenting.pdf.

Gaus, Gerald. "Coercion, Ownership, and the Redistributive State: Justificatory Liberalism's Classical Tilt," http://www.gaus.biz/Gaus -CoercionAndLiberalism.pdf.

George, Robert P. "The Concept of Public Morality." In *The Clash of Orthodoxies: Law, Morality, and Religion in Crisis.* Washington, DC: Intercollegiate Studies Institute Press, 2001.

———. *Making Men Moral: Civil Liberties and Public Morality.* Oxford: Oxford University Press, 1993.

George, Robert P., and Gerard V. Bradley. "Marriage and the Liberal Imagination." *Georgetown Law Journal* 84 (December 1995): 301–20.

George, Robert P., and William L. Saunders. "Romer v. Evans: The Supreme Court's Assault on Popular Sovereignty." *Civil Rights Practice Group Newsletter* 1, 1 (Fall 1996).

Gher, Jaime M. "Polygamy and Same-Sex Marriage—Allies or Adversaries within the Same-Sex Marriage Movement." *William & Mary Journal of Women & Law* 14 (2008): 559–603, http://scholarship.law.wm.edu/wmjowl/vol14/iss3/4Gher.

Gilder, George. *Men and Marriage.* Rev. and exp. ed. of *Sexual Suicide.* Gretna: Pelican, 1992.

Gilreath, Shannon. *The End of Straight Supremacy: Realizing Gay Liberation.* New York: Cambridge University Press, 2011.

———. "Rebuttal: Arguing against Arguing for Marriage." In Nelson Tebbe, Deborah Widiss and Shannon Gilreath, "Debate, The Argument for Same-Sex Marriage," *University of Pennsylvania Law Review* 159, PENNumbra (2010): 28–35, http://www.pennlawreview.com/online/159-U-Pa-L-Rev-PENNumbra-21.pdf.

Girgis, Sherif, Ryan T. Anderson, and Robert P. George. "What Is Marriage?" *Harvard Journal of Law and Public Policy* 34, 1 (2011): 245–87.

———. *What Is Marriage? Man and Woman: A Defense.* New York: Encounter Books, 2012.

Givens, Terryl L. *Wrestling the Angel. The Foundations of Mormon Thought: Cosmos, God, Humanity,* vol. 1. New York: Oxford University Press, 2015.

Glionna, John M. "After Fleeing Polygamist Sect, Boys Face a New World." *Los Angeles Times,* May 8, 2013, http://www.latimes.com/great-reads/la-na-utah-lost-boys-20130508-dto,0,2143256.html story#axzz2qbeEgock.

Goldberg, Jonah. "Abortion and Gay Marriage: Separate Issues; America Has Become More Pro-Life, More Pro-Gun, and More Pro-Gay." *National Review,* http://www.nationalreview.com/articles/343636/abortion-and-gay-marriage-separate-issues-jonah-goldberg.

Goldberg, Suzanne B. "Why Marriage?" In *Marriage at the Crossroads: Law, Policy, and the Brave New World of Twenty-First-Century Families.* Edited by Marsha Garrison and Elizabeth S. Scott. New York: Cambridge University Press, 2012.

Goodin, Robert E. *On Settling.* Princeton: Princeton University Press, 2012.

Goodwyn, Wade, Howard Berkes, and Amy Walters. "Warren Jeffs and the FLDS." *NPR Report,* May 3, 2005, http://www.npr.org/templates/story/story.php?storyId=4629320.

Goody, Jack. *The Development of the Family and Marriage in Europe.* Cambridge: Cambridge University Press, 1990.

Gordon, Sally Barringer. *The Mormon Question: Polygamy and Constitutional Conflict in Nineteenth-Century America.* Chapel Hill: University of North Carolina Press, 2002.

Graff, E. J. *What Is Marriage For: The Strange Social History of Our Most Intimate Institution.* Boston: Beacon Press, 2004.

Griffiths, Paul J. "Legalize Same-Sex Marriage: Why Law & Morality Can Part Company." *Commonweal,* June 28, 2004, https://www.commonwealmagazine.org/legalize-same-sex-marriage-0.

Grisez, Germain. *Way of the Lord Jesus,* vol. 2: *Living a Christian Life.* Quincy, IL: Franciscan Press, 1993, http://www.twotlj.org/G-2-V-2.html.

Grossman, Cathy Lynn. "Should Clergy Be Involved With Civil Marriage? 1 in 3 Americans Say No: Survey." Religion News Service, *HuffPost,* January 26, 2015, http://www.huffingtonpost.com/2014/12/07/clergy-civil-marriage_n_6257774.html.

Grossman, Joanna L. "The Reality Show Sister Wives: Will Its Stars Prevail in Their Civil Rights Lawsuit?" *Verdict: Legal Analysis and Commentary from Justicia,* July 18, 2011, http://verdict.justia.com/2011/07/18/the-reality-show-sister-wives.

Grossman, Joanna L., and Lawrence M. Friedman. *Inside the Castle: Law and the Family in 20th Century America.* Princeton: Princeton University Press, 2011.

———. "Kody's Big Score in the Challenge to Polygamy Law," December 24, 2013, http://verdict.justia.com/2013/12/24/kodys-big-score-challenge-polygamy-laws.

———. "'Sister Wives'": Will Reality Show Stars Face Prosecution for Polygamy in Utah?" *Findlaw,* October 4, 2010, http://writ.news.findlaw.com/grossman/20101004.html.

Hager, Lori D. "Sex and Gender in Paleoanthropology." In *Women in Human Evolution.* Edited by Lori D. Hager. London: Routledge, 1997.

———, ed. *Women in Human Evolution.* London: Routledge, 1997.

Handler, Thomas J. "Do Your Research, and Be Stealthy." *New York Times,* March 21, 2013, http://www.nytimes.com/roomfordebate/2013/03/21/the-power-of-the-prenup/a-stealthy-prenup-can-help-protect-assets.

Hansen, Klaus J. *Mormonism and the American Experience.* Chicago: University of Chicago Press, 1981.

Hartocollis, Anemona. "Jacques Beaumont and Richard Townsend." *New York Times,* August 14, 2011, 13.

Hartog, Hendrik. *Man and Wife in America: A History*. Cambridge, MA: Harvard University Press, 2002.

Hashimoto, Akiko, and Charlotte Ikels. "Filial Piety in Changing Asian Societies." In *The Cambridge Handbook of Age and Ageing*. Edited by Malcolm L. Johnson. Cambridge: Cambridge University Press, 2005, 437–443.

Hetherington, E. Mavis, and John Kelly. *For Better or for Worse: Divorce Reconsidered*. New York: Norton, 2003.

Henrich, Joseph, Affidavit #1, Sworn July 15, 2010, No. S-097767, Vancouver Registry, In the Supreme Court of British Columbia, In the Matter of: The Constitutional Question Act, R.S.B.C. 1996, C.68, etc., http://stoppolygamy.com/court-documents-2/affadavits-witnesses/dr-joseph-henrichs-affidavit-1/.

———. Affidavit #2, Sworn November 15, 2010, No. S-097767, Vancouver Registry, In the Supreme Court of British Columbia, In the Matter of: The Constitutional Question Act, R.S.B.C. 1996, C.68, etc., http://stoppolygamyincanada.wordpress.com/court-documents/affadavits-witnesses/dr-joseph-henrichs-affidavit-2/.

Henrich, Joseph, Robert Boyd, and Peter J. Richerson. "The Puzzle of Monogamous Marriage." *Philosophical Transactions of the Royal Society B* 376, 1589 (March 2012): 657–69, http://rstb.royalsociety publishing.org/content/367/1589/657.abstract.

Hirsch, Fred. *The Social Limits to Growth*. London: Routledge & Kegan Paul, 1978.

Hunter, Nan D. "Marrriage, Law, and Gender: A Feminist Inquiry." *Law & Sexuality* 1 (1991): 9–30.

Hutchinson, Brian. "Charges Laid against Bountiful Leader Winston Blackmore after Judge Rules Charter Should Not Protect Polygamists." *National Post*, August 14, 2014, http://news.nationalpost.com/2014/08/14/na0815-polygamy/#_federated=1.

Institute for American Values. *Why Marriage Matters*. 3rd ed. http://www.americanvalues.org/search/item.php?id=81.

Israel, Laurie. "Bad for Marital Health." *New York Times*, March 21, 2013, http://www.nytimes.com/roomfordebate/2013/03/21/the-power-of-the-prenup/prenups-can-be-bad-for-marital-health.

———. "Ten Things I Hate about Prenuptial Agreements," http://www.ivkdlaw.com/the-firm/our-articles/prenuptial-agreements-and-lawyering/ten-things-i-hate-about-prenuptial-agreements/.

Jaafar-Mohammad, Imani, and Charlie Lehmann. "Women's Rights in Islam Regarding Marriage and Divorce." *William Mitchell Journal of Law & Practice* 4, 3 (April 11, 2011), http://wmlawandpractice.com

/2011/04/11/women's-rights-in-islam-regarding-marriage-and
-divorce/.

Jacobson, Cardell K., and Lara Burton, eds. *Modern Polygamy in the United States.* New York: Oxford University Press, 2010.

Jaffa, Harry V. "Humanizing Certitudes and Impoverishing Doubts." *Interpretation: A Journal of Political Philosophy* 16, 1 (Fall 1998): 111–38.

———. *Original Intent and the Framers of the Constitution: A Disputed Question.* Washington, DC: Regnery, 1993.

———. "Sodomy and the Academy: The Assault on the Family and Morality by 'Liberation' Ethics." In *American Conservatism and the American Founding.* Claremont, CA: Claremont Institute Press, 2002.

James, Scott. "Many Successful Gay Marriages Share an Open Secret." *New York Times,* January 29, 2010, http://www.nytimes.com/2010 /01/29/us/29sfmetro.html?_r=0&pagewanted=print.

Jarvis, Carolyn. "Inside Bountiful: Polygamy Investigation." *16x9,* http:// watchdocumentary.org/watch/16x9-inside-bountiful-polygamy -investigation-video_335e94162.html.

Jessop, Carolyn. *Escape.* New York: Broadway Books, 2007.

John Paul II, Pope. *Familiaris consortio,* 32, AAS 74 (1982) 120, OR, December 21–28, 1981.

Johnson, David K. *The Lavender Scare: The Cold War Persecution of Gays and Lesbians in the Federal Government.* Chicago: University of Chicago Press, 2004.

Johnson, Rebecca. "Reflecting on Polygamy: What's the Harm?" In *Polygamy's Rights and Wrongs: Perspectives on Harm, Family, and Law.* Edited by Gillian Calder and Lori G. Beaman, 97–119. Vancouver: University of British Columbia Press, 2014.

Jones, Craig. *A Cruel Arithmetic: Inside the Case against Polygamy.* Toronto: Irwin Law, 2012.

Jones, Rachel K., and Joerg Dreweke. "Countering Conventional Wisdom: New Evidence on Religion and Contraceptive Use." Guttmacher Institute, April 2011, http://www.guttmacher.org/pubs //Religion-and-Contraceptive-Use.pdf.

Kass, Leon R. "The Other War on Poverty." *National Affairs* 12 (Summer 2012): 3–15.

Katz, Jonathan Ned. *The Invention of Heterosexuality.* Chicago: University of Chicago Press, 2007.

Kim, Michelle. "Bronx Senator, Granddaughter Battle over Gay Marriage. Sen. Diaz Holds Rally against Same-Sex Marriage; Gay

Granddaughter Condemns Stance," May 16, 2011, http://www.nbc newyork.com/news/local/Bronx-Senator-Granddaughter-in-Battle -Over-Gay-Marriage-121865914.html.

Kinsley, Michael. "Abolish Marriage." *Slate*, July 2, 2003, http://www .slate.com/articles/news_and_politics/readme/2003/07/abolish _marriage.html.

Kirk, Marshall, and Hunter Madsen. *After the Ball: How America Will Conquer Its Fear and Hatred of Gays in the 90's.* New York: Doubleday, 1989.

Klarman, Michael J. *From the Closet to the Altar: Courts, Backlash, and the Struggle for Same-Sex Marriage.* New York: Oxford University Press, 2013.

Kopala, M. "Bountiful Is a Detour on the Road to Same-Sex Marriage." *Ottawa Citizen*, January 29, 2005, B6.

Koppelman, Andrew. *The Gay Rights Question in Contemporary American Law.* Chicago: University of Chicago Press, 2002.

Kraemer, Thomas. "Jack Baker & Michael McConnell: Lunatics or Geniuses?" *GayToday.com*, http://gaytoday.com/people/062104pe.asp.

Krause, Harry D., and David D. Meyer. *Family Law in a Nutshell.* 5th ed. St. Paul, MN: Thompson/West, 2007.

Krauthammer, Charles. "Pandora and Polygamy." *Washington Post*, March 17, 2006, http://www.washingtonpost.com/wp-dyn/content /article/2006/03/16/AR2006031601312.html.

Kurtz, Stanley. "The End of Marriage in Scandinavia." *Weekly Standard*, February 2, 2004, 26–33.

———. "Going Dutch?" *Weekly Standard*, May 31, 2004, 26–29.

Larmore, Charles. *Patterns of Moral Complexity.* Cambridge: Cambridge University Press, 1987.

Latter Day Saints. "Plural Marriage and Families in Early Utah." *LDS. org*, https://www.lds.org.

Law Commission of Canada. *Beyond Conjugality: Recognizing and Supporting Close Personal Adult Relationships.* Ottawa: Law Commission of Canada, 2001, http://www.samesexmarriage.ca/docs/beyond _conjugality.pdf.

Lee, Kristen Schultz, and Hiroshi Ono. "Marriage, Cohabitation, and Happiness: A Cross-National Analysis of 27 Countries." *Journal of Marriage and Family* 74 (October 2012): 953–72.

Lee, Patrick, and Robert P. George. *Body-Self Dualism in Contemporary Ethics and Politics.* Cambridge: Cambridge University Press, 2009.

———. "What Sex Can Be: Self-Alienation, Illusion, or One-Flesh Union." *American Journal of Jurisprudence* 42, 1 (1997): 135–57.

Leturcq, Marion. "Competing Marital Contracts? The Marriage after Civil Union in France," June 11, 2011, https://ideas.repec.org/f/ple 448.html.

Lind, Göran. *Common Law Marriage: A Legal Institution for Cohabitation*. Oxford: Oxford University Press, 2008.

Liu, Frederick, and Stephen Macedo. "The Federal Marriage Amendment and the Strange Evolution of the Conservative Case against Gay Marriage." *PS: Political Science and Politics* 38, 2 (April 2005): 211–15.

Loughlin, Sean. "Santorum under Fire for Comments on Homosexuality," April 22, 2003, http://www.cnn.com/2003/ALLPOLITICS/04 /22/santorum.gays/index.html.

Luscombe, Belinda "I Do, I Do, I Do, I Do." *Time Magazine*, August 6, 2012, http://www.time.com/time/magazine/article/0,9171,2120495 ,00.html.

Maccoby, Eleanor E. *The Two Sexes: Growing Up Apart, Coming Together*. Cambridge, MA: Belknap Press, 1999.

Macedo, Stephen. "Against the Old Sexual Morality of the New Natural Law." In *Natural Law, Liberalism, and Morality*. Edited by Robert George. Oxford: Oxford University Press, 1996.

———. *Diversity and Distrust: Civic Education in a Multicultural Democracy*. Cambridge, MA: Harvard University Press, 2000.

———. "Homosexuality and the Conservative Mind" and "Reply to Critics" (Robert George and Gerard Bradley, and Hadley Arkes). *Georgetown Law Journal* 84 (December 1995): 261–300, 329–38.

———. "In Defense of Liberal Public Reason: Are Abortion and Slavery Hard Cases?" *American Journal of Jurisprudence* 42 (1997): 1–29.

———. *Liberal Virtues: Citizenship, Virtue, and Community in Liberal Constitutionalism*. Oxford: Clarendon Press, 1990.

———. "Sexuality and Liberty: Making Room for Nature and Tradition?" In *Sex, Preference, and Family: Essays on Law and Nature*. Edited by David M. Estlund and Martha C. Nussbaum. Oxford: Oxford University Press, 1997.

Macedo, Stephen, and Iris Marion Young, eds. *Child, Family, and State: NOMOS XLIV*. New York: New York University Press, 2003.

Mahar, Heather. "Why Are There So Few Prenuptial Agreements?" Harvard Law School John M. Olin Center for Law, Economics and Business Discussion Paper Series Paper 436, 2003, http://lsr.nellco .org/harvard_olin/436.

Maine, Henry. *Ancient Law*. New York: Dutton, Republished Classics, 2013.

Mansfield, Harvey C. *Manliness*. New Haven: Yale University Press, 2006.
———. "Saving Liberalism from Liberals." *Harvard Crimson*, November 8, 1993, 2.
March, Andrew F. "Is There a Right to Polygamy? Marriage, Equality and Subsidizing Families in Liberal Public Justification." *Journal of Moral Philosophy* 8 (2011): 246–72.
Marin, Mara. "Care, Oppression, and Marriage." *Hypatia* 29, 2 (Spring 2014): 337–54.
Mather, Mark, and Diana Lavery. "In U.S., Proportion Married at Lowest Recorded Levels." Population Reference Bureau, http://www.prb.org/Publications/Articles/2010/usmarriagedecline.aspx.
McClain, Linda C. *The Place of Families: Fostering Capacity, Equality, and Responsibility*. Cambridge, MA: Harvard University Press, 2006.
McDermott, Rose. "Expert Report Prepared for the Attorney General of Canada." In British Columbia Reference Case, submitted July 15, 2010, https://stoppolygamyincanada.files.wordpress.com/2011/04/mcdermott-report.pdf.
———. "Polygamy: More Common Than You Think." *Wall Street Journal*, April 1, 2011, http://online.wsj.com/article/SB10001424052748703806304576234551596322690.html.
McDermott, Rose, Dominic Johnson, Jonathan Cowden, and Stephen Rosen. "Testosterone and Aggression in a Simulated Crisis Game." *ANNALS of the American Academy of Political and Social Science* 614, 1 (2007): 15–33.
McLanahan, Sara. "Diverging Destinies: How Children Are Faring under the Second Demographic Transition." *Demography* 41, 4 (November 2004): 607–27.
McLanahan, Sara S. and Irwin Garfinkel. "Fragile Families: Debates, Facts, Solutions." In *Marriage at the Crossroads: Law, Policy, and the Brave New World of Twenty-First-Century Families*. Edited by Marsha Garrison and Elizabeth S. Scott. New York: Cambridge University Press, 2012.
McLanahan, Sara, and Gary Sandefur. *Growing Up with a Single Parent: What Hurts, What Helps*. Cambridge, MA: Harvard University Press, 1994.
McMahon, Keith. "The Institution of Polygamy in the Chinese Imperial Palace." *Journal of Asian Studies* 72 (November 2013): 917–36.
———. *Polygamy and Sublime Passion: Sexuality in China on the Verge of Modernity*. Honolulu: University of Hawaii Press, 2010.
Metz, Tamara. *Untying the Knot: Marriage, the State, and the Case for Their Divorce*. Princeton: Princeton University Press, 2010.

Miller, Marion Mills, ed. *Great Debates in American History: Civil Rights*, part 2. Np: Current Literature Publishing Co., 1913, http://books.google.com/books/about/Great_Debates_in_American_History_Civil.html?id=3hYOAAAAIAAJ.

Miller, Rich. "Is Everybody Single? More than Half the U.S. Now, Up from 37% in '76." *Bloomberg*, September 9, 2014, http://www.bloomberg.com/news/2014-09-09/single-americans-now-comprise-more-than-half-the-u-s-population.html.

Mill, John Stuart. *On Liberty* (1869), http://www.bartleby.com/130/.

———. *The Subjection of Women*. Edited and introduction by Susan M. Okin. Indianapolis: Hackett, 1988.

Mitchell, J. "AG Greg Abbott: Texas Opposes Gay Marriage Because the State Has an Interest in Procreation?" *dallasnews.com*, July 30, 2014, http://dallasmorningviewsblog.dallasnews.com/2014/07/ag-greg-abbott-texas-opposes-gay-marriage-because-the-state-has-an-interest-in-procreation.html/.

Moats, David. *Civil Wars: The Battle for Gay Marriage*. Boston: Houghton Mifflin, Harcourt, 2004.

———. "Public Reason in Vermont: Public Reason Improvises." *Perspectives on Politics* 1, 1 (March 2003): 131–35.

Montesquieu, Charles de Secondat, baron de. *Persian Letters, with Related Texts*. Indianapolis: Hackett, 2014.

Moore, Roy S., Chief Justice, Alabama Supreme Court. Letter to Hon. Robert Bentley, Governor of Alabama, January 27, 2015, http://media.al.com/news_impact/other/Read%20Chief%20Justice%20Moore%20letter.pdf.

Morris, Ian. *Foragers, Farmers and Fossil Fuels: How Human Values Evolve*. Edited by Stephen Macedo. Princeton: Princeton University Press, 2015.

———. *Why the West Rules—for Now: The Patterns of History, and What They Reveal about the Future*. New York: Farrar, Straus & Giroux, 2010.

Murphy, Mark. "The Natural Law Tradition in Ethics." In *The Stanford Encyclopedia of Philosophy*. Edited by Edward N. Zalta. Winter 2011, http://plato.stanford.edu/archives/win2011/entries/natural-law-ethics/.

"New Harris Poll Finds Different Religious Groups Have Very Different Attitudes to Some Health Policies and Programs," Harris Poll 78, October 20, 2005, http://www.harrisinteractive.com/harris_poll/index.asp?PID=608.

Newport, Frank, and Joy Wilke. "Most in U.S. Want Marriage, but Its Importance Has Dropped: Young Adults More Likely Not to Want

to Get Married," Gallup online, http://www.gallup.com/poll/163802
/marriage-importance-dropped.aspx.

Ngram Viewer online, https://books.google.com/ngrams/graph?content
=sexual+preference%2Csexual+orientation&year_start=1960&year
_end=2008&corpus=15&smoothing=2&share=&direct_url=t1%3B
%2Csexual%20preference%3B%2Cc0%3B.t1%3B%2Csexual%20
orientation%3B%2Cc0.

Nussbaum, Martha C. *From Disgust to Humanity: Sexual Orientation
and Constitutional Law*. New York: Oxford University Press, 2010.

———. "Women in the Sixties." In *Reassessing the Sixties: Debating the
Cultural and Political Legacy*. Edited by Stephen Macedo. New York:
Norton, 1997.

Obama, Barack. *Dreams from My Father: A Story of Race and Inheritance*.
New York: Broadway Books, 2004.

Ober, Josiah L. *Knowledge and Democracy: Innovation and Learning in
Classical Athens*. Princeton: Princeton University Press, 2010.

Offer, Avner. *The Challenge of Affluence: Self-Control and Well-Being in
the United States and Britain since 1950*. Oxford: Oxford University
Press, 2007.

Palmer, James. "Kept Women: Mistresses Are Big Business in China,
Where No Official Is a Real Man without His Own *Ernai*. What's
in It for the Girls?" *Aeon Magazine*, October 10, 2013, http://aeon
.co/magazine/living-together/why-young-women-in-rural-china
-become-the-mistresses-of-wealthy-older-men/.

Parkman, Allen M. *Good Intentions Gone Awry: No-Fault Divorce
and the American Family*. Lanham, MD: Rowman and Littlefield,
2000.

Paulson, Michael. "Pastor Led Son's Gay Wedding, Revealing Fault
Line in Church." *New York Times*, July 13, 2014, A1, 13.

Pew Research Global Attitudes Project. "The Global Divide on Homosexuality: Greater Acceptance in More Secular and Affluent Countries," June 4, 2013, http://www.pewglobal.org/2013/06/04/the
-global-divide-on-homosexuality/.

Pew Research Religion and Public Life Project. "Religious Beliefs
Underpin Opposition to Homosexuality," November 18, 2003,
http://pewforum.org/docs/print.php?DocID=37.

Philips, Bilal. "Monogamy and Polygamy." *IslamsWomen.com*, http://
www.islamswomen.com/marriage/monogamy_and_polygamy.php.

Pinello, Daniel R. *America's Struggle for Same-Sex Marriage*. New York:
Cambridge University Press, 2006.

Pinker, Stephen. *How the Mind Works*. New York: Norton, 1997.

Pope, Stephen J. "The Magisterium's Arguments against 'Same-Sex Marriage': An Ethical Analysis and Critique." *Theological Studies* 65 (2004): 530–65.

Posner, Richard. "Homosexual Marriage." *Becker-Posner blog*, May 13, 2012, http://www.becker-posner-blog.com/2012/05/homosexual -marriageposner.html.

———. *Sex and Reason*. Cambridge, MA: Harvard University Press, 1992.

Putnam, Robert D. "E Pluribus Unum: Diversity and Community in the Twenty-first Century." 2006 Johan Skytte Prize Lecture, *Scandinavian Political Studies* 30, 2 (June 2007): 137–74.

———. *Our Kids: The American Dream in Crisis*. New York: Simon and Schuster, 2015.

Putnam, Robert D., and David E. Campbell. *American Grace: How Religion Divides and Unites Us*. New York: Simon and Schuster, 2010.

Rauch, Jonathan. *Gay Marriage: Why It Is Good for Gays, Good for Straights, and Good for America*. New York: Henry Holt, 2004.

Rawls, John. "The Idea of Public Reason Revisited." In *The Law of Peoples*. Cambridge, MA: Harvard University Press, 2002.

———. *Political Liberalism*. New York: Columbia University Press, 1993.

———. *A Theory of Justice*. Cambridge, MA: Harvard University Press, 1999.

Reeves, Richard V. "How to Save Marriage in America." *Atlantic Monthly* (February 2014), http://www.theatlantic.com/business/print /2014/02/how-to-save-marriage-in-america/283732/.

Regnerus, Mark "How Different Are the Adult Children of Parents Who Have Same-Sex Relationships? Findings from the New Family Structures Study." *Social Science Research* 41 (2012): 752–70.

———. "Queers as Folk: Does It Really Make No Difference If Your Parents Are Straight or Gay?" *Slate*, June 11, 2012, http://www.slate .com/articles/double_x/doublex/2012/06/gay_parents_are_they _really_no_different_.html.

Rhoads, Steven E. *Taking Sex Differences Seriously*. San Francisco: Encounter Books, 2004.

Rosenblum, Nancy L. "Democratic Sex." In *Membership and Morals: The Personal Uses of Pluralism in America*. Princeton: Princeton University Press, 1998.

Sagoff, Mark. *The Economy of the Earth: Philosophy, Law, and the Environment*. 2nd ed. New York: Cambridge University Press, 2008.

Saletan, William. "Back in the Gay: Does a New Study Indict Gay Parenthood or Make a Case for Gay Marriage?" *Slate*, June 11, 2012,

http://www.slate.com/articles/health_and_science/human_nature
/2012/06/new_family_structures_study_is_gay_parenthood_bad_or
_is_gay_marriage_good_.html.

Sanger, Carol. "A Case for Civil Marriage." *Cardozo Law Review* 27
(January 2006): 1311–23.

Savage, Dan. *The Commitment: Love, Sex, Marriage, and My Family.*
New York: Penguin, 2005.

Sawhill, Isabel V. *Generation Unbound: Drifting into Sex and Parenthood
without Marriage.* Washington, DC: Brookings, 2014.

Schaff, Kory. "Equal Protection and Same-Sex Marriage." *Journal of
Social Philosophy* 35 (2004): 133–47.

———. "Kant, Political Liberalism, and the Ethics of Same-Sex Relations." *Journal of Social Philosophy* 32 (2001): 446–62.

Scheidel, Walter. "Monogamy and Polygyny in Greece, Rome, and
World History." *Princeton/Stanford Working Papers in Classics,* June
2008, http://www.princeton.edu/~pswpc/pdfs/scheidel/060807.pdf.

Schneider, Carl E. "The Channeling Function in Family Law." *Hofstra
Law Review* 20 (Spring 1992): 495–532.

Schwitzgebel, Eric. "Thoughts on Conjugal Love," June 4, 2003, http://
www.faculty.ucr.edu/~eschwitz/SchwitzAbs/ConjugalLove.htm.

Scott, Elizabeth S. "Marital Commitment and the Legal Regulation of
Divorce." In *The Law and Economics of Marriage and Divorce.* Edited
by Antony W. Dnes and Robert Rowtham. Cambridge: Cambridge
University Press, 2010.

Scruton, Roger. *Sexual Desire: A Philosophical Investigation.* London:
Weidenfeld and Nicholson, 1986.

Shattuck, Rachel M., and Rose M. Kreider. "Social and Economic
Characteristics of Currently Unmarried Women with a Recent
Birth: 2011." United States Census Bureau, May 2013. http://www
.census.gov/prod/2013pubs/acs-21.pdf.

Sheff, Elisabeth. *The Polyamorists Next Door: Inside Multiple-Partner
Relationships and Families.* Lanham, MD: Rowman and Littlefield,
2014.

Sides, John. "Americans Have Become More Opposed to Adultery. Why?"
The Monkey Cage, July 27, 2011, http://themonkeycage.org/2011/07/27
/americans-have-become-more-opposed-to-adultery-why/.

Simmel, Georg. "The Number of Members as Determining the Sociological Form of the Group I." *American Journal of Sociology* 8, 1 (July
1902): 1–46.

Slark, Samantha. "Are Anti-Polygamy Laws an Unconstitutional Infringement on the Liberty Interests of Consenting Adults?" *Journal
of Law and Family Studies* 6 (2004): 451–60.

Slaughter, Anne-Marie. "Why Women Still Can't Have It All." *Atlantic Monthly*, July/August 2012, http://www.theatlantic.com/magazine /archive/2012/07/why-women-still-cant-have-it-all/309020/.

Slovenko, Ralph. "The De Facto Decriminalization of Bigamy." *Journal of Family Law* 17, 2 (1978–79): 297–308.

Smith, Tom W. "Public Attitudes toward Homosexuality." NORC/ University of Chicago, September 2011, http://www.norc.org/PDFs /2011%20GSS%20Reports/GSS_Public%20Attitudes%20Toward %20Homosexuality_Sept2011.pdf.

Smith, Tom W., and Jaesok Son. "Trends in Public Attitudes about Sexual Morality." Final Report NORC/GSS, April 2013, http:// www.norc.org/PDFs/sexmoralfinal_06–21_FINAL.PDF.

Song, Sarah. *Justice, Gender, and the Politics of Multiculturalism.* Cambridge: Cambridge University Press, 2007.

"South Africa and Polygamy, Swimming against the Tide, President Jacob Zuma Happily Bucks the Trend towards Monogamy." *Economist*, April 28, 2012, http://www.economist.com/node/21553461.

Sperling, Susan, and Yewoubdar Beyne. "A Pound of Biology and a Pinch of Culture or a Pinch of Biology and a Pound of Culture? The Necessity of Integrating Biology and Culture in Reproductive Studies." In *Women in Human Evolution*. Edited by Lori D. Hager. London: Routledge, 1997.

Stacey, Judith. *Unhitched: Love, Marriage, and Family Values from West Hollywood to Western China.* New York: New York University Press, 2012.

Stein, Edward. "Same-Sex Couples, the Future of Marriage, and Consensual Non-Monogamy," paper presented at American Association of Law Schools annual meeting, January 4–6, 2015.

Stern, Mark Joseph. "Judge Upholds Puerto Rico's Gay Marriage Ban in a Comically Inane Opinion." *Slate*, http://www.slate.com/blogs /outward/2014/10/22/puerto_rico_gay_marriage_ban_upheld_by _federal_judge_in_inane_opinion.html.

Strassberg, Maura I. "The Challenge of Post-Modern Polygamy: Considering Polyamory." *Capital University Law Review* 31 (2003): 439–563.

———. "The Crime of Polygamy." *Temple Political and Civil Rights Law Review* 12 (Spring 2003): 353–431.

———. "Distinctions of Form or Substance: Monogamy, Polygamy and Same Sex Marriage." *North Carolina Law Review* 75 (1997): 1501–1624.

Strauss, Gregg. "Is Polygamy Inherently Unequal?" *Ethics* 122 (April 2012): 516–44.

Sullivan, Andrew. "Here Comes the Groom." *New Republic*, August 28, 1989, http://www.newrepublic.com/article/79054/here-comes-the -groom.

———, ed. *Same-Sex Marriage: Pro and Con*. New York: Vintage, 2004.

———. "Three's a Crowd." *New Republic*, June 17, 1996, 10.

———. *Virtually Normal: An Argument about Homosexuality*. New York: Knopf, 1995.

Taormino, Tristan. *Opening Up: A Guide to Creating and Sustaining Open Relationships*. San Francisco: Cleis Press, 2008.

Tenney, Ryan D. "Tom Green, Common-law Marriage, and the Illegality of Putative Polygamy." *Brigham Young University Law Journal* 17, 1 (2003): 141–62.

Thaler, Richard H., and Cass R. Sunstein. *Nudge: Improving Decisions about Health, Wealth, and Happiness*. Rev. ed. New York: Penguin, 2009.

Torcello, Lawrence G. "Is the State Endorsement of Any Marriage Justifiable? Same-Sex Marriage, Civil Unions, and the Marriage Privatization Model." *Public Affairs Quarterly* 22, 1 (January 2008): 43–61.

Tucker, William. *Marriage and Civilization: How Monogamy Made Us Human*. Washington, DC: Regnery, 2014.

Turley, Jonathan, and Adam Alba. Complaint for Declaratory, Injunctive, and Other Relief, in Brown v. Buhman; pp. 37–38, numbered paragraphs 224–29, "Sixth Ground for Complaint: Establishment of Religion," http://jonathanturley.files.wordpress.com/2011/07/brown -complaint.pdf.

United States House of Representatives. Defense of Marriage Act: Hearing on H.R. 3396 before the Subcommittee on the Constitution of the House Comm. on the Judiciary, 104th Cong. 88 (1996).

Vacek, Edward Collins. "Acting More Humanely: Accepting Gays Into the Priesthood." *America: the National Catholic Review*, December 16, 2002, http://americamagazine.org/issue/416/article/acting-more -humanelyaccepting-gays-priesthood.

———. "The Meaning of Marriage: Of Two Minds." *Commonweal* 130, 18 (October 24, 2003): 17–19.

Various. "The End of Democracy: The Judicial Usurpation of Politics." *First Things* (November 1996).

Various. "Sex and God in American Politics: A Symposium." *Policy Review* (Spring 1984): 12–30.

Veaux, Franklin, and Eve Rickert. *More than Two: A Practical Guide to Polyamory*. Portland, OR: Thorntree Press, 2014.

Waite, Linda J. and Maggie Gallagher. *The Case for Marriage: Why Married People Are Happier, Healthier, and Better Off Financially*. New York: Broadway Books, 2000.

Waldron, Jeremy. "Autonomy and Perfectionism in Raz's Morality of Freedom." *Southern California Law Review* 62 (1988–89): 1097–1152.

Wall, Steven, and George Klosko, eds. *Perfectionism and Neutrality: Essays in Liberal Theory*. New York: Rowman and Littlefield, 2003.

Waller, Matthew. "Jessop Given Maximum: 10 Years in Prison, $10,000 Fine." *San Angelo Standard-Times*, November 8, 2011, http://www.gosanangelo.com/news/2011/nov/08/jessop-performed-15-under-age-marriage-ceremonies/.

Walzer, Michael. *Spheres of Justice: A Defense of Pluralism and Equality*. New York: Basic Books, 1984.

Wang, Qi. "Sex, Money, Social Status—Chinese Men and Women in the Whirlwind of Modernization and Market Economy." *NIAS Nytt* (June 2008): 12–14.

Wardle, Lynn D. "Image, Analysis, and the Nature of Relationships." In *Marriage and Same-Sex Unions: A Debate*. Edited by Lynn D. Wardle et al. Westport, CT: Greenwood, 2003.

Wardle, Lynn D., Mark Strasser, William C. Duncan, and David Orgon Coolidge, eds. *Marriage and Same-Sex Unions: A Debate*. Westport, CT: Greenwood, 2003.

Watters, Ethan. *Urban Tribes: A Generation Redefines Friendship, Family, and Commitment*. New York: Bloomsbury, 2003.

Wax, Amy L. "Engines of Inequality: Class, Race, and Family Structure." Faculty Scholarship, Paper 205, 2008, http://scholarship.law.upenn.edu/faculty_scholarship/205.

Wedgwood, Ralph. "The Fundamental Argument for Same Sex Marriage." *Journal of Moral Philosophy* 8 (2011): 246–72.

Weithman, Paul J. "Natural Law, Morality, and Sexual Complementarity." In *Sex, Preference, and Family: Essays on Law and Nature*. Edited by David M. Estlund and Martha C. Nussbaum. New York: Oxford University Press, 1997.

Wellington, Adrian Alex. "Why Liberals Should Support Same Sex Marriage." *Journal of Social Philosophy* 26 (1995): 5–32

West, Robin. *Marriage, Sexuality and Gender*. St. Paul, MN: Paradigm, 2007.

Westermarck, Edward. *The History of Marriage*. London: Macmillan, 1891.

Weston, Kath. *Families We Choose: Lesbians, Gays, Kinship*. Rev. ed. New York: Columbia University Press, 1997.

White, Edmund. "I Do, I Do." *New York Review of Books*, August 14, 2014: 26–28.

Wight, Richard G., Allen J. LeBlanc, and M. V. Lee Badgett. "Same-Sex Legal Marriage and Psychological Well-Being: Findings from the California Health Interview Survey," 2013, http://ajph.apha publications.org/doi/full/10.2105/AJPH.2012.301113.

Wilcox, W. Bradford. "If You Want a Prenup, You Don't Want Marriage." *New York Times*, March 21, 2013, http://www.nytimes.com /roomfordebate/2013/03/21/the-power-of-the-prenup/if-you-want -a-prenup-you-dont-want-marriage.

———. "Marriage Makes Our Children Richer—Here's Why." *Atlantic Monthly* (October 2014), http://www.theatlantic.com/business/print /2013/10/marriage-makes-our-children-richer-heres-why/280930/.

———. "Seeking a Soulmate: A Social Scientific View of the Relationship between Commitment and Authentic Intimacy." Paper prepared for Promoting and Sustaining Marriage as a Community of Life and Love, a Colloquium of Social Scientists and Theologians, October 24–25, 2005, http://old.usccb.org/laity/marriage/Wilcox.pdf.

Wilcox, W. Bradford, and Elizabeth Williamson. "The Cultural Contradictions of Mainline Family Ideology and Practice." In *American Religions and the Family*. Edited by Don S. Browning and David A. Clairmont. New York: Columbia University Press, 2007.

Wilcox, W. Bradford, et al. *Knot Yet: The Benefits and Costs of Delayed Marriage in America*. Report of the National Marriage Project, University of Virginia, http://nationalmarriageproject.org/.

Wilson, James Q. *The Marriage Problem: How Our Culture Has Weakened Families*. New York: HarperCollins, 2003.

———. "Why We Don't Marry." *City Journal* (Winter 2002), http:// www.city-journal.org/html/12_1_why_we.html.

Wilson, Peter J. *Man the Promising Primate: The Conditions of Human Evolution*. 2nd ed. New Haven: Yale University Press, 1983.

Wing, Adrien Katherine. "Polygamy from Southern Africa to Black Britannia to Black America: Global Critical Race Feminism as Legal Reform for the Twenty-first Century." *Journal of Contemporary Legal Issues* 11 (2001): 811–80.

Witte, John, Jr. *From Sacrament to Contract: Marriage, Religion, and Law in the Western Tradition*. 2nd ed. Louisville: John Knox Press, 2012.

Wolfson, Evan. *Why Marriage Matters: America, Equality, and Gay People's Right to Marry*. New York: Simon and Schuster, 2004.

Woodhouse, Barbara Bennett. "'It All Depends on What You Mean by Home': Toward a Communitarian Theory of the 'Nontraditional' Family." *Utah Law Review* (1996): 569–612.

Wright, Robert. *The Moral Animal: Why We Are, the Way We Are: The New Science of Evolutionary Psychology.* New York: Vintage, 1994.

Young, Neil J. "Short Creek's Long Legacy: How a Failed 1953 Raid Shaped the Relationship between Polygamists and the Government." *Slate*, April 16, 2008, http://www.slate.com/articles/life/faithbased/2008/04/short_creeks_long_legacy.single.html.

Zeitzen, Miriam Koktvedgaard. *Polygamy: A Cross-Cultural Analysis.* Oxford: Berg, 2008.

INDEX